THE ROUGH GUIDE TO
Pink Floyd

by
Toby Manning

ROUGH GUIDES

www.roughguides.com

Credits

The Rough Guide to Pink Floyd

Text editing: Michelle Bhatia
Layout: Ajay Verma
Proofreading: Wendy Smith
Production: Aimee Hampson, Katherine Owers

Rough Guides Reference

Series editor: Mark Ellingham
Director: Andrew Lockett
Editors: Peter Buckley, Duncan Clark, Tracy Hopkins
Sean Mahoney, Matthew Milton, Joe Staines, Ruth Tidball

Picture Credits

Alamy 49, 185, Corbis 29, 219, Getty (Hutton Archive) 37, Jill Furmanovsky 18, 82, 89, 92, 96, 99, 105, 106, 117, 128, 143, 148, 149, 165, 166, 170, 176, 203, 204, 209, 212, 215, 277, Movie Store Collection 119 (MGM, Goldcrest Films Ltd, Sony Music Video), 262, Nick Mason archive 3, 14, 16, Redferns 30, 34, 69, 73, 88, 125, 137, 156, 181, 230, Rex 51, 66, 232, 243, 253.

Publishing Information

This first edition published September 2006 by
Rough Guides Ltd, 80 Strand, London WC2R 0RL
345 Hudson St, 4th Floor, New York 10014, USA
Email: mail@roughguides.com

Distributed by the Penguin Group:
Penguin Books Ltd, 80 Strand, London WC2R 0RL
Penguin Putnam, Inc., 375 Hudson Street, NY 10014, USA
Penguin Group (Australia), 250 Camberwell Road, Camberwell, Victoria 3124, Australia
Penguin Books Canada Ltd, 90 Eglinton Avenue East, Suite 700, Toronto, Ontario M4P 2Y3, Canada
Penguin Group (New Zealand), 67 Apollo Drive, Mairongi Bay, Auckland 1310, New Zealand

Printed in Italy by LegoPrint S.p.A

312 pages; includes index

A catalogue record for this book is available from the British Library

ISBN 13: 978-1-84353-575-1
ISBN 10: 1-84353-575-0

1 3 5 7 9 8 6 4 2

Contents

Contents

Introduction:
Wish You Were Here?

If ever there was a band that resisted biography, it is Pink Floyd. They have sold around 200 million records, and their album sleeves are iconic and instantly recognisable. Yet the band can walk through the crowds at their own concerts unmolested and their solo records struggle to sell a fraction of the parent band's worst-sellers.

This anonymity, this enigma, has been, to an extent, deliberate. All the members of the Floyd are inclined to be reserved by nature – or rather, English, middle-class nurture. And lights, projections, props and inflatables have long eclipsed the band as performers at live shows. **Rick Wright** said in 1987, "A Pink Floyd show is not the individuals, it's the music and lights". Indeed, enormous cheers greeted non-member Snowy White as the first musician on stage during the *Animals* tour, while the Surrogate Band of session musicians that opened the *Wall* shows put this confusion at Pink Floyd's conceptual centre.

Then there's the fact that, until the 1986 split between the band's guitarist since 1968, **David Gilmour,** and its bassist, **Roger Waters,** Pink Floyd gave few interviews. "We don't really need the music press and it doesn't need us," a politely bored Gilmour told the *NME* in 1973. Add to that their decision to absent themselves from their own album sleeves: their 1967 debut, *The Piper At The Gates Of Dawn* and 1969's *Ummagumma* are the only albums

to feature the band on their front cover, and even then, the photographer on the former, Vic Singh, described them as "there, but not there", while the latter deliberately confuses the eye as to which member is which. When *Dark Side Of The Moon* appeared, Pink Floyd featured only on the poster included with the album; from *Wish You Were Here* onwards they might as well have not existed. Indeed, drummer **Nick Mason** and keyboardist **Rick Wright** weren't even mentioned anywhere on 1979's *The Wall* package, and Wright's sacking before *The Final Cut* wasn't even perceived as worth mentioning to the public. There but not there. Wish you were here.

But in these attempts to counter the cult of personality that had such a negative impact upon original leader **Syd Barrett**, Pink Floyd have been almost *too* successful. After Barrett was replaced by **Dave Gilmour** with barely a commercial ripple, manager **Peter Jenner** said, "Dave could play better Syd guitar than Syd". Then history repeated itself when the Floyd reconvened in 1986 without Roger Waters.

Despite all those satirical surrogate bands, it was a shock to the group's latter-day leader that fans regarded him as, well, just another brick in the wall. "I was slightly angry that they managed to get away with it," Waters said in 2004 of the resultant reunion album's sky-high sales, and record-breaking tour receipts, "that the great unwashed couldn't tell the fucking difference". Oddly, the sense in the *Wall*-era of **Wright** and **Mason** being replaceable hired hands was reversed in the 80s re-formation, when they were included in the line-up while Gilmour hired others to play their parts. "Jon Carin can do Rick Wright better than Rick Wright can," said Gilmour, of the keyboardist who played alongside Wright on their tours, unconsciously echoing Jenner's opinion of Gilmour's own playing. For this reliance on session musicians and hired lyric writers, Waters called the first Gilmour-led Floyd album, 1987's *A Momentary Lapse Of Reason*, "a forgery". In turn, Gilmour tends to downplay Waters' previous role. He claimed he played much of what was attributed to Waters, pointing out that he served as Waters' stunt vocalist from the off. During 90s performances of *Dark Side Of The Moon*, he would thank Waters "for writing these lyrics", as if that were the full extent of his contribution.

Everything about Pink Floyd is contested. Few facts are entirely certain. Although Waters scrawled "Bollocks!" in green ink across an entire page of the manuscript for Mason's Floyd biography, *Inside Out*. Mason – frustratingly – never tells us which page. While Gilmour's and Waters' accounts of the making of *The Wall* have become increasingly candid, they rarely actually tally. Wright admits that he can't remember anything, so there's no point asking, and Mason – supposedly the group's resident archivist – leaves facts so frustratingly opaque that even his book's *chronology* feels obliged to declare itself "personal".

The point is that Pink Floyd are a bigger entity than any individual. Contrary to the assumption behind the question fans and moguls asked in the early days, "Which one's Pink?", there *is* no Pink. Even Gilmour concedes this: "I think we were greater than the sum of our parts". Apart from anything else, it's actually hard to tell the individuals' voices apart – fans, critics and even the band argue about who sang what. Meanwhile, at the *financial* bottom line, Pink Floyd is a brand, a trademark, a multi-million dollar business that, like Ford or Hoover, has long stopped being connected to any individual. But it's also something less tangible, something that can remain beyond the grasp of partial reunions and solo efforts alike: a mood, an idea, a folk memory ... a mystery.

Enigma is the essence of Pink Floyd's appeal. Enigma, mystery, the intangible can be part of even the most disposable pop song, Natalie Imbruglia's "Torn", for example, or even Britney Spears' "Toxic". But never more so than in the work of Pink Floyd. As **psychedelicists,** they took the listener off into outer space, into inner space, and back to childhood. As **progressive rockers**, they went deeper into the unknown, as well as promulgating a **pastoral** wooziness that was very far from earthbound.

But even when they did come back to earth, addressing tangible, material concerns on *Dark Side Of The Moon*, the sense of mystery remained undimmed. Was it the glacial calm of the music? Or did the lyrics, for all their apparent directness, still somehow slither away from the grasp? Their cultivated vagueness frustrates some critics, but fascinates fans, leaving room for endless re-listens and reinterpretations. A refusal quite to pin down concepts again leaves room for the listener's imagination to expand. Is *Dark Side Of The Moon* about madness or the pressures of modern life? How exactly does "Have A Cigar" fit into *Wish You Were Here*'s theme of absence? Even at their most autobiographically and politically direct, on *The Wall* and *The Final Cut*, The Floyd remain enigmatic, distant, almost disembodied. They possess neither the intimate soul-baring of singer-songwriters nor the sloganeering simplicity of most political acts. Even some of the blander, Gilmour-led later Pink Floyd still manages to evoke this enigma, albeit through memories of imagination rather than imagination itself. That sense of the intangible is integral to Pink Floyd, something mysterious, something fascinating but elusive. There but not there. Wish you were here.

In this fog, this book attempts to identify a few definite landmarks: to clarify biographical facts about the life of Pink Floyd often wrongly reported, from Roger Waters' birth date to when precisely Syd Barrett left the band. It puts the **albums** in career and peer context, explaining how *More* post-dated *Ummagumma* but was released before it, and showing quite what Pink Floyd owe to Crosby, Stills and Nash. *The Rough Guide to Pink Floyd* attempts to get to the bottom of contested information about the **songs**, from who sang lead vocals on "Let There Be More Light" and what was the last song Barrett played on, to whether *The Wall*'s "Nobody Home" really is a dig at Rick Wright. Then there's as much information as anyone could want on the sad business of "What happened to Syd?". There's a full assessment of which **solo albums** best carry the Floyd torch and a full survey of their **collaborations** with other artists, from Kate Bush to The Damned, plus an assessment of their **influence** on everything from prog through punk and grunge to Britpop. Then there's a thorough account of which Pink Floyd music is featured in which **films**, which **soundtracks** are available and are any good, and whether you might be best advised to resort to **bootlegs** to fulfill your Floyd fix. All this plus a guide to Pink Floyd **websites** and Pink Floyd **tribute bands** – there but not there, wishing they were here.

Acknowledgements

Grateful acknowledgements for quotes used herein to all the books, films, programmes and websites either mentioned in the main text or listed in the Books and Websites section, plus the following sources (with apologies to anybody inadvertently omitted): *Days In The Life: Voices From The English Underground 1961–1971*, edited by Jonathon Green (Heinemann), Ian McDonald's *Revolution In The Head: The Beatles' Records And The Sixties* (Pimlico), *Q* Magazine, *Mojo*, *Uncut*, *Rolling Stone*, *Penthouse*, and *The Amazing Pudding* (Floyd fanzine). The book also draws upon interviews with Peter Mew, Barbet Schroeder, Alan Parsons and members of the band and is based upon the author's interviews for this book with Nick Mason, John Leckie, Andrew King, Ron Geesin, Gerald Scarfe, Andrew Bown, Mike Butcher, Mike Leonard, Nigel Gordon, Roger Quested, John "Hoppy" Hopkins and Bob Ezrin. With additional thanks to Mark Blake at *Q* and Mark Ellen at *The Word*.

Dedicated to Rachel, without whom...

About the author

Toby Manning grew up in North Wales and Manchester, before regressing to adolescence in London. He has written for *Q*, *NME*, *The New Statesman*, *Arena*, *The Guardian*, *Select* and *The Word*, and now also manages and produces a band.

Part 1:
The Story

The Early Years
Cambridge beginnings

The Early Years
Cambridge beginnings

Middle-class has never been a very rock'n'roll thing to be. Despite the fact that Britain's art-school bohemian nexus has been rock's crucible since the 1950s, rock's rebels like to present themselves as working-class heroes, even when their street credentials don't withstand much scrutiny (John Lennon, Joe Strummer, Pete Doherty). Musicians that are unabashedly middle class, meanwhile (Coldplay, Keane, Pink Floyd), tend to be sneered at by rock's gutter-snipers as somehow inauthentic.

In the case of **Pink Floyd**, their middle-class background isn't just an incidental biographical fact, it's integral to their music. It's not just that the Floyd sang for much of their career in pronounced Home Counties accents or that they have a propensity for artsy, highfalutin concepts ("Pink Floyd has always been the thinking man's rock'n'roll," says *Dark Side Of The Moon* engineer Alan Parsons). Pink Floyd's middle classness informs their music through the genteel glide that typifies their trademark sound (there are barely ten rockers in the entire Floyd canon) and their glacial delivery, both of which are coolly, infinitely removed from the dirt-and-rattle, Sturm-und-Drang end of rock'n'roll.

Indeed, when rock'n'roll exploded in the five future Floyds' 1950s teenage years, it must have seemed a long, long way from leafy Cambridge to Memphis, from their conformist prep and grammar schools to gritty Sun Studios. And yet these typically middle-class boys felt rock's call as loudly as anyone of their generation. In the sixties they came to epitomize society's changing attitudes, and they went on to become five of rock's most famous exponents.

As its enduring popularity attests, theirs is a music of unique power: comforting yet challenging, laid-back yet thoughtful and – in the darker Roger Waters years – a music with plenty of danger too. But it is music whose essence is perhaps that enduring sense of mystery and enigma, one that has sparked the imaginations of several generations.

Roger Waters

George Roger Waters was not actually a native of Cambridge, but was born in Great Bookham, Surrey, on September 6, 1943. Waters was the youngest of two boys. His father, Eric Fletcher

Waters, a PE and RE teacher (and, in the early years of World War II, a conscientious objector), was killed during the ill-conceived Allied attack on the beachhead of Anzio, Italy, in January 1944. He was 30; Roger was barely four months old. This biographical fact would assume enormous importance in the work of Pink Floyd, influencing *Dark Side Of The Moon* and *The Wall* while utterly dominating *The Final Cut*. As he recalled in both "When The Tigers Broke Free" and the film of *The Wall*, the young Waters was traumatized after he stumbled across his father's uniform and a standard letter of condolence from **King George VI** in a drawer.

After her husband's death Mary Waters moved to Cambridge with her sons, of whom she was fiercely protective in her widowhood – as Waters' song "Mother" attests. She was Scottish (the source of the comic Scottish accent Waters employed on *Ummagumma* and *The Wall*) and believed passionately in the left-wing spirit of the postwar dream in which, having lost so much, she had so much hope invested – political convictions that were to influence her son profoundly.

Waters passed his eleven-plus exam and went to Cambridge County High School for Boys, where he excelled at rugby but not much else. Neither *The Wall*'s "The Happiest Days Of Our Lives" nor "Another Brick In The Wall Part II" present a particularly rosy view of schooldays. Waters later said of his teachers: "Some were just incredibly bad ... just trying to keep [the children] quiet and still, and crush them into the right shape, so that they would go to university and 'do well'."

Despite his later reputation as a rock intellectual, Waters was never much of a scholar. "As a child I never got into the habit of reading. I find it very difficult to read," he has admitted. When he was 13, Waters would lie in bed at night at Rock Road, listening to American Forces Network radio and pirate station Radio Luxembourg, the main source for rock'n'roll in the mid-1950s. Via the station's star DJs – Jimmy Saville, Jimmy Young and Alan Freeman – he absorbed the music of **Bill Haley** and his British counterparts **Tommy Steele** and **Billy Fury**, and, in time, **Elvis Presley**. The experience would feed into the storyline of Waters' 1987 solo album *Radio K.A.O.S.* Although there were no musical influences from within his family, Waters remembers listening to Gilbert and Sullivan's operettas (see *The Wall*'s "The Trial") and to balladeer Frankie Laine (also audible in Waters' work), as well as trad jazz (which isn't). At 14 he was given a Spanish guitar by his mother and although he took a few lessons, by his own admission he never pushed himself to practice (a lifelong attitude), only really gaining interest in playing music in his late teens with the advent of **The Beatles** and **The Rolling Stones**.

In later years Waters was anti-militarist and anti-authoritarian, but as a youth he served as a naval cadet-spending weekends at HMS Ganges, a cadet training base in Suffolk, and attaining the rank of Leading Seaman. He has never been a pacifist and he has a lifelong fondness for bloodsports. "I liked guns ... I used to shoot for the school,

Floyd's Cambridge

Cambridge appears the consummate middle-class town – leafy, largely white-collar, and centred upon one of the country's oldest and most prestigious universities. Pink Floyd have maintained a life-long connection with Cambridge, where their three leaders – **Syd Barrett**, **Roger Waters** and **David Gilmour** – all grew up. Even Londoner **Rick Wright** bought himself a country pile near Cambridge with his *Dark Side Of The Moon* millions. Cambridge's ancient university makes for a dominant student population that contributes to the town's aura of comfortable bohemia. Crucially, compared with larger or more industrial conurbations, Cambridge remains close to nature. The leafy river Cam runs through it, the unspoilt Grantchester Meadows is a short punt-ride away, and the inhospitable marsh-land of the fens is nearby.

The Floyd remained Cambridge boys long after they became part of the hip London underground or even after joining the international jet set. Most of their cohorts came from Cambridge: **Storm Thorgerson**, their future designer and the director of several 1990s Floyd concert films, was at school with Barrett and would later utilise a Cambridge scene on the cover of Floyd's *Division Bell* album; **Aubrey "Po" Powell**, Thorgerson's partner at the design company Hipgnosis; future second guitarist **Tim Renwick**, who was also at school with Barrett; roadie **Alan Stiles** (of "Alan's Psychedelic Breakfast" fame); *Dark Side Of The Moon* sax-man **Dick Parry**; and scenester **Ian Moore** (Emo), who would be employed by David Gilmour as caretaker for decades. "Most of our friends are people we've known from before the time when we were successful," Gilmour has said.

Many of Syd Barrett's songs referred back to Cambridge. "Arnold Layne", for example, concerns a local sixties underwear thief and "Flaming", "Scarecrow" and "The Gnome" hark back to more innocent days frolicking in Grantchester Meadows. Barrett himself long ago returned to Cambridge, never to leave again; Waters and Gilmour have carried their Cambridge heritage with them to London, Hampshire, Greece and beyond. The town's influence is most notable in Pink Floyd's post-Barrett pastoral songs such as "Grantchester Meadows", "Cirrus Minor" or "Fat Old Sun" (all of which relate directly to Cambridge) and the later, more edgy wartime pastorale of "Goodbye Blue Sky". Apparently, for Waters, the lines in "Brain Damage" about the lunatic on the grass refer to Syd Barrett and the lawn behind King's College Chapel, and Gilmour's lyric for 1994's "High Hopes" – at the time of writing, the last song created by Pink Floyd – again recalls the fenland scenes of his youth.

Pink Floyd's Cambridge comes wreathed in a hazy nostalgia. Stories about their early Cambridge years are vague, incomplete and often contradic-tory. Obviously, these events took place a long time ago, and although a surprising number of the Floyd's clique are alive today (by comparison with, say, the **Rolling Stones**' circle), the communal laboratory of drug experimentation of the 1960s has fuzzed a few memories – if not eradicated them altogether. All this, combined with a veneration of childhood typical of the acid generation, makes Pink Floyd's Cambridge something rather magical: an arcadia of music, games, picnics by the Cam and lazily strummed acoustic guitars … there but not there. Wish you were here.

The Story

What Roger did on his year off

During his year off in 1962, Roger Waters hitchhiked across Europe and into the Middle East. This, he has since claimed, was a formative experience for him, and formed the basis for a 2003 song, "Leaving Beirut" (released only on the Internet). Invited to stay with strangers – a one-legged man and his hunchbacked wife – the young Waters was given the only bed they had. "They were unbelievably hospitable," he has said. "It's only through those chance encounters that we are truly able to live even momentarily in the skin of another human being, by something so shocking happening as somebody being that poor, that deformed, and that kind. It's those moments that shape our lives."

small-bore shooting … I think there's something in me that makes me want to kind of dominate people anyway…" He was considered haughty and overbearing by his peers, as he would be throughout his life, and, after becoming intolerably rebellious and truculent, was eventually given a dishonourable discharge.

Upon leaving school in summer 1961 (the only sixth-former not to become a prefect), Waters attended Manchester University to study mechanical engineering. Unenthused, he took a year out, becoming chairman of CND's local youth group in Cambridge in 1962. An acquaintance of his, Syd Barrett (another alumnus of Cambridge County High School for Boys), was by this time playing guitar with singer **Geoff Mott** (apparently not his real name), a gangling youth some years senior to Barrett who had a rebellious reputation as a result of having been expelled from school. Waters regularly attended the **Mottoes'** practices and gigs, even organising one – a CND benefit at the Friends Meeting House on March 11, 1962. Although Waters claims to have played with the band at other times, there is actually no evidence he did.

Syd Barrett

Roger Keith Barrett was born on January 6, 1946 at 60 Glisson Road, Cambridge, the third child of five. His father, Dr Arthur Max Barrett, was a police pathologist and a medical expert on cot death. Max was a music lover, a member of the Philharmonic Society and the proud owner of a grand piano, so there was always music in the house when Roger was growing up, and the family often indulged in singsongs around the piano. Dr Barrett was also artistic, enjoying watercolour painting, and was something of a naturalist, who wrote several books on fungi. According to Barrett's Cambridge friend **Nigel Gordon**, Max Barrett also suffered from bouts of mental illness. Barrett's mother, Winifred Flack, was a catering manageress five years her husband's senior. The pair met – family legend had it – atop a haystack on a hot summer's day in the Essex countryside in 1930.

In 1951, when Roger was four, the family moved to 183 Hills Road, Cherry Hinton, Cambridge. By all accounts, Roger was a sunny and good-natured child but was prone to tantrums. His sister Rosemary was his closest companion. "You never knew what he was going to do next," she later said, citing him getting lost on Snowdon on a family holiday to North Wales. Roger Waters' mother taught Roger Barrett at Morley Memorial Junior School. He learned piano from the age of eight and, with Rosemary, won a school piano duet competition, although he gave up the piano soon afterwards. Inspired by his older brother, Alan, who was in a skiffle group, he took up the ukulele and, at the age of

The Pinks and the Blues

The blues – the stark, simply crafted music of poor black Americans, with its distinct harmonic vocabulary of flattened fifth and seventh notes ("blue notes") – underlay the youth revolution that swept Britain and America during the mid to late 1950s and caught the young Floyds up in its wake. From blues evolved first the more driving, uptempo rhythm'n'blues (acts such as **The Coasters**, **Etta James** and **Fats Domino**), which in turn evolved into both soul and rock'n'roll. It also underpinned the British beat boom spearheaded by The Beatles.

Another crucial ingredient in the beat boom was the advent of skiffle (**The Beatles** began as a skiffle act), an uptempo blues-folk hybrid whose British popularity was concurrent with the mid-fifties advent of rock'n'roll. Played largely on home-made instruments such as broom-handle bass and washboard, skiffle democratized music and – unlike, say, trad jazz, which demanded a high degree of technical expertise – suggested to British teenagers that musicianship was within their grasp.

Pink Floyd mainly encountered the blues via the rock'n'roll that coincided with their teens (Nick Mason reports that **Elvis**'s 1956 singles compilation *Rock'n'Roll* was the first album purchase of "at least three members" of the band) and by way of the hits of R&B/rock'n'roll hybrids such as **Bo Diddley**, the British skiffle boom and, in time, **The Rolling Stones**. Although Pink Floyd were, of course, named after two Delta bluesmen, **Pink Anderson** and **Floyd Council**, it's hard not to suspect that the young proto-Floyds were not quite the pure blues enthusiasts they later made out. And the Floyd were considerably less blues-based than their American psychedelic contemporaries Grateful Dead or Big Brother and the Holding Company – or even Jefferson Airplane or The Byrds.

Nevertheless, Pink Floyd's patented slide guitar sound has its origins in blues, as does the open tunings Barrett – and Gilmour – would later use. Barrett's solo work would often revert to blues ("Terrapin"; "Maisie"; "Bob Dylan's Blues"), as did the post-Barrett Floyd ("More Blues"; the jam in *Zabriskie Point*; the improvised blues they used to end their seventies sets with; and "Young Lust"). Waters claims "the blues is at the root of everything" he does, and that it is what he most enjoys playing, something which would enable him to bond with the similarly blues-orientated **Eric Clapton** during the latter's tenure in Waters' band in 1985.

eleven, his parents bought him a banjo.

The young Barrett performed unremarkably at school outside his art classes, although he managed to pass the eleven-plus exam, which secured him a place at the grammar school on his street – Cambridge High School for Boys – in the same year as Storm Thorgerson and two years below Roger Waters. Barrett continued to take little interest in schoolwork, however, and was regarded as rebellious by his teachers. Much like Waters with his incongruous cadet career, Barrett did a stint as a boy-scout patrol leader, with future Floyd stunt guitarist **Tim Renwick** as one of his charges.

Finally, when he was 14, Roger's mother bought him his first guitar – an acoustic, with which he would play along to **The Shadows** and **Buddy Holly** records. A year later Barrett bought his first electric guitar and built his own amplifier in the DIY skiffle spirit. Popular with girls for his good looks and wit, he was going out with one **Libby Gausden**, a relationship that would continue intermittently for several years. But in 1961, when Roger was 16 and in his final year of school, Max Barrett died of cancer, aged 52. "His father's death affected Roger a lot," said Rosemary. "They had a sort of unique closeness." In the diary Roger kept, the entry for December 11 was left blank.

Afterwards, Mrs Barrett addressed their now more straitened circumstances by taking in lodgers, but also encouraged her youngest son's musical activities to distract him from his grief. Barrett began to host ad hoc musical assemblies of friends in the house basement. An aspirant bohemian, Barrett began to take an interest in both blues (Lightnin' Hopkins and Snooks Eaglin were popular with his Cambridge crowd) and beatnik-favoured jazz, and began frequenting the El Patio café and the Riverside Jazz Club in the Anchor Coffee Bar where existential trendies hung out. An ancient drummer (some sources say bassist) named Sid Barrett was a regular player there, and the name stuck to the younger Barrett. Nigel Gordon recalled that "he was a very cheerful boy", with "an Ariel sort of quality – a child-like innocence." From the basement jams, the newly re-monikered Syd formed Geoff Mott and the Mottoes in spring 1962, with Barrett on guitar, performing numbers by **The Shadows** and **Chuck Berry**. Roger Waters was an occasional visitor to these sessions, speeding up Hills Road haughtily on his new motorbike. Shortly after the CND gig in March 1962, the Mottoes split when Geoff Mott joined the **Boston Crabs**, who eventually became the first of a burst of Cambridge beat groups to gain a record contract (their version of the **Lovin' Spoonful**'s "You Didn't Have To Be So Nice" gained some radio play in 1965).

David Gilmour

David Gilmour was born on March 6, 1946 – exactly two months after Barrett – in Grantchester Meadows, a well-to-do suburb on the River Cam. His father, Doug Gilmour, was a professor of genetics; his mother, Sylvia, was a schoolteacher who later became a film editor.

They were easy-going and permissive parents – described by some contemporaries as bohemian – and they encouraged their four children's musical abilities. Though his brother Peter was a guitarist, it took Dave some time to get the bug.

Gilmour attended the Perse private school, also on Hills Road. "It was a very disciplined school which I didn't enjoy," he later confessed. He was another devotee of Radio Luxembourg, and the first single he bought was **Bill Haley**'s "Rock Around The Clock" in 1954. When Dave was 13 a neighbour gave him his first guitar, a Tatay, and Gilmour started learning how to play from the popular book and record set his parents bought him by American folk revivalist and guitarist **Pete Seeger**. Gilmour later described Seeger as one of his "all-time favourite people". Never especially academic, after secondary school young Dave went to study modern languages A-levels at Cambridge Technical College in September 1962. Although, much to his academic parents' disappointment, he didn't finish the course, Gilmour would in time become a fluent French speaker.

Bohemia: Barrett meets Gilmour

In September 1962, Roger "Syd" Barrett took up a place at Cambridge Technical College art department. Here he was again regarded as rebellious, often getting thrown out of classes for such antics as playing the guitar with his feet during lectures. Despite such attention-seeking behaviour, friends from the time reported that Barrett always had a very secret side. His time at the college brought him into closer contact with Dave Gilmour and they became the centre of a local, arty, bohemian set.

This crowd spent their free time at tech playing guitars. Gilmour, – known as "Fred" to Barrett – was technically the more competent, teaching Barrett Stones riffs he'd worked out. "I don't want to go into print saying that I taught Syd Barrett everything he knows 'cause it's patently untrue," Gilmour has said, "but there are one or two things in Syd's style that I know came from me." Specifically Gilmour is probably referring to Barrett's use of that blues staple, the slide: he used a glass bottleneck to sound the strings. Whether or not Barrett's very individual, un-bluesy use of the slide really can be laid at Gilmour's door is another question. Gilmour certainly showed little inclination towards using this style prior to replacing Barrett in the Floyd.

The arrival of The Beatles in the winter of 1962/63 made a huge impact on Barrett. "Storm, man, this is it," he told his old school friend Storm Thorgerson. Barrett began to tell friends he wanted to be a pop star (a term then without its modern freight of manufactured-ness) rather than a painter, and began to perform Beatles songs at his bohemian crowd's parties and during picnics by the Cam, which were fuelled by newly discovered cannabis. During 1963 he was hanging out at the hip crowd's Criterion pub, and becoming a big Rolling Stones fan. He and Libby Gausden saw an early performance of theirs in a tiny village hall in rural Cambridgeshire, where he got chatting to **Mick Jagger** at the bar afterwards. He and Gilmour also saw **Bob Dylan** play that year.

Barrett was then beginning to write his own

songs: "Effervescing Elephant" is one friends remember hearing – later to surface on his second solo album. Although they played the occasional acoustic gig together, it was Gilmour who was the musical star at that time, playing in semi-pro bands such as **The Newcomers** (from January to October 1963) and **The Ramblers** – he was now proficient enough to hire himself out to bands for gigs. Barrett, meanwhile, played bass with **Those Without** in summer 1963 and guitar with **The Hollerin' Blues** the following summer, performing Bo Diddley and Jimmy Reed material.

Increasingly, Syd Barrett was starting to stand out, even among his bohemian crowd. He was witty, a talented artist, and something of a dandy who wore sunglasses in winter. "From the time I came to know him until the time he 'turned', Syd was fantastic," Gilmour recalled. "There wasn't a single person who didn't like him, think he was

brilliant or wasn't certain he was going to be a success at something."

Barrett now began to think beyond Cambridge, applying to study at **Camberwell of Arts College**, London. To Barrett's dismay, his interview, in November 1963, took place on the same day his beloved Beatles were playing Cambridge. Showing a discipline he would not always possess, he attended the interview and was accepted at the college.

Art schools have always played a crucial part in the British pop scene: Pete Townshend, John Lennon, Keith Richard and Ray Davies were all art school alumni. Art schools have long been a magnet for outsider-types who disdain conventional aspirations. When an 18-year-old Syd Barrett arrived to join the art school elite in summer 1964, his old Cambridge acquaintance Roger Waters was already a London lag of some two years' standing.

Mason, Wright and Sigma 6

Upon his return from his year off in 1962, Waters took a series of aptitude tests at the National Institute of Industrial Psychology, which led him to architecture. "It didn't sound as dull as mechanical engineering," was his verdict. And so he was apprenticed to an architect's firm over the summer and, in September, arrived at **Regent Street Polytechnic**, based at Little Titchfield Street, off Oxford Street. Waters was uninterested in his architecture course, however, irritating lecturers with his challenges to their

regimented, rote-learning teaching methods. "It was just like school," he said.

In his second term, in early 1963, Waters encountered Nick Mason, whose Austin Chummy he had noted and requested to borrow. Mason told him it was off the road, but Waters spotted him driving it days later. It was, Mason later said, a typical action that walked the "thin line between diplomacy and duplicity".

Nicholas Berkeley Mason was born in Birmingham on January 27, 1944, the only boy of four children born to Bill and Sally Mason. Sally was a competent pianist and Bill was a documentary filmmaker, a keen collector of gadgets and vintage cars, and a racing enthusiast (passions his son inherited). Although Bill had been a Communist and a shop steward, Nick's upbringing was more affluent than his future bandmates'. He was brought up in a large house in Downshire Hill, Hampstead, complete with swimming pool, and had tried out piano and violin before he had even started school. He dates his musical awakening to the age of twelve, tuning in, like Roger Waters, to Radio Luxembourg. The first album he purchased was Elvis's *Rock'n'Roll*, aged 13, when he also saw the best Britain could come up with in response to Elvis – **Tommy Steele** – at a variety show. He was given a set of wire brushes by a friend of his father's and took up drums in a neighbourhood band called **The Hotrods,** playing variants upon the theme tune of *Peter Gunn*, a late-50s/early-60s detective series. In the same year, Mason was sent to an expensive prep school, Frensham Heights, in Surrey, where he would meet his future wife, Lindy Rutter.

Mason and Waters hit it off, discovering they had shared musical and political inclinations. But although Waters and his Cambridge girlfriend **Judy Trim** went on CND marches from Aldermaston, Oxfordshire, to London in protest at the H-bomb, Lindy and Mason only joined them on the outskirts of London. The cosseted Mason was very impressed with the more streetwise Waters, who had the words "I believe to my soul" Letrasetted to his guitar and who lived in a rough squat off the King's Road, Chelsea, for a time. Sharp-tongued and witty, Waters was also extremely competitive, excelling at table tennis and pool.

Later in 1963, the pair joined a band called **Sigma 6**, formed by fellow students **Clive Metcalfe** (on bass – though pictures have shown him playing guitar) and **Keith Noble** (on vocals). Noble's sister Sheila occasionally sang and a fellow student called Rick Wright sometimes played piano (if the pub they were playing had one), though it's said Wright also played rhythm guitar and Waters played lead guitar. Wright also attests to finding Waters intimidating.

Richard William Wright is the oldest member of Pink Floyd: born on July 28, 1943 to Bridie and Cedric Wright in **Elton John**'s home town of Pinner, Middlesex. Rick's father, Robert, was chief biochemist for Unigate Dairies, and Rick was brought up in Hatch End on the outskirts of London, with his two sisters. He played piano, trumpet and trombone as a schoolboy and, after breaking his leg at the age of ten, the young Wright taught himself the guitar, inventing his own fingering. He attended the exclusive Haberdashers' Aske's school, and became something of a jazz buff (complete with bowler hat), venturing out to see **Humphrey Lyttelton** and **Kenny Ball** at Eel Pie Island and later recalling that the only time he ever queued for tickets was to see **Duke Ellington** when he was 17. Without any real passion for the subject, Wright enrolled at Regent Street Poly to study architecture in September 1962. By autumn 1963 he had joined Sigma 6 with Waters and Mason.

Abdabs, Lodgers and The Tea Set

In early 1964, Sigma 6 morphed into **The Abdabs** (sometimes known as The Screaming Abdabs). Their line-up was the same, with Wright's girlfriend **Juliette Gale** sometimes singing blues standards with the band. They performed at student parties and received their first press in the Regent Street Poly magazine (the headline leading to the band being mistakenly called the Architectural Abdabs). In the article Waters said that "[blues] doesn't need practice, just basic understanding" – future bandmates would continually bemoan Waters' refusal to practice. Clive Metcalfe's friend **Ken Chapman**, a fellow student, briefly became

The Abdabs, aka The Screaming Abdabs

their manager, writing some songs for them and setting up an audition with a song publisher, but to no avail.

At the end of the academic year in summer 1964, Juliette Gale married Rick Wright and they decamped to Brighton. Noble and Metcalfe opted to become a duo. Wright dropped out of his course and went off travelling in Greece.

Although the chronology is confused in everyone's mind at this point, it appears that in spring 1964 Waters and Mason moved to a ground floor flat in the house of **Mike Leonard**, a Regent Street Polytechnic architecture lecturer. A keen gadgeteer and amateur musician in his thirties, Leonard set up and ran a sound and light workshop at Hornsey College of Art, where he worked part time. Waters occasionally worked as Leonard's assistant, from which his interest in the combination of lights and music developed. Leonard purchased a Farfisa organ and played with the pair that winter while Wright was on his travels, being replaced upon Wright's return. At their few gigs the group was sometimes billed as **Leonard's Lodgers**. Wright then began to attend the London College of Music.

September 1964 saw the arrival at Regent Street Poly (and Stanhope Gardens) of another Cambridge High School for Boys alumnus and friend of Barrett's, **Bob Klose**. Klose had played in a Cambridge band called **Blues Anonymous** and was a proficient, jazz-oriented guitarist, so the roles in the band were reassessed, Waters being demoted to rhythm guitar. Their frontman was **Chris Dennis**, an RAF dental assistant who also had a Cambridge connection,

having played in The Redcaps. He also – crucially – possessed a PA, and the band played the occasional gig at college hops, supporting visiting bands. Dennis was posted to the Gulf in late 1964, but Mason says there were plans afoot to replace him before then. Syd Barrett had recently arrived in London and was a regular visitor to the house. "Chris didn't feel quite right – we just wanted Syd in the band," Mason explained.

Mike Leonard recalls Barrett as "a very charming fellow, with a lightness and a sparkle about his personality that was uplifting", someone who was "always playing with words" and "always strumming Bo Diddley riffs". With Barrett now handling rhythm guitar and vocals, Waters was demoted again, to bass. "I was never a bass player", he later said. "I've never been interested in playing the bass. There was always this frightful fear that I could land up as the drummer."

Although they continued to play the same Bo Diddley and Stones songs, Waters saw Barrett's takeover as the group's defining moment: "He was the key that unlocked the door to rock'n'roll for me." Now known as **The Tea Set**, around this time they failed an audition for *Ready Steady Go*. They played the Countdown club, Kensington, in February 1965, while entering (and losing) various band contests that July. At some point during 1965 they entered a studio for the first time, a friend of Wright's giving them free downtime. They recorded **Slim Harpo**'s R&B standard "I'm A King Bee" plus three Barrett songs, "Double O Bo" (a mash-up of Bo Diddley rhythm and the

Crazy days at Stanhope Gardens

007 theme, later revisited on "Lucifer Sam"), "Butterfly" (aka "Flutter By Butterfly"), and "Lucy Leave", which were pressed on a small number of vinyl copies, the first and last of which were pressed as a 7" acetate and have been regularly bootlegged. Intriguingly, Wright had a song published and recorded for an act called **Adam, Mike & Tim** at this time.

Barrett now moved to Earlham Street in Covent Garden with various Cambridge alum-ni – aptly enough, on the corner of Cambridge Circus. **Jean Simone Kaminsky**, the leaseholder, made ends meet by printing arty pornography. Other key members of their circle included **Peter Wynne Wilson** and **Susie Gawler-Wright**, "The Psychedelic Debutante", who would later provide light shows for the Floyd.

With both his tastes (jazz) and his lifestyle (square) running counter to Barrett's, Klose left the band in the summer of 1965, though

Mason cites parental pressure regarding his failing studies as the main reason. Klose later said of Barrett: "He had almost too much talent, if such a thing is possible. And also this strange charisma."

Jokers Wild

Meanwhile, back in Cambridge, David Gilmour formed a more long-lasting aggregation, Jokers Wild, featuring ex-Mottoes drummer **Clive Welham**. One of the few professional bands on the limited Cambridge circuit, Jokers Wild's signature tune was Wilson Pickett's "In The Midnight Hour". Gilmour rented a small flat in Mill Road in the centre of Cambridge, as his father had moved to Manhattan, and the band played gigs at US military bases, gaining a residency at the Victoria Ballroom (opening for acts such as **The Animals** and **Zoot Money**). Gilmour – tall, extremely good-looking and with the wholesome, well-fed air of the Home

Counties boy – earned additional cash as a male model.

The band gigged throughout late 1964 and 1965, and during the autumn of that year they self-financed the recording of a five-track, one-sided album at Regent's Sound Studios in London, which they sold privately at gigs. This artefact can nowadays fetch around £400, and features competent versions of **Chuck Berry**'s "Beautiful Delilah", **Frankie Lymon & The Teenagers**' "Why Do Fools Fall In Love", plus two **Four Seasons** tracks – "Sherry" and "Big Girls Don't Cry". This recording (or perhaps the lissom Gilmour himself) caught the eye of singer-songwriter and music industry mogul **Jonathan King**, who had connections at Decca Records. King produced a single featuring versions of **Sam and Dave**'s "You Don't Know What I Know" plus "That's How Strong My Love Is", which – scuppered by the re-release of the originals – was never released.

The Pink Floyd sound

All sorts of changes were underway in the summer of 1965 – both among the future Floyds and within the culture at large. As term ended that July, Waters was told to take a year out of his course and gain some practical experience. Mason also began a year's work experience for his girlfriend Lindy Rutter's father at his architectural office near Guildford. Shortly afterwards the couple moved to Sidney Street, Chelsea.

Also that summer, Barrett began an affair with **Lindsay Corner** and had his first acid

trip in the Cambridge garden of his friend **Dave Gale**, along with **Ian "Emo" Moore** and possibly **Storm Thorgerson**. It was liquid LSD 20, dropped onto sugar cubes, but so haphazardly that they took rather large doses. Barrett picked up an orange, a plum and a matchbox, hoarding them in a corner, and stared at the fruit, which he said represented Venus and Jupiter. Thorgerson would later pay homage to this event by adding an apple, a plum and a matchbox to the cover design of the twofer reissue of Syd's solo albums (see p.231).

Gilmour on stage in Jokers Wild

Barrett was shaken by the experience, feeling he'd witnessed the majesty of the universe and was determined to put this experience into his songs.

That August, Barrett and others travelled to **St Tropez** in a Land Rover, hooking up with Dave Gilmour (the start of a long connection for Gilmour with the south of France). While in St Tropez, Gilmour and Barrett were arrested for busking Beatles' numbers on the streets. The pair later travelled on to Paris, camping outside the city for a week and visiting the Louvre.

Back in London, the Cambridge set began taking acid regularly. Friends later recalled an occasion from this period of experimentation when Barrett and another friend ended up naked in the bath chanting: "No rules, no rules". "Having no rules was something Syd had a thing about," said Ian Moore. Thorgerson said that Barrett was "always experimenting", that he had "a very open sort of mind", and was "empirical to an almost dangerous degree". Such restlessness and questioning could easily tip over into a lack of discipline or self-control – from this perspective, Syd's disdain for rules could be seen as his undoing. "Syd didn't need encouraging. If drugs were going, he'd take them by the shovelful," Gilmour has said, which somewhat tempers Waters' comment that people were "feeding him acid".

As a consequence of this drug use, the Cambridge set also became interested that summer in **Sant Mat**, a Sikh sect. Storm Thorgerson, by now also ensconced at Earlham Street, and Syd went to meet the sect's guru in a London hotel; while Thorgerson joined the sect, Barrett was turned down for being too young. Thorgerson sees this as a deeply significant event in Barrett's life, as he was profoundly upset by this rejection.

Perhaps it was because of his rejection by Sant Mat that Barrett began to pursue music with greater commitment when everyone returned to London in autumn 1965. Holed up in the proto-hippie haven of Earlham Street, Barrett began writing more songs, "Bike" being written around this time. It's also commonly held that the band became **The Pink Floyd** that autumn, although all the recorded gigs of this period have them billed as "The Tea Set".

With Klose's departure having deprived them of their most accomplished musician, Barrett, Waters, Mason and Wright simply couldn't compete with the countless other R&B outfits playing a similar repertoire. They also had relatively few songs, and improvisation was one way of extending the set long enough to get paid. Jazz-lover Wright, who had never cared for R&B, was pleased with this shift: "With Syd the direction changed, it became more improvised around the guitar and keyboards. Roger started playing the bass as a lead instrument, and I started to introduce more of my classical feel." But Waters said, in 2005, that "all that sort of 'let's stretch things out and be experimental' didn't have very much to do with Syd." Their future manager, **Andrew King**, corroborates this: "That all came from Roger. Perhaps because Roger only *knew* one chord." Mason has a rather different recollection. "He's laid claim to it? Was that before or after he invented the wheel? It always felt to me that most of the ideas were emanating from Syd at the time. Roger might have picked it up and run with it – Roger's very good at that."

How Pink Floyd got their name

Mason claims the band's name change was necessitated by the discovery of an identically monikered band on a bill at an airforce base. Although Barrett later claimed the name "Pink Floyd" was transmitted to him from a flying saucer while he was sitting on a ley-line at Glastonbury, the more banal truth was that, back home in Cambridge the previous summer, flicking through some old blues records, Barrett hit upon the idea of combining the first names of two obscure veteran Georgia bluesmen – **Pink Anderson** (1900–74) and **Floyd Council** (1911–76).

The Story

Perhaps, rather than being down to one individual member, the whole band simply tapped into this more experimental approach from the cultural ether. Pop music was in a distinct phase of transition. From 1965–66, **The Beatles** – closely followed by The Stones – hugely expanded the palette and potential of guitar-based pop. December 1965's *Rubber Soul* had incorporated elements of Indian music (the sitar on "Norwegian Wood", the Stones replying in May 1966 with "Paint It Black"), baroque classical (the string quartet on "Yesterday", echoed by the Stones on February 1966's "As Tears Go By"), and even vaudeville (hinted at on "Drive My Car", to be pursued on the next year's "Good Day Sunshine"). Showing the influence of **Dylan**, several British bands had far outstripped the banal love-song lyrics of earlier beat music for something altogether more ambitious (The Beatles with "Help" and "In My Life",

The Stones with "Satisfaction", "Nineteenth Nervous Breakdown" and "Mother's Little Helper"). **The Kinks** meanwhile – a key and oft-overlooked influence upon Pink Floyd – were beginning to establish a much more English variant on R&B-derived beat music, in songs such as "Well Respected Man" and "See My Friend", in 1965, and peaking with March 1966's "Dedicated Follower of Fashion". Change and experimentation were not just in the air: they were staples of the very scene in which the proto-Floyd now found themselves immersed. They played at the 21st birthday party of Storm Thorgerson's girlfriend, Libby January, in Cambridge in October 1965. Also on the bill were Jokers Wild and a then-unknown **Paul Simon**. Gilmour jammed with The Tea Set and they all got so drunk that Barrett attempted to whip off a tablecloth, sending everything crashing to the floor.

The Underground
1965–68

The Underground 1965–68

The stories of Pink Floyd and the British psychedelic underground are intrinsically entwined. Being "the movement's house orchestra", as Roger Waters put it, the Floyd were at the creative heart of the drug-fuelled social and artistic movement that became known as the counterculture. Their sad experiences with Syd Barrett became a microcosm of that movement's darker aspects, of the social and artistic fallout from the excesses that created it.

At first, however, psychedelia was all sunshine, childhood regained and love. Lots of it. Love for your brother, love for mankind, and – after the introduction of the contraceptive pill in 1961 – a whole lot of love for the opposite sex. But there were many other crucial factors in the development of the underground. It was both a reaction to the stuffy conformity of the 1950s ("the generation gap") and a product of the early 1960s economic boom, which had given young people more spending money. Student radicalism had been energized by American support for black civil rights, British campaigns against the H-bomb and protests on both sides of the Atlantic against the war in Vietnam. And, from 1963 onwards, acid began to change the way popular culture looked and sounded.

The Counterculture and The Spontaneous Underground

The self-styled Spontaneous Underground was the first proper outgrowth of this new (counter) culture. The avant-garde art movement Fluxus (of which Yoko Ono was a member) had staged "happenings" in New York – semi-spontaneous amalgams of art and music – but little was actually known in the UK about the US counterculture. Perhaps unsurprisingly, this British equivalent was organized by two Americans, **Steve Stollman,** brother of Bernard, who owned New York's ESP Records in New York (label of such legendary musical insurrectionists as The Fugs and Sun Ra) and **Joe Boyd,** then heading the UK wing of Elektra Records. This Sunday afternoon event took place at the **Marquee Club,** Wardour Street. Initially called the Giant Mystery Happening, it ran from February until April 1966 and was a deliberate attempt to establish a "scene" – advertising its audience as "poets, pop singers, hoods, Americans, homosexuals (because they make up 10 percent of the population), 20 clowns, jazz musicians, one murderer, sculptors, politicians and some girls who defy description..." A who's-who, then, of the marginal and the non-conformist, it was to become a haven of kaftans, face and body paint, old movies, projected light blobs, LSD... and giant jellies. The Spontaneous Underground became the centre of British counterculture. Acts that performed there included Johnny Byrne (an *Emmerdale Farm* scriptwriter, who went on to co-write the novel *Groupie* with fellow scenester Jenny

Fabian); poet Spike Hawkins; **Donovan** (singing to six sitars – he later couldn't remember having performed); free-improv group **AMM**; African drummers; and a lady who "performed" having her hair cut. The Floyd, however, became the house band, playing at almost every event. "They played sheets of sound", remembers "Hoppy" Hopkins, "like a jam session between musicians of different schools."

In March The Pink Floyd played the Essex University Rag Ball and a key Floyd component fell into place. A film, which had been shot by a paraplegic man as he travelled around London, was projected while the band played, and from here on the Floyd took an increased interest in combining visuals with music. Meanwhile, a sociology lec-

The Beat generation

The example of the American Beat generation was crucial to the British underground scene. **Allen Ginsberg**, **Jack Kerouac** and **William Burroughs** formed a loose bohemian confederation defined by openness to sexual, narcotic and artistic experimentation and a love of black American music. For Roger Waters, "The beat generation in North America ... made some kind of connection between blues and intellect ... which produced the melting pot out of which all the kind of middle-class English rock'n'roll developed."

As such, a key conceptual forerunner of the British underground was the International Poetry Incarnation held at the Royal Albert Hall on June 11, 1965. The event was organized by **Barry Miles**, who ran the progressive Indica Bookshop and Gallery with financial

help from Peter Asher. Asher's sister was going out with **Paul McCartney**, and the Indica became the centre for an artsy bohemian nexus. Indeed, **John Lennon** later met Yoko Ono there. With American countercultural figures like Andy Warhol present, this event was filmed by **Peter Whitehead** (of whom more later) and featured readings by Beats **Lawrence Ferlinghetti** and **Gregory Corso**, culminating in Ginsberg reciting his poem *Tonite Let's All Make Love in London*. The event was a considerable success, with 7,500 people turning up, combining various incipient strands in the British social ether: anti-authoritarian politics, sexual liberation and a veneration of drugs as a tool for personal expansion. "It was a hinge, a node," says cultural catalyst and photographer **John "Hoppy" Hopkins**. The only thing missing was music.

Joe Boyd

An American associate of folk-singer **Tom Rush**, Joe Boyd became an assistant to Elektra producer **Paul Rothchild**, before he moved to London to head up Elektra's UK division in November 1965. Here his first proper job was facilitating and producing the recordings of supergroup **The Powerhouse** (Eric Clapton, Stevie Winwood, Jack Bruce, Paul Jones) for the *What's Shakin'* sampler. The personable Boyd entered the heart of the underground music scene, producing scenesters AMM's debut, and co-founding the UFO club that December. When he became involved with Pink Floyd's career in 1967, he formed **Witchseason Productions** for the express purpose of producing the Floyd. He also then produced an abortive single for **Soft Machine**, "She's Gone". In retrospect, this could have been the start of an entirely different career. But after Boyd recorded "**Arnold Layne**" with The Floyd, the band signed to **EMI** and Boyd was passed over. Consequently, Boyd's production career took a very different turn: that of folk rock.

turer named **Peter Jenner** who was employed at what later was to become a hotbed of sixties radicalism, the London School of Economics, had started a fledgling record company called **DNA**, alongside his friends Joe Boyd and Hopkins. Their only release so far was *AMMMusic* by Marquee regulars AMM (nominally produced by Jenner and Hopkins). Jenner, an arty, radical figure who had been hitherto sniffy about pop music, began casting around for a pop group to bail out the money-losing label.

Jenner believes he saw the Floyd play at the Marquee. Their set-list at the time still included R&B staples such as "Roadrunner", "Louie Louie", Bo Diddley's "You Can't Judge A Book By Its Cover" and Chuck Berry's "Motivating", alongside long improvised sections. Jenner recalls that his "ears were tweaked because, during very straightforward blues songs ... they would go off into these psychedelic interludes." Afterwards Jenner tracked the band down to Stanhope Gardens. Told they were actually thinking of breaking up due to lack of gigs and Barrett's interest in painting, legend has it Jenner said he could make them "bigger than The Beatles". But at this point the Floyd were more interested in their impending summer break, and it was agreed to reconvene in September.

Andrew King, a friend of Jenner's from Westminster Public School, was working in the education and training department for British European Airways at the time. ("I could still be doing that job today and no one would notice," he once revealed. "Most of the time I was in bed.") He had even less interest in pop music than Jenner did, but he did have some money his grandmother had left him. When Jenner asked him if he wanted to get involved, in that era of easy employment, King gave up his job without a second thought. Without even having seen the band.

Countercultural revolution

That summer Barrett, installed at Earlham Road, played **The Mothers of Invention**'s *Freak Out!*, **The Byrds**' *Fifth Dimension*, and **The Fugs**' and **Love**'s debuts endlessly. All were seminal 1966, proto-psychedelic albums which began to influence Barrett's tunes as much as R&B previously had. The riff from Love's "My Little Red Book" informed that of "Interstellar Overdrive" (included in the band's set by the autumn) while the tune's free-form central section (and that of the same era's "Pow R Toc H") owed something to **Zappa**'s free-form freak-outs and to the Byrds' "Eight Miles High". All of these were, of course, American influences – but the key British psychedelic document also emerged that summer. **The Beatles**' *Revolver* followed up the implications of their previous B-side "Rain" in June, combining Indian elements with one-chord experiments, tape effects with vaudeville, and nursery rhyme singalongs with stinging, propulsive guitar pop. **The Kinks**' Englishness also came into full flower with "Sunny Afternoon" hitting #1 that June – not psychedelia per se, but a key influence on Barrett's songwriting style.

At the time Barrett's reading reputedly consisted of Grimm's *Fairy Tales*; Tolkien's *The Hobbit* and *Lord Of The Rings*; Carlos Castaneda's *The Teachings Of Don Juan* (a hippie bible); *The I-Ching*; and works by Aldous Huxley, William Burroughs, Aleister Crowley alongside plenty of science fiction – all forward-thinking proto-hippie fare. And Barrett was writing at an incredible rate, creating not just the songs that would comprise *The Piper At The Gates Of Dawn*, but most of those on his later solo albums. From similarly catholic and eclectic ideas emerged the **London Free School**. It was based in West London's Notting Hill, a neighbourhood with a large West Indian community, and the area's cheap rents were fast making it a countercultural enclave. The Free School, brainchild of local "Hoppy" Hopkins, with help from Jenner, was a kind of anti-university – the idea being that what they considered the authoritarian, conformist credo of conventional education could be unlearned. If it sounds vague, that's because it was – even Hopkins called it a "pretty unstructured idea". But it did have the effect of bringing an embryonic hippie scene together. It also led to the **Notting Hill Fayre**, later to morph into the Notting Hill Carnival.

With the Free School newsletter costs putting him in debt, Hoppy organized a benefit called the **Sound and Light Workshop** at All Saints Hall, Powis Gardens, on September 30 1966. The Free School booked their friends' new charges, the Floyd (billed as "London's farthest-out group") and several other bands to play. One night, an American nudist couple, Joel and Toni Brown – associates of acid guru Timothy Leary - brought their projector along and cast slides onto the band as they played. The idea of the lightshow caught on, both with the Floyd and within the psychedelic culture. At the Free School, a one-off became a regular "happening"; with visiting artists throwing paint over Hopkins' piano and the Floyd playing each time. "By the third week people were queuing around the block," said Hoppy Hopkins. "Somehow it seemed to touch a raw nerve of anticipation."

Another key component of the underground was the creation, by Hopkins and Barry Miles, of *International Times*, or *IT*, the UK's first underground newspaper, which was run from the basement of the Indica Gallery. For its launch, on October 15, they booked what had become the underground's two favourite bands – **The Soft Machine** and The Pink Floyd, and hired the Roundhouse. This was an old railway building that had been taken over by playwright Arnold Wesker and other left-wingers, with the intention of turning it into a populist arts centre – but the project had run out of steam. The event put the Roundhouse on the map as much as it did *IT*.

The venue was approached by an incredibly narrow staircase and boasted only two toilets, which meant incredible queues and overflowing latrines that night. For those lucky

Pink Floyd and Soft Machine

Pink Floyd and Soft Machine were the leading lights of the British psychedelic scene. They released their debut albums within six months of each other, and both were far more removed from R&B than other psychedelic acts. Both employed improvisation to a much greater degree than other bands, and Soft Machine later headed towards jazz. Robert Wyatt, the Softs' drummer and vocalist, has said that the Floyd had a much greater "sense of pop music", and that "their formula could be reduced to a single much more easily." However, Floyd influenced the Softs in subtle ways. On their debut, both Wyatt and Kevin Ayers (vocals) were only in transition between American and English accents; it's arguable that their decision to stick to their own accents thereafter was influenced by Barrett. Certainly Syd's guitar technique influenced original Softs guitarist Daevid Allen, a style he took with him to his next band, Gong.

As it was, both bands lost their primary songwriter after their debuts – Ayers and Barrett both going on to equally eccentric solo careers.

Barrett played on an unreleased version of Ayers' "Singing A Song In The Morning" in November 1969 (available on the 2003 reissue of Ayers' *Joy Of A Toy*). Soft Machine contributed the backing to Ayers' "Song For Insane Times" (*Joy Of A Toy*) and Barrett's "No Good Trying" and "Love You" (1970's *The Madcap Laughs*), as well as a version of "Octopus" that remained unreleased until EMI's 1994 *Opel* compilation. Ayers later wrote "O Wot A Dream" (from 1973's *Banamour*), a lyrical and stylistic tribute to Barrett.

Then, when Wyatt broke his back, it was the Floyd who arranged the benefit gig at The Rainbow in November 1973, to help pay his medical bills, performing *Dark Side Of The Moon*. The event raised £10,000. Soon after, Nick Mason produced Wyatt's riveting 1974 album *Rock Bottom* – Wyatt returning the favour by singing on Mason's 1981's *Fictitious Sports*. More recently, Dave Gilmour, who played on Wyatt's 2004 album *Cuckooland*, presented him with his Lifetime Achievement Award at the 2005 *Mojo* Awards.

The Story

enough to gain entry, there were experiences and sights such as a Buick done up in pop art-style, a showing of **Kenneth Anger**'s cult mystic film *Scorpio Rising*, and the inevitable enormous jelly, which the Floyd managed to run over with their van. Among the audience were **Paul McCartney** dressed in Arab costume and **Marianne Faithfull** in a nun's habit mini-dress (earning her the "shortest and barest" award). With 2,500 people packed into the space, this was by far the Floyd's largest show to date, and they utilized all their tricks: the Free School light show, abetted by a primitive lighting machine created by Jenner and King; Barrett using a cigarette lighter as a slide and rolling ball-bearings down the neck of his guitar (both learned from watching AMM at the Marquee) to set up waves of feedback; and, as a climax, blowing the power altogether during "Interstellar Overdrive". It was an event that seemed to fuse all the divergent ingredients of the underground. "Very cold, very dirty but very nice", Hopkins summed up.

"It's totally anarchistic", Roger Waters told a disapproving *Sunday Times*, "but it's co-operative anarchy … it's definitely a complete realisation of the aims of psychedelia." *Melody Maker* said they needed more of their own material: "psychedelic versions of "Louie Louie" won't come off." Indeed, by the time they played the Free School later that month, "Louie Louie" was gone, though they retained Chuck Berry's "Gimme A Break" and Bo Diddley's "I Can Tell". Their performances throughout October and November were increasingly improvised and increasingly packed.

Blackhill Enterprises

At the end of October, the four members of the Floyd, along with King and Jenner, set up Blackhill Enterprises, named after a cottage King had bought on the Welsh borders of Herefordshire in 1964, with money he'd inherited from his grandmother. It was a six-way split of profits, as opposed to the usual management 20 percent of everything: very much a sign of the communal, one-for-all times.

To staff Blackhill, Jenner simply turned to the lodgers in his Edbrooke Road house: **June Child** (who later married Marc Bolan) became Blackhill's secretary, while **John Marsh** became unpaid lighting assistant. Barrett's flatmate **Peter Wynne Wilson** was appointed road manager, though – because he had theatre lighting experience, his main duties were the signature light show, assisted by his girlfriend **Susie Gawler-Wright**.

King's first management act was to spend £1000 on buying the band new equipment, which was promptly stolen after Wright – who earned additional cash by unloading the gear – left it in their van overnight in Regent's Park, near his flat in Leinster Gardens. The managers' next task was to create some demo recordings. These were recorded at the Thompson Private Recording Studio, Hemel Hempstead, in November 1966 and comprised "I Get Stoned" (aka "Stoned Alone", a poppy number), "Let's Roll Another One", "Lucy Lee In Blue Tights" ("what a drag, you're a slag/in blue tights"), and a 15-minute version of "Interstellar Overdrive". "That was the first time I realized they were going to

write all their own material," says King. "Syd just turned into a songwriter, it seemed like overnight."

Both new booking agent **Bryan Morrison** (an old-fashioned hustler who had managed The Pretty Things) and Joe Boyd suggested investing in better quality recordings, which later led to Boyd producing the Floyd's debut single. In November, via Morrison's agency, they started to gig outside London. On the 18th, they played their first of many bizarrely titled concerts, **Philadelic Music For Simian Hominids**, a multimedia event organized by former landlord Mike Leonard at Hornsey College of Art (scene of the first student occupation the following year). The following

night they played at Canterbury Technical College with a 15-foot tinfoil Buddha behind them. They attracted much press attention. Rick Wright was quoted as saying: "There is probably more coordination between us than any other pop group. We play like a jazz group."

They continued to play the Free School for the next two weeks before playing at **Psychodelphia Versus Ian Smith** at the Roundhouse on December 3, organised by the Majority Rule for Rhodesia Campaign ("Bring your own happenings and ecstatogenic substances," said the flyer, "drag optional") and an Oxfam benefit at the Albert Hall – their biggest venue to date.

UFO

Another product of Hoppy's imagination, **UFO** (pronounced "you-foe" by those in the know) was inspired by the runaway success of the Free School events. "If you light a fire and it burns brightly, you look around for more fuel," says Hopkins today. It was located beneath the Blarney Pub on Tottenham Court Road. Joe Boyd booked the groups and DJed and the Floyd became the resident band. Jenny Fabian said: "The Floyd were like our local consciousness come to life. It was as though they'd always been there … poets from the cosmos." It's intriguing now to see what dandies the Floyd members were back then – a band later

Waters in 1967

so synonymous with dressing down – in their stackheeled Gohills boots, cravats, scarves and stripey trousers.

Unusually UFO went on all night because of lack of public transport after midnight, although there was no alcohol (hardly necessary given the quantities of acid around). Again there were coloured lights, Chinese animations, avant-garde films by Kenneth Anger, as well as a whole melting pot of music. In addition to the Floyd, regulars included **The Third Ear Band** (later to be Floyd's label mates on Harvest), **The Purple Gang**, whose song "Granny Takes A Trip" (named after a hip Kings Road clothes store) was produced by Boyd and would become an anthem for the scene (Barrett had, as it happens, been one of the first to sport Granny Takes A Trip clothes.) Psychedelic rock band **Tomorrow** were also key participants; their drummer **Twink** later worked with Barrett. Such was the communality at UFO that on the day after the Stones' drug bust, the entire club marched out to picket the *News Of The World* newspaper.

Barrett began to detune his guitar for psychedelic effect, and often used three different Binson echo units in a row (a trick he'd learned from AMM), creating a field of sound. "Everything was so rosy at UFO," Barrett later said. "It was really nice to go there after slogging around the pubs and so on. Everyone had their own thing." The Floyd's own thing was their light show. Wynne Wilson was pulling out all the stops – experimenting with stretching condoms around the projector, using a polarizer for a Polaroid effect.

If UFO was mainly for the hip cognoscenti, the band's regular Thursday gigs at the Marquee captured a more mainstream crowd searching for what *Time* magazine had dubbed "Swinging London". Mason says the band were never entirely comfortable there. They finished off the year by playing the Roundhouse's New Year's Eve All Night Rave, supporting **The Who** and **The Move**. *The Daily Mail* covered the event. "Teenagers celebrating the New Year at two psychedelic pop music sessions in London were risking permanent damage to the ears," they claimed. "The Pink Floyd group occasionally reached 120 [decibels] at the 'Freak-out'." Quite how they figured this out is unclear.

For all the flash and spectacle, Nick Mason has since been sceptical about the actual music: "There was a hell of a lot of rubbish being played in order to get a few good ideas out."

Tonite Let's All Make Love In London

At the start of 1967, Syd Barrett was seeing a girl called **Jenny Spires**. She was one of a sequence of Syd's girlfriends from Cambridge (she later married his future Stars bandmate, Jack Monck) but unbeknown to Barrett she had had an affair with another Cambridge alumnus, filmmaker **Peter Whitehead**, who had shot a 1965 tour documentary on The Rolling Stones. Spires persuaded a reluctant Whitehead (who had previously thought the Floyd sounded "like bad Schoenberg") to utilize the Floyd for a film about the swinging London scene, *Tonite Let's All Make Love In London*, named after the Ginsberg poem. In February, at a cost of £80, Whitehead took the band into sound engineer John Wood's Sound Techniques studio in Chelsea, with Joe Boyd. There they recorded a 16:46 minute version of "Interstellar Overdrive", ending up recording an additional 11:50 minute extemporisation, "Nick's Boogie". Whitehead filmed it and the footage was used in both *Tonite* and a later video release, *London 1966–67*. Whitehead later conceded that "they were just completely welded together, just like a jazz group."

On February 1, 1967 the Floyd turned professional, giving up their ailing studies. As they began to tour further around the country, regional audiences proved less receptive, pelting the band with beer mugs at Dunstable and pouring beer from the balcony. The press, however, were dazzled by their light show. "If we have to have some kind of definition, you could say The Pink Floyd were lights and sounds," Waters told *The Kentish Gazette* in March.

Arnold Layne

Despite having signed **Love** in the US and Boyd's protégées **The Incredible String Band** in the UK, Elektra head Jac Holzman drew the line at the Floyd. Boyd instead negotiated the band an advance from Polydor, but booker Bryan Morrison persuaded Jenner and

King to try to start a bidding war between Polydor and EMI – who had also expressed an interest – over an independently financed recording.

So in February the band returned to Sound Techniques with Boyd to record their first single. Although "Matilda Mother", "Chapter 24" and "Interstellar Overdrive" were also recorded, "Arnold Layne" was deemed the most appropriate. "We knew we wanted to be rock'n'roll stars and we wanted to make singles," Mason later said, "so it seemed the most suitable song to condense into three minutes without losing too much." They also recorded "Let's Roll Another One", changing its title to the less controversial "Candy And A Currant Bun". Barrett was put out by this decision, but Waters overruled him – an interesting insight into the dynamic between the two. Although most perceived Barrett as the driving force, King noted Waters' strong contribution from the off – organizing, thinking up schemes, talking to the press. "Roger had enormous drive and determination from the beginning," says King. "If he'd stuck at architecture, he'd be as famous as Norman Foster by now. He didn't have much musical knowledge, but he was very drawn to all that avant-garde experimental stuff." More rooted in R&B than some of their original material, "Candy" nevertheless has a certain charm, boasting similar Duane Eddy guitar to "Arnold", but also a rather too similar organ solo. The band's managers, who felt that Wright had a tendency to repeat himself, dubbed his approach "Fry's Turkish Delight".

Barrett – always fey – sounds fantastically camp here.

Bryan Morrison's bidding war idea paid off, for EMI outbid Polydor by offering £5000 to their £1500. The offer was too good to turn down, but it effectively cut Boyd out of the agreement – EMI possessing a strict staff producer system. The deal, unusually, also included an album development clause, giving the Floyd unlimited studio time at EMI Studios (later to become known as Abbey Road, following The Beatles' album of the same name) in exchange for a smaller royalty percentage. After an attempt to re-record "Arnold Layne", however, the original Boyd version was used.

Blackhill, meanwhile, were able to invest in some proper office space below Andrew King's house in Alexander Street, Bayswater, having utilized Jenner's house for some ten months. "Arnold Layne" was released on March 11, accompanied by a promo film by **Derek Nice**. Often wrongly attributed to Peter Whitehead, it was never shown until the 1980s, when both the solo Waters and reformed Floyd played it on tour. Waters is perhaps the most comfortable in front of the camera, but the clip of the Floyd frolicking with a mannequin on East Wittering beach on the south coast manages to suggest both an innocence and – with Wright and Waters both dressed as undertakers – something a little more sinister.

Pirate station Radio London refused to play the song, deeming it "smutty", although the supposedly stuffy BBC did not – in an attempt to get licences and become legitimate, the

60s pop and Englishness

Pete Brown, lyricist for **Cream**, once described "Arnold Layne" as "the first truly English song about English life", and admitted that Cream's January 1969 hit "White Room" would not have occurred without it. But his comment is inaccurate. Influential as Barrett's strain of Home Counties English whimsy may have proved, a certain strain of Englishness was simply in the 60s ether.

"Arnold Layne" didn't emerge until March 1967, by which time **The Kinks** had long established a very English approach to their music, starting with the *Kwyet Kinks* EP in September 1965. The set pursued a less abrasive approach to their early singles. One song, "A Well-Respected Man", drew on the English vaudeville tradition and found **Ray Davies** singing in a plummy English accent about the kind of stuffy conservative who disapproved of beat groups. Davies quickly followed this with "Dedicated Follower Of Fashion", in March 1966, which turned the satire back upon his own peer group of swinging London hipsters, again singing in an English accent and using a jaunty music-hall style. "Sunny Afternoon", a #1 that summer, and "Dead End Street" in November, consolidated the style to which The Kinks would stick for their entire career.

By contrast, **The Beatles** were relatively slow on the uptake. Although Americans imitated The Beatles'

English accents, the four Liverpudlians maintained a distinctly American idiom until *Rubber Soul*, on which tracks such as "Norwegian Wood" and "Girl" occupied an indistinct, Euro-American territory. "Paperback Writer" in June 1966 was their first expression of a more English sensibility, with English reference points (the *Daily Mail*) and something resembling an English accent. This style reached full flower with "Eleanor Rigby" in August 1966, and elsewhere on *Revolver* ("For No-One", "Yellow Submarine"), before peaking with the "Strawberry Fields Forever"/"Penny Lane" single of February 1967, which combined Englishness with childhood – a key component of English psychedelia in general, and the Floyd in particular. All this, of course, would be alloyed in *Sgt Pepper* that June.

Inevitably, **The Rolling Stones** weren't far behind, with the baroque English strains of "Lady Jane" in June 1966, and "Ruby Tuesday", in January 1967. Although this style wouldn't outlast The Stones' much underrated (and partly Floyd-inspired) *Their Satanic Majesties Request* album of November 67, plenty of others were at it. **The Who**'s mini-opera, *A Quick One*, and #3 hit "Happy Jack" of December 1966 are two good examples; **Kaleidoscope** released the gorgeous, baroque "Flight From Ashiya" that spring; whilst fellow Londoners' **Blossom Toes**' *We Are Ever So Clean* was a release chock-full of English whimsy.

pirates were trying to out-prude the establishment. Reviewing "Arnold Layne", the *NME* said it had an "offbeat weird lyric and blockbusting sound", venturing that "with all their publicity, [it] could well be a hit." *Melody Maker*'s response was that "The Pink Floyd represent a new form of music to the English

pop scene, so let's hope the English are broadminded enough to accept it with open arms." In an interview with *Melody Maker* Barrett said, "'Arnold Layne' just happens to dig dressing up in women's clothing. A lot of people do. So let's face up to reality." Perhaps Barrett had picked up on something – some months later, the Stones delivered their dragged-up promo film for "Have You Seen Your Mother Baby, Standing In The Shadow?"

"Arnold" went into the chart at #20, with a little hyping help from their management, and a *Top Of The Pops* appearance was filmed. But the single slipped several places, and it was never broadcast.

The Piper At The Gates Of Dawn

During February 1967, The Pink Floyd had begun recording their debut album in Studio 3 with EMI staffer **Norman Smith**, in between gigs and tours around the country. Smith started working at EMI Studios in 1959, as assistant to Beatles producer **George Martin**. After Martin's departure to create his own company, Smith remained with EMI imprint Parlophone and continued to engineer Beatles sessions, harbouring ambitions to produce.

EMI boss Beecher Stevens later said he regarded Smith as "a firm hand on the sessions", and the company issued a press release distancing The Pink Floyd from psychedelia. "The Pink Floyd does not know what people mean by psychedelic pop and are not trying to create hallucinatory effects on their audiences."

Conspiracy theorists among Floyd fans maintain that this was part of an attempt to water down the Floyd's more challenging, countercultural elements. In fact, the Floyd themselves had been regularly denying they were a psychedelic band since January.

Still, much criticism has been made of Norman Smith's production, suggesting that he curbed the wildness of The Pink Floyd's live sound to create something more conventional and pop-orientated. "That's probably true," Andrew King has said, "but it's also what everyone wanted." "We all want to be pop stars," Barrett informed Canadian radio that summer. However, Smith has tended to play into the hands of his critics, by his later dismissal of the Floyd, describing the sessions as "sheer hell", and disparaging Barrett's inconsistency and the musical abilities of the other members. He said that Waters "made more interesting noises with his mouth" than his bass; that he had to step in for Mason on a drum roll (which is apparently true); and that Wright was "not as good as he thinks he is". "I don't know when Norman started hating the Floyd," says Andrew King. "He got paid overtime and got his house recarpeted!" Management, band and indeed Smith's comments nearer the time suggest the sessions

The Floyd under psychedelic lights

The I Ching and "Chapter 24"

This *Piper* song's lyric is derived from the 5,000-year-old Chinese Taoist book, the **I Ching**. A popular pastime among proto-hippies, "reading" the *I Ching* involved throwing coins six times, performing a complex series of sums, and then referring to the chapter of the book suggested by the final figure. It was revered both as part of a general respect for the oriental during this time, but also for opening the participant to chance. Syd Barrett was given his copy by the mother of **Seamus O'Connell**, in whose house on Tottenham Court Road he lived upon first arriving in London in 1964. Chapter 24 of the book (and the lyrics of the song) concerns the phases of time and finding your true path – both quite poignant themes in the light of Syd Barrett's subsequent history. Barrett took the lyric almost verbatim from **Richard Wilhelm**'s 1924 translation.

were relaxed and efficient, a view backed by the fact that several songs ("The Gnome" and "The Scarecrow") were recorded in one take.

Although no technical master, Nick Mason, like Ringo Starr before him, had perfected a distinctly personal sound. It was tom-tom heavy, using mallets rather than sticks, it was drenched in dramatic echo, and was given extra impact by Smith's Ringo-learned wheeze of damping the drums with teatowels. "You can't imagine Pink Floyd without those tom-toms and the beaters – that's the sound," commented Peter Jenner. As for Waters, his basic, driving bass was integral to the sound – and both Joe Boyd and Eric Clapton were admirers. Rick Wright meanwhile was, according to Jenner, "the musical backbone ... the one who could help find the harmonies, who could sing in tune." Indeed Wright used to tune both Waters' bass and Barrett's guitar onstage.

Whatever he may have said since, at the time Norman Smith and The Pink Floyd were in perfect accord, a fact reflected by Smith not only letting the band record the unprecedented nine-minute freak-out "Interstellar Overdrive" (see p.179), but gamely making it one of the *first* things he recorded with them. In fact Smith maximized the weirdness of the track by overdubbing one entire performance over another. King concurs: "Norman was wonderfully tactful and reserved and made sure it was there on tape. He was never one of the chaps, but he never said: 'You've got to do this, you've got to do that.'" Smith allowed the established barrier between band and producer to be breached. "In that respect Norman was just brilliant, because he let us join in," Mason later admitted. "Some of the studio staff, the engineering department, were extremely disapproving."

Barrett got especially involved in the mix. Jenner remembered him throwing levers on the boards up and down apparently at random, "making pretty patterns with his hands" while Smith sat contentedly by. Furthermore, there is little that is conservative about "Astronomy

The Fabs and The Floyd

When The Pink Floyd were recording *Piper* at EMI Studio 3 with former Beatles engineer Norman Smith, The Beatles themselves were recording *Sgt Pepper's Lonely Hearts Club Band* in Studio 2. On March 21, 1967 at 11pm, what should have been a momentous meeting occurred, when Smith took the Floyd in to meet The Beatles (then working on "Lovely Rita"). "It was like meeting the Royal Family," said Waters. Most report the atmosphere as cool. "A shame", says Ian McDonald, in his definitive Beatles book, *Revolution In The Head*. As he points out, "At this stage, the Floyd's music more closely resembled The Beatles' than any other group in the country."

Both Lennon and Barrett shared a love of wordplay, of the absurd, of the childlike – all tendencies alloyed by acid, a drug that both Lennon and Barrett were experimenting with at this time. (Indeed, Lennon is sometimes said to have been tripping during their meeting – although some have cast doubt over whether he was actually present.) For both, the results were almost disablingly potent, firing their imaginations but also dulling their ability to interact socially. In Lennon's case this change would only be temporary.

The pair also shared an intuitive approach to musical form. Lennon's characteristic, unconventionally abridged or elongated bars moulded songs to mood, a practice echoed by Barrett's work. Its intensity became rather disturbing by the time of Barrett's solo albums, when his intuitive musical sense had become an eccentricity that bordered insanity.

Yet it was **Paul McCartney** who was the Floyd's main advocate among The Beatles. He called their debut "a knockout", and apparently dropped into UFO to check them out with Lennon, but he was also generally supportive of the underground via the Indica Bookshop/Gallery, and had created a new tolerance to outré ideas within EMI. Given all this, it is odd that McCartney's contributions to the spoken sections of *Dark Side Of The Moon* should have been considered too cagey to be used. The Beatles and Floyd camps did eventually collaborate, however, when Dave Gilmour played guitar in McCartney's **Rockestra** on his 1979 *Back To The Egg* and then again on "No More Lonely Nights" (UK #2, October 1984) – and on his 1999 covers album *Run Devil Run*.

Domine", "Pow R Toc H" or "Flaming" (see p.180). Smith's pop nous also served the band well, his arrangement of the vocal harmonies on "Matilda Mother" bringing out its dreamlike tenderness and his swathing of "Chapter 24" in keyboards and harmonies endowed it with a delicacy the Floyd would later frequently employ in their pastoral pieces. And although the arrangements of the more twee numbers are questionable, Smith was only enhancing a tweeness that was already extant, rather than

creating it. If Smith's intention had really been to create a mainstream pop album, he fell very far short of such an aim, the album boasting only one chorus for its entire duration.

14-Hour Technicolor Dream and Games For May

While recording in April and May, The Pink Floyd continued to perform on evenings and at weekends, their advance having financed the purchase of a fashionable Ford Transit van.

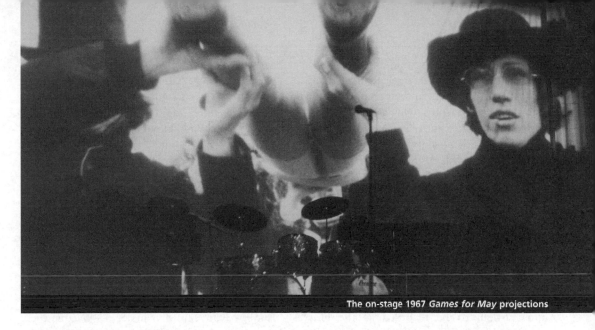

On April 29 came the 14-Hour Technicolor Dream at Alexandra Palace, a Barry Miles and John Hopkins-organised fund-raiser for the troubled *International Times*, which had suffered a police raid and the snatching of all their equipment. "It was double or quits," says Hopkins, "... because of the cultural tidal wave, it was really well attended [10,000 people] though we lost more money than we gained." This was despite never actually paying Alexandra Palace for the hire of the venue. Joints were handed out from a fibreglass igloo, there was a helter-skelter, a performance by **Yoko Ono**, music from future Floyd-collaborator **Ron Geesin**, **Arthur Brown**, **Soft Machine** and **The Pretty Things**, while The Beatles were among the audience. The Floyd played as dawn streamed in through the huge east-facing windows, two tracks being relayed by BBC TV. "That event was the peak of acid use in England," Jenner recalled. "Everyone was on it ... the bands, the organisers, the audience ... and I certainly was."

On May 12, 1967, they were booked to play at the prestigious **Queen Elizabeth Hall** on London's South Bank, an event they called *Games For May* which was billed as "space-age relaxation for the climax of spring – electronic composition, colour and image projection, girls and The Pink Floyd." Concerts lasting more than half an hour were almost unheard of in those days, and the South Bank rarely booked pop groups. But the event came about through King's and Jenner's connections with the classical establishment, and it helped create an acceptance for the band beyond the counterculture. It also paved the way for Floyd's future live spectaculars.

As well as Barrett writing a song especially for the event, there was an elementary quadraphonic sound-system, and taped nature noises. The noises of Mason sawing a log were amplified and Waters chucked potatoes at a gong while thousands of soap bubbles were pumped out by roadies. One of the crew threw daffodils into the audience while dressed up as an admiral. The venue managers complained about the mess, and the group were consequently banned from the Queen Elizabeth Hall. "The audience which filled the hall was beautiful ... and to enjoy them was alone worth the price of a ticket," gushed an unusually effusive *Financial Times*. "When you add in the irrepressible Pink Floyd and a free authentic daffodil to take home", the review continued, "your cup of experience overflows." Barrett declared, prophetically, that: "In the future, groups are going to have to offer more than a pop show. They are going to have to offer a well-presented theatre show."

See Emily Play

The song "Games For May" was shortened and retitled, to be recorded as the Floyd's next single, "See Emily Play". With the band struggling to repeat the immediacy of "Arnold Layne", Norman Smith took the band back to Sound Techniques on May 21 to try to recapture Joe Boyd's magic. "It was a bit galling at the time," said Boyd later. This creative pinnacle of the early Pink Floyd found a dark, negative reflection in its leader's psyche.

Barrett's old pal, Dave Gilmour, back briefly from his travels in France, stopped by the Emily sessions. "Syd didn't seem to recognize me and just stared back," he recalled. "I'll go on record as saying that that was when he changed. It was a shock. He was a different person. I assumed he'd had too much of the old substances..." Equally, **Rosemary Barrett**, then a student nurse in London, met her brother shortly after the release of "Emily". "He'd changed so much that I just couldn't reach him. The brother I knew had disappeared." Andrew King said that his eyes "became these great empty dark pools", and that "it felt quite sudden." Although, as he pointed out, "the traditional wisdom is that it was triggered by too much acid," King believes "there was something else ... something to do with his relationships with people."

Unaware of what was brewing behind the scenes, the single's reviews were celebratory. *Record Mirror* called it "Pink Floyd's best so far", predicting "a substantial hit". *NME* found "Emily" to be "crammed with weird oscillations, reverberations, electronic vibrations and fuzzy rumblings", though the magazine also detected "a pleasant mid-tempo tune that's appealingly harmonised" – one that "Should register!" It did. "See Emily Play" climbed to #6 at the end of July in the BBC chart, with other charts placing it in the Top 5. The band were booked on *Top Of The Pops* three times. The first time, Barrett appeared in Granny Takes A Trip satin and velvet (see p.30); a week later, the clothes were creased and he was unshaven; the third week he arrived in his finery only to exchange them for some filthy rags, refusing to do the show. "He didn't want to know," Waters said. "He got down there in an incredible state and said he wasn't going to do it. We finally discovered the reason was that John Lennon didn't have to do it, so he didn't."

Dark side of the Summer of Love

As the summer progressed, Barrett's behaviour became still more unpredictable. On one occasion he abandoned his Mini, engine running, at a traffic light after spotting something in a shop window. The Pink Floyd returned to UFO for the first time in some months on June 2. Joe Boyd later described seeing Syd that night. "I looked right in his eye and there was no twinkle, no glint," he said. "It was like somebody had pulled the blinds – you know, nobody home." It's a comment later referenced by Roger Waters on *The Wall*'s Barrett-inspired song, "Nobody Home". *IT* reported that the Floyd "played like bums" that night.

As it was, the shadow Barrett cast over the Summer of Love was not the only one. John Hopkins was arrested for marijuana possession ("I was on their hit list," he claimed), Soft Machine's **Daevid Allen** was denied re-entry into the UK and **Mick Jagger** and Keith Richard had been imprisoned on drug charges. UFO had its Blarney lease terminated after police inter-

vention and a shift to the Roundhouse never recaptured the old magic. The Establishment had clamped down on the counterculture. And arguably, weakened by drugs, disorganisation and the appeal of profiting from a commercially viable scene, the counterculture *allowed* itself to be clamped.

Although the Floyd didn't suffer directly from this clamping down, the shift into the commercial world brought its own share of problems – for their fragile leader in particular. The Floyd continued to tour relentlessly (80 shows between May and September) and to be hassled for the hits by mainstream audiences indifferent to the underground. They began to play a number called "Reaction In G", whose thrashy improvisations faced down the pop fans. More amusingly, spoofing **Timothy Leary**'s "tune in, turn on, drop out" dictum, they put an ad in *Melody Maker* proclaiming, "Turn up, Shell Out, Get Lost" (Waters' hand surely lay heavy upon this). Following a series of tacky "What's your favourite colour?"-type interviews in magazines, booked on the *Saturday Club* radio programme in London, on July 28, Barrett walked out of the studio saying, "I'm never doing this again." That night they played UFO and again refused to perform their hits. Waters explained, "The sort of records we make today are impossible to reproduce on stage so there is no point in trying." It's notable that Waters was now handling much of the press without Barrett.

For Barrett's state was getting worse. While people can speculate endlessly on whether drugs (or indeed fame) caused his illness or whether

Piper's release and reviews

During the Floyd's holiday, EMI released *The Piper At The Gates Of Dawn* on August 4, 1967 – the tail end of the Summer of Love. The album was named by Barrett after a chapter in **Kenneth Grahame**'s *The Wind In The Willows*, in which the book's animal heroes encounter the god Pan. The artwork was designed by Barrett and the front cover was taken by **Vic Singh**, a friend of Patti Boyd's, who had lent him a prism lens belonging to her husband, **George Harrison**. "They were so abstract and undefined, transparent," Singh recalled. "They're very like that lens … there, but not there." The album spent fourteen weeks on the album chart and reached #6. *Piper* got good reviews, receiving four stars in both *NME* and *Record Mirror*, the latter saying that it featured "mind-blowing sounds" and was "performed extremely well", while **Paul McCartney** told the press it was "a knockout". But The Who's **Pete Townshend** summed up the attitude of the underground when he later complained that "it had so little to do with what they did live," describing it as "like bubblegum – Mickey Mouse music." However, Joe Boyd (who had reason enough to dislike the album) called it "a great album" and "really well produced". It has also remained a favourite among the Floyd: "I love listening to it, just to listen to Syd's songs," Rick Wright has said. "It's sad in a way as well, because it reminds me of what might have been." Although the definite article remained on the album sleeve, from the end of July The Pink Floyd were referring to themselves simply as Pink Floyd.

they were the catalyst for an extant condition, probably the last thing he needed was to move to 101 Cromwell Road, Kensington, with his girlfriend Lindsay Corner and a crowd of acid acolytes that summer – "The catastrophic flat where Syd got acided out," in Jenner's words. "Acid in the coffee every morning, that's what we were told," he continued. "He had one of our cats, and they gave the cat acid." Barrett took to locking up Corner, who had to be rescued by June Child and Juliette Wright.

When The Pink Floyd made what should have been a triumphant return to Alexandra Palace for the **International Love-In** on July 29, Barrett was in a terrible state. Catatonic, he had to be dragged onstage by Waters and June Child. The event would be recalled in Waters' "Comfortably Numb" lyric. "I don't think

Syd played a note," remembers Andrew King. "You could pretend it was some sort of a freak-out but there was no Syd – just standing there looking limp – terrible." Fearful, the promoter demanded the return of the fee, and Child hastily drove the band away the second they'd left the stage. Barrett's condition was mirrored by the event itself, which, with violent bouncers, gangs of hostile locals, and a stabbing in the car park, further reflected the outside threats to the Summer of Love.

Telling the press Barrett was suffering from "nervous exhaustion", Blackhill cancelled the band's engagements for August, prompting a headline from *Melody Maker*: "Pink Floyd Flake Out." The managers then arranged a holiday for the Floyd and their partners with the underground scene's house doctor, **Sam**

Hutt (later better known as the alt.country singer **Hank Wangford**), on the Spanish island of Formentera where some of the Cambridge set had settled. It was not a success. Snapshots show Barrett looking lost and distanced from proceedings.

Following up the hit

There was intense pressure to follow up the success of "See Emily Play", so the Floyd were hustled back into the studio. "Scream Thy Last Scream" could not have been a less likely successor if it had been trying – a slice of insane genius, yes, but hardly chart material (see p.184). It was never completely finished and Andrew King has pointed to Nick Mason doing the lead vocals as indicative of Barrett's parlous state. Significantly, Roger Waters' "Set The Controls For The Heart Of The Sun" was also laid down on the same day, though it was never considered as a single. "It was obvious, looking back, that Roger was going to do stuff," recalls King. "But everyone was too busy watching Syd to watch Roger."

The managers were more enthusiastic about "Jugband Blues". Recorded on October 19, 1967 at De Lane Lea in central London, Barrett asked Norman Smith to book a Salvation Army band for the session. "He wanted a massive Salvation Army freak-out, but that's the only time I can remember Norman putting his foot down," remembers King. The end result featured written horn parts as well. Smith and the band blocked this painfully autobiographical song from being a single. "The most alienated, extraordinary lyrics", says King. "It's

not addressed to the band, it's addressed to the whole world. He was completely cut off." (See p.187)

The band also recorded Rick Wright's "Sunshine" (later "Remember A Day") in the same month. A deliberate – and quite successful – attempt to emulate the feel of "Emily", it wasn't quite direct enough to be considered as a single. But it's interesting that both Waters, and Wright's material was now being worked on – a sense of all hands to the pump compounded by the fact that it was Norman Smith who drummed on this track, rather than Mason.

"We totally pressured him to produce a single," says King of Barrett. "We had to keep the ball rolling. The gigs were drying up. We thought we needed more airplay." Barrett, however, was now ensconced in another acid palace, in Richmond, and was growing ever more remote. According to King, when asked for advice about the Syd situation, Norman Smith's response was: "Why doesn't he write more songs about animals?"

Within days of an impending US tour, Barrett finally came up with the poppier "Apples And Oranges", which Pink Floyd recorded hurriedly. "That was grim," says King, "an indifferent song – if there hadn't been so much pressure it would have been reworked into something else." Days later, they recorded Rick Wright's "Paintbox". A charming piece of lightweight bubblegum psyche – like a lightweight "Day In The Life", King rightly believes it's a better song than "Apples". But, wispy and fragile as its writer, it highlights why Wright, despite being

Barrett's second in command, would not go on to be his replacement. So hurried were these sessions that both songs were mixed by Smith in the Floyd's absence.

Tours and tribulations

The US was far from being at the Floyd's feet at this time: *Piper*, retitled *Pink Floyd* in the US and denuded of its weirder tracks, had scraped up to #134 in the album charts while their singles had made zero impact. There was clearly work to be done. Due to visa problems the band arrived later than planned, resulting in a number of cancellations. Their first US date therefore was at Winterland, San Francisco on November 3, supporting Janis Joplin's Big Brother & The Holding Company. Despite the Floyd's American label dubbing them "The Light Kings of England", Peter Wynne Wilson's lightshow looked weedy in the bigger American venues ("like a Sunday school picnic" says King), while Barrett simply stood there, arms at sides, occasionally blowing a referee's whistle.

On it went. Arriving in LA, Barrett realized he had forgotten his guitar. To add to the calamities, he then fell into a swimming pool and left his wet clothes behind. Booked on *The Pat Boone Show*, Barrett simply stared at the MOR entertainer during their scheduled chat. And, having acquired at Vidal Sassoon what Waters would later call "the obligatory Hendrix Perm", Barrett spent such an age primping his new hairdo at Santa Monica's Cheetah Club that the others went onstage without him. Unable to get the desired look, he finally settled on a combination of lavish quantities of Brylcreem topped off

with some crushed Mandrax tablets. The effect, to his dumbfounded colleagues, was of "a man melting before our very eyes," says Mason. And Barrett simply stood there, on stage, staring – with his detuned guitar. Waters smashed his borrowed bass to pieces in frustration at the end of the show.

The following night, on Dick Clark's *American Bandstand*, Barrett kept closing his lips during a mimed performance of "Apples And Oranges" leaving Waters and Wright to fill in – Waters looking deeply resentful, Wright like was trying to guide everyone safely through. On another TV show Barrett simply walked off the set. The band had gigs and TV slots booked on the east coast, but, because of Barrett's condition, King decided they should bail out. With everyone increasingly frustrated by what felt like Barrett's sabotage of the band's career, Waters apparently demanded King solve the "Syd problem" on the flight back home. "I hadn't a fucking clue what to do," King admits. "We hoped that Syd would get better. That was the wreckage to which we were all clinging."

Apples, oranges and Jimi Hendrix

Barely pausing for breath, on November 14, the band then commenced a prestigious sixteen-date British package tour with **Jimi**

Hendrix, **The Nice**, **The Move** and **Amen Corner** (whose vocalist, **Andy Fairweather-Low**, would later collaborate with Waters). There were no album promotional tours in those days, just the rock equivalent of a music-hall revue, meaning each band played only for twenty minutes, often doing two shows a night. Indeed, the Floyd were once threatened with expulsion by the promoters for going twenty seconds over time. Their set-list often consisted solely of "Interstellar" and "Set The Controls". After having refused to play their hits, one show at Glasgow Green's Playhouse (later the Apollo) found them being bombarded once again with beer glasses.

EMI released "Apples And Oranges" on November 18. Initially Barrett told the press, "It's unlike anything we've done before. It's a happy song, and it's got a touch of Christmas." It was favourably reviewed by *NME* as "the most psychedelic single the Pink Floyd have come up with," though *Melody Maker* warned it was "pretty hard to get a hold of". "Apples" singularly failed to set the charts alight; Barrett's response was that he "couldn't care less". Waters later unfairly laid its failure down to Norman Smith: "It was destroyed by the production. It's a fucking good song." The truth is it was an OK song, adequately produced, which sounded commercial only in comparison with its more out-there competitors. At its heart something was strangely lacking.

Barrett was miserable throughout the tour, Hendrix ironically dubbing him "laughing Syd Barrett". Several times, he refused to go onstage or simply didn't show up, leaving it to The Nice's guitarist Dave O'List to stand in. "We staggered on", Mason said, "thinking we couldn't manage without Syd. So we put up with what can only be described as a fucking maniac." Waters said: "His live performances were useless. He was working out so many things none of us understood."

The gigs continued to dry up. Blackhill was experiencing money difficulties and Barrett's behaviour began to be seen as not just a personal or musical problem but also a business one. Partly as a consequence, Barrett's ally Wynne Wilson – on a draining retainer – was sacked from lighting duties, to be replaced by his deputy (and Jenner's lodger) **John Marsh**. Again looking for a single to sort them out, the band recorded the Barrett-penned "Vegetable Man" at De Lane Lea. It was a dismal song, lacking any discernible tune, with a chorus bellowed by everyone (including managers) and a lyric that (all too painfully) went, "I've been looking all over the place/for a place for me/But it ain't anywhere/ It just ain't anywhere." "It was too dark," said Jenner. "Vegetable Man" remained unfinished, as did "She Was A Millionaire". "That was the one that got away," says King, "the hit they were looking for."

The band began discussing finding another guitarist for live shows to cover Barrett's parts. **Jeff Beck** was one name mooted to join them (something that would not occur until 25 years later when Beck contributed to Waters' *Amused To Death*). Their old friend Dave Gilmour, however, was a more likely candidate.

The five-man Floyd

Dave Gilmour had spent the Summer of Love in France, playing with bassist **Rick Wills** and drummer **John "Willie" Wilson** as, first, **Flowers** and then **Bullitt** (both would play on Gilmour's France-recorded debut solo album ten years' hence). Their fortunes had hardly been flourishing. They had their equipment stolen in Paris and had to resort to threats when club owners failed to pay them. And their renditions of current chart hits were not exactly inspiring. They arrived back penniless, unable even to afford petrol for their van, having to push it off the ferry.

Gilmour's colleagues returned to their parents in Cambridge while Gilmour went to London, camping out in a Fulham bedsit. There are unconfirmed reports he formed a band at that time called The Crew, with future **Spooky Tooth** member **Gary Wright** and future Kevin Ayers bassist **Archie Leggett**. Others say he was driving a van. When he attended a Floyd gig at the Royal College of Art on December 6, Nick Mason sounded him out about joining the band.

Barrett seems to have had his own ideas about expanding the line-up – telling Waters he wanted a sax and banjo player to join, and at another point wanting to augment it with female vocalists. In *Pink Floyd: In The Flesh* writers Povey and Russell speculate that proposals such as this – alongside Barrett performing perfectly capably in rehearsals for *American Bandstand* and on a *Tomorrow's World* show

filmed that December – suggest something more complex was afoot. They suggest that Barrett was pre-empting the band's shift away from the pop psychedelic sound he'd spearheaded and was forcing them into regicide. The knowing lyric of "Jugband Blues" would also fit this theory. Appealing as this argument is – making of Barrett a more empowered figure – it isn't really sustained by subsequent events in Barrett's life and career.

The Barrett Floyd recorded another *Top Gear* session, broadcast on December 31, which included the most commonly bootlegged versions of "Vegetable Man" and "Scream Thy Last Scream", alongside a hesitant "Jugband Blues". At Olympia on December 22, Barrett again stood on the spot, staring, hands hanging limply by his side.

So, at the start of 1968, Gilmour got the call. "I loved the first album, but I thought the gigs were pretty interminable," Gilmour said later. "It was too anarchic. I was all for music-ing things up a bit." Gilmour's first gig with the Floyd was on January 12 at the University of Aston, Birmingham, during which Barrett stood on the stage as the roadies dismantled the kit, reciting a soliloquy from *Hamlet*. The five-piece played four shows that month, announcing the change as part of an intention "to add further experimental dimensions to its sound". But even with Gilmour covering his parts, Barrett still proved impossible to play with. Then, on the way to Southampton in their equally unreliable Bentley Rolls, someone – it's never been revealed who – apparently asked: "Shall we pick up Syd?" to which someone else – again, unnamed – said, "Fuck it, let's not bother." Barrett's last gig with the band was on January 20, 1968 at Hastings Pier, Sussex.

Sidelining and split

Although Barrett was enthused by a mooted plan to give him a Brian Wilson-like role as an off-road songwriter, the first results were not auspicious. Barrett brought in a song to Abbey Road entitled, "Have You Got It Yet?" But every time he played it, it was different, and the others couldn't follow. And each time, of course, they would return to Barrett's chorus of "Have You Got It Yet?" Waters calls it "a real act of mad genius".

Barrett may have contributed to some or all of "Let There Be More Light", "Corporal Clegg" and "See Saw" (all recorded that January); King's memory is that Barrett contributed the slide solo at the end of "Light". "Syd was considered inoperative, but then you'd be in the studio and he'd do that slide guitar and you're just gobsmacked." But Barrett was definitely absent from February 1968 onwards, when a reconfigured four-man Floyd recorded Wright's "It Would Be So Nice" and Waters' "Doreen's Dream" (later "Julia Dream"). Note how, amidst this leadership uncertainty, both Waters and Wright were level-pegging compositionally, with Waters just having the edge – indeed it was announced in early February that Waters' "Clegg" would be their next single.

During this uncertain time, encouraged by Bryan Morrison, they plugged away at Europe,

a strategy that would later pay good dividends. Pink Floyd recorded a series of promotional clips for Belgian TV and for French TV a few days later.

There was, says King, a series of "horrible band meetings with Syd present and not present". He remembers "being horrified about the way people would talk about Syd in the third person when he was there in the room". (At one point, it was even suggested Barrett see hip 1960s psychotherapist **R.D. Laing** – but he professed himself unable to help.) A meeting on March 2, between Waters and Barrett, proved crucial – the point at which Waters decided to terminate the band's association with Barrett altogether. Waters asked the managers what they intended to do, and Jenner and King opted to stay with Barrett. Says King: "We thought Pink Floyd had no future without him. I wasn't convinced they'd have strong enough material. I underestimated Rick, but everyone has always underestimated Rick. But foolishly, what I certainly didn't spot was the way in which Roger would turn himself around." The Floyd's relationship with Blackhill Enterprises was dissolved on March 2, 1968, though nothing was announced until April 6.

With Wright having been a second vocalist to Barrett, and the band's best musician prior to

The Story

Blackhill after the Floyd

If Peter Jenner and Andrew King's decision to back Barrett rather than the Floyd suggests a lack of business savvy, it was actually more suggestive of their instinctive grasp of cult attractions. Blackhill thereafter made a career out of managing English eccentrics who accrued small but devoted followings. And in their defence, it *was* Barrett who had written almost all the songs, sang them and played lead guitar. Moving on, they managed **Marc Bolan** (though lost him before he hit the big time) before championing **Edgar Broughton**, **Kevin Ayers**, future Floyd collaborator **Roy Harper**, experimental progsters **Slapp Happy** (whose Anthony Moore also later worked with the Floyd), **The Clash**, **Ian Dury** and **Billy Bragg**. Jenner and King also produced many of these acts.

Gilmour's arrival, he was the most obvious candidate for post-Barrett leader. This is certainly what their former managers assumed, and King denies a common story that Backhill tried to persuade Wright to leave with Barrett. The newly configured Floyd turned their management over to agent **Bryan Morrison**, and then – after Morrison sold his agency to NEMS later in 1968 – to his henchman **Steve O'Rourke**.

Both Gilmour and Mason have since admitted to some guilt over Barrett's sacking. "We probably did hang on to him for our own ends," says Mason today. "If we'd parted with him earlier, we'd have sunk without trace. But I don't think we could have saved him. Almost certainly the drugs drove him into a state, but we don't really know. And there was no cry of help from Syd." The situation was intensely awkward. Wright was actually sharing a flat with Barrett at the time and had to lie about his activities. At one show Barrett turned up with his guitar, and at the hippie club of the moment, **Middle Earth**, he stood at the front of the stage and glared at Gilmour throughout. "It

was a paranoid experience," said Gilmour, "it took me a long time to feel a part of the band." It's said that Barrett also regularly arrived at the studio to see if the band needed him to play anything. Within months he was back in Cambridge in psychiatric care.

The hippie dream was in retreat; Syd Barrett's situation was one of many sad endings to a hopeful era. It was a situation movingly depicted by Waters in a song "Incarceration Of A Flower Child" that remained unrecorded until **Marianne Faithfull** sang it in 1999.

It Would Be So Nice

For a time, the post-Barrett Floyd were in something of a mess, the burden of songwriting and leadership undecided, and Gilmour far from integrated into the line-up. "I was, quite honestly, a little on the outside through it all. I certainly didn't feel like a full member," said Gilmour. It can't have helped having to mime Barrett's parts on TV shows.

Buying time, and bowing to label pressure for a single, they abandoned announced plans to release Waters' "Corporal Clegg" and turned to Wright's "It Would Be So Nice" instead. As if seizing a leadership opening, Wright plugged away at the song almost single-handedly throughout March, adding layers and layers of keyboards and vocals. A mere six days after Barrett's official departure, on April 12, "Nice" was released, with Waters' "Julia Dream" on the B-side. *Record Mirror* called it "their best yet" while *NME* declared, "Could be a big hit". It wasn't.

Within mere weeks Waters, now living in Pennard Mansions, Shepherd's Bush, with **Judy Trim**, was telling *Melody Maker*, "I don't like the song or the way it's sung." Certainly the sickly chorus overestimates its own charm in putting itself at the start of the song, and the jaunty Beatlesy verse is whimsical without the necessary wit. As for the singing, Waters is presumably alluding to the fact that Wright overdoes the Barrett-esque overenunciation trick, leaving the chorus a jumble of fussy consonants. Waters' "Julia Dream", was, interestingly, rather Wright-esque, and, with its spacey organ chord coda and folk textures, hinted at both the progressive and pastoral styles the band would pursue in their next phase. As such, the single can be seen as a key moment in the shift in power towards Waters, who was, if the less conventionally musical, by far the more competitive of the two.

Finishing off Saucerful

Pink Floyd appear to have spent April taking stock of what they had. Waters blocked Barrett's "Vegetable Man" and "Scream Thy Last Scream", but they did retain his "Jugband Blues". They also had Wright's "Remember A Day", the only song from *Saucerful* other than "Jugband" on which Barrett definitely plays, and Waters' "Set The Controls For The Heart Of The Sun".

Aside from singing lead on three tracks, Gilmour contributed relatively little – he only really got to play guitar properly on "Corporal Clegg". The title track was the first thing the Floyd recorded without Barrett that they felt truly happy with, and one of only two tracks on the album to become staples of the post-Barrett set list ("Set the Controls" having been played live since the autumn). With insufficient songs to fill *Saucerful*'s last twelve minutes, they cobbled together several extant pieces. Gilmour recalled, "Nick and Roger drew it out as an architectural diagram, in dynamic forms rather than in any sort of musical form, with peaks and troughs." If this comment would come to seem pointed in the light of future developments (Gilmour as the musical focus, Waters the non-musical conceptualist), at the time Gilmour was enthusiastic, "That was the first clue to our direction forwards, from there. If you take *Saucerful Of Secrets*, *Atom Heart Mother*, then *Echoes*, all lead quite logically towards *Dark Side Of The Moon*." Norman Smith was reputedly sceptical, telling them, "You just can't do this, it's too long. You have to write three-minute songs," according to Wright. What's more surprising is that EMI had even allowed them to continue at all without their principal songwriter.

In May the Floyd pursued further European

dates and TV spots, a show in Rome turning to chaos when the police responded to the Floyd's pyrotechnics by letting off tear gas. Their Dutch tour of June often found them playing three shows a day, sometimes to schools – putting on a cheap and cheerful affair. The band also recorded their second movie soundtrack around this time, at De Lane Lea, for *The Committee*, a film by Peter Sykes (see p.260), starring Manfred Mann's Paul Jones. Another film, *San Francisco*, directed by Anthony Stern, utilized an old, 15-minute version of "Interstellar Overdrive". They recorded a second session for *Top Gear* on June 25, which included "Julia Dream", proto-"Eugene", "Murderistic Women" (sans scream), "Let There Be More Light" and "The Massed Gadgets Of Hercules" (a truncated "Saucerful"). By June Waters was being referred to in the press as the band's leader.

Saucerful Of Secrets is released

Pink Floyd continued to tour the UK into June, appearing regularly at Middle Earth and playing the first free concert ever held in Hyde Park, on June 29, alongside **Roy Harper** and **Jethro Tull**, organized by Blackhill. The band allayed the fears of the Ministry of Works by saying, "Our music is very soothing. If any litter bins get kicked in it won't be because of us." Then doyen of the underground, **John Peel** said later that it was "the best outdoor event [he'd] ever been to – their music then suited the open air perfectly. It was a religious experience." Given that Peel had been cynical about the Floyd's post-Barrett future, this was a definite turning point.

A Saucerful Of Secrets was released on the same day. For the cover, they employed the services of their old friends **Storm Thorgerson** and **Aubrey Po Powell**, both of whom had graduated from the Royal College of Art and were now working under the name Hipgnosis; they had already produced album covers for British blues godfather **Alexis Korner** and **Free**. This relationship with the band would last the rest of the Floyd's career. Gilmour later said: "We try and keep everything we can within the framework of our own friends."

Reviewing the album *IT* found "little new here", decrying "See Saw" as "unimaginative" and the title track as "boring", although it concluded that it was nevertheless "a record well worth buying". *NME* gave it three stars, but again regarded "Saucerful" itself as "boring". *New Society* meanwhile called it "a cosmic elegy for anyone who seeks truth". Although *Saucerful* hit #9 in the UK charts, it didn't chart in the US.

That July and August of 1968 saw Floyd return to the States for their first proper tour following the abortive Barrett foray. It was still something of a patched-together affair, involving much waiting around in a motel in Seattle while further dates were booked and equipment was scrounged off other acts.

Live in New York City, 1968

Here Jimi Hendrix came to their rescue, and The Soft Machine and The Who were regular cohorts. Although the Floyd went down well in New York, the dates had no impact on the performance of either the album or its US-only single "Let There Be More Light". They followed this with yet another European tour in September.

Point Me At The Sky

The Barrett era was drawn to a close with the release of "Point Me At The Sky", recorded that November. They even gamely made a promo film, dressed up in World War II flying suits. Upon its December release, *NME* called it "intriguing and absorbing ... the best Pink Floyd single in a long time", but it was another commercial failure. As such, "Point Me At The Sky" and its B-side "Careful With That Axe Eugene", closed one era, but opened another simultaneously. When "Point Me" failed to chart, Pink Floyd finally drew a line under their pop career: they did not issue another British single for eleven years. As such, alongside **Led Zeppelin** and **King Crimson**, they were pioneers in the notion of the "album band".

A persistent carp among dedicated undergrounders is that the other, "straight", Floyds sacked the psychedelic Syd Barrett in order to become pop stars. Comments by the band, distancing themselves from the underground, hardly helped, Mason once telling *Mojo* magazine: "We weren't loyal supporters of the underground. Even then, we were occupied with being a band, going the route. The underground was a launch pad."

But Pink Floyd's pop career was clearly Barrett's doing – however he may have felt about it later – and Waters was the architect of their aural experiments from the start. And as they now decided to abandon the pop single after the failure of "Point Me", it was Waters who led the band into the experimental phase announced by "Saucerful" and "Careful With That Axe". Looking back, the lyrics of "Point" now seem to signal this shift, with their tale of a man's decision to leave the world behind and launch himself into space. This metaphor makes Mason's choice of the words "launch pad" doubly intriguing. For Pink Floyd were using psychedelia as a launch pad indeed: to fly off into stranger territories that left the concerns of the pop charts far, far behind.

Set The Controls
1969–72

Set the controls
1969–72

The idea of "progression", of pop music "moving forward" was everywhere in the press, pubs and student unions of Great Britain in 1969. The term "progressive" was initially applied to any music that ran with psychedelia's expansion of 1960s beat music – ambitious blues outfits like **Cream** and **Jethro Tull**, as well as post-*Sgt Pepper* "symphonic rock" acts like **The Nice** and **The Moody Blues** who came to dominate conceptions of the term. These progressive groups were rock not pop, musicians not entertainers, album artists not singles acts, and their audience comprised serious students not fickle "pop-pickers", listeners not dancers – and student unions became an important platform for this new music.

Pink Floyd's first major work post-Barrett, *A Saucerful Of Secrets*, had already revealed their penchant for big concepts and complex structures, putting them at the vanguard of progressive rock. At the start of 1969, although **The Moody Blues** were in full symphonic flight, **Genesis** and **Yes** were still in post-psychedelic embryo, and pomp-rock princelings **King Crimson** wouldn't perform publicly until the summer. If Waters was this era's conceptualist, then Wright was its prime musical mover: both wanted to pursue the progressive implications of *Saucerful*. "Pink Floyd is about taking risks and pushing forward," was a typical Waters utterance of the time.

This phase of Pink Floyd's career lasted from 1969 until 1972 and was, tellingly, one from which only two tracks were chosen by the band for 2001's 26-track retrospec-

tive, *Echoes*. It was a time of exploration, of experiment, of searching, even if at times that search just showed how lost they were. "It was a genuine attempt to find a new way forward," said David Gilmour later, "beyond the diktat of the three-minute pop song." But although they were at prog rock's front-line, the Floyd largely eschewed the literary and philosophical pretensions of their prog peers: Nick Mason would later pointedly say of their most progressive piece, *Atom Heart Mother*, "It's not the story of the Bible set to music or anything!" For, as the survivors of 1960s battered utopianism turned inwards to spiritualism on the one hand, and outwards to space on The other, so too did their music. Like Yes and the Moody Blues, Pink Floyd, in their quiet way, actually did both. For it's important to remember that Pink Floyd's

The Story

progressive period was also their pastoral period, a time when they regularly pursued acoustic, folk-tinged music as well as space-rock epics. And so, although they never sounded so far out again, neither did they ever sound so innocent.

Ummagumma and More

Although the Floyd had begun recording an ambitious, progressive follow-up to *Saucerful Of Secrets* as early as October 1968, the project was announced to the press on January 25, 1969. The album was to "feature each member on their own for a quarter of the record" (*Record Mirror*), with Wright reported as already having finished his section. By February 15, Nick Mason, newly married to long-term girlfriend **Lindy Rutter** and now resident in Camden Town, claimed to have finished recording two versions of his piece. Gilmour said Waters was – with typical prog portentousness – writing "one or two songs about conception and birth with a science-fiction touch." One of these was "Embryo", already recorded for the BBC on December 2, 1968. The song became a set regular throughout 1970 and 1971. Meanwhile, Gilmour, had completed part of his piece by the same December 68 session (as "Baby Blue Shuffle in D Major") but was said to be then "still at the ideas stage" on the rest of it.

Completion of this project was abruptly postponed that January when Pink Floyd were asked to provide the soundtrack for the film *More*, directed by **Barbet Schroeder**. He was a minor member of the *nouvelle vague*, a group of radical leftist film critics-turned-filmmak-ers centred upon the magazine *Cahiers Du Cinéma*. These critics – including Francois Truffaut and Jean-Luc Godard – went from analysing classic Hollywood movies to redefining cinema's possibilities on screen. The Floyd, keen to widen the European audiences that had already helped them through their post-Barrett slump, accepted.

The More recording sessions

More was a negative exploration of hippie subculture. Set on the island of Ibiza, the film shows sexual, moral and narcotic freedom quickly giving way to betrayal, criminality and hard drugs. Perhaps, given their experiences with Barrett, the Floyd were receptive to the film's anti-drug, anti-counterculture message. Perhaps they were just receptive to the £2,400 proffered. Wright later confessed, "We didn't really like the film." The soundtrack was written and recorded in just over a week in January and February, in-between touring commitments, at Pye Studios, London, with engineer **Brian Humphries** (who would go on to work on *Ummagumma*, *Wish You Were Here* and *Animals*). "I don't really like working under that sort of pressure," Waters later said, "but it can help you by focusing your ideas." It certainly focused Waters, the bass player, writing, on the spot, the majority of the songs.

The whole band only played on six numbers, with Wright the most regular absentee. Disgruntled by this distraction from "real music", Wright came up with little for the score. And when he did, he stuck to the progressive *Saucerful* archetype – the group-credited instrumentals "Quicksilver" and "Main Theme" have Wright's fingerprints most prominently upon them, alongside an avant-garde extemporisation with Mason, "Up The Khyber". But he contributed no songs and added vocals only in the background of "Ibiza Bar". "As an album, I didn't much like it," Wright has said, while other reports even suggest he considered leaving the band at this point – he certainly discussed the desire to make a solo album. Compositionally, Gilmour didn't contribute much more than Wright (his first solo composition, "A Spanish Piece", is a flamenco doodle), though the fact that he sang lead on every vocal track and had a vast increase in solos throughout pointed to his increasing importance in the line-up. Although both Gilmour and Wright later deprecated Waters' songwriting skill, the truth is Waters came up with the goods, pushing Floyd simultaneously towards the pastoral ("Green Is The Colour" and "Cirrus Minor") and a harder rock sound ("Nile Song" and "Ibiza Bar"). Mason acknowledges that, "Roger has always known how to work, which is quite an unusual characteristic in rock'n'roll." He also admits than "when Syd went, [Roger] really did just become a songwriter." Waters notably later called the sessions "really good fun". It was the first – and last – time such a comment would be made of a Floyd recording session.

Finishing Ummagumma

Devoting a half side of vinyl to each member of the band was a typically hubristic concept of the progressive era – and never really made much sense. According to EMI engineer **Peter Mew**, the four-way split was "a product of chaos, of not quite knowing what to do". There was "a sense on one hand of 'Oh my God', and on the other of an excitement, a notion of forging new frontiers". The idea, it seems, was to create some substantial new material for a live set that was now getting stale.

But although Pink Floyd were voted sixth favourite group in *Melody Maker*'s 1969 poll, the group's individual members – no virtuosos in this age of technical prowess – showed nowhere in the instrumental categories. In terms of song composition, meanwhile, Mason and Gilmour had absolutely no track record, and Gilmour has always given the impression he was hustled into the project. Certainly he soon foundered. Struggling with lyrics, he rang Waters for help. Waters curtly refused. Was Waters shoring up a potential power-base? (Mew reports that "Roger had assumed the helm at that point.") Or was the arch conceptualist just keen to stick to the concept?

Waters divided his slot between a flimsy pastoral song, "Grantchester Meadows", and a throwaway tape-effects experiment. Mason

The show must go on

As the 1960s nudged the 1970s, Pink Floyd increasingly concentrated on the "show" part of the term "live show". Theatricality was in the progressive air post-*Sgt Pepper*, and the band had been discussing the idea in interviews as far back as 1967. Always heavy on the light show and with a propensity for titling their performances, the Floyd built on the previous year's **Games For May** approach. This was largely Roger Waters' instigation, consolidating his position as ideas man and de facto leader. Indeed the "musicians" (Gilmour and Wright), as opposed to the "architects" (Waters and Mason), were a little resistant to this theatrical approach, feeling it detracted from the music. "Roger was interested in the grand plan," Rick Wright expanded. "Mainly because of Roger, each tour we did, the show got bigger." The history of post-Barrett Pink Floyd is, says Mason, "Dave's desire to make music, versus Roger's desire to make a show". Of course, Waters' conceptual approach would become so spectacularly successful that none of them were to tamper with the formula in the decades that followed.

The first of the reconfigured Floyd's spectaculars, **More Furious Madness From the Massed Gadgets Of Auximenes**, was held at the Royal Festival Hall, April 14, 1969, the same location as *Games For May* two years previously. Premiering their new pseudo-classical suites, *The Man* and *The Journey* (see p.158), the show featured a silver-painted sea monster lumbering up the aisle, the band sawing logs and banging nails onstage, and roadies brewing tea during the interval (while the band apparently slept). This show also debuted their Azimuth Co-ordinator. A "pan-pot", made by Abbey Road boffin **Bernard Speight**, it utilized four large rheostats and a lever to pan instruments' sounds through speakers around an auditorium. The Floyd enhanced the effect by adding extra speakers at the back as well as the front. "A very important step for us..." said Mason afterwards. "If we can develop this kind of thing into an even bigger and better stage ... we will be going in the right direction."

The Floyd continued to tour essentially the same show around Britain for the next month, before conducting their first headlining tour of Britain that June, climaxing at the prestigious Royal Albert Hall on June 26, entitled **The Final Lunacy**. The band were joined on *The Journey* by the Royal Philharmonic's brass section and the Ealing Central Amateur Choir, conducted by Norman Smith. A gorilla wandered through the audience, a cannon fired, and members of the band sawed wood on stage before a pink smoke bomb exploded at the end. With such Establishment venues and collaborators, the Floyd could by now be said to be "overground". As they refined their show's theatrics throughout this period, they also regularly talked about a planned "theatrical project". "We don't like being held back by the fact we're a rock group," Gilmour told *Music Now* in December 1970.

created a melange of unmusical percussion, while Wright opted for cod-classical with "Sysyphus". It is interesting how amenable the supposedly conservative Norman Smith was to this foolishness, offering percussion assistance to Wright and flute arrangements to Mason. They finally completed the studio album by the end of April 1969.

There had been talk of *Ummagumma* being a double album, with the second disc featuring a major work involving all members but, with time running out, they decided instead upon a live second disc, as a final fling for some of the more doddery items in their set-list. They began taping shows for this purpose the same month: at Bromley Technical College, Mothers in Birmingham and the College of Commerce in Manchester. As a result of various technical and performance hitches, elements of the Birmingham and Manchester shows were combined for the version of "Saucerful" and most of the vocals were re-recorded in the studio. The group always felt that the live album never quite represented the Floyd at their performing peak.

Moon Landings and More

As an indication of the band's increasingly Establishment-friendly status, the BBC invited Pink Floyd to soundtrack the **Apollo 11** space mission TV transmission, broadcast on an *Omnibus* special titled *What If It's Just Green Cheese?* The event was broadcast on July 10, and a version was also shown on German and Dutch TV later in the month. With the band's evocative "Moonhead" improvisation accompaniment, the event was a momentous piece of promotion for the band.

As they mixed *Ummagumma*, they also recorded a Waters track entitled "Biding My Time", and Gilmour and Waters spent three days working on Syd Barrett's debut solo album (see p.231). A busy month also saw the release of the *More* soundtrack. Despite the band's lack of promotion, the album was reasonably well received, with *Grass Eye* saying it was "radically different to their music as heard on stage, an album of understatement". *More* went to #9 in the UK after its release on July 27 and the film (unreleased in Britain because its sexual content and portrayal of drug use fell foul of the censor) expanded their audience in Europe, especially in France where it was a substantial hit. Neither film nor soundtrack made much impact in the US, where the film received a restrictive certificate. "Pink Floyd helped the movie a lot, and it helped them because the movie was a big hit," Schroeder commented. "They were a little pissed off – they work on records for one year, and here they do it in two weeks and it does just as well." For Schroeder, "Roger was always the number one man." He continued: "It was obvious that he was the creative force ... Yeah, he was sharp and curt, but if you're getting results, where's the problem?"

The Floyd finally took a two-week holiday during August. Waters married his long-term Cambridge girlfriend Judy Trim – a teacher, amateur potter and left-wing activist – and the couple settled into a terraced house in New North Road, a then desolate area of Islington, North London, with six Burmese cats. In a rare insight into the private life of a Floyd, Waters extolled the virtues of marriage, telling *Disc And Music Echo* that "a family is the most important thing in life, even if only in terms of one's biological function of having kids, which is all life's really about" – he didn't "believe in life after death or any of that stuff." The couple would remain childless, however, eventually splitting up in 1975.

Pink Floyd followed this break with a two-month tour of Europe. At a performance at the Amougies festival, Belgium, on October 25, they were joined onstage by prog kingpin **Frank Zappa** during "Interstellar Overdrive". A film of this event, entitled *Music Power*, is available on bootleg.

Release of Ummagumma

Ummagumma was released on October 25, 1969 on EMI's hip new progressive rock imprint, Harvest. It was housed in another fine Hipgnosis sleeve, depicting the band members in interchangeable poses in a picture-within-a-picture. This mirroring of positions and poses (inadvertently?) suggested a changeable anonymity – it was both an odd cover for an album that uniquely highlighted the bandmember's *individual* skills and also one of the more memorable artifacts of the

Hipgnosis' pic-within-a-pic sleeve for Ummagumma

era, perhaps designed simply to be visually trippy. *IT* called it "a really magnificent package", while *Record Mirror* called it "a truly great progressive album". The album was considered such a benchmark that some journalists would unfavourably compare *Dark Side Of The Moon* with *Ummagumma*.

Ummagumma fared equally well with the public, beating *More*'s performance by hitting the UK Top 5 and gaining their best chart placing so far in the US (though it was still only #74). "It was a very valid experiment and it helped me," Rick Wright told *Beat Instrumental* in January 1970. "[But] I think that maybe Roger feels that if we'd all worked together it would have been better." Waters confirmed this in *Disc And Music Echo* that August: "It would have been a better album if we'd gone away, done the things, come back together. I don't think it's good to work in total isolation." After the progressive rock era was over, the others' opinions were radically revised, Wright later calling his own contribution "pretentious", and Gilmour saying, that "it was just an experiment" and that they "didn't know where [they] were going in terms of recording". Mason now calls it "a very, very flawed album" that shows they "work slightly better as a group than as individuals".

The Zabriskie Point soundtrack

The Floyd conducted a brief British tour in November 1969, but of the *Ummagumma* tracks, only "Grantchester Meadows" and "The Narrow Way" became set-list regulars. The band closed the year by spending December in Rome working on the soundtrack for **Michelangelo Antonioni**'s film *Zabriskie Point*, an exploration of the Californian radical hippie scene. The band's involvement came about after the director, in London during October 1966 for the shooting of his film *Blow Up*, saw their performance at the Roundhouse for the *IT* launch. It was a prestigious commission – although rock soundtracks to films would become commonplace, the Floyd were the first British group to be entrusted with the soundtrack for a major production.

Antonioni had established his reputation as a director of "anti-cinema", rebelling against neo-realism with an emphasis on internalized action, his films exploring alienation and non-communication. He was notoriously difficult to please, as the Floyd found out. "We could have finished the whole thing in about five days, because there wasn't too much to do," Waters later recalled of the

Geesin's Body

In October 1969 Nick Mason introduced Roger Waters to a Scottish experimental composer and jazz enthusiast named **Ron Geesin**. They hit it off and became golf partners. (Waters is a very keen – and very good – golfer with a remarkably low handicap.) Geesin had played piano and banjo in a trad jazz band, but had put his keyboard and string skills to increasingly eccentric ends, making a quirkily experimental album at the age of 23 in his home studio, entitled *A Raise Of Eyebrows*. This had been an influence on Waters' "Several Species…" on *Ummagumma*. Recommended to director **Roy Battersby** by DJ John Peel, Geesin was asked to provide the soundtrack for a documentary about the wonders of the human organism entitled *The Body*. Asked for songs as well as instrumentals, Geesin thought of Waters, seeing him as "the creative force of the band", someone who possessed "that manic flare to do something crazy and make it a piece of art."

Waters and Geesin recorded the album mostly separately, in February and March 1970. Interestingly, Pink Floyd *en masse* play – uncredited – on the album's final track, "Give Birth To A Smile", which, with its black backing singers and sense of revelation, closely prefigures *Dark Side*. Despite Waters' professed dislike of his own voice, he handled more lead vocals on this album than he'd ever done before. This must have been a confidence booster for him, for there would never again be another Floyd album without a Waters vocal.

Geesin's friendship and working methods had a profound effect upon both Waters and Mason. Mason credits his interest in sound effects to Geesin, alongside his ability to splice tape for editing, while Waters became increasingly interested in home recording, employing Judy Trim's potting shed in their garden for the purpose.

9pm–8am sessions. "We did some great stuff, but he'd listen and go, 'Eet's very beauteeful but eet's too sad', or 'Eet's too strong'. You'd change whatever was wrong and he'd still be unhappy. It was hell, sheer hell." But Waters and Mason both also recalled enjoying their MGM-financed stay in the upmarket Hotel Massimo D'Azeglio, and the fine dining they indulged in between sessions.

With Antonioni mainly interested in "Careful With That Axe, Eugene" (remade for the film as "Come In Number 51, Your Time Is Up"), the other tracks used were "Heart Beat Pig Meat", an extemporisation around a speeded-up heartbeat, and "Crumbling Land", which Gilmour described as "a kind of country & western number which he could have gotten done better by any number of American bands." Indeed, Antonioni scrapped much of what the Floyd had done and supplemented the score with those very west coast and country-rock acts Gilmour referred to: **Kaleidoscope**, the **Youngbloods** and the **Grateful Dead**.

This exploration of country and west coast sounds would actually play an important part in the development of Pink Floyd. Furthermore, despite its poor reception, the film – released in March 1970 – helped spread the Floyd word in the US, where the band would increasingly concentrate their attention. Later, Wright commented, "We really dug the film, but we didn't agree with the way he used the music." The band made it clear, however, that they were keen to do more music for films, Gilmour saying, "we like to do film scores because it's an overall concept, not just a string of songs."

Big tours

The Floyd played their biggest show to date on September 12, 1970 – to half a million people at Bois de Vincennes, Paris. But an indicator of quite how rushed everything had become was that their tour commenced on September 26, several weeks prior to the album's release. Bringing along their own brass section and choir they bemused promoters with their refusal to have support acts.

Their performance at the Fillmore East, New York, on September 27 attracted counterculture-friendly classical composer **Leonard Bernstein**. He was "bored stiff" by "Atom Heart Mother" itself, but liked the rest of the show. The piece also soon earned them the honour of being the first rock band to perform at the Montreux Classical Music Festival, and it was announced that September that the band would work with **Roland Petit**'s ballet company on a piece featuring ballet legend **Rudolf Nureyev**. This was a typical progressive-era project. Gilmour said, "It's something no one from our field of music has ever done." Mason, more cynically, later said, "I think we liked the idea of being a bit posh. The high culture thing really helped." The project was to be based on

Marcel Proust's seven-volume *À la recherche du temps perdu*. Each Floyd attempted to read the Proust classic, but Gilmour gave up after just eighteen pages; the competitive Waters got the furthest. By the end of their European tour, Petit had replaced the Proust idea with *Arabian Nights*. Nothing initially came of this although it would reappear in two years' time.

Their performance at the Fillmore West, San Francisco, on October 21 featured a Floyd-less spot for the choir. *Rolling Stone* claimed: "The music of Pink Floyd evokes images of cold, clear, far interstellar regions, of black moving water, of the exhilarating bleakness of the moon," while their show at the Santa Monica Civic Centre on October 23 prompted the *Los Angeles Free Press* to call it "the most successful integration of rock and formal music... the sound of the future". The *LA Times* was

less complimentary wondering "why the four human components of Pink Floyd bother to come out on stage at all, when computers could hardly fail to make as interesting use of their arsenal of gadgets."

During this tour, members of the band consistently distanced themselves from the underground – or what remained of 1960s radicalism. Waters said, in an interview with the *Vancouver Free Press*, that he thought it "a bit unfortunate that these people pick on rock and roll as the start of their process to get rid of profit-oriented society", asserting that "music can't be free," that "it costs fortunes to put on festivals." Gilmour was careful to dissociate the band from drugs; Mason meanwhile rejected the more militant aspects of hippiedom: "My emotional reaction is that I don't go along with it. We're not a committed band."

Atom Heart Mother

When Syd Barrett's Floyd-assisted *Madcap Laughs* album came out in January 1970, its creator gave a few interviews that March. "When I went away I felt the progress the group could have made," he said. "But it made none, none at all, except in the sense that it was continuing." For someone as supposedly emotionally askew as Barrett, this hurtful remark seemed not entirely innocent. But the Floyd appear to have both forgiven him (Gilmour and Wright squeezing in production sessions for his second album between Floyd commitments) and to have

taken his point. Now intent on progressing rather than simply continuing, and with a projected animation project with **Alan Aldridge** (of *Yellow Submarine* fame) having fallen through, they decided to create their most ambitious music yet: a side-long suite. After the atomized *Ummagumma*, they felt that this should be both a collaborative effort and self-produced. "They wanted an epic piece to play live, to go a bit further than the restraints of a simple band on stage," says sessions engineer **Alan Parsons**. "The concept of a band and a choir was something that appealed to them." Norman Smith received a token executive producer credit.

Gilmour devised the piece's main melody, initially known as "Theme From An Imaginary Western", which was supplemented by Wright and Waters, by which time it was known as "Epic". An early version, provisionally entitled "The Amazing Pudding" (later the name of a Floyd fanzine) was premiered in Cottingham, Yorkshire, as early as January 17, 1970, and was played in Britain and Europe until March. Featuring Gilmour reprising his "Eugene" falsetto, it was on the whole barely distinguishable from "Embryo" and other jam-inclined pieces of that era.

An interesting indicator of simmering tensions was revealed in a Gilmour interview with *Disc And Music Echo* on February 21, 1970 in which he disavowed Waters' musical leadership ("he doesn't do any more in the musical direction than the rest of us") and called him "a pushy sort of person". Indeed, after arguing with each other about what to do with the piece, the band brought in Waters' and Mason's mate **Ron Geesin** to help with brass and choir arrangements.

Geesin was given a tape of the entire piece to work with. Both Gilmour and Wright visited his Notting Hill home studio in April to work on the melodies before going off on a US tour throughout the rest of April and May. While Geesin says Wright "offered a few chord progressions for the choral bit", he is disparaging about Gilmour's contribution. In turn, Gilmour has not only downplayed Geesin's

role, but compelled the publishers of Cliff Jones's *Echoes* book to remove reproductions of Geesin's melody alongside his own. "I obviously hit a bit of a nerve there," says Geesin today. Egos aside, the end results sound like a collaboration, with Geesin cleverly developing Gilmour's good idea.

The band returned in June. Mason and Waters laid down a backing track with a shaky tempo that, due to EMI directives about new tape stock, couldn't be corrected, only redone, which time wouldn't allow. "Suddenly it dies back a few digits," says Geesin (of the fluctuation in the piece's speed). "Not much, but enough to make it cumbersome to deal with. When we came to put the stuff on top, we had to go with that. It was a cockeyed way of doing it."

Furthermore, on the day the choir were to record the funky section ("Funky Dung"), Mason told Geesin that his score had misplaced the first beat of the bar throughout. "If there had been time and I'd been a bit more streetwise and sharp", Geesin says, "I'd have said 'Just give me quarter of an hour and I'll move all the bar lines!'" So the piece had to be performed one beat out. What's more, the backing track's uneven tempos meant that recording the Abbey Road brass became nightmarish. Alan Parsons, who engineered the sessions said, "Geesin is a very talented guy but he had written a score which was almost unplayable." Geesin began to lose control of the sessions.

Contrary to many reports, Geesin says the Floyd were very much present throughout the recording, "sitting in the control room biting their fingernails thinking 'Who let that nutter in here?'" Exhausted, Geesin finally conceded conducting chores to choir leader **John Aldiss** – no stranger to prog rock, having worked with composer and Mike Oldfield collaborator **David Bedford**.

For all these reasons Geesin was never happy with the finished piece. "Black jazz like Duke Ellington or Count Basie, they tend to attack things a bit more, lean into it," he commented. "Being a classical conductor, John Aldiss wouldn't know how to lean into the beat. And so it got a bit puddingy."

The Floyd premiered the Geesin version of "Atom Heart Mother" on June 27 at the Bath Festival, Somerset, complete with choir and orchestra. Despite their scheduled slot being pushed back from 10pm to dawn, and a pint of beer being spilled down a tuba, the event was a success. As recording continued between tour dates throughout July they performed AHM again for a BBC **John Peel** broadcast at the Paris Cinema, London, on July 16, when it was finally accorded its title. Minutes beforehand Geesin had suggested they find a name from the *Evening Standard*, so Waters picked up the paper, saw an article about a woman kept alive with an atomic heart, and the suite got its name. It was then played at Blackhill's free festival in Hyde Park, Geesin being so upset by the performance that he left midway in tears.

The Floyd then took the piece to France, hiring a villa near St Tropez to base band, crew and families (both Wright and Mason now having small children). They played the Festival International Jazz d'Antibes on July 26, among others. Mason has said that the atmosphere wasn't quite the idyll painted in Waters' later "San Tropez", with Mason upbraiding Waters in front of Waters' wife for on-the-road infidelity, even though he had behaved just as badly himself. So much for the Floyd's gentlemanly reputation, and Waters' paeans to family life. Late in July, the Floyd provided the PA for the Isle of Wight festival, Gilmour reportedly mixing Jimi Hendrix's performance.

In a candid interview that August, with *Disc And Music Echo*, Waters provided an insight into the man behind the distinctive persona that was beginning to emerge in his songs, "I'm frightened of other people … if you lower your defence, someone jumps on you. I find myself jumping on people all the time and regretting it afterwards." It's an exposition of the sentiments of "If" on *Atom*, also outlining the defensive humanism which would increasingly inform his work. "I haven't even really begun to find out how to relate myself to the rest of the world. But I do have a kind of nagging optimism about the possibility of people coming together."

Recording continued into August, in which month they worked on Gilmour's "Fat Old Sun" (containing a noticeable Hendrix influence) and Waters' "If" (cut from similar musical cloth to the songs on *The Body* he was concurrently mixing). But once again, as deadlines approached, they were short of sufficient material to fill an album. Waters recalled, "We were all frantically trying to write songs,

The Story

and then I thought of doing something on the rhythm of a dripping tap." This grew to encompass the section from *The Man* in which roadies boiled kettles and fried eggs on stage. **Alan Stiles** was selected from their crew to provide voice-over for the piece. "'Psychedelic' was Nick's baby," says Alan Parsons. "He recorded all the sound effects at home in his kitchen at Highbury…This tape would start with pouring milk on cereal, take one, egg frying, whoops, egg frying take two." The band weren't entirely happy with the piece even at the time. Gilmour said: "'Alan's Psychedelic Breakfast' never achieved what it was meant to. It was … the most thrown together thing we've ever done." Wright added, "It's rather pretentious, it doesn't do anything. Quite honestly it's a bad number."

AHM release and reviews

For the cover of *Atom Heart Mother*, Hipgnosis again excelled themselves. Attempting to do something anti-cosmic, anti-prog, and – possibly – running with the fashionable idea of the earth mother, **Storm Thorgerson** sent a photographer into Essex to photograph the first cow he saw. The cow was called Lulubelle 3. "It's the ultimate picture of a cow," said Thorgerson. This time Thorgerson boldly omitted both the band's name and the title from the cover, prompting one EMI executive allegedly to scream, "Are you trying to destroy this record company?" This anonymity – allied to a cover whose down-to-earthness was itself eccentric – only added to the band's enigma.

EMI soon came on board, creating a live cow photo-opportunity in the centre of London for promotional posters and Capitol in America slapped huge bovine billboards over LA's Sunset Strip. Their first album to be released in then fashionable quadrophonic sound, *Atom Heart Mother*'s reviews were mixed. *Sounds* said it "still has that mysterious, intangible feel that has always been the essence of Pink Floyd music" and *Melody Maker* called it "their best yet" but thought the title track "too long, without sufficient strong ideas". In the States, *Rolling Stone* said, "Try freaking out again, Pink Floyd," while describing the second side as "English folk at its deadly worst". *Rock* called it "a new step for Floyd – a fusion of rock and romanticism…they've succeeded in breaking out of the 'cosmic' mould and into a conscious earthiness." It also impressed filmmaker **Stanley Kubrick**, who requested use of the title track for his forthcoming *A Clockwork Orange* – the Floyd refused. Released on October 10, 1970, *Atom Heart Mother* bettered the Floyd's previous chart performance in the US with a #55 placing. In Britain, the album scored them their first #1.

In an interview with *Melody Maker* that November, Wright declared the album "much simpler to listen to than *Ummagumma*", deeming it "more emotional, a sort of epic music in fact", but, strangely, at the same time he disparaged other attempts to combine orchestras and rock groups: "It does not work at all because people are trying to combine rock and classical music. The two go together like oil and water." Waters told *Sounds* that summer that he thought *Atom Heart Mother* "by far the best, the most human things we've done". Mason now calls it a "cul-de-sac" while Gilmour is more dismissive still, "[It] sounds like we didn't have an idea between us. At the time we thought that *Atom Heart Mother*, like *Ummagumma*, was a step towards something or other. Now I think they were both just a blundering about in the

dark." Wright agrees, "At the time I thought we were making the most incredible music in the world. But looking back it wasn't so good." These harsh judgements of a worthy experiment can perhaps partly be put down to the conservatism that comes with age.

A UK tour immediately followed, with *Sounds* hailing them as "Britain's No 1 truly progressive pop band" after their performance in Brighton's Big Apple in December.

Meddle

Despite all this popular success and Establishment approval, 1971 dawned with considerable dissatisfaction within the band. Mason told *Disc And Music Echo*, "We must start on new things. We've always had this bigger concept in mind." More directly, Roger Waters had moaned to *Melody Maker* in December 1970, "I'm bored with most of the stuff we play. There's not much new stuff, is there?"

The problem of their live set had not been solved by either *Ummagumma*, or *Atom Heart Mother*. "Summer '68" was never played live, "Alan's Psychedelic Breakfast" and "If" lasted one performance apiece, and the need for an orchestra on "Atom Heart Mother" made it a cumbersome live proposition.

Waters was right: there was no new stuff even when they reached the studio. In between UK live dates that January, they went into **Abbey Road** and attempted various methods

of bump-starting material. First they recorded parts separately with no reference to what the others were doing, then played the tapes simultaneously. "It was pretty avant-garde and pretty useless," says Mason. Then they recorded a whole series of snippets as "Nothing Parts 1-36". During this Waters came up with the riff for "Fearless" while Wright chanced upon the piano note that, put through a **Binson echo unit** at Waters' suggestion, ultimately became the basis for "Echoes".

Having then in Gilmour's words "[gone] away to think about them", in March they took a complete diversion. Inspired by "Alan's Psychedelic Breakfast", they now spent valuable studio time trying to create new material using scissors, egg-slicers, cigarette lighters and elastic bands. Apart from the potential for being utterly unmusical, had the practical problems of recreating such foolishness live not struck them? "We

Roger Waters with a big gong

got three or four tracks down," Gilmour said later, "but it'd be very hard to make any of them really work as a piece of genuine music." Strange that. Engineer **John Leckie** says of this period, "They were searching for things. Searching for sounds and songs. There was a lot of time sitting around fiddling. People not speaking. It always took hours and hours getting the right sound. Anything but play the bloody thing. They seemed to have infinite time."

Gilmour said at the time, "Basically we're the laziest group ever. Other groups would be quite horrified if they saw how we really waste our recording time ... Now we are letting things take a natural pace. We're refusing to take any pressure on the album. If people ask us about a release date, we just tell them that they can have it when it is ready." This was perhaps bravado however: others report the Floyd feared being dropped. Indeed frustration did leak out at this time. "What we must do is Get Ourselves Together," Mason told *Beat Instrumental* in April.

For all this, they managed to get the basis of "Echoes" recorded that April. Starting with Wright's echoing piano note, Gilmour – playing an increasingly integral role in the band – followed this with the opening mournful guitar phrase, while Waters and Mason were essential in structuring what Waters came to call, an "epic sound poem", using the experience gained from creating *Atom Heart Mother*. Waters was also responsible for the lyrics, significantly shifting his initial emphasis from outer space to under water. The resultant 25-minute piece was in sufficient shape to premiere at, of all

places, Norwich Lads Club on April 22, 1971 as "Return Of The Son Of Nothing", not the Crystal Palace Garden Party of May 15 (as often reported). During the South London event an inflatable octopus rose from the lake and the volume of the speakers killed all the fish.

In the midst of all this came the preparation of *Relics*. Reports suggest variously that the band viewed this compilation (released in May 1971) as a cash-in on EMI's part, and that the band were crucially involved in compiling it. Certainly Nick Mason supplied the splendid Heath Robinson-inspired cover drawing.

During May the Floyd only played six dates, leaving themselves some proper recording time. With Abbey Road having failed to upgrade to sixteen-track recording, they decamped with their tapes and Leckie to **George Martin**'s AIR studios in August, adding Gilmour's spacey, seabird effects in the middle section of "Echoes". Here they also came up with what became "One Of These Days", Gilmour playing a crucial role in composition (see p.194).

Gilmour then created "Seamus" single-handedly. While looking after former **Small Faces** singer **Steve Marriott**'s dog (Seamus), he brought him to the studio and the dog began to howl when Gilmour played harmonica. "I guess ["Seamus"] wasn't really as funny to everybody else as it was to us," Gilmour later said. "Seamus" is of note only because it gave Gilmour a chance to rehearse his American accent.

With Gilmour now grown in confidence, a certain amount of friction developed between him and Waters. Leckie observes, "There was

Pompeii

It sounds like the ultimate prog rock conceit. A rock concert in a majestic classical setting (the 2000-year-old amphitheatre ruin of lava-petrified **Pompeii**), with a touch of the otherwordly (the bubbling sulphurous lakes and hissing steam-vents of Mount Vesuvius), plus a mad professor's workshop of electronic equipment and a band playing grandiose, twenty-minute soundscapes to no audience but a film crew and the petrified corpses of Pompeii – and you have a near volcanic piece of progressive folly.

In fact, it wasn't actually Pink Floyd's idea. As so often, someone brought the idea to them – in this case aspirant French director **Adrian Maben**, who had the idea of an "anti-Woodstock film". Thus on October 3, 1971, the band flew to Naples and filming began. For this they played what had become an increasingly static stage set, for one of the last times. As such the performance – and the film – served as both a celebration of – and a farewell to – their progressive rock phase.

If the project allowed cynics to insert their own jokes about ossification, petrified audiences and dusty set-lists – as Nick Mason says in the film, "We're in danger of becoming a sort of relic of the past" – the band would soon have the last laugh thanks to *Dark Side*'s success.

In fact, due to various technical mess-ups, the Pompeii footage had to be augmented by additional footage shot in a Paris studio in December. By the time Pompeii came out, it was itself a relic of the past: first shown at the Edinburgh Festival in September 1972, though never released in that form, it was already an album behind (*Obscured By Clouds*, released in June). And with a planned premiere at the Rainbow pulled at the last minute by the Rank organisation, by the time the film finally emerged in 1974, *Dark Side Of The Moon* had already conquered the world. And – attempting to bring Pompeii up to date – Maben interspersed footage of the band making *Dark Side* with the original Pompeii material. This makes the film a curious patchwork of the old and the new, revealing a band in uneasy transition, bidding farewell to the past, uncertain quite what the future will bring. The band made almost no money from the film, and when, after a New York *Dark Side* show, a mogul told Waters how much he had made from the film, that mogul was escorted from the building.

always that tension between Roger and Dave. Roger was the leader, he took command, he sat at the desk, and Dave always objected. Sat at the side and was grumpy."

They continued to tour Europe throughout June, Waters facetiously introducing "Return Of The Son Of Nothing" variously as "The March Of The Dambusters", "Looking Through The Hole in Granny's Wooden Leg" and "We Won The Double".

The group took time out for recording that July, relocating to the 24-track Morgan Sound Studios. Here they remixed "One Of These Days" to sound more electronic and added the Liverpool home crowd singing "You'll Never Walk Alone" on "Fearless". With time running out, they also came up with material for the other side of the album. Typically Waters was the only one to arrive with a complete song – "San Tropez" (inspired by the Floyd's expedition to the South of France the previous summer). Indeed tape op **Mike Butcher** recalls Waters "telling everyone what to play, right down to the drum part. He also insisted on playing guitar as he said the chords were too complicated for Gilmour. All very bureaucratic." Waters also now added lyrics to a new composition of Gilmour's – "A Pillow Of Winds" (a title derived from Mah Jong, a game popular with the group).

That August, Pink Floyd conducted their first tour of Japan, where they were presented with fake gold discs and acquired a lifelong devotion to sushi. Then it was on to Australia, where they met George Greenough, whose surf film *Crystal Voyager* would be a recurring visual at future Floyd shows, then Hong Kong, and back to the UK, flying through a massive thunderstorm over the Himalayas (intensifying everyone's fear of flying). After mastering the album at the end of August, a European tour began on September 18 in Montreux.

Mason at his Vitruvian Man kit in 1971

Meddle Tour and Release

On October 15 Pink Floyd began yet another US tour, once again prior to the release of the album it was supposed to promote. And once again, there wasn't quite as much new mate-

rial as might have been hoped: although "One Of These Days" and "Echoes" became live set staples, neither "Winds", "Fearless", "San Tropez" nor "Seamus" were ever played live. "Eugene" and "Saucerful" would have a few more airings yet.

Meddle was finally released on November 13, 1971, in a cover which featured a photograph of an ear under ripples of water, intended to be suggestive both of the lyrics of "Echoes" and of sound-waves. Thorgerson: "Nobody owns up to having designed it. I didn't design it." The title was a last minute decision partly inspired by a sense of satisfaction at what they'd produced (as in "medal").

Reviews were primarily positive. *NME* said it was "an exceptionally good album", "Echoes" being "the zenith which the Floyd have been striving for". In the States, *Rolling Stone* said, "*Meddle* not only confirms lead guitarist David Gilmour's emergence as a real shaping force with the group", but concluded, "*Meddle* is killer Floyd from start to finish ..." while *Billboard* inaccurately predicted "heavy FM play". Although *Meddle* hit #3 in the UK, it charted lower than *Atom Heart Mother* in the States (at #70).

Gilmour later said, "[*Meddle*] was a clear forerunner for *Dark Side*, the point when we first got our focus." That focus essentially entailed a refinement of *Atom Heart Mother*: a more coherent sidelong suite in "Echoes", a second side again composed of shorter, pastoral songs, this time showing a more American west coast orientation, alongside hints of American accents. America was clearly more and more in this once most English of bands' sights.

Continuing to tour the States throughout November, they were now dusting down the increasingly criticized Pompeii-style set list. At one US show they put down a request with a weary, "We'll never play 'Astronomy Domine' again." And in a January 72 issue of *Sounds* Waters admitted the band was at a crucial juncture, saying, "I think we're coming down to earth a bit, a bit less involved with flights of fancy and a bit more involved with what we as people are actually involved in." "They were desperately hungry," recalls John Leckie. "They were searching for things. And all that time they were searching for *The Dark Side Of The Moon* really."

What happened to Syd?

One of David Gilmour's most winning characteristics is that he has never ceased to help, praise and acknowledge the man he replaced in Pink Floyd. Whether or not guilt plays a part in his supportiveness, David Gilmour doesn't actually need to see that Barrett gets his royalties, to include generous selections of his songs on Floyd compilations or to make statements such as, "He's on a different level of existence from the rest of us mere mortals. He's right up there with the McCartneys and Dylans of the world." Indeed, because Gilmour had worked with Barrett at very close quarters as producer, one might imagine that Gilmour would have a more jaundiced, myth-deflating view of the matter.

After both Barrett and **Peter Jenner** split with Floyd in April 1968, Jenner took his new charge into the studio to record some solo tracks that May. "I had seriously underestimated the difficulties of working with him," Jenner later said, having failed to capture any vocals on "Golden Hair", "Late Night", "Clowns And Jugglers" (later "Octopus"), "Swan Lee" or "Lanky". By further sessions in June and July, most of these tracks were beginning to sound promising, however, especially "Swan Lee" and a new version of "Clowns And Jugglers". A long jam entitled "Rhamadan" was never properly committed to tape.

Barrett was, however, in a mess, allegedly taking heroin, breaking up with girlfriend Lindsay Corner and going off on a frantic drive round the UK in his Mini, ending up back in Cambridge in psychiatric care.

To some extent recovered, Barrett, in New Year 1969, took on the tenancy of a three-bedroom mansion flat in Egerton Road, Earls Court, with artist **Duggie Fields**. The flat was so near Gilmour's that Gilmour could see right into Barrett's kitchen. Deciding to recommence his musical career, Barrett contacted his old label, EMI, and was passed on to **Malcolm Jones,** head of EMI's new progressive label, Harvest, who – after Norman Smith and Jenner declined – opted to produce the album himself. They began recording in April 1969 at Abbey Road Studio 3. After a successful first solo session, Barrett brought along musicians to the next: drummer **Jerry Shirley,** of Humble Pie, and **Willie Wilson,** drummer from Gilmour's old band, Jokers Wild – this time on bass. But communication with Barrett was not easy. Jones: "It was a case of following him, not playing with him. They were seeing and then playing so they were always a note behind." Shirley: "He gave the impression he

knew something you didn't. He had this manic sort of giggle."

A similar situation resulted when **The Soft Machine** were brought in to overdub existing recordings, **Robert Wyatt** recalling, "We'd say, what key is that in Syd? And he would simply reply 'Yeah', or 'That's funny'". Jones finally began to lose faith when Barrett spent hours over a tape of motorbike noise for "Rhamadan". On one occasion Barrett told his flatmate he was off "for an afternoon drive" and instead followed the Cambridge set to Ibiza (legend has it he skipped check-in and customs, ran out onto the runway and tried to flag down a jet). His friends spotted him on the beach in filthy clothes and with a carrier bag full of money.

It was during this trip that Barrett asked Gilmour for help in the recording sessions (Jones insists this was not, as often reported, due to panic on EMI's part). In two sessions Gilmour – with Waters – remade "Clowns And Jugglers" from The Soft Machine's version as "Octopus", recorded "Golden Hair" and "Long Gone" (probably with Wright playing the vibes and organ parts), plus the acoustic "Dark Globe". Much to Barrett's dismay there was a long gap while Floyd mixed *Ummagumma*. Further acoustic tracks were recorded towards the end of July: "Long Cold Look", "Feel" and "If It's In You", Gilmour and Waters making the controversial decision to record these songs largely as Barrett played them in the studio, complete with false starts and manic comments from Barrett. They also decided to exclude the

The Story

completed – and much more together – Jones-produced "Opel".

Barrett painted the floor of his Egerton Court bedroom orange and purple for the **Mick Rock**-photographed/Hipgnosis-designed cover. The naked girl on the cover was just one of Barrett's string of casual affairs, an Eskimo girl called Iggy. Released in January 1970, Jones was shocked by the finished album. "I felt angry. It's like dirty linen in public and very unnecessary and unkind." Gilmour also later regretted this, admitting there may have been a self-justifying motivation, "Perhaps we were trying to show what Syd was really like. But perhaps we were trying to punish him." *Melody Maker*'s review commented on "the mayhem and madness representing the Barrett mind unleashed", whereas *Disc* called it "an excellent album to start 1970". Even Waters went into print saying, "Syd is a genius." Barrett himself said, "It's quite nice but I'd be very surprised if it did anything if I were to drop dead. I don't think it would stand as my last statement."

With the album selling a respectable 6,000 copies in its first month, Barrett recorded a session for BBC Radio 1 show *Top Gear* on February 24 with Gilmour and Shirley. In this flurry of activity, sessions for a second album began, with Gilmour producing and playing bass, Rick Wright on keyboards and Jerry Shirley again on drums. Gilmour later said, "It was murder." **"Baby Lemonade"** and **"Gigolo Aunt"** were attempts at getting Barrett to play and sing to an existing backing track, losing, felt Gilmour, some essential Barrett-ness; the chaotic **"Rats"** was solo

Syd that was overdubbed later by other musicians as best they could to his shifting tempos. Shirley: "He would never play the same tune twice. Sometimes Syd couldn't play anything that made sense; other times what he'd play was absolute magic." Barrett would issue such instructions as, "Perhaps we could make the middle darker and maybe the end a bit middle afternoonish. At the moment it's too windy and icy."

This was taking place while the Floyd were starting *Atom Heart Mother* and at various points Barrett went to spy on the Floyd as they recorded. Syd finished the album in July and the album released in November 1970 (the cover derived from drawings Barrett had made while in Cambridge many years before). However, it received more muted reviews than its predecessor. *Beat Instrumental* (Feb 1971) said, "Syd Barrett is capable of much greater things than this. He sounds flat on most of his vocals and the instruments give the impression that only one track of the stereo is actually working."

Shortly afterwards, with Gilmour and Shirley, Barrett made his first stage appearance since leaving Floyd two-and-a-half years earlier. Seemingly terrified, he played four numbers before making an abrupt exit. Meanwhile, his domestic situation at Egerton Road was deteriorating. There was a constant stream of hangers-on and groupies – even people living in the hallway. Partly to avoid them, Barrett shut himself in his room, which began to stink. His relationship with Fields wasn't helped when Barrett set the kitchen on fire when cooking chips. Fields said: "It was like being with a child."

Barrett still occasionally behaved violently, once throwing a young woman called Gilly, with whom he was having a casual affair, across the room when she didn't want to go to Gilmour's house. Another young Cambridge woman, 19-year-old model **Gala Pinion**, was an important relationship of his, and the subject of "Wined And Dined". Barrett had actually met her through his previous girlfriend, Lindsay Corner. "Syd was very good looking and had this sort of mad attractiveness about him," Pinion said later. "He had the most extraordinary eyes and when he looked at you, you felt hopelessly caught." Pinion worked at the Chelsea drug store, later moving into Barrett and Fields' living room.

On one occasion when Barrett ran into Waters in Harrods he dropped his bags and raced outside. The bags were full of hundreds of children's sweets. Barrett began going back to Cambridge for longer periods, leaving Fields with a house full of the hangers-on until finally, he locked his room with all his stuff inside, declared he was going to become a doctor (like his father) and left with Pinion for the basement of his mother's house in Cambridge. There they lived for a time in the 8ft by 8ft, barely 5ft-high L-shaped room. Despite Barrett's obsessive jealousy (even following her to work to spy on her) and violent rages, the couple became engaged. However, at a big family get-together to celebrate, Barrett poured soup over Pinion (according to some accounts) and went upstairs and shaved off all his hair. Some months later, with the violence increasing, Pinion left him, and Barrett

Syd Barrett, 1969

formally broke off the engagement by letter, signing it R.K. Barrett.

Thereafter Barrett cut himself off from most people, although David Gilmour visited him occasionally. He would reappear regularly in London, however, and did a session for *Sounds Of The Seventies* (a contemporary music BBC radio show). In an interview with *Beat International*, he said, "It's a nice place to live really – under the ground," apparently unaware of both its echo of his old role as underground princeling and of Mole in his beloved *Wind In The Willows*. He also gave a *Melody Maker* interview, saying of the Floyd, "Their choice of material was always very much to do with what they were thinking as architectural students. Rather unexciting people, I would've thought." And during this time Barrett was still talking about recording a third album.

With no further sightings, rumours circulated during 1971 that Barrett was dead or in prison, prompting a statement promising a single with "friends in the business who are members of well-known groups".

Surprisingly, Barrett now formed a new band with his neighbour **Twink**, formerly of underground colleagues **Tomorrow** and fellow EMI act **The Pretty Things** (their *SF Sorrow* was also produced by Norman Smith at Abbey Road, concurrent with *Piper*; in 1999 Gilmour would play guitar on a re-creation of the album) plus bassist **Jack Monck** from **Delivery**. Calling themselves **Stars**, they debuted at East Road café, Cambridge. Monck: "He had great natural ability but no discipline. He never practised. He didn't like … trying to live up to what he used to be." Stars were booked, before they were ready, to support MC5 at Cambridge Corn Exchange. "What the audience saw was a man disintegrating before their eyes, a piece of bad theatre, except it wasn't make believe – it was happening for real," Monck said. *Melody Maker* sent journalist Roy Hollingsworth, who wrote: "It was like watching somebody piece together a memory that had suffered the most severe shell shock." Barrett turned up at Twink's house with the *MM* article and said he was quitting. He then went berserk at Hills Road, smashing furniture and smashing his head into the ceiling.

Nevertheless, he still had another crack at a third album with Peter Jenner at Abbey Road. It was disastrous. Afterwards Barrett again went haywire in the basement and ended up back in hospital. Still, he showed up, uninvited, at a local gig by ex-Cream bassist Jack Bruce, and nonchalantly jammed with him onstage. Meanwhile, in the early 1970s, his income grew with the *Relics* compilation in May 1971; Bowie's cover of "See Emily Play" in 1973; and the reissue of *Piper* and *Saucerful* as *A Nice Pair* the same year.

Bothered by the stream of callers to the Cambridge house, Barrett returned to London in 1972 in quest of anonymity, renting two flats in the exclusive Chelsea Cloisters, off Kings Road, living on the ninth floor and keeping a room full of musical equipment three floors below. There he primarily watched television and raided his fridge, leaving the flat only to visit his publisher, **Bryan Morrison**, whenever the rent was due. On one of these occasions, when Morrison refused his monthly royalty cheque, Barrett vaulted over the desk and bit his finger. Barrett is believed to have gone to see a performance of *Dark Side Of The Moon* at least once during this time.

Fan interest continued to grow, culminating in a 1974 *NME* article by **Nick Kent** and the re-release of Barrett's solo albums as a twofer the same year, though Barrett slammed the door in Storm Thorgerson's face when he attempted to photograph him for the cover. Thorgerson instead utilized the matchbox, orange and plum that had played such a significant part in Barrett's first acid trip back in Cambridge (and arguably, his condition thereafter).

In November 1974, Jenner again booked Barrett into a studio, but Barrett arrived with a stringless guitar, and when someone handed him his lyrics typed up in red ink, Barrett thought it was a bill and tried to bite his finger, just has he had done with Morrison a couple of years before. The material was "extremely weird", according to Peter Jenner, and no vocal tracks were ever attempted. "It was pretty untogether," recalls engineer **John Leckie**, "he kept wandering off and kept unplugging his guitar. He was pretty vacant, didn't really say anything, or look at you."

Syd's retirement: 1975–present

Barrett kept the Chelsea Cloisters apartment for eight years, obsessively buying televisions then giving them and his music gear away to the staff, along with the odd £300 tip. He also still intermittently had violent episodes, once smashing the door of his flat off its hinges, and on another occasion he appeared in a dress. Jenner told a radio interviewer, "It's tragic that the music business may have a lot to do with doing him in. I think we have a lot to answer for – myself and everyone else involved with him."

By 1975 Barrett was distinctly fat, partly due to his fondness for sitting alone in pubs drinking Guinness. He had also shaved off all his hair again. It was now that he visited Floyd during the recording of *Wish You Were Here*. **Roy Harper** claims Barrett also turned up at the Knebworth festival when they played the album, though Gilmour thinks otherwise. "The idea of Syd being this spectre hanging over us is complete shit."

That same year, DJ **Nicky Horne** tried to interview Barrett who answered the door in his pyjama trousers, announcing, "Syd can't talk." Frustrated by the lack of income generated by his charge, Bryan Morrison commented at this time, "He doesn't want to be bothered: he just sits there on his own watching television all day and getting fat." In an interview on Montreal Radio, Rick Wright said, "I don't know what he's like in his head because he does not talk at all. It's very sad. He can't relate to anyone … The drugs don't cause these things. Drugs are just a catalyst."

Barrett moved back to Cambridge in 1980 to live the life of an almost total recluse, bar his long, eight-mile walks and trips to the supermarket and the occasional door-steppings by journalists. His mother died in 1991 and he continued to live at the house, needing for nothing given the royalties still pouring in from his back catalogue. Roger Waters has been uncharacteristically generous in his praise of his former bandmate. "It's the humanity of it all that is so impressive. It's about deeply felt values and beliefs and feelings. Maybe that's what *Dark Side Of The Moon* was aspiring to. A similar feeling."

In 2001 the book *Psychedelic Renegades*, featuring photographs of Barrett taken by Mick Rock from 1969 to 1971, was published. Rock managed to get 320 copies signed by Barrett and he also reprinted his 1971 *Rolling Stone* article in full. Barrett's words were almost

The Story

unbearably moving, jumbled up, but still making some kind of lopsided, sad sense. "I'm disappearing ... I'm treading the backward path. Mostly I just waste my time. I'm full of dust and guitars." His verdict on the Floyd was, "It's always been too slow for me ... I mean, I'm a fast sprinter." And his judgement on himself was even more pertinent, "I don't think I'm easy to talk about. I've got a very irregular head. And I'm not anything that you think I am anyway."

Thereafter, Roger Barrett spent his time gardening, writing a book about the history of art, listening to jazz (never rock), photographing flowers, painting them, and then destroying the canvases. The intrusion of journalists and fans was said to trigger depressive episodes, while his erstwhile Pink Floyd colleagues kept away at his family's request. Although rumours that Barrett had been invited to join the Live 8 reformation were rubbished by Gilmour, Waters did, touchingly, dedicate "Wish You Were Here" to Barrett onstage.

Barrett's influence had continued to be pervasive: notably within the 90s Britpop movement and the noughties' indie scene, while a screen biography of his life, *Crazy Diamond*, directed by Peter Medak, has been mooted, and he was an eerily prescient presence in Tom Stoppard's 2006 West End theatrical hit, *Rock'n'Roll*, cast as the antic spirit of the 60s counterculture. But Barrett's reality was very far removed from such fancies: suffering from stomach ulcers, unable to care for his diabetes since his mother's death in 1991, Barrett's physical health was deteriorating. Although he was doorstepped on his 60th birthday, he died at home six months later, on July 7 2006, apparently from complications related to the condition. Mysterious to the last, even this cause of death was later revealed to be inaccurate: Barrett actually died from pancreatic cancer. Equally, Barrett's old friends couldn't even find out when the funeral was, which was held, aptly enough, away from the media's attention. "I've been doing this funny sort of grieving in a vacuum," said his former manager, Andrew King, "for someone who really has become an imaginary person".

"Imaginary" is the right word: because by his very elusiveness Barrett captured people's imaginations. With his strange, lovely songs, with his wild improvisations, with his looks, with his mad antics, with his very withdrawal from the world. And in death, as in life, he will continue to do so.

Eclipse
1972–76

Eclipse
1972–76

One in five UK households owns a copy of *Dark Side Of The Moon*. It still sells 8,000 copies a week in the US alone. At any given second, the album is playing somewhere in the world. Its all-conquering "everyman" popularity seems all the more extraordinary given that it was made by a band that only a few years previously had been releasing ten-minute drum solos and cod-classical suites to an underground fanbase.

But *Dark Side Of The Moon* hardly appeared to the band in a flash of light. The record that caused such a huge shift in Pink Floyd's fortunes was a long time coming – fifteen months from conception to completion. And it would also be a long time going – a commercial monolith that was the making of the band and, ultimately, nearly the breaking of them too. "The only reason we stayed together after [*Dark Side*] was fear and avarice," said Waters later.

Both lyrically and musically *Dark Side* represents a return to earth after the Floyd's – and everyone else's – failed attempt to extend 60s utopianism via the early 1970s "progressive" ideal. In its lyrics, madness (Barrett's?) is seen simply as the end result not of a spiritual search but of material pressures – money, travel, human conflict ("Us & Them") – and more abstract but nevertheless mundane pressures such as time and

mortality. The ongoing Vietnam War, the activities of the IRA and the backlash to sixties "permissiveness" represented by **Mary Whitehouse**'s reactionary Festival of Light were all contemporary symbols of the defeat of 1960s ideals.

In the album's music, progressive rock is drawn upon in the segued suites of songs, but they're largely excised of their excesses, trimmed to three- or four- minute durations, and grounded in melodies and strong choruses. Prog also provided a useful model in that *Dark Side* finally found a home for a whole series of fragments. But rather than being a rummaging through used laundry by a band who didn't have enough new material for an album, *Dark Side* seemed to draw upon the past in order to summarize it, and – in the words of its original title – *Eclipse* it. The album would, in turn, prove very hard itself to eclipse.

Dark Side Of The Moon and side projects

After yet another American tour, in October and November 1971, the band reconvened at a rehearsal studio in Broadhurst Gardens, West Hampstead. With a major British tour booked from January 1972 onwards and concerts already booked throughout most of the next year, time was tight.

So, to start with, they sifted through old tapes. Wright came up with the unused piano chords from "The Violent Sequence" recorded for *Zabriskie Point* (and given a few live airings as an instrumental in 1970) and another he'd been pootling about with for a year or so, which became known as "Religion". Gilmour, by his own admission, brought in no new songs. But Waters was on a roll, bringing in a strange, loping 7/8 riff he'd written on acoustic guitar (an embryonic "Money"), a lyricless "Time" and the prototype of "Brain Damage", which he'd been playing at the *Meddle* sessions at which he called it "The Dark Side Of The Moon". Perhaps it was this Barrett-inspired song that gave Waters the Big Idea for the album.

Gilmour has called this "the moment" – when Roger Waters came into Broadhurst Gardens with the idea of "putting it all together as one piece with this linking theme he'd devised". It is, however, a moment that, in typical Floyd fashion, is contested: Mason insists it occurred in his Camden kitchen. The concept has also been variously described. Waters initially flippantly called it "life with a heartbeat an' that", pointing out that "then you can have other bits: like all the pressures which are anti-life." Wright said, "It was about one's fear, it was about the business." Gilmour described it as "the specific idea of dealing with all the things that drive people mad". Enthused by the idea, the band drew up a list of themes: encroaching old age, death, fear of flying, money and violence.

It was agreed that Waters would write all the lyrics, which he did quickly, coming up with words to "Time", "Breathe" and "Us And Them" within a month. Much has been made of Waters' new lyrical directness, but he had used such an approach before ("Biding My Time", "If", "Free Four"), and although he curtailed his more whimsical poetic flights here, the words are still far from the confessional directness of the album he often cited as inspiration, **John Lennon**'s *Plastic Ono Band*. And although it later irritated Waters that *Dark Side* was misinterpreted as containing cosmic meanings, the fact is that there's still a certain elliptical, mysterious element to the words alongside the literalism.

Though the others weren't to know it at the time, this decision to let Waters write the lyrics was one that would have enormous ramifications for the Floyd. For a start, the lyrics were key to the universal success of *Dark Side Of The Moon*, this new directness and simplicity striking a chord with the post-1960s generation. "He wanted … to get away from all the psychedelic warblings and say exactly what he wanted for the first time," said Gilmour. But in doing this they were also delivering Pink Floyd over to Waters' personal worldview – a general faith in humanity often undercut by a deep and acerbic cynicism. Perhaps smarting from later accusations of misanthropy, in the nineties and beyond, Waters repeatedly emphasized the project's humanism: "Despite the rather depressing ending … there is an allowance that all things are possible, that the potential's in our hands." Nevertheless, in the knife-edge sarcasm of "Money", the bitter ironies of "Us And Them", the caustic hints of "Breathe Reprise" and that downbeat ending, lay the distinct seeds of something more acerbic.

What's more, Pink Floyd were implicitly giving Waters a position of leadership. Gilmour has since regretted this, while remaining philosophical about his own abilities – and work ethic. "Roger worked all sorts of hours on the concept and the lyrics while the rest of us went home to enjoy our suppers."

That said, the musical contributions of the others were absolutely vital to *Dark Side*'s success, with Wright, particularly, at his creative peak (though, once the royalties started pouring in, all four bickered about precisely who had done what).

Road-testing the Moon

The first attempted performance of what was then still known as *Eclipse* was at Brighton Dome on January 20, 1972, with the Floyd's first integrated light show since 1968. Waters had made a tape loop for "Money" of coins chinking and paper tearing using his wife's potter's wheel, but the tape snagged, stopping the performance. So the first completed performance took place the next day at the **Portsmouth Guildhall**. Pink Floyd continued to play the piece for the next few weeks, culminating in four shows at the Rainbow on February 17–20, the piece by now titled *Dark Side Of The Moon, A Piece For Assorted Lunatics*. A "mind and sense-stunning experience" enthused the *NME*. "A magnificent production." The *Sunday Times* described them as

"dramatists supreme". But the group weren't entirely happy with the piece. Mason later recalled, "I didn't really have any sense at first that *Eclipse* was anything particularly special … there was quite a lot of padding."

At this point "Time" was much slower, lacking its later VCS3 drone and was sung in harmony by Wright and Gilmour on the verse. "Great Gig" was called "Religion", and was played on organ not piano. It also featured taped readings from the Biblical Book of Ephesians and a recital by the broadcaster and journalist **Malcolm Muggeridge**, best known as a presenter of religious programmes and supporter of **Mary Whitehouse** in the censorious Festival of Light campaign. (In "Pigs (Three Different Ones)", Waters would later

Waters and Gilmour live and happy

Recording Obscured By Clouds

Aptly enough *Obscured By Clouds* blocks out the view at this point. As released, it's the link between *Meddle* and *Dark Side Of The Moon*. As actually recorded, it's just a work-job tangent written and recorded after *Dark Side* had begun.

Having already recorded one soundtrack for Barbet Schroeder (*More*), the Floyd were glad to be asked to work with him again, despite being busy with *Dark Side*. This time it was to a soundtrack for a bigger-budget film, *La Vallée*, about hippies searching for an earthly paradise in the New Guinea rainforest. As sensible middle-class boys approaching 30 in a rock world still associated with youth, the band were simply feathering future nests. "I know it sounds silly now", admits Gilmour, "but we thought of films as one of our possible futures." "I was aware they were working on something they were devoting an immense amount of energy and time to," Schroeder recalls. "What they were doing with me was of a very different nature. Something that had to be done very quickly."

Sessions were recorded at the Chateau D'Herouville near Paris, in the last week of February and again in March after their Japanese tour. As ever, the band had nothing prepared. "We sat in a room, wrote, recorded, like a production line" Gilmour recalled. "Very good for one to work like that sometimes – under extreme constraints of time and trying to meet someone else's needs." As it was, the experience of writing *Dark Side Of The Moon* had obviously energized them. Gilmour recovered his

make his feelings about Mrs Whitehouse very clear.) Closer to the eventual "Any Colour You Like" was "Scat", another instrumental jam, featuring Gilmour scat-singing along to his guitar solo.

During the tour Waters wrote **"Eclipse"**, to pull the whole piece together. It was first added at the **Leicester De Montford Hall** show of February 10, making this, technically, the full premiere of *Dark Side Of The Moon*. A less useful by-product of this road-testing was that their Rainbow performance was issued as a bootleg and racked up substantial sales before the Floyd were aware of it – some say 100,000 copies – a full year before the album's official release.

The VCS3

The VCS3 was a synthesizer designed by Peter Zinovieff and a team from the **BBC Radiophonics Workshop** (also responsible for the *Dr Who* TV theme that Floyd referenced on "One Of These Days"). Unlike the Moog synthesizer, the Voltage Controlled Studio initially lacked a keyboard so was much harder to programme, as well as being bulky. Zinovieff eventually came up with a version small enough (the Synthi A) to fit in a suitcase, which also contained a keyboard in the lid of the case.

The Floyd utilized the VCS3 on almost every track of *Obscured By Clouds*. Mostly played by Gilmour, it was used to harmonise with Wright's Hammond on both "Burning Bridges" and "Mudmen". Oddly, the latter wasn't actually used in the film's "mudmen" sequence, but is used in the film as the middle section of "Burning Bridges".

Meddle form and Wright wrote his first actual songs in some time. As ever, Waters was everywhere, skilfully matching lyrics to footage, coming up with the jaunty "Free Four", and adding the VCS3 synthesizer to "Absolutely Curtains".

Nevertheless, there was a lot of waiting around for inspiration. Such was the boredom that the roadies put on shows for their employers' entertainment. Chris Adamson (the "I've been mad for fucking years" voice on *Dark Side*) attempted to eat a stone of raw potatoes in one sitting – he got through two-and-a-half pounds before giving up. Waters later spoke of the stresses and tensions that surfaced. "We pretend they're not there. We certainly don't face up to them in an adult way."

After a disagreement with the film company the band retitled the soundtrack *Obscured By Clouds*, from a line from the film. After the success of *Dark Side*, the movie was re-released with the Floyd's title appended as *La Vallée (Obscured By Clouds)*. The film received mixed reviews, many accusing it of being clichéd and superficial. Response to the album, released on June 3, 1972, was more positive. *NME* said it contained "no musical epics, just beautiful songs" while Gilmour's playing was "impeccable", and *Melody Maker* said, "It contains some of the most aggressive instrumentals the Floyd have ever recorded, as well as some dreamy melodic songs." The Floyd, meanwhile, touring the States from April 14 to May 4, found the album picking up the first substantial US radio play of their career – especially "Free Four" – which would pave the way for *Dark Side Of The Moon*.

Recording Dark Side

Just before *Obscured By Clouds* was released, recording proper for *Dark Side Of The Moon* began on June 1, though it was now once more titled *Eclipse*. Often erroneously thought to have been Abbey Road's first 24-track recording, *Dark Side* was actually recorded on 16-track, sometimes using two machines to accommodate the sheer weight of overdubs. "Us And Them" was the first track recorded, and Gilmour immediately made his presence felt, taking over the lead vocal and adding layers of Beatles-like guitar arpeggios. He also made "Money" his own with his assertive vocal, improvised guitar line, and his variance of wet (echoey) and dry sounds in the mix. He was all over "Time" with another blinding improvised guitar solo and a far more assertive vocal. When it came to recording "Great Gig In The Sky", which Wright had been developing since the live shows, Gilmour responded by echoing the pedal steel part of "Breathe". The band would end up tinkering with these tracks over a full six months.

After this bout of recording, the Floyd took a full two months' holiday, before decamping for their second, fifteen-date US tour of the year on September 8, taking the retitled *Dark Side Of The Moon* with them. They returned to the studio in October for a further nine days' recording, getting down "Brain Damage" and "Any Colour You Like", now stripped of Gilmour's sync'd vocal.

It was then that Floyd made the key decision to add female backing vocals to the album, adding a soulful warmth to the recordings (though the women reported the atmosphere among the frosty Floyd was anything but warm). Gilmour again played a key role here, directing the vocalists' "ad libs". It was also now that **Dick Parry**'s sax was added to

both "Money" and "Us And Them". An old Cambridge friend of Gilmour's, jazzer Parry's contribution added what Mason later admitted was a "commerical sheen". But after the band dropped recording dates to play a War On Want charity show at Wembley Park, they were far from finished and had to pack up for a two-month-long European tour on October 10.

A Balletic interlude...

In the midst of all this came a typically bizarre Floydean tangent – the belated fulfilment of their longstanding agreement to score a ballet for choreographer **Roland Petit**'s company Ballets de Marseilles. "Again, we were interested because we thought of it as one of the possible ways to extend the scope of what we could do in the future," said Gilmour later.

At one point Wright suggested to the press that *Eclipse* (aka *Dark Side*) could be used for the project. Finally it was decided to once again redeploy older material – "a cheap and cheerful solution", as Mason put it. Petit devised choreography for "One Of These Days", "Eugene", "Obscured", "When You're In" and "Echoes", and the band backed the dancers in a show billed as **Pink Floyd Ballet** in Marseilles from November 20 to 26, then in Paris for four shows in January and another four in February. "In the end the reality of these people prancing around in tights in front of us didn't feel like what we wanted to do long term," Gilmour said later.

During all this, serious business machinations were underway. Long unhappy with

EMI's US division, Capitol, and aware of how strong the album was, **Steve O'Rourke** proposed withholding *Dark Side* from the US. As a result, EMI executive **Bhaskar Menon** flew to Marseilles to pledge proper promotional support – support that proved crucial in *Dark Side*'s success. But although Capitol got *Dark Side*, the band signed a deal with **Columbia** for all subsequent US releases. They just forgot to tell Menon.

Back to the Dark Side

Mason and Gilmour both claim that Chris Thomas was brought in early in 1973 to arbitrate between Gilmour and Waters. The pair were apparently at loggerheads over the sort of sound the album should have. Thomas was a seasoned studio hand who'd worked on The Beatles' White Album and produced Procol Harum (and went on to produce everyone from Roxy Music to the Sex Pistols and Elton John). His claim that he was brought in as a producer is rejected by both Gilmour and Waters. Thomas's sleeve credit reads "mixing supervised by". But the pair's testimony to Thomas's lack of involvement in the album's recording is inaccurate, if only for the one case of "Great Gig In The Sky".

"Great Gig" had been an instrumental, variously called "Religion" and "The Mortality Sequence", until a matter of weeks before the sessions for *Dark Side* were completed. At Waters' suggestion, it was decided to use a vocalist. Parsons recommended EMI staff songwriter and session singer **Clare Torry**, whose other main claims to fame were being a "stunt vocalist" on various *Top Of The Pops* cover albums of chart hits (often working with then-sessioneer **Elton John**) and singing the theme tune to the 1970s BBC sitcom *Butterflies*. When Torry arrived at

Fab side of the Floyd

If you're going to go big, who better to draw upon than the biggest band of them all? For the influence of **The Beatles** is all over *Dark Side*: from the chromatic "Dear Prudence" riff on "Brain Damage", to the arpeggios on "Eclipse". Already recording at The Beatles' studio, they got Beatles collaborators **Alan Parsons** (apprentice engineer on *Abbey Road*) and **Chris Thomas** (engineer and occasional producer on *The White Album*) in to help them. The overblown Leslie kaleidoscopic effect on the guitar on "Any Colour You Like" also suggests The Beatles, although Gilmour says he had **Eric Clapton**'s work on Cream's "Badge" in mind (a song that twice hit the British charts – in April 1969 and again in October 1972, while Floyd tinkered away with "Any Colour..."). In point of fact, of course, The Beatles' **George Harrison** both co-wrote the song with Clapton and played its signature arpeggios.

The Story

the studio she was given a blank sheet, and after attempts to improvise lyrics failed to meet with band approval, she let rip with a cavalcade of wordless vocal wails. Worried she'd gone too far, Torry went into the control room to apologise. The Floyd typically gave no indication of their feelings. "Other than Dave Gilmour I got the impression they were infinitely bored with the whole thing," Torry admitted. "When I left I remember thinking to myself: 'That will never see the light of day'."

But the Floyd were actually very pleased. Indeed, Wright has since attested that, "It sends shivers down [his] spine – it's got something that's very seductive." Torry was paid a double fee for working on a Sunday (£30), but she later sued EMI and Pink Floyd for a co-writing credit, settling out of court in April 2005 for an undisclosed sum.

Thomas says that at this stage in the recording the spoken passages had not been added. At Waters' instigation, cards with questions such as "When was the last time you hit someone?" or "What do you think of death?" were placed in an empty studio, and various people who happened to be at Abbey Road – roadies, doormen, musicians, wives, even such luminaries as **Paul** and **Linda McCartney** – were ushered in to answer the questions. Intriguingly, the intimidating empty studio brought out the best in the non-musicians while the McCartneys' remarks were guarded beyond use.

These passages proved to be absolutely crucial additions, cohering the concept and mak-

The Cover of Dark Side Of The Moon

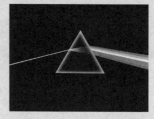

Inspired by Rick Wright's request for something "simple, clinical and precise", **Hipgnosis** prepared seven different designs. "[It] took about three seconds", said Thorgerson, "in as much as the band cast their eyes over everything, looked at each other, said in unison, 'That one' and left the room." The prism that Pink Floyd chose, drawn by artist **George Hardie**, was a reference to the Floyd's light show, while the triangle apparently symbolized "mad ambition".

The prism, incidentally, contained no indigo – a deliberate anti-realist touch. The spectrum becoming a monitored heartbeat on the inner gatefold was Waters' idea, tying into the album's opening sound effect. Thorgerson pursued the triangle theme further, travelling to Giza in Egypt to photograph the pyramid for the album's poster. The cover (which has seen various changes for subsequent reissues) was crucial to the album's success – a bold, simple image that's instantly recognisable.

ing it accessible. It is these that open the album, "I've been mad for fucking years" is Floyd road manager **Chris Adamson**, the crazed laughter is longstanding roadie **Pete Watts** (both are regularly attributed to **Roger The Hat**), and the "I know I've been mad, I've always been mad" line is Abbey Road doorman **Jerry Driscoll**. Driscoll's contributions practically *made* the album. He also provided "I'm not frightened of dying" in the middle and "There is no dark side of the moon, really; matter of fact, it's all dark" at the end. Driscoll was eventually paid a session fee for his contribution.

"Speak To Me" was also created at this late juncture. It was not a recording as such but a collage of the album's various sound effects. The heartbeat at the beginning and end of the album was another vital addition: "It sets the mood for the music which describes the emotions experienced during a lifetime," said Gilmour. It's an idea so obvious, it's odd no one had thought of it before. Mason created the effect with a soft beater on a padded bass drum. Played at the kind of pulse-rate which would indicate catatonia in an actual human being, this effect is quintessential Pink Floyd: human but mechanical, lethargic but tense, obvious yet mysterious. *Dark Side Of The Moon* was finally finished on February 19, 1973.

Dark Side Released

With everything now in place, the band were upset when EMI launched the album to the press at the **London Planetarium**. Not only did it hinder their attempts to jettison the "space rock" tag, but the album was played in stereo rather than quadraphonic sound. Only Rick Wright turned up – the others being sardonically replaced with cardboard cut-outs.

Reviews were mostly positive, though *Melody Maker* (admitting *Ummagumma* was their favourite Floyd album) said, "Oh what a waste of wonderful talent – nine months in the making and only one good side?" But *Sounds* was unequivocal, gushing that it would "unreservedly recommend everyone to *The*

Dark Side Of The Moon." **Lloyd Grossman** of *Rolling Stone* called it "a fine album with a textural and conceptual richness that not only invites but demands involvement". By this time Floyd had established a rule of only playing three-week tours, to minimize disruption to their family lives.

From March 4, 1973, Pink Floyd performed seventeen US dates, the peak of which was a show at New York's Radio City Music Hall on March 17, with **Andy Warhol** one of many luminaries in attendance. New lighting designer **Arthur Max**'s effects were particularly impressive, with the band making a dramatic entry rising up through the stage through pink steam.

Get it on... burn a gong: metallophone pyrotechnics as *DSOTM* is toured

During "Saucerful", a gong burst into flames; for *Dark Side*, the Floyd were augmented with backing singers **The Blackberries**; and an aircraft launched across the auditorium during "On The Run", crashing into the stage in an explosion of smoke.

Despite the sky-high expectations of everyone associated with the Floyd, Gilmour, with typical English self-effacement, bet manager Steve O'Rourke that *Dark Side Of The Moon* wouldn't crack the US Top 10. But when it was released on March 10 in the US, it climbed to #1 on the Billboard chart – an unprecedented achievement for the Floyd. Strangely, when released worldwide on March 24, it only peaked at #2 in the UK (although it bagged the #1 slot in France and Belgium). Not that the band were worrying: US success was the significant thing. After its sole week at the US top spot, *Dark Side* took up residence in the US album chart for the next consecutive 591 weeks, conclusively beating the previous record set by **Johnny Mathis**, whose *Greatest Hits*, had racked up 490 weeks.

Dark Side on CD

The album was given another lease of life when first issued on CD in 1985, *Dark Side*'s pristine production being just the kind of record stereo snobs wanted on the latest format. And people have kept on buying it. Even in 2001, two reissues down the line, it was still racking up sufficient sales to be America's two-hundreth best-selling record of the year, and the 2003 thirtieth anniversary edition boosted sales all over again – which are now reckoned to sit at around 34 million.

Dark Side of The Wizard of Oz

In a collective fit of moon madness, many believe that *Dark Side Of The Moon* is intended to be listened to while watching the 1939 version of *The Wizard of Oz*. Daft as this sounds, there's no denying that film and album complement each other well (start the CD at the MGM lion's third roar), but the idea does rather smack of people with way too much time on their hands. Talking of which, David Gilmour actually tried it himself once. "It seemed to bear no relation when I tried it," he commented. "I mean, it can only last for the first forty minutes. What's supposed to happen for the rest of it?"

There was one dissenting note sounded in the British press, however. In *NME*'s summing up of 1973's *Dark Side* phenomenon in its review of the year, **Ian MacDonald** complained that though "it's a passively compassionate view of the world as seen by the British post-acid youth generation" it is also a "record company 'product'" and pointed out that "the Floyd are making money through transmuting this view into popular music". He found it "a depressing piece of work ... ponderous, humourless, hopeless, apathetic".

The Floyd themselves remain proud of the album, if bemused by its ongoing success. "Everyone thought it was the best thing we'd done to date," said Nick Mason,

"but there's no way that anyone felt it was five times as good as *Meddle*, or eight times as good as *Atom Heart Mother*." Waters rationalised it to *Spin*: "[the album is] comforting to people because it gives you permission to feel it's all right to be going crazy." Waters doesn't regard it as their best album, though he still calls it "a great piece of work".

Gilmour and wife-to-be Ginger

Dark Side's Dark Side

"*Dark Side Of The Moon* finished the Pink Floyd off once and for all," was Roger Waters' summation of the legacy of the band's biggest album. A curious pronouncement, but in fact, the downside of success kicked in almost immediately.

In May 1973, Pink Floyd's American *Dark Side* tour took them to the US heartlands for the first time. Suddenly, rather than being greeted with respectful silence, the Floyd were greeted with shouts and whoops – and demands for "Money", the "hit", which must surely have reminded them of the shouts so many years before for "Emily". The mood was far from happy. Tour photographer **Jill Furmanovsky** said, "You never knew with the Floyd if you were *persona grata* or *non grata*. Even the individual members of the band weren't always sure if they were in the band or not ..."

Then, upon their return to the UK, and the need to return to the round of writing and recording a follow-up, the enervation that so often accompanies massive success kicked in. "When you're fifteen ... the pinnacle that you see ... is the Big Album. The #1 in Billboard," Waters told Capital Radio in 1976. "And once you've done that, a lot of your ambitions have been achieved." All four members of the Floyd fell into creative stasis, doing nothing for a full three months – their longest holiday since 1966.

Gilmour, Mason and Wright all availed themselves of the perks of success. Gilmour bought a Notting Hill house to complement his Royden retreat and expanded his already impressive collection of guitars (he would eventually acquire the very first Fender Stratocaster ever made). Wright bought a country pile in Royston, near Cambridge, and began to collect Persian carpets: he recalls that the leftist Waters gave him "an incredibly hard time" for buying the house. Mason bought a place in posh Highgate and added to his collection of vintage cars. All three bought holiday homes – Wright and Gilmour on the Greek islands of Rhodes and Lindos, Mason in the South of France. None of them much enjoyed the exponential expansion of Pink Floyd the business, though it at least meant they were able to donate some money to their beloved **Monty Python** to finance their Holy Grail film.

Aside from a couple of European shows in October, the Floyd's sole gig until June 1974 was a benefit to raise money for Soft Machine's **Robert Wyatt**, who'd been paralysed in a fall from a tower block window. In early 1974, Mason produced Wyatt's *Rock Bottom* album. Gilmour, meanwhile, met a country rock act, **Unicorn**, during an impromptu jam of Neil Young's "Heart of Gold" at the wedding in Kent of his Cambridge friend Ricky Hopper. He recorded Unicorn's demos at his Essex home studio that summer and then produced their *Blue Pine Trees* album (released in 1974). That same summer, Gilmour became involved in the career of **Kate Bush**, recording the thirteen-year-old prodigy at her parents' house and recording her demos at his home studio in August with help from Unicorn.

Despite having been the first to talk about a solo album, back in 1969, Wright did nothing musical for the remainder of 1973, mostly partying at his country house. In retrospect, this seems ominous, an early warning of Wright's gradual withdrawal from the band. Waters too had sunk into a malaise. As a socialist, he was uncomfortable about his new wealth. "I wasn't stupid enough ... not to understand that the minute I left it in the bank that I was a capitalist," says Waters. "I sort of heart-searched a bit about that... But I definitely took the decision that I wasn't going to immediately divvy it out among the poor and needy, I was going to buy a car!" Indeed, he also bought himself a country pile of his very own a mere six months after chiding Wright for doing so. He did, however, elect to give a proportion of his proceeds to a charitable trust. But with his marriage to Judy crumbling, it was clear that money didn't buy anyone love, let alone happiness. (*The Wall*'s "Don't Leave Me Now" is thought to refer to this unhappy time.) Already inclined towards solipsism, Waters was distanced further by wealth, and his close contact with hit-hungry audiences and bean-counting businessmen did little for his love of humanity. When Waters emerged from this unproductive phase, cynicism and misanthropy would do battle with his long-held humanism for supremacy in his work.

Writer's block and on-tour ennui

After all this, it's little surprise that when Pink Floyd finally reassembled for the first ten days of October 1973, they were stuck for ideas. So stuck that they returned to their *Household Objects* idea. The rest of the year was wasted tying elastic bands to tables to recreate bass sounds, tapping bottles to imitate tablas, twanging cheese graters for percussion, and recording chords from multiple wine glasses, managing to get only three tentative rhythm tracks on tape. "It'd be very hard to make any of them really work as a piece of genuine music," said Gilmour afterwards.

Finally, rehearsing in a depressing, windowless space in King's Cross in spring 1974 for an impending tour of France, two tracks finally came. Waters' "Raving And Drooling" was indicative of his increasingly negative mindset, and appeared to address the Floyd's new mass audience in unsympathetic terms. "**Shine On You Crazy Diamond**" was sparked by a mournful four-note guitar phrase. "I found it by accident but it stirred something in me," Gilmour recalled. The phrase prompted Waters to pen a poetic, unusually passionate lyric to Syd Barrett.

During the summer the Floyd came up with another new number for their forthcoming British winter tour. Set to a jazzy Gilmour chord sequence, "Gotta Be Crazy" was a prototype of "Dogs" (which appeared on *Animals* in 1977) and was, again, reflective of Waters' negativity – the lyrics dealt with the corporate shill in only slightly less murderous terms than "Dogs" ultimately would. They also embellished and extended "Shine On". They now had what they felt was a complete album: the twenty-minute "Shine On" as side one, "Gotta

The Story

Bitter Love

Setting new records for audience attendances, Pink Floyd's 1974 French tour was a sell-out in more ways than one. Two years previously Pink Floyd had agreed to a deal with a French soft drinks company, **Gini's Bitter Lemon**. Failing to read the small print, they didn't realize that any future French tour would involve an accompanying circus of "trendsetters", comprising models and bikers carrying gigantic Gini Bitter Lemon signs. The band were horrified by this, and Waters wrote a song about the experience, "Bitter Love" (unrecorded and never released). All their profits were donated to charity. Nevertheless, the band all sported Guinness T-shirts throughout the tour and lent their name to an Avis advert.

Be Crazy" and "Raving And Drooling" as side two. Gilmour said that the songs were "tons better now than … on the French tour" but that "it seems to have got harder", wondering whether "it's because [they were] trying to go one better every time."

Keen squash players Mason & Wright (with racquet)

The Floyd spent time at Elstree in September and October 1974 filming visuals for the tour with Hungarian director **Peter Medak** (known for his *A Day In The Death Of Joe Egg*, and later *Let Him Have It*) and incorporating animation by **Ian Eames**. Projected onto a circular screen, these visuals included flashing aircraft and car lights, a planet hurtling towards the audience during "On The Run", squadrons of flying, animated clocks for "Time", slow-motion footage of the London rush hour set against images of black South African miners, shots of politicians apparently singing along to "Brain Damage" and, naturally, an eclipse of the sun. The combined technical jiggery-pokery required a crew of 35. Mason later called this "a gloomy period for the band".

They had personnel problems, too. **Pete Watts** was fired after seven years because of drug problems and **Arthur Max**, who replaced him for a while, alienated the team with his volatile temper. After a series of technical mishaps, the Floyd brought in **Brian Humphries** to oversee the sound. Mason recalls performances as erratic, the band "more interested in booking squash courts, than perfecting the set".

And the incipient press backlash was bolstered by **Nick Kent**'s *NME* review of their four nights at The Empire Pool, Wembley, in November, which called them "incredibly tired and bereft of creative ideas", suggesting they

leave the machines to play the music. Having distanced themselves from the press since *Dark Side* the Floyd now became actively hostile towards them. It has since emerged that at this time each member was threatening to leaves and had told Steve O'Rourke as much.

Wish You Were Here

When Pink Floyd returned to Abbey Road's upgraded Studio 3 in early 1975, the situation was no better. Members of the band took it in turns to be late to the sessions. "It got very laborious and tortured and everybody seemed to be very bored by the whole thing," Waters said later. "Nobody was really looking each other in the eye … it was all very mechanical."

Gilmour was particularly irritated with Mason's playing and attitude and was finding Waters harder to work with. "Roger was getting crosser. There was much more drama between us." Although Wright had spoken to the press the previous November about new material he wanted to include on the new album, it seems that this did not meet with group approval: it was certainly never used. Mason has no memory of Wright submitting anything.

Waters convened a group meeting (he even took notes) and suggested that they scrap two songs and attempt to make the album an expression of the band's current condition. He outlined a concept album about absence, using "Shine On" as a starting point – people being there but not there. "[Syd's] just a symbol of all the extremes of absence some people have

to indulge in because it's the only way they can cope with how fucking sad modern life is – to withdraw completely", he explained. Gilmour wanted simply to record the tracks they'd already written and road-tested and Wright was hardly enthused by the concept either. "Roger's preoccupation with things such as madness and the business is something that I didn't feel nearly so strongly about," he later said. But Waters got his way and – always working quickly when the conceptual bit was between his teeth – came up with three new lyrics to fit the new idea.

The first of these, "Have A Cigar", lambasted the part the music industry had played in Barrett's condition. The lyric "By the way, which one's Pink?" was a question the band were genuinely asked by record execs – and fans – throughout their history. "Cigar" was included in the set for Floyd's American tour of April 18–27, sung by Waters with Gilmour. The set still also prominently featured "Crazy" and "Raving", suggesting a holding operation while new material was created. These huge arena shows sold out in hours, breaking all box-office records in the US. They were a colossal operation, involving a convoy of articulated trucks for the thirty tonnes of equipment and seventeen-strong crew, plus a private jet for the band. As if acting out a part prescribed by "Cigar", their former label, Capitol, issued a promotional compilation to radio stations, *Tour 75*, to boost back-catalogue sales.

In the gap before their second 1975 US tour there were two more bouts of recording in early May and June during which it was decided to scrap "Crazy" and "Drooling" and to record new material. "Welcome To The Machine" presented both the music industry and Pink Floyd's musicians as machines, and the central song concerning absence, "Wish You Were Here", emerged – unusually, as an independent Waters lyric, galvanized by a Gilmour melody that matched the lyric's wistfulness. Again, the professed sentiments could be seen as being addressed as much to Waters' current bandmates as to his old bandmate, Barrett.

On the last day of recording before a US tour – June 5, 1975 – **Syd Barrett** himself turned up at the sessions. As the Floyd were trying to finalise a mix for "Shine On You Crazy Diamond", a song urging Barrett to emerge from the darkness, it was supremely ironic they should fail even to recognize the bloated, bald man in string vest, nylon shirt and Terylene trousers that shambled around the studio. They assumed he was one of Abbey Road's army of anonymous engineers.

The incident remains typically shrouded in mystery. Both Gilmour and Waters have laid claim to finally recognizing him; others say it was another visitor from the past, former manager **Andrew King**. And although many biographies state it was Dave Gilmour's wedding day, and that the reception was held in the Abbey Road canteen, both Mason and John Leckie deny this. What Barrett said to his former bandmates is equally unclear. Some say he declared that the song sounded "a bit old". So did he recognize the implicit tribute to himself? And if so, was it the words themselves that brought it home to him, or Wright's quotation of "See Emily Play" at the end? Wright says Barrett kept asking when it was his turn to play, although it's also said that Barrett seemed surprised that they should want to play the track back again, apparently asking "Why bother? You've already heard it once!" Was this a comment on the Floyd's laboured approach to composition? Or was Barrett too lost inside his own skull for such barbed comments?

This incident has spurred the Floyd to some eloquence. Waters once said he was "in fucking tears". "Seven years of no contact and then to walk in while we were actually doing that particular track," Wright has said. "Coincidence? Karma? Fate? Who knows, but it was very, very, very powerful," he continued. Mason said that they were all "a little disturbed by his arrival", and that "Guilt was one feeling." "We had all played some part in bringing Syd to his present state, either through denial, a lack of responsibility, insensitivity or downright selfishness," he felt. A snapshot Mason took of Barrett on the day shows him looking hunted, frightened and lost – one of the most haunting images from the entire Floyd story.

Back In The USA

The day after Barrett's visit the Floyd set out on another fifteen-date North American tour. The show used a pyramid-shaped stage with an inflatable roof – conceived by Waters and designed by **Mark Fisher** and **Jonathan Park** – intended to ascend at the end of the performance. However, at the first show, in Atlanta, the thing failed to work, was cut free altogether in Pittsburgh and was cut to ribbons by souvenir-hungry fans. At a show at Boston Gardens on June 18, Floyd roadies and local fire marshals played a game of cat- and-mouse over attempts to set off secreted boxes of pyrotechnics.

Waters hated the tour. "I don't think there was any contact between us and them [the audience]. I don't like all that superstar hysteria, I don't like the idea of selling that kind of dream 'cos I know it's unreal 'cos I'm there. I'm at the top ... I am the dream and it ain't worth dreaming about." This rather suggests it was around then that Waters wrote "Welcome To The Machine", and laid the foundations of *The Wall*.

In June, David Gilmour had found time to take Kate Bush to AIR studios to record some tracks for submission to EMI. He also spent much of July in discussions between Bush's family and EMI, negotiating the terms of her contract. On July 5, for Floyd's performance at the Knebworth Festival, back in the UK, **Roy Harper** joined Pink Floyd onstage to sing "Have A Cigar". The World War II Spitfires that flew over the audience put the keyboard out of tune during "Shine On" and the performance immediately fell to pieces. Knebworth also saw the Floyd's last complete performance of *Dark Side Of The Moon* (its 385th) until the Gilmour line-up revived it in 1994. The press gave the show the worst reviews of the band's career, and The Floyd would not play any further British shows until 1977.

Finishing Wish You Were Here

During July, the Floyd applied the finishing touches to *Wish You Were Here*. As usual, these were crucial. At the very least the vocals on "Shine On You Crazy Diamond" were done now, though judging by the American performances, it sounds as if Gilmour's opening guitar solo had been entirely reconceived. "Wish You Were Here" and "Welcome To The Machine" were probably started from scratch. Following the US tour, Waters felt drained, later confessing that he "didn't have an ounce of creative energy left" and that "those last couple of weeks were a real fucking struggle." His vocal for "Shine On", in particular, was troublesome, veering out of pitch so often that it had to be dubbed line by line. Waters had been struggling to sing "Have A Cigar" on the US tour: when it came to recording it, he found it virtually impossible. Indicative of ongoing poor band relations, Gilmour refused to sing the vocal as it was too "complaining". With the band's friend and maverick folkie **Roy Harper** being a regular visitor to the studio, recording his own *HQ* album down the corridor at the time, Harper offered to have a go at the song himself. The band were pleased

Listening back to *Wish You Were Here* in 1975, with Roy Harper (left)

with the results, but Waters later regretted the decision, saying "It didn't sound like us anymore."

Once again, when they got properly stuck in to recording, very little was left to chance. *Dark Side* tour vocalists **Venetta Fields** and **Carlena Williams** were brought in to boost the chorus of "Shine On You Crazy Diamond", and sax man **Dick Parry** was brought back. Even **Stephane Grappelli** – violinist with Django Reinhardt's Hot Club in the 1930s, and now a jazz legend, who was recording at Abbey Road – played a violin part, though his

input (to "Wish You Were Here") is barely audible. Though less central than on *Dark Side*, sound effects were again used to link the tracks on the album: another loony chuckle on "Shine On", another throbbing VCS3 pulse on "Welcome To The Machine". More adventurous was the way the solo at the end of "Have A Cigar" deliberately replicates the sound of a stereo malfunctioning, while the intro to "Wish You Were Here" begins as if through a transistor radio, complete with interference from other stations – a snatch of dialogue, a surge of classical music – recorded

The Roy Harper connection

Roy Harper is a singer-songwriter whose address book far outweighs his sales. In the late 1960s, the volatile Harper fitted in perfectly with Peter Jenner and Andrew King's Blackhill cast of English eccentrics. Harper's 1970s albums (mostly produced by Jenner, recorded at Abbey Road and released on Harvest) are classics – wordy, ambitious and melodically intricate, essaying practically their own genre of prog folk, while never attaining more than cult status, except among other musicians.

Acquainted with the Floyd since the sixties, Harper first worked with them when Gilmour contributed guitar to his *HQ*'s "The Game", with Harper returning the favour by adding vocals to the Floyd's "Have A Cigar". As a songwriter, Harper has much in common with Roger Waters: cynical, acerbic, thoughtful, left-wing, anti-Establishment, entirely English. Harper, however, is both a less disciplined lyric writer and a more ambitious composer, which is probably why he gelled so well with David Gilmour as a writing partner. Their first effort was "Short And Sweet", on Gilmour's eponymous 1978 solo album and recorded by Harper on his 1980 *Unknown Soldier*. They worked together regularly thereafter (see Collaborations p.245). Harper sang on Gilmour's 1984 *About Face* album, helping with lyrics and writing another track that appeared on Harper's 1985 album *Jugula* as "Hope".

A less complimentary Harper influence occurs on Waters' "One Of My Turns", however, inspired by witnessing Harper lose it before the Floyd's Knebworth appearance in July 1975 – he destroyed his trailer. As such it fitted perfectly both with Waters' interest in madness and the pampered rock star's alienation from ordinary life: different rules of behaviour apply if you're famous, or even, as in Harper's case, just notorious.

on Gilmour's car stereo. In the event, *Wish You Were Here* turned out to be both a refinement of the *Dark Side* sound and a farewell to it. The rich vocal harmonies and keyboard layers that had dominated their last three albums had their last gasp here. With Waters' solo voice increasingly taking over thereafter, disharmony would now dominate.

Cover, release and reviews

Wish You Were Here's cover did a brilliantly oblique job of suggesting the album's contents. Packaged in a blue or black plastic sleeve, the album artwork was itself absent, identified only by a sticker on the cover of robots shaking hands (alluding to "Welcome To The Machine"). Inside this self-effacing packaging, **Hipgnosis**'s four photos for album sleeve and inside jacket hinted at the theme of absence and nodded to the band's hippie past with their depiction of the four elements: earth (the bodyless businessman), fire (the businessman burning), air (the veil) and water (the splashless diver).

The album was finally released on September 15, 1975. Reviews were mixed at best. *Sounds* said it was "light years better than *Dark Side Of The Moon* … We're not dealing with songs on a record any more but environments, creations of mood through specific textures of sound."

The Story

One of the "four elements" photos from *Wish You Were Here*

But *Melody Maker* said the Floyd were in a "creative void" and that the album "lacks imagination". It criticised both Waters' "dubious qualities as a lyricist" and the "extremely poor" standard of musicianship. In the US, *Billboard* bizarrely called it "their best effort since *Atom Heart Mother*", though *Rolling Stone* called them "just another conventional rock and roll band ignoring their strengths of self-analysis in order to gain entry to an arena in which they aren't equipped to do battle".

Bettering *Dark Side*, *Wish You Were Here* went to #1 in the US and #2 in the UK, but its total sales to date of around 12 to 13 million is far below those of *Dark Side* and indeed of *The Wall*. *Wish You Were Here* has emerged as the favourite Floyd album of both Rick Wright and David Gilmour. But it closed another phase in Pink Floyd's career, a phase that was both the commercial cumulation of their progressive years and a complete break from them. They created a triumph that eclipsed almost all that went before it. But then they almost collapsed trying to eclipse that. It was also, crucially, a period when they inadvertently created a new leader in Roger Waters. For although the last notes of the *Wish You Were Here* album belong to Rick Wright, it would be his final Floyd composition for 19 years.

Bricks in The Wall
1977–82

Bricks in The Wall
1977–82

The second half of the 1970s was a dark time for Pink Floyd. A time when business threatened to take over from music; a time when this most studio-orientated of bands landed in a mess trying to run their own studio; a time when these multi-million-sellers found themselves financially crippled. The Floyd managed to pull their second-biggest selling album out of this gloom and business chaos, sometimes even drawing from it for inspiration. But struggles for power and a messy hiring-and-firing policy ultimately caused the band's dissolution.

If such cynical, materialistic concerns were a long way from the idealism of the 1960s, then they were at least reflective of society at large, now in the depths of its "Me Decade". By 1976 – with economic recession kicking in, unemployment rising, and punk's nihilism ridiculing sixties idealism – the weary melancholy of *Dark Side* and wistful cynicism of *Wish You Were Here* had hardened into an angry bitterness. Or it had, at least, in Roger Waters. He had always been imaginative and hard work-ing, but this new anger caused ideas to pour out of him, until he was dominating the band's music credits and lead vocals, planning their stage shows and even designing their album covers. Less interested in concerts and visuals, Gilmour was not quick to come up with competing material, while Rick Wright had neither the strength of personality or the material to make his presence felt. Pink Floyd was, during this period, very much Roger Waters' show. The rest were just bricks in The Wall.

Britannia Row

Pink Floyd's business empire began in 1975 in a converted church hall at 35 Britannia Row, off Essex Road, Islington. It was initially used to store sound and lighting equipment between tours, though a scheme to hire out the equipment never really got off the ground. The band gradually added office space, a demo studio, and – at Waters' insistence – a billiard room. The studio was upgraded to 24-track by the end of '75, tested by Mason as engineer on jazz trumpeter **Michael Mantler**'s *Hapless Child* (see p.239).

The Story

With the contract they had with EMI, granting them unlimited studio time, about to expire, this slow-working band began to upgrade the studio to professional standard, wary of spiralling studio costs. The interior was designed by Mason and Jon Corpe, a friend of Waters from Poly, in an austere windowless breeze-block schema. Waters' comment on completion in May 1976 was that "It looks like a fucking prison." As such it was an appropriate setting for a grim era both outside and inside the studio, and for the grim trio of albums the band made in it.

There was little good news around in 1976. Waters and Judy Trim had split up the year before, Waters moving from North to South London. Thieves broke into Gilmour's Essex home and stole £7000-worth of guitars in April. On August 2 the band's former road manager (and *Dark Side* voice), **Pete Watts** was found dead in a band-owned house in Notting Hill. The verdict was "death from drug addiction". He was 30.

Animals

Surprisingly, both Gilmour and Mason have called the *Animals* sessions "cheerful". Said Mason: "I enjoyed making this album more than *Wish You Were Here*. There was some return to a group commitment, possibly because we felt that Britannia Row was our responsibility."

Animals was recorded between April and December 1976. The band began, as usual, by picking at leftovers, namely "Gotta Be Crazy" and "Raving And Drooling" from the 1974 tour. It was as they worked on these that Waters hit upon his new concept, a **George Orwell**-derived anthropomorphic state-of-the-race address. He added a recent song, now called "Pigs", about the ruling classes; retooled the lyrics of "Crazy", which became "Dogs", about ruthless businessmen; and completely overhauled "Raving" as "Sheep", about the apathetic masses. Entirely apt for the troubled late 70s, with racism endemic and industrial unrest erupting across the UK, it was a concept as grim as it was crude. In Waters' worldview, unlike Orwell's, almost no one had any saving graces.

Waters' damning view of mankind was not mitigated by his bandmates' contributions – or lack of them. Gilmour, who had just become a father for the first time, brought in no new compositions, and neither did Wright. The keyboard player gives a rather contradictory explanation. "Recording *Animals* [Waters] started rejecting what I came up with. But it was partly my fault ... because I didn't push my material or I was too lazy to write anything." Elsewhere, Wright more candidly admitted to being distracted by marital difficulties and suffering from a "writing block". What's more, Mason says he doesn't remember Wright bringing things in – "If people brought stuff in it tended to get used."

Wright didn't bring much to the instrumental fray either. Gilmour's guitar often took parts Wright had covered in concert versions. Indeed, Gilmour amply compensated instrumentally for his lack of compositions, adding aptly corrosive and expressive guitar throughout and often playing bass as well (on "Sheep" and – by the sound of it – "Pigs").

For all their retrospective reports, tensions certainly simmered during the sessions. Waters accidentally wiped an entire Gilmour guitar solo on "Dogs", to Gilmour's fury. And Gilmour was again disgruntled when Waters came up with a new tune, "Pigs On The Wing" late in the sessions. Waters' rationale for including the last song actually made perfect sense: "Without 'Pigs On The Wing' *Animals* would have just been a kind of scream of rage." The song instead offers hope through human love – a Floyd first. This may have had something to do with Waters having fallen for **Carolyne Christie**, niece of the Marquis of Zetland. But, because copyright royalties were allocated per *number* of songs, rather than by length, the addition meant that Waters would receive the lion's share of the album's royalties – even though the track Gilmour had co-written, "Dogs", took up 40

percent of the album's length. "Dave wasn't happy that Roger got a bigger share," says Mason. "It resulted in a big argument at the end." Which perhaps explains a rather fraught and unusual turn of events.

The band had decided to add musicians for the next tour, including guitarist **Snowy White**. He would later join **Thin Lizzy** and enjoy a 1982 UK hit with "Bird Of Paradise", also performing at Waters' Berlin *Wall*. When White arrived at Britannia Row to audition, Waters co-opted him to play a solo on "Pigs On The Wing" on the spot. No guitarist, bar Gilmour, had featured on a Floyd track since Barrett's departure. As it was, White's incongruous-sounding solo was axed when the song was split in two – though that would hardly have satisfied Gilmour, because splitting the song gave Waters an even greater share of royalties than before. Even if this wasn't simple one-upmanship, the ruthless apportioning of credits was certainly a long way away from *Dark Side's* "band-like" behaviour, when credits were given for instrumental contributions and to boost band morale. The materialistic 1970s had now very much eclipsed the idealistic 1960s.

Animals' cover

For the first time in nearly ten years, Pink Floyd were unimpressed by **Hipgnosis**'s ideas. Among the images rejected was that of a small boy interrupting his parents having sex. Waters, unsurprisingly, provided the solution. Driving

every day to Britannia Row, he passed Battersea Power Station. An imposing 1930s art deco building on the river's south bank, designed by **Sir Giles Gilbert Scott** (who also designed the red telephone box), it had long been defunct.

Waters decided they needed a shot of the station with a 40-foot inflatable pig flying by – an allusion to "Pigs On The Wing".

The cover design could have been created in the studio, but Thorgerson – ever in pursuit of verisimilitude – had it done for real on December 2, 1976, with an inflatable pig constructed by Zeppelin-makers **Ballon Fabrik**. The press were invited to observe and a marksman was on hand should the pig break free. There wasn't, however, sufficient helium for lift-off and so the team reassembled the next day, sans marksman. On this occasion, the pig did indeed break free, and was carried off by the wind. Reports that it was picked up by air traffic control at Heathrow Airport are erroneous: the pig later landed safe and sound in a farmer's field. So, Hipgnosis had to mock-up the pig flying past the power station in the studio after all. So much for verisimilitude.

Release and reviews

Animals was launched to the press at Battersea Power Station on January 19, 1977. The Floyd did not attend, the album was played only once, and journalists were forbidden to take notes. Common practice in the new millennium, back then such behaviour would have seemed a deliberately insulting move to an increasingly hostile press. Yet *NME* declared *Animals* "one of the most extreme, relentless, harrowing and downright iconoclastic hunks of music to have been made available for public perusal this side of the sun … great, generous healing rock music". *Melody Maker* called *Animals* "punk Floyd", hailing its "intense

and savage humanism", while *Record Mirror* went so far as to relate the album's concept to the preview event itself – with record company executives as dogs and reviewers as sheep. "The lyrics are strong, bitter and ask questions, the music is powerful at times, and the album is powerful, thought-out and may disturb you."

US reviews were considerably less positive. *Rolling Stone* called it "warmed over, spaced out, heavy metal". It concluded, "Floyd has turned bitter and morose." *Playboy* opined, "The trite lyrical execution, punctuated by oinks and barks, is for the birds. 'Dogs' unleashes the best melody in an album otherwise devoid of sustaining substance."

Animals was released on January 23, 1977 (February 3 in the US) and went to #2 in the UK and #3 in the US. Although eminently respectable, eventually shifting four million copies Stateside, this still represented an album on album decline in sales from the heights of *Dark Side Of The Moon*. At the time, Nick Mason declared the album his favourite, "with the possible exception of *Saucer*", but Waters expressed doubts – "It doesn't gel cohesively either musically or conceptually…" However, he now says, "*Of course Animals* is supposed to be funny! The humour in these situations is something that hasn't been expressed." Neither Wright nor Gilmour is fond of the album: they played nothing from it after they reformed Floyd in the 1980s. Although many regard *Animals* as the third of a trilogy that began with *Dark Side*, Waters has accurately declared *Animals* a precursor to *The Wall*.

Live and in the flesh

Having played not a single show throughout 1976, Pink Floyd now went on tour on the day of release for six months. The tour started in Dortmund and saw the band playing stadiums for the first time. The Floyd wanted to ensure that the back row saw as much as the front, and they made their heaviest use yet of props. These included a flying pig that exploded over the audience, an inflatable nuclear family (complete with 2.5 kids) and fireworks which, when exploded, released sheep-shaped parachutes. For the complete performances of *Wish You Were Here*, they now added animation from **Gerald Scarfe** for the first time. Scarfe had been a satirical political cartoonist since the 1960s and, having seen his 1973 film *A Long Drawn Out Trip*, Mason and Waters asked him to draw a cartoon for their 1975 tour programme. Here Scarfe created the crushing insect-like Machine and a naked, sexless body falling through air which becomes a leaf for "Welcome", and a man gradually being

Waters live (on guitar) in 1977

Snowy White on guitar, live in 1977

the band in sync with the films, distancing him even further from the audience. He hated the environment, especially the restiveness of audiences that had usually been waiting several hours for the band to arrive. "It's very difficult to perform in that situation with people whistling and shouting and screaming and throwing things," he later said, but added "... it was a situation that we have created ourselves out of our own greed." Indicative of the growing spaces between Floyds, Waters arrived separately at shows by helicopter, never attending pre- or post-show parties.

Onstage Waters showed his disaffection by shouting out, in the middle of "Pigs", the number of shows they had played, as if impatient for the tour to be over. Then, at **Madison Square Gardens** on July 3, he lost his temper over a firework thrown on stage, "You stupid motherfucker ... just fuck off and let us get on with it." Three days later, at the final show, in Montreal, Waters cracked completely.

Some accounts say a fan was climbing up the storm netting, others that Waters himself beckoned him forwards; Waters says the fan wouldn't stop shouting; Mason says he was calling for "Eugene". But what everyone agrees is that Waters finally spat full in the fan's face. Gilmour was so disgusted with this that he didn't return to the stage for the encore; Waters himself was profoundly shocked at his own behaviour – which he regarded as a "fascist" gesture. The fan in question has never come forward to clarify the incident.

eroded by a sandstorm for "Shine On". These animations suited the songs' ideas perfectly. British reviews were increasingly negative, however, with *Melody Maker* suggesting the band might as well "hire puppets to stand on stage with Floyd masks on". As later developments revealed, Roger Waters agreed entirely.

The Floyd added even more props for the tour's US leg in late April, including the nuclear family's refrigerator and Cadillac. They ironically dubbed these far-from-intimate shows "In The Flesh". It says a lot that sessioneer **Snowy White**'s arrival on stage for the opener, "Sheep", was confused by audiences for the arrival of the Floyd themselves. It was probably this that gave Waters the idea of the "surrogate band" in *The Wall* (see p.170).

In the litigation-obsessed US they constantly ran into problems with power and safety regulations. The capacity for technical mishaps was enormous, and Waters wore headphones to keep

"I hate Pink Floyd" – Pink Floyd and Punk

Such was the perception of Pink Floyd among the punk generation, that when aspirant svengali **Malcolm McLaren** spotted **Johnny Rotten** sporting a customized Pink Floyd T-shirt with the words "I Hate" scrawled before the band's name, he promptly auditioned him for the **Sex Pistols**.

Thus whenever post-punk got a bit too arty, "sounds like Pink Floyd" was as negative an insult as could be uttered, being duly applied to John Foxx's **Ultravox**; **Wire**'s 1978 album *Chairs Missing*; and **Magazine**'s 1979 *Secondhand Daylight*.

Yet punk was far more influenced by Pink Floyd than anyone liked to admit. The Sex Pistols themselves tried to get Syd Barrett to produce their debut, storming into Chelsea Cloisters, the serviced apartment block Barrett had booked into for a few weeks. They got as far as his apartment door but he didn't respond. **The Damned** also tried to get Barrett to produce 1977's *Music For Pleasure*, before making do with Nick Mason instead. Pistol pal **Siouxsie Sioux** wasn't far behind, citing "Arnold Layne" as an influence on the Banshees' 1980 third album, *Kaleidoscope*. Of course, another punk denizen who professed to hate Pink Floyd, **Bob Geldof**, not only came to star in a Pink Floyd movie, but was the architect of their 2005 reunion.

Breathing space: solo projects

Punk exploded on to the British music scene in 1975–76, initially as a purely live phenomenon: the first punk single, The Damned's "New Rose", wasn't released until October 1976 even though a whole host of new bands – the Sex Pistols and The Clash being the best known – had become firmly established by spring that year. From late 1976 onwards, however, punk was where it was at on vinyl as well as live – and the punks made a point of how much they hated the Floyd and how they were going to consign them to the dustbin of history.

But punk didn't actually have much impact upon Floyd. It neither killed them off, like dinosaur peers **Emerson, Lake & Palmer**, nor did it have any effect on their music (the bleakness of *Animals* notwithstanding). Although Mason produced The Damned's *Music For Pleasure*, he veered in the opposite direction afterwards, next producing *Green*, an album by arch-hippy, former Gong guitarist **Steve Hillage**.

David Gilmour couldn't have seemed more aloof from punk, spending the winter of 1977–78 at Super Bear Studios, high in the Alpes Maritimes in France, working on a solo album very much in the "old Floyd" vein. Intended to be an antidote to the Floyd's "complete perfection", Gilmour said it was "born from a crazy desire to express [himself]", wanting to be "as natural as possible", saying Pink Floyd was "not all [his] life any more." "I know what I give to our sound, and [Waters] knows it, too," he told *Rolling Stone*. "It's not a question of him forcing his ideas on us," he continued. "I get my ideas across as much as I

The Story

want to. They would use more of my music if I wrote it." A rather different tune to the one he'd be sounding retrospectively.

And one that is rather different to the recurring sentiments of his album. Given the chance to write lyrics for the first time since 1972's "Childhood's End", Gilmour's songs bristled with dissatisfaction. But three leftovers from the sessions would become better known than anything on the album itself, later used for "Comfortably Numb" and "Run Like Hell" on *The Wall* and "Signs Of Life" on *Momentary Lapse Of Reason*. The imaginatively titled *David Gilmour* sold half a million copies and climbed to #29 on the US chart. In Floydean terms, it was a flop.

Gilmour was followed into Super Bear that January by Rick Wright. He had had a curious time since the *Animals* tour, bizarrely managing to get into a fight with a local police official after a party at his villa in Rhodes in August. That he was also making a solo album was less odd, given his feeling that he'd been blocked by Waters during the *Animals* sessions. What *was* strange was quite how poor it was. In fact, though Wright was never much of a lyricist, *Wet Dream*'s words were more interesting than its music (see p.236). On "Holiday" he sang of a man who is unsure "who he is or where he stands." He was probably talking about

Money

It's typically ironic that, having berated the industry's bean-counters, the Floyd should, in September 1978, find themselves in financial trouble. For **Norton Warburg**, their advisers since 1976, had been mismanaging their money. As a way of avoiding tax, Norton had persuaded the band to invest in various venture capital enterprises, including carbon-fibre rowing boats (Carbocraft), pizzas (My Kinda Town), a floating restaurant (Willows Canal), a hotel (the Moorhead, in Devon), a children's shoe company, car-hire, a skateboarding firm (Benjyboards) and Cossack Securities.

Many of these went under, at a loss to the Floyd of either £1.6 million (said Warburg), or £3.3 million (said Floyd). As a result of additional mishandling, the company left the Floyd liable for tax on money they had actually *lost*. And with high earners paying 83 percent tax under the Labour government, the Floyd were saddled with a crippling, multi-million-pound tax bill. To make any income from the next tax year, both to live and to pay the back-tax, the band would need to leave the country and become – as so many 1970s rock stars had – tax exiles.

In September 1978, the Floyd ended their agreement with Norton Warburg, charging a team of accountants to recover their uninvested cash, while Norton sold off its holdings. When the company finally crashed in 1981, founder **Andrew Warburg** fled to Spain. His company's activities didn't just affect rock royalty: they deprived countless ordinary people of their pension funds. Upon his return to the UK in 1982, Warburg was arrested and served three years in prison for fraudulent trading and false accounting. Mason says, "We felt galled. Just feeling that we'd been mugged. We thought we were a bit cleverer than that."

himself, with regard to his relationship to his wife Juliette – but he might as easily have been talking about his role in Pink Floyd. "*Wet Dream* was rather amateurish," Wright said later. "It wasn't very well produced and the lyrics weren't very strong, but at the end of the day, I think there's something rather quaint about it." Audiences disagreed. *Wet Dream* made even less impact upon the charts than *David Gilmour*. If either wright or Gilmour had any illusions of a commercial life outside Pink Floyd – and thus by extension, beyond Waters' control – they were dashed by these two failures.

Building The Wall

As if to trump Gilmour's and Wright's solo efforts, Waters returned from his own sabbatical in July 1978, with not one but *four* albums' worth of material for the others to hear. He played 90-minute demos of both *The Pros And Cons Of Hitchhiking* & *The Wall* and suggested they choose which they wanted to do. Everyone but Steve O'Rourke preferred *The Wall*.

The story of *The Wall* is that of a rock star and the psychological "bricks" that build up over his lifetime – the death of his father in the war, an overprotective mother, an unfaithful wife – until he becomes first mechanical, then comatose and finally insane. The storyline contained elements of Waters' life and elements of Barrett's, as well as drawing on the Floyd's collective experience on the *In The Flesh* tour. The Wall itself was also suggestive of a deeper social alienation, a relative of The Machine on *Wish You Were Here*. Envisaged from the off as a stage show, it was an idea Waters had been discussing for several years. His most downbeat concept yet, it was again perfect for its doomy times.

Gilmour later called Waters' recordings "unlistenable" and Wright complained that they were "musically very weak indeed", with every song "in the same tempo, same key, same everything". Wright thought, "Oh no, here we go again – it's all about the war, about his mother, about his father being lost." He did, however, concede that Waters had the material, while he and Gilmour had none, but also implied that only financial pressures obliged them to produce anything. Mason also later disparaged the demos but admitted, "It was obvious even then, this was a major new work." He was also the only member to admit how unusual it was for this most unprolific of bands to be presented with such a vast amount of material (*The Wall* alone was enough for a triple album). What he didn't acknowledge, however, was that *The Wall* was unlike anything they'd ever done before. It was closer to rock opera than concept album, a project on a scale that Gilmour and Wright – stale from stunningly unambitious solo albums – couldn't begin to conceive.

Waters' wife Carolyne, with whom he now had a son and who was expecting another baby, was a former employee of the American producer **Bob Ezrin**. And as the band began to work on the material at Britannia Row in autumn 1978, Waters called Ezrin, inviting him to stay at his country house. He played him the demos. Ezrin recalls, "It was very formative, but good enough for me to know it was going to be a very important project." Waters told Ezrin his job was to be his production partner so he didn't have to deal with the other members of the band. "He made it sound like they would be nothing but dead weight and Dave would be extremely difficult, whereas it was the other way around. The only one with any attitude was Roger!"

For a start Waters had failed to mention to Ezrin that Gilmour would be co-producing – "and by the way, that reduces your royalty" – and, secondly, that the band had also brought in Judas Priest and Heatwave producer **James Guthrie**, who in turn hadn't been told about Ezrin's involvement. Ezrin insisted Guthrie be demoted to engineer. "Ghastly", recalls Mason, "Steve [O'Rourke] had to unravel that." With Mason having already ceded his production credit, a wrangle now went on over Wright's, before the keyboard player finally backed down. Money was never far from the surface in this materialistic era.

Ezrin now had an all-night session with Waters' tapes, writing a movie synopsis, just as The Who's manager/producer **Kit Lambert** had for *Tommy*, the project's obvious precursor (right down to its World War II scenes

and lead character's catatonia). Among Ezrin's changes were naming the lead character Pink Floyd and making him younger, "No one wants to know about an ageing rock star. The character needed to be more of an everyman, a gestalt. I thought we already had one of those – 'Pink'" (as in "Which one's Pink?" from "Have A Cigar").

So when the others objected to "When The Tigers Broke Free" being too World War II-specific to fit Ezrin's version, it was dropped. "They would like to believe that the making of *The Wall* was a group collaboration [but] it was in no sense a democratic process," Waters sniffs. "Rick didn't have any input at all. Dave played the guitar and wrote music for a couple of songs … Ezrin's input was big." (In fact, Gilmour co-wrote three songs, while Waters, characteristically, underestimates the importance of his considerable vocal and production input.)

Ezrin's biggest input at this point was to realize the music for "The Trial", "Is There Anybody Out There?" and "Stop!" (similar to his work on **Alice Cooper**'s 1975 *Welcome To My Nightmare*). Waters had told him at the outset: "You can write anything you want – just don't expect any credit." Ezrin says: "I went in with an understanding, I really did – I wasn't sitting there counting notes. But I put my foot down on "The Trial", 'cause I literally walked in with that." It would be Ezrin's sole credit.

"It became my job to be the interface between Roger and the rest of the band," Bob continues. "I had to fight for there to be some Dave songs on the record, and if I hadn't

Bob Ezrin

Bob Ezrin is largely associated with heavy rock. But his CV is more interesting, arty and eclectic than that implies. Born in Ontario, Canada, in 1949, Ezrin became **Alice Cooper**'s producer and keyboard player on his breakthrough 1971 album, *Love It To Death*, as well as the same year's *Killer*. Bringing subtlety to Cooper's theatrical heavy rock, Ezrin penned the music to the brilliant "My Stars", from 1972's *School's Out*, and was co-writer of 1973 hit "Elected" and live favourite "I Love The Dead", as well as "Steven" on 1975's *Welcome To My Nightmare*, plus the rock opera *Alice Cooper Goes To Hell* in 1976 and *Lace And Whiskey* in 1997. In between he worked on **Poco**'s country-rock *Crazy Eyes* (which would have appealed to Gilmour) and **Lou Reed**'s *Berlin* in 1973 – more to Waters' taste, if only for ranking alongside *The Wall* as one of the most miserable albums of all time.

Ezrin became in demand for reproducing the Cooper magic elsewhere; from **Aerosmith**, (for their second, career-making album *Get Your Wings* in 1974), then **Kiss** (for 1976's consolidating *Destroyer*). Ezrin again brought a degree of subtlety to this crude act, co-writing almost every track, including their first ballad, "Beth", a top-ten US hit.

Shortly before *The Wall*, Ezrin worked on Genesis singer **Peter Gabriel**'s 1977 debut, which gave him a 1977 British hit single in "Solsbury Hill". After *The Wall*, Ezrin reteamed with Gilmour for 1984's *About Face*, produced (and co-wrote) all of glam metallers **Hanoi Rocks'** *Two Steps From The Move* the same year, working with **Rod Stewart**, **Berlin** and **Joe Cocker** before reuniting with the Gilmour Floyd in 1987 (jilting Waters in the process). Although Ezrin still produces, he has diversified into digital media, co-founding 7th Level in 1993 and founding Enigma Digital in 1999, later becoming vice-president of Clear Channel.

we wouldn't have had 'Comfortably Numb'." Encouraged by Ezrin, the guitarist dug up his solo album's demos. "I still remember when he played it just how beautiful and ethereal and otherworldly it sounded," says Bob. Waters was less impressed, but pressured by Ezrin, "took the challenge and returned with just stunning poetry". "The hairs on my arms still stand up when I remember the first time I heard it," Bob confides.

From the same demos came the basis for "Run Like Hell", its new disco beat deriving from Ezrin, who'd been recording next door to disco/pop outfit **Chic** in New York, and whose commercial savvy was tweaked by the hit genre. Although Gilmour was unimpressed by disco, the beat suited his tune perfectly and was left to await Waters' lyrics. The guitarist's only new contribution was "Young Lust", which remained an instrumental on the demo completed by the end of 1978, which found *The Wall* almost entirely present in embryo bar "Nobody Home" (see *Under Construction* p.229).

France

At the start of 1979, the Floyd took stock. Addressing their dire financial situation, **Steve O'Rourke** had negotiated a major publishing deal with Chappell and another with Sony, whereby Pink Floyd's percentage points would be increased if they completed an album in time for an end-of-year release. O'Rourke now persuaded the band to relocate abroad to complete the album. This would avoid tax and would get round problems with studio technology: despite Ezrin's and Guthrie's upgrading, **BritRow** just wasn't up to the job. And so, at the start of April, the Floyd relocated en masse to the South of France, to **Super Bear** studios, which had its own accommodation, tennis court and pool.

Although they were living the rock-royalty tax-exile life, this was a tense time, especially between Waters and Gilmour. "Roger is a very difficult man," says Ezrin. "He's very hard on himself. And that translates into being quite hard on other people." Not least Ezrin, who he ribbed mercilessly about his lower royalty rate, to the extent of making button badges for the band saying "NOPE" – "No Points Ezrin". "Roger's a bully. He has a way of instilling self-doubt in everyone – by deferring his own self-doubt," says Ezrin.

Indeed, such difficulty was Waters having with his vocals at Super Bear's high altitude that he gave over the chorus of "Mother", half of "Hey You" and all of "The Show Must Go On" to Gilmour. "Roger won't ever win a vocalist of the year award," says Ezrin. "Dave was the voice of Pink Floyd." Even so, this time Waters was bullishly determined to sing the majority of this album, so he and Ezrin decamped to a second studio, **Miraval**, fifty miles away, to concentrate on vocals.

During this tense time Waters also bullied Mason, who couldn't master "Mother", and who eventually simply decamped to Le Mans with O'Rourke to pursue his motor-racing hobby. But the person who took the bulk of Waters' bullying was Rick Wright. Wright simply wasn't coming up with keyboard parts. While Mason says Wright was "sitting around doing bugger all because it just wasn't time to do the keyboards yet", Ezrin disputes this. "I recall trying to get some stuff from Rick," he remembers. "And I was disappointed by some of the stuff that was coming out. But Roger was being so hard on him that Rick was seizing up. We were setting him up for failure and making him feel like a piece of crap." Ezrin believes his own presence – as an accomplished keyboard player – exacerbated the situation. "I feel very badly for that."

But things were about to get a whole lot nastier. With time running out on the CBS deadline and mixing in Los Angeles impending, Waters demanded Wright cut short his Greek holiday to complete his keyboard parts in LA before the rest of the band arrived. Wright refused. Apoplectic, Waters told O'Rourke he wanted Wright out of the band or he'd pull the plug on the whole enterprise.

Wright's demotion from producer and his crumbling marriage to Juliette – plus the financial implications of refusal (which would have made him responsible for the band's financial woes) – conspired to make Wright quit. But why did the others accede to such a drastic step? Gilmour has said he didn't agree with Wright's ousting, whilst Mason says now "We were probably all as cross as Roger was," he adds, by way of explanation of the Wright affair. "It was a pretty desperate deadline and Rick was refusing to help." As it was, most fans remained unaware of the departure of one of the Floyd's founder members until the credits of *The Final Cut*, four years later.

Los Angeles

On September 6, 1979, Pink Floyd shifted operations to Los Angeles, with families and nannies in tow. They went first to Cherokee Studios for further recording, then to the Producer's Workshop to mix. Crucial recording was done at this stage. "One Of My Turns" had Waters' groupie monologue redone by a local girl, with Ezrin bringing in guitarist Lee Ritenour when Gilmour, curiously, "couldn't think of a good part to play". Ritenour also bolstered "Mother", "In The Flesh" and "Comfortably Numb," while Gilmour, struggling with acoustic guitar instrumental "Is There Anybody Out There", brought in classical guitarist Ron di Blasi (again curious, because it's quite a simple sequence).

With Wright remaining in Greece, Ezrin brought in Freddie Mandell and Peter Wood to supplement Ezrin's own keyboard parts. Consequently, Wright doesn't play on most of the album's signature songs. With Mason again also often absent, working on a solo album (later released as *Fictitious Sports*) in New York, Ezrin got Jeff Porcaro to redo Mason's "Mother" drum part and double "In

The Flesh?". Gilmour later claimed this was the moment Waters began to wonder whether Mason too was dispensable. But with Gilmour covering many of Waters' bass parts, surely, all this use of session musicians showed that, instrumentally, *everyone* in the Floyd was, in a paradoxical kind of way, dispensable? If this was something only Waters realized at the time, Gilmour ultimately came to the same conclusion himself. The previous album, *Animals*, marked the last time a "pure" Pink Floyd was ever committed to disc.

The Wall's backing vocals were now finessed by Beach Boy Bruce Johnston, Toni Tenile (of seventies soft rockers Captain and Tenile) and others, a plan to use all the Beach Boys falling through once they got wind of *The Wall*'s content. And now, for the first time ever, the Floyd were also boosted by orchestration. Ezrin had commissioned composer Michael Kamen to record orchestral parts at New York's Columbia Studios while the band worked in LA. Kamen, whose credits included the musical *Godspell* (1973) and Janis Ian's *Between The Lines* (1977), had worked with Ezrin on a 1978 album by Tim Curry of the *Rocky Horror Picture Show* but had also, crucially, been David Bowie's Musical Director on the *Diamond Dogs* tour. As well as working on Floyd's *The Final Cut*, Kamen went on to score *Lethal Weapon* and the *Die Hard* films, as well as co-writing Bryan Adams' enormous *Robin Hood* hit "Everything I Do". God rest his soul.

Still showing signs of clinging to the "old" Floyd, Gilmour was resistant to the orchestrations, particularly when it came to

"Another Brick In The Wall"

Haunted by what was a mere fragment on the Brit Row demo, Ezrin sniffed a hit single. The Floyd were very anti-singles, so he had to set to work behind their backs. First, he extended the song, repeating the first verse to create a second, then conceived the idea of putting children on it.

After Griffiths got the call, he made the two-minute walk to Islington Green Comprehensive School from Brit Row, striking a deal with music teacher **Alan Renshaw**. He offered free recording for the school orchestra in exchange for the fourth-form children's work. The recording took the duration of one missed lesson – forty minutes. After this part was added to the track Ezrin called Waters into the room. "When the kids came in on the second verse there was a total softening of his face." Waters said, "It was great – exactly the thing I expected from a collaborator."

"Comfortably Numb". Ezrin himself had orchestrated this track, Waters backed him up and an ungentlemanly shouting match ensued at an Italian restaurant in North Hollywood. "The only thing I'd really argue with Roger over was my own music," said Gilmour later, "With his music, I wouldn't bother." The pair's relationship never really recovered.

As with *Dark Side*, the sound effects were recorded at this late stage. Waters tore around a car park in a Ford van so Mason could record tyre squeals for "Run Like Hell", and **Nick Griffiths** worked through a list of effects back at Britannia Row, including the entire staff chanting "Tear down The Wall", crockery smashing, and the real sound of buildings being demolished. Most important of all, Griffiths also got the children of Islington Green school to sing on "Another Brick In The Wall".

Release and reviews

For *The Wall*'s cover, Hipgnosis were now passed over altogether. **Gerald Scarfe**, who'd been at work on animations for the stage show since spring 1978, got the gig instead, Waters phoning from his French villa to request a simple black-and-white cover, Scarfe being left to design the gatefold himself, adding manic splashes of cartoonesque colour. Because of a rather charged oversight, neither Wright nor Mason was credited anywhere on the package (later corrected). So up against *The Wall* were they that various last-minute changes to the running order also occurred, too late to correct on the sleeves.

If the situation wasn't already sufficiently tense, there were now record-company hassles. CBS haggled over percentages until the band threatened to withhold the album. The record company threatened to take it by force – and then the studio was burgled. Just to fan the flames, CBS's head of promotion reacted badly to the finished record, which had cost $700, 000 to make.

In the UK, "Another Brick In The Wall Part 2" was released two weeks ahead of the album proper as a trailer. The Floyd's first UK single in eleven years more than did its work. The single went straight to #1 in the UK, and did the same upon release in January 1980 in the US. The single generated massive tabloid controversy. The *Daily Mail* criticised the use of children from a school with a bad educational record singing an anti-education song. The *News Of The World*, meanwhile, accused the band of exploiting the children by not paying them a fee, nor even giving them complimentary copies of the album. Consequently, head teacher **Margaret Maden** banned the children from appearing on *Top Of The Pops* or in the promotional video.

The song also caused controversy in apartheid South Africa when it was adopted by black schoolchildren as part of a school boycott – single and album both being banned by the government. And in the final act of controversy, in 2004, original choir members were persuaded to claim for performing royalties. Despite headlines stating they were suing Floyd, they were instructing the Performing Artists Media Right Association to collect royalties on their behalf.

The Wall was released on November 30, 1979, shifting a million copies in its first two months, and hitting the US #1 (where it stayed for 15 weeks). In the UK, where, post-punk, the Floyd were still unfashionable, it landed at #3. British reviews were unanimously bad, *Melody Maker* saying, "Waters might wear his heart bravely on his sleeve, but he often ends up with his feet in his mouth, choking on his own platitudes..." *NME* called it a "seamlessly fatalistic piece of work" a monument of "self-centred pessimism– hopelessly clichéd". In the US *Rolling Stone* called it "unremittingly dismal and acidulous", but with "a stunning synthesis of Waters' by now familiar thematic obsessions that leaps to life with a relentless lyrical rage". Indicative of Floyd's importance beyond the rock market, even *Time* magazine afforded the album space, describing Waters' lyrics as "a kind of libretto for Me-decade narcissism", saying "the album may succeed more on the sonic sauna of its melodies than the depth of its lyrics."

The Wall went on to sell 23 million copies. "I thought it was a very good concept at the time," Gilmour has since said. "With the benefit of hindsight I found it a bit whingeing." Mason also has reservations, but calls it "an extraordinary piece of work". *The Wall* is, however, Waters' favourite Pink Floyd album. Citing the "extraordinary coincidence" of twice gaining mass success (with *Dark Side* and *The Wall*), Waters believes he tapped into some kind of universal consciousness. "I experience the fact of writing as a kind of passive experience. I've often had this pregnant feeling that it's allowing this thing to come out that's only partly to do with me."

The Wall tour

Plans for *The Wall* live shows went back to the album's conception. Initially the idea had been simply to have a huge wall between band and audience, but the concept gradually metamorphosed into something completely different. At work since January, **Mark Fisher** and **Jonathan Park** visited the Floyd in France in summer 1979 to present sketches. Scarfe, meanwhile, created animations to project onto the wall, and inflatables were made of Pink's mother, his wife, a schoolmaster and a judge, with the mother depicted as a grotesque harridan whose arms turned into bricks and the wife a harpy with flaming hair – reflecting an underlying misogyny in the concept. Scarfe also had the task of visualizing Pink himself, who he conceived as "a vulnerable pink prawn – a creature without his shell".

As the band prepared for the live show, Waters and Ezrin suddenly had a falling out. Interviewed by a friend from an American magazine, Ezrin leaked details of the show. A breach-of-contract suit was threatened. He was also banned from the shows, though in the event he paid for his ticket and watched it in New York, where he was reduced to tears (by the emotional content, that is, not the animosity of his former clients).

The show was rehearsed for two months at Culver City Studios, LA, with Gilmour as musical director and James Guthrie as sound engineer. Oddly, Rick Wright was now hired as a session musician on a fee. It opened with the "surrogate band" dressed in grey – **Peter Woods** on keyboards, **Willie Wilson** (formerly of Gilmour's Jokers Wild and Quiver) on drums, **Andy Bown** on bass and **Snowy White** on guitar – each wearing life-masks of the real Floyd's faces. They then served as back-up musicians for the rest of the show. Bown recalls everyone being made very nervous by Waters' arrival after working with the "very approachable" Gilmour. Andy Bown broke the ice, after Waters played a bum note, by saying, "If you're going to play like that, I want smaller billing." The pair became friends. "He likes it better if you stand up to him," says Bown.

The 33ft-high wall of cardboard "bricks" was built up during the performance, with the last brick being placed at the end of "Goodbye Cruel World", before the intermission. After initial performances of the second half were deemed static, two new sequences were added. For "Nobody Home", a gap opened in the Wall to reveal "Pink" (Waters) in his hotel room, audibly flicking TV channels, and for "Comfortably Numb" Gilmour dramatically played his solo on top of the wall. The climax was the wall's destruction, the entire cast then playing "Outside The Wall".

The Wall was performed only 29 times in all, deliberately targeting "small" 16,000-seaters rather than the enormo-dromes that had partly sparked the concept. This was in spite of an offer of a million dollars to play Philadelphia's RFK Stadium. When Waters refused, the other

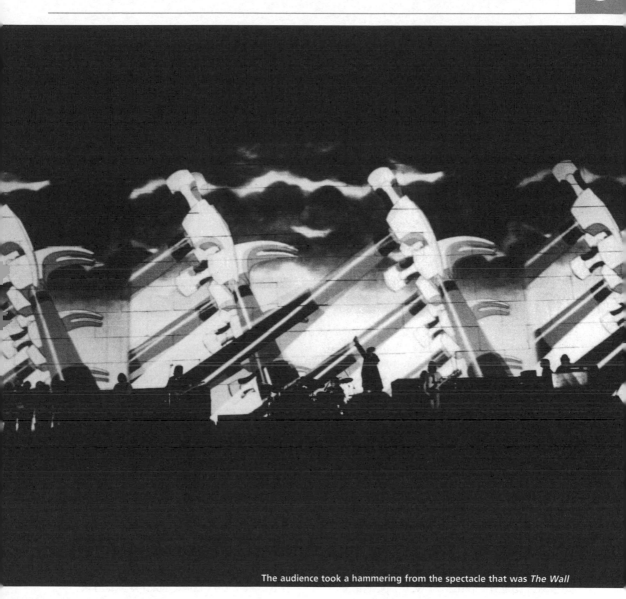

The audience took a hammering from the spectacle that was *The Wall*

The Story

three considered doing the show with Bown covering Waters' parts. The plan came to nothing, and the actual shows comprised five nights in LA, four at Nassau Coliseum in New York, five at Earls Court (released as *Is There Anybody Out There* twenty years later), seven in Dortmund in February 1981, plus four more at Earls Court from June 13 to 17 to allow Scarfe and Michael Seresin to shoot footage for the film.

For the band, however, the writing was now well and truly on the wall. Backstage each member had an individual Portakabin. They also had individual after-show parties. The irony of *The Wall* was that, with the shows so phenomenally expensive to stage and the band losing $45,000 a night, Rick Wright collected a (substantial) session fee regardless, as a hired hand. It must have provided a small, sad consolation to the estranged keyboard player who saw these shows as a "kind of final goodbye". He confesses: "I'm not sure how I did it. I must have completely blanked out my anger and hurt ... In the English stiff upper lip manner, we just got on with the job." To cap this irony, these shows actually proved to be not Wright's goodbye but more Waters'. He wouldn't play another show with Pink Floyd for 25 years.

The Wall movie

While the tour was underway, Waters pitched the idea of a film of *The Wall* to EMI's film division. To his surprise, they declined. Realizing that the name Pink Floyd, all-conquering in the world of music, wasn't sufficient in the film industry, Waters decided he needed an insider onside. He contacted British director **Alan Parker**.

Parker came into film via copywriting adverts, ending up directing slick commercials and going on to write and direct *Bugsy Malone* in 1976 and the hit *Midnight Express* in 1978, receiving Oscar nominations for Best Picture and Best Director. His next film *Fame*, spawned the hit 1980s TV series. When Waters approached him, Parker was impressed both with the concept and the "weird psychopathic quality" of **Scarfe**'s animations, and agreed to be the producer of the project. Flying to Dortmund to see the live shows, Parker was struck by Waters' "almost demonic control of the proceedings".

Waters wrote a screenplay and, in February 1981, Parker, Waters and Scarfe put together a seventy-page book to sell the film to backers. This synopsis had Waters as lead character and included such scenes as Pink being "kneed in the balls by anonymous people on tube trains", during "Comfortably Numb", as well as ample live Floyd footage. Scarfe's primary contributions were a lyrical World War II animated sequence for "Goodbye Blue Sky" and the grotesques of "The Trial". "It was all very hazy," recalls Scarfe, "we didn't know what it would be."

And they say TV's bad for you... Bob Geldof plays "Pink" in *The Wall* movie

physical unpredictabili-ty", Parker approached **Bob Geldof,** singer with the **Boomtown Rats,** who'd recently had two #1 UK hits with "Rat Trap" (October 1978) and "I Don't Like Mondays" (July 1979). When told of the offer in a cab, punk-reared Geldof reportedly said, "Fuck that. I fuck-ing hate Pink Floyd." Bizarrely, this conversa-tion was overheard by Roger Waters' brother, who, by an astonish-ing freak coincidence, was driving the cab. Keen to break into film, however, Geldof

Parker appointed his long-time director of photography, **Michael Seresin** as co-director with Scarfe, but attempts to film at Earls Court that June were disastrous. "The rushes looked like they'd been shot through soup," said Parker. "With five live shows it had five chances, all muffed." Parker decided that the solution was to direct the film himself, drop-ping Seresin, along with the live sequences, redeploying Scarfe as designer, and engaging his usual producer, **Alan Marshall**. Parker was apparently unconvinced by Waters' acting abilities – and so the search began for a new Pink. Struck by his "dangerous quality and

was persuaded to screen test, despite seeing Waters' lyrics as "social-conscience-stricken millionaire leftism". Although Waters was doubtful, Geldof got the role, Waters having to content himself with a cameo as a witness at Pink's wedding.

MGM now agreed to back the film if Pink Floyd underwrote the final cost. Parker assembled a team, among them *Tommy* and *Quadrophenia* choreographer **Gillian Gregory** plus actor **Bob Hoskins** and a young **Joanne Whalley** playing a groupie. Almost no one had a speaking part.

There had been intense rivalry between

Waters and Parker from the start. "We were all paranoid, all under stress, three megalomaniacs in a room together," described Scarfe. Waters viewed Parker's direction as too mainstream, although some of his own ideas (the crowd's heads blowing off at the rally, for instance) proved unworkable. Waters called it "the most unnerving, neurotic period of [his] life, with the possible exception of [his] divorce in 1975". Eventually Parker effectively banned Waters from the set by suggesting he take a six-week holiday at the start of the shoot.

Filming began on September 7, 1981, at Pinewood Studios (the sign on Parker's door read, "just another prick on *The Wall*"), the concert scenes were filmed at Wembley Stadium, and the wartime Italian beach scenes were shot on Saunton Sands, near Barnstaple, Devon. In the usual spirit of Floyd recycling, this same beach was later redeployed on the cover of *Momentary Lapse Of Reason*. The rally was filmed at the Royal Horticultural Hall, Victoria, with its authentic fascist-style architecture. This scene featured real skinheads, and there were small skirmishes between them and Floyd fans hired as extras. Geldof proved a success – dedicated, with a physical and facial expressiveness perfect for the part. Waters conceded, "He's doing it a hell of a lot better than I ever could have done."

But when Waters returned at the editing stage, the tensions erupted, with Waters walking off the film and Gilmour having to act as unlikely conciliator. "It was a nightmare," Waters said. "We just screamed and screamed at each other." Parker was drained by the film, later calling it, "one of the most miserable experiences of my creative life".

When it came to the soundtrack, Waters was left alone to tweak various songs for the film. Parker agreed to add "When The Tigers…", a solo Waters performance, alongside Michael Kamen's orchestrations and the Pontardulais Male Voice Choir as an overture to the film. Released as a single in August 1982, the bleak, uncompromising song unsurprisingly failed to confirm Pink Floyd as pop hit-makers, limping to #39 in the UK chart.

Waters' ultimate view of *The Wall* film was that it was "unremitting in its onslaught upon the senses" and thus uninvolving. "I felt, who gives a shit?" The film was released on July 14, 1982 under the tagline, "The Memories, The Madness, The Music…The Movie." Reviews were poor, *Monthly Film Bulletin* calling it "a vacuous, bombastic and humourless piece of self-indulgence", *Sight & Sound* dubbing it a "feature-length TV commercial", in which "Waters flounders in woman-hating self-pity". *Time Out* said, "All in all, it's just another flick to appal." While the film was given an AA rating (over 14s) in Britain, The Motion Picture Association of America gave it a limiting R (Restricted) rating upon its release in the US on August 6, 1982. Even so, the film grossed a respectable $22.24 million and went on to accrue cult status in the video age.

Although Parker, Hoskins and Whalley all went on to further success in the industry, Geldof only made one more film, the flop

A collection of great power bases

With Waters' attention consumed by *The Wall*, it was left to Gilmour to respond to CBS's demand for a new compilation. But in supervising November 1981's *A Collection Of Great Dance Songs*, Gilmour quietly established a power base within Pink Floyd as custodian of their back catalogue. He also made a point about his own musical importance in the band: as the tapes to *Dark Side* were still owned by Capitol, Gilmour re-recorded "Money" completely single-handedly. He also pointedly brought Thorgerson back into the fold for the cover. In all, then, a subtle realigning of the Floyd into a pre-Waters-takeover mould.

Number One (1985), before his attentions were famously diverted elsewhere. In his capacity as Live Aid/Live 8 organiser Geldof would, of course, play an unexpectedly large role in Pink Floyd's later history.

Spare Bricks

By 1983, the Pink Floyd that had existed since 1968 existed no more. Recently divorced from both Juliette Gale and his band, Rick Wright was in Greece with his new wife, Franka, sailing his yachts and looking after his children. But his absence did nothing to improve relations in the group.

Talk of releasing a film soundtrack resulted in the collection of offcuts from *The Wall* entitled *Spare Bricks*. Gilmour was unhappy: having already rejected songs on quality grounds once, why revive them? Certainly *Spare Bricks* is hardly an inspiring concept, but the songs themselves are better than Gilmour's opinion of them. (For the record, the *Spare Bricks* were "Your Possible Pasts", "The Hero's Return", "One Of The Few" and "The Final Cut", all of which appeared on *The Final Cut*.) Gilmour requested time to come up with his own material but Waters, citing the slow speed at which Gilmour worked, refused.

As for Mason, he was even less involved than on *The Wall*. Having founded **Ten Tenths** to promote the photographing of his Ferraris and Bugattis for magazines, books, films and adverts, he began to win historic car races (sometimes partnered by Steve O'Rourke). His participation in Le Mans in 1983 was covered on British TV's *Life Could Be A Dream* documentary, which also included additional footage of the Floyd at Crystal Palace and Pompeii.

The Story

The Final Cut

When the Falklands War broke out in April 1982, Roger Waters, now resident in East Sheen, London, was presented with a new idea. Many of the _Spare Bricks_ songs focused on the experiences of the teacher character from _The Wall_. Like Waters' father, he served in the airforce in World War II, but, unlike Waters' father, returned to participate in the post-war dream of peace and prosperity, represented by **Clement Attlee**'s 1945 Labour government and its establishment of the welfare state. Waters began to write a series of songs that posited Britain's attack on Argentina as emblematic of Britain's – or more specifically, Conservative Prime Minister **Margaret Thatcher**'s – betrayal of the post-war dream: rolling back the welfare state to return to a time when, under Thatcher's hero, **Winston Churchill**, Britain was an imperial world power. For socialists like Waters, Thatcher's policies were undermining Britain's economic and moral foundations.

Gilmour liked these new songs even less than the old _Wall_ songs, finding them too baldly political and lacking in Floydean enigma. Waters gave him a deadline to come up with new material – Gilmour missed it. "Dave still feels that he was frustrated by Roger", says Mason, "that he could have written more given a bit more time and a bit more encouragement." But he acknowledges, "It's not Roger's job to encourage Dave…" though his implication is that it's one of the responsibilities of leadership.

Waters now essentially repeated the same manoeuvre he'd executed on Wright three years previously, threatening to shelve the entire project unless Gilmour let him make the album he desired. He also suggested putting out _Final Cut_ as a solo record, but Mason and Gilmour refused. "They know songs don't grow on trees," said Waters later. Gilmour called all this "the lowest point in our Pink Floyd career for me personally. [Roger had] got to a sort of megalomaniac stage where he could not tolerate anyone else having any real say in what was going on." Waters actually concurs, "_The Final Cut_ was absolutely misery to make. We were all fighting like cats and dogs. We were finally realizing – or accepting, if you like – that there was no band." As a result of all this bad feeling, Gilmour took his name off the production credits (although he insisted he still receive his producer's royalties).

With Waters writing and singing almost every song (Gilmour has no co-writes and sings only one song, "Not Now John", while he even has relatively few featured guitar solos), _The Final Cut_ represented a complete reconfiguration of Pink Floyd. **Michael Kamen** became Waters' co-producer in Gilmour's stead, alongside **James Guthrie**; Kamen and **Andy Bown** effectively replaced Wright. Then, towards the end of the sessions, Mason was dropped in favour of sessioneer **Andy Newmark**, for "Two Suns In The Sunset". Then Waters told Mason that he wouldn't receive any credit he did for his work capturing church bells and plane sounds for sound effects. Mason says: "This was megalomania. It was a case of either convince everyone else or make everyone do what you want to do. I definitely felt like I was being pushed around." This was a sad situation for such former friends – Mason was even godfather to Waters' son Harry.

The album was laborious in every respect, recorded in eight different studios over six months from June to December 1982. Waters recorded most of his vocals in his home studio, **The Billiard Room**, perched on the billiard table. On one occasion, when Waters was struggling with a vocal track, a frustrated Kamen started scribbling on a note pad. Waters stormed into the control room demanding to know what Kamen was writing. He was writing, bizarrely, "I must not fuck sheep" over and over again. Later, when Kamen was part of Waters' touring band, Waters had a T-shirt made up in mirror writing bearing just that.

Once again Waters took charge of the album's art direction, using his brother-in-law, *Vogue* photographer **Willie Christie**. The artwork included an image of a soldier standing to attention in a poppy field, a knife sticking from his back, and a film canister tucked under his arm – a reference both to the betrayal of soldiers by their leaders, and to Waters' feeling of betrayal by Alan Parker over *The Wall* movie.

Release and reviews

Dedicated to Waters' father, **Eric Fletcher Waters**, *The Final Cut* was released in the UK on March 21, and in America on April 2, 1983. In the UK, *The Guardian* called it "messy, overblown and awkward", *Melody Maker* said, "Its failure is stupefying and its self-satisfaction nauseating. A milestone in the history of awfulness." *NME* called it "flabby, inconsolable rhetoric. The expression of a man who loathes the demands of rock and roll, yet is unable to move beyond them." In the States, *Rolling Stone*'s Kurt Loder called it "art rock's crowning masterpiece". But *Creem* magazine called it "an artistic failure. The music is dull, and Waters' vocals often sound like the mutterings of a street lunatic."

Perhaps it was surprising that such a gloomy, arty album as *The Final Cut* made it as far as # 6 in the US charts, let alone # 1 in the UK. "It sold three million copies", said Waters, "which wasn't a lot for Pink Floyd. But it's absolutely ridiculous to judge a record solely on sales." Gilmour has been famously dismissive of the album, claiming there are only three good songs on it, calling it "a weak album, musically". "*The Final Cut?*" he asked in 2002, "we should have called it *The Final Straw*." Even Waters later called it "deeply flawed", dismissing his singing, though he has since softened towards the album.

Although live performances were announced in November 1983, Waters changed his mind. Pink Floyd appeared to be on indefinite hold. "As usual I was sort of in denial", Mason says, "thinking maybe at some point everything will warm up again, whereas the writing was on the wall that Roger wanted to head off and do stuff on his own." Andy Bown says, "Roger wanted to do less work, and he said 'next year I might play some golf'. In retrospect he

5

saw the band was going to stop." But in an interview in *Sounds* that March, Waters said that rumours the band were breaking up were "nonsense", although he did also say to *Rolling Stone*, "I could work with another drummer and another keyboard player very easily. The future of Pink Floyd depends very much on me." Which rather confirmed that he viewed his colleagues as little more than session men, to be hired or fired at will. In May Gilmour admitted to *Sounds* there had been arguments during *The Final Cut*, resulting in him "coming off" the production credits, and distancing himself from the end result: "It's not personally how I would see a Pink Floyd record going." This was an extraordinary comment for a band member to make mere months after the release of an album. If only people had recognized it, this was the moment at which this incarnation of Pink Floyd effectively died. And as an epitaph, *The Final Cut* was a fittingly downbeat, dark conclusion to a downbeat, dark era.

Which one's Pink?
1984–2006

Which one's Pink?
1984–2006

Boosted by the arrival of the CD, the record companies' back catalogue sales were running at forty percent of all sales by the late 1980s, and grew higher in the 1990s. Responding to this nostalgia boom, bands as diverse – and estranged – as The Velvet Underground, The Eagles, The Sex Pistols and The Who all re-formed.

But Pink Floyd were the first re-formers, the pioneers of looking backwards. For, although the gap between *The Final Cut* and *A Momentary Lapse Of Reason* was no longer than that between *The Wall* and *Final Cut* (four years), Pink Floyd had to all intents and purposes broken up in 1983. Gilmour re-formed the band in 1985 and, in order to claim that *he* was Pink (as it were), returned to a pre-Waters takeover approach, thus largely reconfiguring Pink Floyd as an oldies act. Bitterly contesting this re-formation, a struggling, solo Roger Waters revived *The Wall* in its entirety in 1990, as if to counter-prove that *he* was Pink. Five years later his former Floyd colleagues, in turn, performed *Dark Side Of The Moon* in its entirety. In the twenty-first century these nostalgic live re-creations of entire albums became an industry standard, indulged in by Brian Wilson, Patti Smith and Suede.

And then finally, in 2005, we got the full re-formation of all four classic-era Pinks. Perhaps *because* of the waters that had flowed under the bridge between these warring parties, this reunion did not feel as hollow as so many others. Which one was Pink? Well, for those brief, emotive fifteen minutes, they all were.

About Face vs Pros And Cons

"There are three people who are in what is laughingly called the Pink Floyd," David Gilmour told *Rolling Stone* in 1984, "and none of us have any plans at the moment to work together on any project." Indeed, barely had they finished *Final Cut* than Waters, Gilmour and Mason all turned their attentions to solo work.

Recording his second solo album in Paris, Gilmour called in **Bob Ezrin** as co-producer midway through the sessions, pointedly saying afterwards that "It's very pleasant to work without having to argue to get your way." The album featured lyrical contribu-

David Gilmour and Roy Harper live in 1984

tions by new celebrity pal **Pete Townshend** and among those featuring Gilmour's own lyrics were two tracks seemingly addressed to Waters: "You Know I'm Right" and "Near The End". Issued in March 1984, *About Face* was adjudged by *Rolling Stone* "not bad at all, but – except for Pink Floyd cultists – not essential either". The album only made #32 on the US charts and #21 in the UK, selling, like its predecessor, *David Gilmour*, a mere half a million copies.

Gilmour toured to promote the album, without any of the signature Pink Floyd visual effects. In the band was saxophonist **Raphael Ravenscroft** (who'd just worked with Waters) and Mott the Hoople/Bad Company guitarist **Mick Ralphs**. Although the ensuing tour documentary was called *After The Floyd*, Mason joined Gilmour for "Comfortably Numb" at Hammersmith Odeon. Although the concert sold out he couldn't fill a small cinema in Birmingham, and ticket sales were so poor on some North American dates that shows were cancelled. He described the experience as "depressing". "I've made this record and

done this tour to see if it was possible for me to continue without Pink Floyd," he said. You have to guess that the answer was a "no".

Roger Waters meanwhile had turned his attention to the very song-cycle the Floyd rejected back in summer 1978, *The Pros And Cons Of Hitchhiking*. Waters summarized the concept thus: "Within the context of these dreams, the subconscious is weighing up the pros and cons of living with one woman within the framework of a family – against the call of the wild." Waters achieved an incredible coup by replacing Gilmour with one of the world's most famous guitarists – **Eric Clapton**. Waters and Clapton shared a love of the blues and Clapton's wife Patti was a friend of Waters' wife Carolyne. It must have helped that Clapton expressed amazement that Gilmour had ever denigrated Waters' bass playing.

Upon release in May 1984, reviews of *Pros* were unanimously con. *NME* asked: "Did Roger actually *try* hitchhiking?" and "Wasn't somebody sensible enough to mow the old bore down?" *Melody Maker* declared it: "The work which marked out Roger Waters' determination to be his own man ... as powerful and as hard to take as a Munch painting of a screaming mouth." Even *Final Cut*-defender Kurt Loder's *Rolling Stone* review said *Pros* reduced "Waters' customary bile to musical bilge ... a strangely static, faintly hideous record. You can count the melodies here on Mickey Mouse's fingers." Waters himself has remained uncharacteristically muted about the record, consistently defending "Every Strangers

Eyes", and commenting, "It's the only record I've made that was only about sex." *Pros And Cons* fared only marginally better than *About Face*, making #13 in the UK and #31 in the US, but ultimately, largely matching its competitor's sales record.

To promote the record, Waters mounted an ambitious spectacle in Floyd vein, beginning on the very day Gilmour's tour ended and using new animations from **Gerald Scarfe** and film sequences by director **Nicolas Roeg**, alongside a super-sized bedroom stage-set, complete with 40-foot TV, designed by Floyd regulars Jonathan Park and Mark Fisher. The shows also employed both saxophonist **Mel Collins** (who'd worked with Rick Wright) and guitarist **Tim Renwick**, an old Cambridge friend of Gilmour's and a mainstay of folk rockers Quiver and Al Stewart's band. Renwick found Waters to be "totally charming" at first but during the tour felt that he "created a sort of angst" and that he seemed "to thrive on [tension]". Clapton, meanwhile, felt "stifled" and left after the tour's first leg, taking Renwick with him to join his band, their places taken by **Andy Fairweather-Low** and **Jay Stapley**. At this point, Sony withdrew tour support and financiers backed out of a projected tour film. *Rolling Stone* regarded the shows – which included much Floyd material – as "a petulant echo, a transparent attempt to prove that Roger Waters was Pink Floyd". Certainly he wasn't convincing the public. Tickets sold as poorly as they had for Gilmour's show, and the expensive staging meant Waters lost £400,000 of his own money. "I thought that out there

in Recordland, people did kind of identify me with quite a lot of the work that went into "the Floyd, he complained, but the buggers aren't going out and buying the tickets. Which I'm very surprised by." Nick Mason went to the Earl's Court show in June 1984 and was depressed by the experience. "That was my part being played by someone else … I realized I could not quite so easily let go and watch the train roll on without me."

If the result of this Gilmour-Waters standoff was a commercial draw, Gilmour now looks like the victor. For Waters, with his irascible, impatient demeanour, stumbled over that crucial 1980s notion of networking: having lost Clapton and Renwick, he now alienated the increasingly influential MTV. By contrast, the new, networking Gilmour wooed the station, and received regular airings of his videos, whilst doing guest spots for his musical peers with an open-mindedness that bordered on the undiscriminating. He played with Townshend, **Paul McCartney** and **Bryan Ferry** (see p.247), appearing at **Live Aid** in Ferry's band, which included keyboard player **Jon Carin**. Gilmour took Carin's number, and the pair later jammed at Gilmour's home studio. Gilmour, via his younger brother Peter, also produced **Dream Academy**'s debut album alongside singer **Nick Laird-Clowes**, who provided another useful number for the address book, as did the band's bass player, **Guy Pratt**.

And the other two? Well, the Greek-exiled Wright was working with Fashion's **Dave "Dee" Harris** as Zee, united by an interest in the Fairlight synthesizer (although Wright would later call it "an experiment that didn't work out"). Mason, meanwhile, had set up a company called **Bamboo Music** with former 10cc/Mike Oldfield guitarist **Rick Fenn** to provide music for films and adverts. They, in turn, recorded an album, *Profiles*, at Britannia Row, released in August 1985, Gilmour contributing vocals to "Lie For A Lie". Mason and Fenn would also write the score for *Life Could Be A Dream* (a 27-minute profile of Mason) and *White Of The Eye* by cult director **Donald** **Cammell**. When Mason began to take flying lessons, Gilmour soon followed suit, as did manager O'Rourke, Mason buying a De Havilland Devon twin-engined aeroplane with Gilmour. Inevitably, they talked about the possibility of a new Pink Floyd album. By November 1985, Mason was publicly declaring himself open to the idea; flop solo album behind him, Gilmour was, aptly enough, doing an about-face on the subject. Waters claims it was also discussed with him, but that he had no interest in the idea.

Waters walks

Now things get complicated. For, as the others were warming to the idea of a Floyd album, in June 1985 Waters was negotiating with **Steve O'Rourke** over the apportioning of Floyd royalties. When O'Rourke told the others about this, Waters, feeling betrayed, decided to terminate his management contract. However, being part of Pink Floyd™, Waters was unable to act independently, and Mason and Gilmour refused to free him from his contract with O'Rourke. Mason says, "We probably could have resolved it much more amicably by letting Roger out of his management contract. Unfortunately we were all paranoid by then and saw it as a plot to establish the fact Pink Floyd couldn't exist without him." To his later regret, Waters hubristically offered them the Pink Floyd name in exchange for letting him go, convinced they'd never re-form. "You'll never fucking do it," were, allegedly, his precise words. For reasons Mason is now unclear on, but which suggest it was down to bullishness after being insulted, they still refused to let Waters out of his contract. So, in order to rid himself of O'Rourke, Waters had to "leave" the band officially. Thus, in December 1985, Waters wrote to EMI/CBS requesting they release him from his contractual obligations as a member of Pink Floyd. Waters' "departure" was not reported to the press, just as Rick Wright's departure had never been officially announced.

When The Wind Blows; Radio K.A.O.S

Now managed by former Rolling Stones minder **Peter Rudge**, Waters immediately commenced work on his first official release as a solo artist. *When The Wind Blows*, a cartoon book by **Raymond Briggs** relating an elderly couple's experience of nuclear war, was being made into a film for television, the couple voiced by John Mills and Peggy

Ashcroft. When the original soundtracker-of-choice, David Bowie, couldn't fit the job in to his over-committed schedule, Waters agreed to take over (with tracks by Squeeze, Paul Hardcastle and Genesis later added). Waters' half of the album was credited to Roger Waters and the Bleeding Heart Band, essentially his *Pros* tour band, plus guest vocalists **Paul Carrack** (Ace, Squeeze; later Mike and the Mechanics) and a returning **Clare Torry** ("Great Gig"). Carrack later said, "Roger can be quite nasty and obviously he's a control freak, but I never minded either of those things. In fact they kept me on my toes." Indeed on Waters' next tour, the team were issued with T-shirts asking, "Am I really cost-effective?" in mirror-lettering.

The nuclear theme continued on Waters' second solo album proper, *Radio K.A.O.S*, recorded with the same personnel (including Carrack and Torry) and conceived, like *The Wall*, as album, stage show and film. Indeed, the storyline of the album was partly inspired by working on *The Wall*, when Waters had met DJ **Jim Ladd** of Los Angeles radio station KMET and had recorded the Pontardoulais Male Voice Choir for "When The Tigers Broke Free". An American DJ and a Welsh mining community are both integral to *Radio K.A.O.S.* The album also found a home for some still unused spare bricks from *The Wall*. In February 1986, Waters rang *The Wall*'s producer **Bob Ezrin**. "I've broken up the band, and I'd like to discuss a solo project with you," Ezrin reports him saying. "Come

to England immediately. I'm a much kinder, gentler person and I'd very much like [us] to work together." But, by April, Ezrin had backed out. Waters was "becoming much more demanding and controlling", and Ezrin didn't want to disrupt his five children's education by working in the UK again for an unspecified length of time. "It's my way or the highway with Roger," says Ezrin.

Shortly afterwards, Ezrin says he received a phone call from David Gilmour announcing, "The band is carrying on without Roger"). Gilmour went on, "Do you mind if I come and play some songs for you?" With Gilmour agreeing to split recording between the UK and Ezrin's LA domicile, Ezrin remarks, "It was such a contrast, so easy and so human."

Waters ultimately made *Radio K.A.O.S* with hi-tech producer **Ian Ritchie** who had produced Pete Wylie and Wham!. The *Tommy*-esque concept concerned Billy, an idiot savant from a depressed Welsh mining town, who develops a knack for psychically tuning into radio waves, learning to control the world's most powerful computers, and staging a mock nuclear attack. Waters himself admitted, "I realized half-way through that, as a narrative, the album was doomed." The album was put together in The Billiard Room recording studio in Waters' house in Barnes, West London,1 and took a year to make. During that time, the first Floyd warning shot came across the bows in June 1986, when O'Rourke filed a suit against Waters, demanding £25,000 in retrospective commissions.

The Floyd re-form

Paradoxically, it was Waters' very dismissal of the Floyd reconvening without him that made the others determined to do just that. "Once Dave absolutely got the message that Roger was saying 'You can't go on without me', Dave got the hump and said 'Yes we can'," says Mason. "Being both an opportunist and being a bit miffed at the idea that we weren't allowed to carry on without Roger, I absolutely said 'yes'."

Learning of these sessions, in summer 1986, Waters found Ezrin's resignation from *K.A.O.S* too much of a coincidence. "He thought it was a conspiracy", says Ezrin, "that we were trying to derail his project so ours could come out first. Just paranoid – we weren't anywhere near smart enough!" In fact very little progress had been made so far on a Floyd album. Gilmour and **Jon Carin** had been working on a tune the keyboardist had laid down the previous year. But then, that summer, Pink Floyd's original keyboardist, Rick Wright, reared his head. Still living in Greece and sailing his 45-ft yacht *Gala* (named after his daughter), he played occasionally with local traditional musicians, but had produced no music since playing in Zee. Hearing Gilmour was considering re-forming Floyd, Wright realised he wanted in. That summer, when Gilmour was on holiday at his own Greek villa on Lindos, Wright approached him. It must have been a strange feeling for a founder member to have to petition the "new" boy for work – even stranger that Gilmour should be so vague in his response. Gilmour said he would get back to him.

Back in the UK, that September Bob Ezrin came aboard – literally, as operations moved to Gilmour's converted houseboat studio, The Astoria, on the Thames near Hampton. Mason describes Ezrin's role in the project as "to support David by acting both as a catalyst and as a kind of musical personal trainer". Ezrin added a hook to Carin's tune, which became "Learning To Fly". It was "the defining moment, no question", says Ezrin, "a signature Floyd song".

But work soon languished. **Michael Kamen** confirms Waters' claim that Ezrin called the sessions "a disaster" at the start of 1987. Meanwhile, CBS executive **Stephen Ralbovsky** said the same thing, telling Gilmour that the material was "not Pink Floyd enough" (despite later denials). "It was a kick in the ass," says Ezrin. "We wanted to make sure that we were favourably compared for artistic and business reasons – and we weren't there yet."

Gilmour, at Ezrin's instigation, reworked the music and also tried to address the album's conceptual and lyrical shortcomings, which both conceded were caused by Waters' absence. "We lost our primary lyricist", says Ezrin, "there's no mystery about that, and basically we were auditioning, to see if there was somebody who could put themselves in a Pink Floyd frame of mind. Of course, if everyone was playing nicely together in the sandbox, the preference would have been to keep the whole damn thing together. And I'd like a pony too!"

Gilmour tried to write with 10cc's **Eric Stewart**, Liverpudlian poet **Roger McGough** and Canadian songwriter **Carole Pope**, who says the best song was a conciliatory one towards Roger Waters called "Peace Be With You". The song was never used. "Sorrow" may perhaps also address Waters, but in less complimentary terms. The guitarist spent a week sailing upriver, recording the instrumental parts, with Ezrin going out in the early hours to record the lapping water that opens the album. It was perhaps from this that the album's linking motif of the river emerged.

Finally Gilmour formed a writing partnership with **Anthony Moore** – who, as a member of avant-garde 1970s band **Slapp Happy**, had also been managed by **Peter Jenner**. Led by Moore, "Learning To Fly" acquired words, inspired by Gilmour's flying lessons (which often prevented him showing up for work with Moore). The song was also obviously a reference to Gilmour's new role piloting the Floyd. But it was at this point that Waters attempted to bring the new Floyd crashing back down to earth.

Writs and Wright

On October 31, 1986, Waters took out a High Court injunction to dissolve the Pink Floyd partnership and terminate the group altogether. In his submission – released to the press – he described Pink Floyd as a "spent force creatively", saying, "It is only realistic and honest to admit that the group has in practical terms disbanded and should be allowed to retire gracefully from the music scene."

Gilmour was furious – surprising all who knew him with his assertiveness. His lawyers put out a press release of their own. "Naturally we will miss Roger's artistic input. However, we will continue to work together … We are surprised Roger thinks the band is a 'spent force creatively' as he's had no involvement in the current project. We would prefer to be judged by the public on the strength of the forthcoming Pink Floyd album." For the notoriously

media-shy, tight-lipped, gentlemanly Floyd, this was a quite extraordinary exchange.

Was Gilmour's decision to take up Wright on his offer to participate in the new Pink Floyd prompted by Waters' injunction? Certainly Waters thinks so, and even Gilmour said, "I thought it would make us stronger legally and musically." Mason says, "He was absolutely brought in to strengthen Pink Floyd's case." Wright appears not to have arrived at the sessions until as late as February 1987, by which time almost everything had been recorded. Wright simply backed up a few Hammond parts and added a few vocal harmonies, notably on "Sorrow". His one solo was rejected. What's more, Wright was not reinstated as a full member: Mason says it was because there was a clause in his leaving agreement that prevented him rejoining; Gilmour says the other two had put up the money and didn't want a third part-ner. So, once again, Wright was put on a wage (albeit at $11,000 a week, a good one). And once again, Mason was not much more help.

"Both Nick and Rick were catatonic in terms of their playing ability at the begin-ning," Gilmour later said. "Neither of them played on this at all really. In my view, they'd been destroyed by Roger. Nick played a few tom-toms on one track. Rick played some tiny little parts. For a lot of it, I played the keyboards and pretended it was him." Mason was irritated. "I'd deny that I was catatonic. I'd expect that from the opposition, it's less attractive from one's allies. At some point, he made some sort of apology." But he cedes that Gilmour was fiddling with the thing because he was "extremely nervous about what was going to happen and how it would be perceived".

In April 1987, Waters' lawyers discovered that, as the partnership had never been con-firmed in writing, a dissolution couldn't affect Gilmour and Mason's plans. Waters now tried a different tack: to establish that Pink Floyd Music "must act in accordance with the unani-mous wishes of the group" – effectively giving himself a power of veto over use of the name. Mason claims he understood Waters' predica-ment and the danger of his solo career being eclipsed by the Floyd brand name, but also felt "aggrieved that after twenty years I thought I was being told to quietly lie down, roll over and retire". Others commented on the ironic parallels with the Barrett situation of twenty

years previously when Waters thought noth-ing of continuing the band that had previously been someone else's vision.

"Roger is a dog in the manger and I'm going to fight him," Gilmour told *The Sunday Times*. "No one else has claimed Pink Floyd was entirely them. Anybody who does is extreme-ly arrogant." Waters simply accused the new Floyd of greed. "The lure of the dollar is a very powerful lure," he said. There was a ring of something near the truth when Gilmour said, "I haven't spent twenty years building up my name. I've spent twenty years building up Pink Floyd's name." But there was a degree of revisionism in Gilmour's assertion to *Rolling Stone*, "We never assumed that it was defunct … Our assumption was that we would do another record." Each antagonist now tried to downplay the role of the other in Pink Floyd: "Which one's Pink?" again. Gilmour denigrat-ed Waters' musicality; Waters said that "Dave doesn't have any ideas" and that "Nick can't play." Mason now reflects that "It's funny how much time – particularly when things turn nasty – is spent trying to evaluate who did what" and consoles himself that "at least Roger always seemed to be even more horrible about Dave" than himself.

The feuding Floyds issue became *Rolling Stone*'s biggest selling 1987 issue. And strange-ly, instead of destroying their patented enigma, the very haziness, the dizzying panoply of opin-ion and agenda-boosting selective memory only served to deepen the Floydean mystery.

Finishing A Momentary Lapse Of Reason

In spring 1987, Pink Floyd relocated to Los Angeles' A&M studios, where many of Mason's and Wright's parts were redone by session musicians. "I hadn't played seriously for four years and didn't even like the sound or feel of my own playing," Mason later said. "Perhaps I had been demoralized by the conflict with Roger." "There were times when we just needed something when Nick wasn't present or finding his way to when he was playing. It just took a while to get his stride back," says Ezrin. Ultimately a total of fifteen session musicians were employed on the album, a fact much criticized by Waters, despite the fact that *The Wall* features almost the same number. Arguably the approach is simply Bob Ezrin's way. And this time No Points Ezrin also made sure he got his points.

Planning responses to Waters' suit, Gilmour spent almost as much time in conference with lawyers as he did in the studio. "It certainly hampered the proceedings," says Ezrin. "Maybe that was the intention – to set us back time-wise."

For the album was taking an age. They agonized for aeons over the title. *Of Promises Broken, Signs Of Life* and *Delusions Of Maturity* were all rejected as gifts to nay-sayers (read: Waters), but finally a phrase from the lyrics of the track "One Slip" was settled upon: A Momentary Lapse Of Reason". Some might say this wasn't much of an improvement.

Meanwhile, Gilmour brought back Floyd stalwart **Storm Thorgerson** (by now a film-maker), whose other-worldly shot of beds on a beach (inspired by the line "visions of empty beds" from "Yet Another Movie") was classically Floydian in the *Wish You Were Here* vein. As usual, the picture was not faked, meaning that when it rained, the 800 beds had to be taken in, then laid out all over again. On the inside cover, Wright is listed in the smaller print of the session musicians, and only Gilmour and Mason appear in the David Bailey-photographed portraits.

Radio K.A.O.S vs Momentary Lapse

Released on June 15, 1987, *K.A.O.S* fared worse than *Pros And Cons*, reaching #25 in the UK and #50 in the US, to mixed reviews. *Sounds* called "The Tide Is Turning" "a tidal wave of slurpy sentiment", although *Rolling Stone* said the album was "by no means perfect but powerful". Waters later said, "Between Ian Ritchie and myself we really fucked that record up. We tried too hard to make it sound modern. Also the part where Billy pretends that he's just started the third world war I now find faintly embarrassing." Him and us both.

Releasing three albums in three years, Waters' solo career was off to a characteristically bloody-minded start, although plans for a *K.A.O.S* film soon foundered – and he was very soon to face competition from the new incarnation of his former band.

Pink Floyd's *Momentary Lapse* was released only months later, on September 13, 1987, and although reviews were hostile to indifferent – *Sounds* said it was "back over the wall to where diamonds are crazy, moons have dark sides, and mothers have atom hearts" – it was a huge commercial success. It shot to #3 in both US and UK charts, selling over four million copies overall. A relieved Gilmour took the success as a vindication of his "music first, lyrics second" policy. "*Dark Side Of The Moon* and *Wish You Were Here* were so successful not just because of Roger's contributions, but because there was a better balance between the music and the lyrics. That's what I'm trying to do with *A Momentary Lapse*." The album's singles did well too, and "Learning To Fly" was the world's first CD-only single.

Gilmour later said, "I don't think it's the best Pink Floyd album ever made, but I gave it my best shot." Mason reflected, "It is a very 'careful' album with very few risks taken ... I feel ever so slightly removed from it." More predictably, Waters said in *Rolling Stone*, "*Lapse Of Reason* was a forgery. If one of us was going to be called Pink Floyd, it's me."

Delicate Sound Of Thunder vs Radio K.A.O.S tours

The re-formed Floyd's live shows had been plotted for some five months. Initially promoters wouldn't touch them. Not having toured for six years, no one knew whether there was any demand for a Pink Floyd live show, although Gilmour also claimed Waters wrote to every promoter in America, threatening legal action if they put Floyd tickets on sale. Even manager O'Rourke wasn't willing to invest, and so Gilmour and Mason simply put in £1.65 million of their own money, with Mason hocking the 1962 GTO Ferrari bought in 1973 from his *Dark Side* millions. "No half measures", said Gilmour, "if you're going to do it, make it big."

Crucially though, they gained the support of Canadian promoter **Michael Cohl**, who'd promoted The Rolling Stones' 1980s tours, and who took the risk of one night at a Toronto 60,000-seater. When it sold out in moments, he added two more nights with the same result. Suddenly promoters started calling the Floyd's bookers back.

And, despite supposedly being the music as opposed to the "show" man, Gilmour went for a traditional Floyd spectacular from the start. When Floyd regulars Mark Fisher and Jonathan Park refused to work with the re-formed Floyd, opting to work on Waters' K.A.O.S tour, Gilmour engaged **Paul Staples** instead, who designed a black box within which the band played, and which highlighted the projections. They also redeployed the inflatable pig, circumventing Waters' copyright on it by – literally – giving it balls. They now required a crew of a hundred.

In August, a few weeks ahead of the album's release, Pink Floyd – plus supporting sessioneers – rehearsed for four weeks at Toronto's Pearson

A ballsy pig watches the Pink Floyd live show in 1989

Airport in an aircraft hangar. This was the first time that Carin had actually met Wright, the man he'd stunt-doubled. "What I saw in his face was a lot of pain. Back then, Rick was as shot as everyone says." Alongside Carin was Cambridge/Waters alumnus **Tim Renwick** on guitar; **Guy Pratt** on bass; two 1980s extroverts — saxophonist **Scott Page** and percussionist **Gary Wallis**; plus backing singers **Margaret Taylor** and **Rachel Fury**. They also brought in Bob Ezrin to offer advice.

On August 15 Waters arrived in Toronto with *Radio K.A.O.S.* The tour had begun in Providence, Rhode Island, three days before, with his regular band, plus Carrack (who sang many of the Gilmour songs), Clare Torry (who sang "Great Gig") plus DJ Jim Ladd, who pointedly hailed a Floyd medley with "words and music by Roger Waters" (inaccurately in the case of "Great Gig"). Although Waters banned Floyd alumni from attending, Scott Page managed to slip through to watch the show, reporting back that it sounded nothing like Pink Floyd. Nevertheless, it was a conceptually imaginative show, presented in the format of a radio broadcast, with a telephone in the audience so fans could call in like *K.A.O.S* hero Billy. Tickets were not selling well, however – especially in comparison with the buoyant Pink Floyd cavalcade. "I'm competing against myself and I'm losing," Waters said, bitterly.

For Pink Floyd's tour, which began in Ottawa on September 9, was a crushing commercial juggernaut that rolled into 1988 and 1989. In New York the band played an unexpected early morning blues and R&B set at an East Village bar. In Atlanta – recorded for an abortive live album and video – Gilmour added a third singer, **Durga McBroom** (from Blue Pearl), and her sister **Lorelei** eventually replaced Margaret Taylor. The set list ignored the Waters-dominated *Final Cut* and *Animals* altogether, the pre-*Dark Side* period being represented only by "Echoes" (dropped after the first show) and "One Of These Days". What's more, according to Gilmour, Wallis and Carin were initially covering all of Mason's and Wright's parts, but by the end of the tour Mason and Wright were back on form. "That tour brought them back to being functioning musicians. Or you could say I did," said Gilmour. He was beginning to sound almost as bumptious as his old rival Roger Waters.

Back in Europe, Floyd's performance by the Berlin wall sparked riots on the East. In Moscow the band played the biggest rock show ever staged in the USSR, playing five nights to a 30,000-capacity Olympic Stadium. The live album of the tour, recorded at Nassau Coliseum in August, *Delicate Sound Of Thunder*, released on November 22, 1988, didn't fare as well as previous Pink Floyd albums, only hitting #11 in both the US and the UK and selling three million copies. But that was still a considerable improvement on anything Waters had managed since leaving.

And the tour was far from finished. Floyd went to New Zealand and Australia – their first visit since 1971. Back in Europe again, in Venice on July 15, 1989, 200,000 fans swarmed St Marks Square for a free concert performed on a floating stage in the Grand Canal. The city became overcrowded and Michael Kamen was unable to get through the crowds to play. The Floyd ended up paying $2 million to the city in compensation.

Pink Floyd grossed $135 million on the Delicate Sound Of Thunder tour – making it the most successful musical tour of all time. In *Forbes* magazine's chart of the world's highest paid entertainers, Pink Floyd ranked seventh, ahead of all other rock groups. Mason later called the tour "the most enjoyable ever".

Rebuilding The Wall

In the midst of this, Waters' lawyers finally advised him against pursuing the Pink Floyd case any further. So, on December 23, 1987, he and Gilmour met at Gilmour's houseboat, with their accountants, to forge an out-of-court agreement. Waters would be freed from his contract, while the others could continue to work under the name Pink Floyd. Waters retained rights to the inflatable pigs and *The Wall* concept.

As well as beginning to write music for **Etienne Roda Gil**'s opera, *Ça Ira*, inspired by the French Revolution, Waters returned to the studio between legs of his tour with the same band and – essentially – the same concept, as *K.A.O.S.* But although there was talk of a 1989 release, the album was shelved as Waters entered into another dispute with his record company. This allegedly concerned the company's support of Pink Floyd in preference to his solo work.

Certainly there was something competitive about his next project. Waters had once said that he would never again perform *The Wall* unless the **Berlin Wall** came down. Yet now he began talking to Jonathan Park about potential new locations for restaging the show, from the Sahara Desert to Utah's Monument Valley. Then Waters met Leonard Cheshire. A 72-year-old war hero, Cheshire was the most decorated Royal Air Force bomber ever, and had founded the Cheshire Homes for the Disabled. In September 1989, Cheshire launched the Memorial Fund for Disaster Relief and contacted Live Aid promoter Mike Worwood, because he wanted to put on a show to raise money. Worwood recommended Waters. Cheshire and Waters instantly hit it off, the death of Waters' father at Anzio providing a crucial link. And then, in November 1989, the Berlin Wall really did come down, and the solution seemed obvious: to stage *The Wall* at the wall. Waters said he was "In no sense going to Berlin to celebrate what I consider to be the victory of capitalism over socialism. I'm going to celebrate the victory of the individual." Asked about the show's use of Nazi imagery in National Socialism's capital, Waters said, "Clearly everybody understands that that's satire."

Various locations were researched before the former no-man's-land of Potsdamerplatz was decided upon. The production cost £7.5 million, and featured an even bigger wall than the original stage show's larger Gerald Scarfe inflatables (the teacher alone was 120ft high), plus an enormous all-star cast, though Waters' former Floyd colleagues were notably absent. "I have no more respect for them," Waters announced. Instead *The Wall* was performed by **The Scorpions, Cyndi Lauper, Sinead O'Connor, Joni Mitchell, Bryan Adams, Van Morrison,** actor **Albert Finney,** an East German symphony orchestra and the marching band of the Combined Soviet Forces (conducted by Michael Kamen).

On July 21, 1990, the crowd of 350,000 made it the biggest concert ever held on German soil. Although the show went out live, technical hitches meant footage from the dress rehearsal had to be included for O'Connor's "Mother", with Waters reduced to doing a tap dance routine in front of the biggest crowd of his career. The show climaxed, not with the downbeat "Outside The Wall", but the aptly anthemic "The Tide Is Turning". The notably truculent O'Connor refused to stay for a restaging for the TV version. Looking back on the event Waters said, "It's not something I'd ever try to do again."

The Wall – Live In Berlin album was poorly reviewed and reached #27 in the UK chart and #57 in the US. It did little either for Waters' career, or the charity – making merely a tenth of its projected £5 million – something Gilmour made much of. "I suspect that the motivation for putting *The Wall* show on in Berlin was not charitable," he sniffed. But this time Pink Floyd couldn't compete: their sole concert of 1990, at the similarly star-studded Knebworth Park benefit for the Nordoff-Robbins Music Therapy charity the following August, was, literally, a wash-out, with rain ruining the entire event.

Amused To Death

The origins of Roger Waters' *Amused To Death* extend right back to *Radio K.A.O.S,* of which it was intended to be the second part. This idea was vetoed by EMI, at which point Waters signed worldwide to his US company, Columbia. The eventual five-year gap between *K.A.O.S* and *Amused* was the biggest gap in any Floyd member's productivity thus far. During this time, Waters began a new relationship with American actress **Pricilla Phillips,** divorcing Carolyne in 1992, and marrying Phillips in July 1993.

Meanwhile Waters tweaked the album's concept after reading Neil Postman's anti-television polemic *Amusing Ourselves To Death; Public Discourse In The Age Of Show Business.* Waters: "Most of the songs developed from watching television and checking out what's been going on around the world." He began recording in The Billiard Room and at Abbey Road, then relocated to the US, where he and producer **Patrick Leonard** assembled an impressive cast, including **Jeff Beck** on lead guitar ("a charming man; a real sweetheart", according to Waters, **Rita Coolidge** as co-lead vocalist, plus Eagle **Don Henley** (at whose Walden Woods benefit concert he would appear the following year). Waters professed himself uninterested that former Madonna producer Leonard had worked on *Momentary Lapse*. "I liked the cut of his jib: whatever Pat had done before didn't interest me." Waters updated much of the material with references to the Gulf War and "**Too Much Rope**" contained a dig at Bob Ezrin ("each man has a price, Bob, and yours was pretty low"). "Isn't that childish?" laughs Ezrin now, "listen to that! That's just amazing."

Released on September 1, 1992, *Amused To Death* received the best reviews of Waters' solo career. *Billboard* called it "one of the most provocative and musically dazzling records of the decade". It was also Waters' best commercial performance so far, making #8 in the UK and #21 in the US. But this wasn't good enough for Waters, who had said he'd only tour if the album sold two million copies. It shifted half that number. The album remains close to Waters' heart, however. He ranks it alongside *Dark Side* and *The Wall*. "*Amused To Death* is, I think, a kind of classic masterpiece. I don't think there is any question that if that record had Pink Floyd written on the front of it, it would have done huge numbers." And lest anyone be in any doubt, he added, "Pink Floyd was four people and as those four people are no longer working together, in my mind that band doesn't exist any more." In November 1993 Waters' manager **Mark Fenwick** sternly contradicted rumours that Waters was to rejoin Pink Floyd.

Biding his time

In 1990 Gilmour divorced **Ginger**, his wife of fifteen years. After the divorce he had several brief liaisons – a parallel with his professional life at the time, which consisted of innumerable session appearances – before he met *Sunday Times* journalist **Polly Samson** through mutual friends. She was the former partner of poet and playwright Heathcote Williams and mother of his child, and, at 28, was 16 years Gilmour's junior. It was probably Samson's influence that led to the previously apolitical guitarist joining a protest outside the Israeli embassy against the imprisonment of **Mordechai Vanunu**, the Israeli technician who revealed nuclear secrets to *The Sunday Times*: he sang a specially written song. Gilmour and Samson married during The Division Bell tour, and the couple later had two children, Joe and Gabriel.

The same year, Gilmour joined Mason and O'Rourke in **La Carrera PanAmericana**, a sports car race in Mexico. Gilmour crashed his and O'Rourke's C-type Jaguar, and O'Rourke suffered compound fractures of his leg. A film of the event was as a result not quite the document it was intended to be.

Pink Floyd also contributed music for the film – mostly taken from *Momentary Lapse*, but there were also some new tracks created at Olympic studio in Barnes, in November 1991. The film was released in 1992 (see p.266).

The Division Bell

Inevitably, Waters would again be eclipsed by his old colleagues – their *Division Bell* following hard (in Floyd terms at least) on the heels of *Amused To Death*. Pink Floyd started recording in January 1993 – returning to a remodelled Britannia Row – and attempting to return to their earlier, jamming ethos to create material organically. This time Wright and Mason were involved from the off, and Wright had co-writing credits on five numbers. The album's two instrumentals, "Cluster One" and "Marooned", were the main products of these jams. But Gilmour was also finally getting better at producing material to demand and the band ended up with forty pieces to consider. "I think Dave came at this with less self-doubt than he may have had on the first one," says Ezrin.

After the Britannia Row sessions, the band and Ezrin converged for three months on Gilmour's houseboat. Once again, however, the sessions slowed down. "We started off great guns, then lost momentum," said Ezrin. Then during a break, Gilmour wrote "High Hopes". "Until then everything seemed too intellectual," said Ezrin, 'High Hopes' took the plastic off the furniture."

At this point in the proceedings, Gilmour's lyrics were given a polish by Polly Samson (though he was also assisted by **Nick Laird-Clowes** of the Dream Academy). "That made a huge difference," says Ezrin. "Now it was not just a lyricist but someone who was part of the family. We were all a bit careful at first. Later she was just part of the team."

Rick Wright, now resident in a Kensington town house, with a third wife, **Milly**, also came up with some music. "Anthony Moore wrote the lyrics to 'Wearing The Inside Out' after talking to Wright. Rick is so internal, he's Pink Floyd's quintessential Brit," said Ezrin. "He has the greatest difficulty saying what he feels." What he feels about the financial arrangements, where he is still not on as high a royalty rate as Gilmour, has also been left unsaid, in public at least.

This became the album's theme: communication and the lack of it – a particularly pertinent topic for all Floyds involved. The band went to Olympic Studios to complete the album, augmented by their usual back-up team of Wallis, Carin and Renwick, with old pal Dick Parry making a return. Backing vocals came courtesy of a full-throated team of **Durga McBroom, Sam Brown, Carol Kenyon, Jackie Sheridan** and **Rebecca Leigh-White**. Michael Kamen again provided orchestration. As usual, there was a stash of sound effects. "Cluster One" had noises from beneath the earth's crust, "High Hopes" featured a buzzing fly that recalled "Grantchester Meadows" and "Keep Talking" featured the voice of **Stephen Hawking** sampled from a BT advert. "It was still a problem to finish the thing," Ezrin recalls, "just getting everyone to pay fucking attention and finally get it done. Everyone's lives were even more complicated than during *Lapse Of Reason*."

There was the usual kerfuffle over what to call the album, still untitled as late as July 1994. Mason favoured *Down To Earth*; Gilmour *Pow*

Dave Gilmour, Rick Wright and Bob Ezrin at the houseboat, 1993

Wow. The solution came from author **Douglas Adams** (*Hitchhiker's Guide To The Galaxy*), when he and the Floyds went out to dinner. Adams said he would give them a title in exchange for a £5,000 contribution to the Environmental Investigation Agency. Adams drew their attention to a line from "High Hopes" about the bell rung in the House of Commons to warn MPs that a vote – a division – is about to occur.

Gilmour duly stumped up the cash. For the cover, Thorgerson came up with the idea of a pair of heads forming a single head. As per the traditional Thorgerson approach, these had to be properly constructed in both stone and metal, after which they were installed in a field near Ely in Cambridgeshire for the photo shoot, covered in camouflage netting to avoid press discovery.

Released on March 30, 1994, *Division Bell*

made #1 in both US and UK charts – a Floyd first – and it went on to sell more than four million copies. *Q* said, "They remain unique and uniquely enigmatic. Should be just the job for Floydies and a striking listen for anyone else who bumps into it." *Rolling Stone* was more critical, "The band seems to be padding at every opportunity. Consequently the *Division Bell* will only satisfy the most ravenous Pink Floyd fans."

"I really like *The Division Bell*", said Gilmour afterwards, "although I wouldn't say it's an immediate album." He later said, "It sounds much more like a genuine Pink Floyd record to me than anything since *Wish You Were Here*." Wright said, "I think it's a much better album than the last one. It's got more of the old Floydian feel. I think we could have gone further, but we are now operating as a band." It was left to Waters to provide the negative reaction: "Just rubbish … nonsense from beginning to end."

Division Bell tour

Touring began at Joe Robbie stadium, in Miami, on the same day the album was released. A year long, it consisted of 107 shows, all in the very stadiums whose anonymity had inspired *The Wall*. This time **Mark Fisher** was brought back into the fold to help with the staging, though not, significantly, Jonathan Park. They also brought back **Peter Wynne**, their old acid era cohort. Staging innovations this time included a giant mirror ball, glowing drum sticks for Gilmour and Wallis, and new films by Storm Thorgerson. This time the crew totalled a staggering 200 and for the first time the tour was sponsored – by Volkswagen.

Production rehearsals were held at Norton Air Force Base near San Bernardino. At Mason's urging, they elected to perform *Dark Side* in its entirety, an indication of the band's heritage orientation. It was first performed on July 15 at Pontiac Michigan. Carin remarked, "Playing *Dark Side* is not about expressing yourself, it's about retrieving people's memory of the original. You have to be respectful." The set-list also included "Astronomy Domine", unplayed for two decades. The Floyd's growing legion of conspiracy theorists' pulses were sent racing when, at a New Jersey show on July 18, the words "Enigma Publius" were flashed out by the light show.

After the States, they played at Mexico City on April 9 and 10 – the Floyd's first time in Latin America. In Italy, paparazzi were waiting at the airport – and continued to wait long after Gilmour, Mason and Wright had got onto the bus unrecognized – proof of their continuing anonymity. When they played a series of homecoming shows in Earls Court that October they actually invited Waters to play with them. According to Gilmour, Waters politely declined. One ex-member of Pink Floyd who did show up that night, however, was **Bob Klose**, who was reunited with his old bandmates backstage.

The band didn't enjoy this tour as much as Delicate Sound Of Thunder, and Gilmour said he wouldn't enter a sponsorship agreement again. "Any money I made from it went to charity. We should remain proudly independent." There was one further live document, *Pulse* (released in 1995), which repeated the *Division Bell*'s feat of hitting both US and UK #1. Then, from the point of view of Pink Floyd as an active recording or touring organisation, that was that.

Silence

The years from 1995 to 2005 found the Pink Floyd story slowing to a virtual standstill. With the band shelved indefinitely its members made few forays into the studio or onto the stage. But although the "Which one's Pink?" sparring continued both in interviews and in vague back-catalogue custody battles, there was, in retrospect, some concurrent easing of hostilities and a slow reconfiguration of battle-lines.

David Gilmour concentrated on family life, fathering a further three children. Rick Wright quietly issued a solo album, *Broken China*, in November 1996, co written and produced by Anthony Moore. Its subject was mental illness. In 1994 Waters began working on a stage adaptation of *The Wall*, alongside his ongoing opera about the French Revolution. Initially writing music for **Etienne Roda Gil**'s French libretto, Waters agreed to essay an English translation in 1997. He and Pricilla had a son, Jack. In 1995 Mason bought **Camilla Parker-Bowles**' Wiltshire mansion, where he brought up his twin sons, helicoptering between there, his Hampstead house and his London office.

Mason was notably absent when Wright and Gilmour played "Wish You Were Here" (with Smashing Pumpkin **Billy Corgan**) at the band's **Rock'n'roll Hall of Fame** induction ceremony in January 1996; Waters was not present either. Gilmour did however invite the bassist to his 50th birthday party in March, although Waters didn't reply.

Roger Waters' first new music since *Amused* came in 1998, co-writing "Lost Boys Calling" with soundtrack legend **Ennio Morricone** for *Legend Of 1900*. This was followed by a return to the live arena in 1999, with Jon Carin crossing sides to join him, apparently with Gilmour's blessing. Waters played a new song, "Each Small Candle", among solo and Floyd material, with Texan **Doyle Bramhall** as Gilmour's latest stand-in. Showing the benefits of years of therapy, Waters told *Q*, "I feel I've worked through a lot of my own issues in the last ten or twenty years and I now feel more inside myself." He talked about "feeling the truly reciprocal nature of the arrangements between me and my audiences". He was putting *The Wall* behind him. Indeed he told this writer, "the misanthropic urge is a powerful one. Oh there's absolutely no question that I've succumbed to it. It's something one needs to apply oneself to all the time."

In a similar spirit of post-*Wall* conciliation Rick Wright went backstage after Waters' Wembley show on June 16, although Waters was quite rude to him. Nevertheless, the fact that the tour's 2000-released live document, pointedly titled *In The Flesh*, was produced solely by **James Guthrie** suggested a loosening of the reins. *Rolling Stone* called it, "a Pink Floyd cover band featuring the original bass player". *Q* said, "A couple of hours negotiating … Waters' fears, paranoia and loathing can still prove a slog."

There wasn't much sign of a thaw when Waters blocked a projected BBC Sessions album, however, or when Gilmour oversaw the most comprehensive Pink Floyd compilation yet during 2000 – and Waters infuriated the guitarist by voting only for his own material. Spurred perhaps both by this and *In The Flesh*'s claim to the back catalogue, Gilmour now made his own return to the live arena, **Robert Wyatt**'s Meltdown in London in June 2001, and another Royal Festival Hall performance in January 2002, featuring a guest appearance by Wright and **Bob Geldof** doing Waters' vocal on "Comfortably Numb". Alongside covers of Syd Barrett songs, Gilmour's set contained a sole new song, "Smile". Which is what Gilmour continued to do, distancing himself from the driven, irascible figure of *Momentary Lapse* and presenting himself as "the jolly, happy one" in his increasingly rare interviews. Betraying as much sympathy as hostility, Waters commented: "Dave's mask is very thick and efficient. I hate to think of the pain underneath it all, under the benign, everything's-cool-man exterior." In early 2002, Gilmour sold his Georgian mansion in Maida Vale, London, to Earl Spencer, contributing the resultant £4.5 million to the Crisis homeless charity. He appeared on *Desert Island Discs* in April 2003, and in November that year, Gilmour was made a CBE – every inch the benign Establishment figure. He owns a villa in Greece and a farmhouse in Sussex, and estimates of his worth range from £60 million to £75 million.

Waters went quiet again after the 2000 shows, still working on the musical *Wall* and his opera at his Kimbridge Manor estate in Hampshire and doing a lot of hunting and fishing. "Some of us are gatherers and some of us are hunters," he said. "I need the mud of a river oozing between my toes." Indeed, Waters formed a hunting supergroup with **Eric Clapton** and **Stevie Winwood**, convening for regular shooting holidays at Stanage Castle in the Welsh Marches, all three decked out in plus fours. Another Establishment figure, Waters has wealth valued at £78 million.

In January 2002 Nick Mason (whose wealth is estimated at £50 million) was holidaying on the Caribbean island of Mustique when, during a beach picnic, he was suddenly grabbed from behind by a pair of hands. It was Waters – and a typically challenging Waters approach. They talked all afternoon and met up several times later. "It felt terrific to make peace with one of my oldest friends," said Mason. "A large amount of emotional baggage got dumped at Mustique customs."

In February 2002, following his 2001 divorce from Pricilla, Waters toured again, with his dreadlocked son Harry now on keyboards, and introduced another new song, "Flickering Flame". Waters asked Mason to do a guest spot at his Wembley Arena show on June 27, his "old friend" playing on "Set The Controls For The Heart Of The Sun". "Working with Roger again had been a joy," said Mason. Waters then read the manuscript of Mason's *Inside Out* book, and they met up so that he could offer his comments. That Waters, like Gilmour, used green ink for his comments suggested that the pair actually have more in common than either might care to contemplate. Although extensively rewritten to appease him, David Gilmour was rumoured still to be unhappy with the book's flippant tone (see p.275). The thaw still had a way to go.

After releasing a compilation of his solo material, *Flickering Flame*, everywhere except the US and the UK, in May 2002, Waters performed a benefit concert in October for the Countryside Alliance's campaign against the Labour government's hunting ban. He also joined **Don Henley** at a charity tribute to the recently deceased *Billboard* editor Timothy White, with Henley taking Gilmour's part on "Comfortably Numb" (the **Scissor Sisters** had a hit with a novelty dance version of the song shortly afterwards). Waters then moved, with his fiancée, filmmaker **Laurie Durning**, to a mansion in the Hamptons, upstate New York (his daughter, **India Waters**, being a resident of the city), where his neighbours include Puff Daddy. Galvanized by the Gulf War into finally putting out some music, Waters released two songs on the Internet in July 2004, "Leaving Beirut" and "To Kill The Child".

Having released nothing since 1994, Gilmour, ten years on, said there were no plans for a Pink Floyd album. "It's not anywhere in my list of things I ought to think about. It just isn't relevant at this stage," said Gilmour. "I really don't feel ready to lift all that weight again." Asked about Waters, Gilmour replied, "I don't really have any feelings about him". Mason, meanwhile, said in August 2002: "I like the idea of re-forming for something enormously worthwhile such as another Live Aid."

In October 2003 **Steve O'Rourke** died. Putting aside differences Mason, Wright and Gilmour played "Fat Old Sun" and "Great Gig In The Sky" at his funeral in Chichester Cathedral, with Clare Torry singing, despite her court case with the Floyd still being unsettled. Long alienated from O'Rourke, Waters did not attend.

And, with no hint of new Pink Floyd product it began to seem as if the band O'Rourke had managed for over thirty years had also gone to that Great Gig in the Sky. But, as with all things Pink Floyd, nothing would be quite that straightforward.

Live 8

If the announcement of Bob Geldof's Live 8 was surprising enough, the announcement that Pink Floyd would re-form for the occasion was simply astonishing – and indeed, for many fans it came close to eclipsing the real purpose of the event.

The Pink Floyd website carefully said, "Roger Waters will join Pink Floyd to perform at Live 8," while Gilmour said, "Any squabbles Roger and the band have had in the past are so petty in this context … if re-forming for this concert will help focus attention then it's got to be worthwhile." A statement from Waters added, "It's great to be asked to help Bob raise public awareness about third world debt and poverty. Also, to be given the opportunity to put the band back together again, even if it's only for a few numbers, is a big bonus." Again, note the careful wording: that both warring Floyds were

Pink Floyd's former manager, the late Steve O'Rourke

essentially keeping to their positions of the last 20 years was also indicative of quite how much pushing and pulling had gone on behind the scenes in order to achieve this reconciliation.

For, despite rumours and wistful comments from Mason about re-formation, the Waters-Gilmour standoff didn't have any real reason to end. As it was, Geldof conceived the idea ("that world audience; those sales"), cornering Gilmour at his home. Gilmour still refused, keen to concentrate on a solo album. Wright, despite some apprehension, agreed. (Mason: "I think he was worried Roger might throw him out of the group again."). Waters rang Geldof, surprisingly positive about the idea, asking "what's old Grumpy up to?" Geldof told him Gilmour wasn't playing, so Waters, astonishingly, rang Gilmour. This time, Gilmour, equally stunned, acceded. Geldof was ecstatic, "Not that I can stand you cunts, but you've made an old retro punk very happy. 'Cos I never liked the music, really."

To a crowd of 205,000 and a massive global audience of millions, the classic line-up of Pink Floyd came on stage to the iconic sound of the

The temporarily reunited Pink Floyd, at Live 8

Dark Side heartbeat. An aged, shorn Gilmour was the main focus for the opener, "Breathe", looking tense. Wright was the invisible man yet again for the duration of the song. There but not there. Waters, on the other hand, was if anything, *doubly* there, bouncing up and down, striding around the stage and indulging in the number one band no-no: mouthing the lyrics when not singing as if to assert that *he* wrote the songs. Rather than appearing petty it was actually rather charming.

Interestingly, unlike all the other artists appearing on the day, the Floyd chose to play only one number that had been a hit for the Floyd themselves, which was "Money". Then, as Tim Renwick struck up the intro to "Wish You Were Here", Waters took the mic, saying, "It's actually quite emotional standing up here with these three guys after all these years. Standing to be counted with the rest of you. Anyway, we're doing this for everyone who's not here, but particularly, of course, for Syd." It was fitting that at this historic reunion, Pink Floyd's original leader – forever there but not there – should be invoked. Waters sang one verse, voice hoarse and ragged, the moment all the more moving for it, while all four Floyds were wreathed in dry ice (again – there but not there).

They ended with every Floyd fan's wet dream, "Comfortably Numb", the ultimate song of the intangible. Waters and Gilmour traded vocals with a sympathy long ago mislaid, and Gilmour perfectly replicated his soaring, momentous guitar solos. All four hugged – somewhat awkwardly – at the conclusion. Which one was Pink that night? Well, just for those fifteen minutes, they all were.

According to HMV, sales of *Echoes* the following week rose by 1343 percent, while Amazon reported increases in sales of *The Wall* at 3600 percent, *Wish You Were Here* at 2000 percent and *Dark Side Of The Moon* at 1400 percent. Gilmour declared his intention to donate the profits to charity. The offers of remuneration for a further re-formation tour became sillier by the hour.

Waters sent out mixed signals to these approaches. "I didn't mind rolling over for one day, but I couldn't roll over for a whole fucking tour," he said at one point; at another, "I hope we do it again. If some other opportunity arose, I could even imagine us doing *Dark Side Of The Moon* again – you know, if there was a special occasion. It would be good to hear it again." He even said, "Never say never" to the idea of a new studio album. Mason is unequivocal. "I'd love to do it," he says.

But Gilmour has been equally unequivocal. He later called the experience "like sleeping with your ex-wife" and Mason now concludes, "Dave felt it was a good thing to do and was happy to do it. At some point he and Roger might resolve their differences ... Roger is a different guy, I think he's worked out lots of demons. I think as long as we didn't try to create new material, just going out and playing would be easier. But Dave really isn't up for it."

2006

For ten years after the *Division Bell* album, very little happened in the world of Pink Floyd. In the year since, very little hasn't happened. If Roger Waters' opera had been rumbling on so long it was beginning to sound like a convenient excuse for not issuing a real album, then suddenly, on October 4 2005, it was a reality. *Ça Ira* was reviewed respectfully in the classical press and hit number one on the classical chart. For the first time Waters' face was deemed sufficiently recognisable to sell magazines.

By the time Pink Floyd were inducted into the UK Music Hall of Fame (by **Pete Townshend**), a familiar fragmentation had returned. Gilmour and Mason appeared in the flesh, but Wright (in hospital following eye surgery) did not, while Waters, launching *Ça Ira* in Rome, appeared on a video screen. There but not there. Wish you were here.

David Gilmour was, as ever, not to be outshone by his rival. He released a new solo album on his 60th birthday – March 6, 2006. And indeed, rather than being eclipsed by Live 8, *On An Island* benefited hugely from the resultant attention. Enjoying excellent reviews, Gilmour's album hit number one in the UK album charts, if only for a week, while also reaching a highly respectable 6 in the US (though its tenure in the top 50 was brief). Gilmour's visage was suddenly also now deemed sufficiently recognisable to sell magazines. He also announced that he

would be touring for the first time since *The Division Bell*. Intriguingly, his touring band included not just Floyd regulars **Guy Pratt**, **Jon Carin** and **Dick Parry**, but also one Rick Wright too. Gilmour billed himself as "the voice and guitar of Pink Floyd". Mason was thus the only key member of the *Division Bell* team not involved.

We will probably never know what machinations went on behind the scenes during this period, but shortly after Gilmour began his tour, it was announced that Roger Waters would also be playing live – with Nick Mason. And performing *Dark Side of the Moon*, to boot. Gilmour having patently rejected such a proposal, the surprise was that Mason had "gone over to the *Dark Side*", heralding what had long been hinted at – another reconfiguration. The two line-ups, each with two members of the four-man Floyd, did not however style themselves as Pink Floyd; though Waters, perhaps following Gilmour's lead, billed himself as "the genius and soul of Pink Floyd".

Just to add to bitter fun, he later revealed that he'd invited Wright to join him and Mason. Perhaps sensibly, Wright opted to stick with his employer of the previous 20 years, while claiming that his energy was to be saved for a solo album (just drop that one in casually, why don't you!). Wright's oft-time keyboard stand-in Jon Carin, however, actually signed up with both factions. You really couldn't make this stuff up.

Then to cap it all, in the midst of all this activity, Syd Barrett died. With his death making the national news, suddenly this ultimate of cult artists was a household name. His face could sell magazines. On tour at the time, outshone by the Crazy Diamond at the peak of their solo careers, both Gilmour's and Waters' tributes to their old boss were somewhat muted. The official Pink Floyd management saying, "the band are naturally very upset and sad to learn of **Syd Barrett**'s **death**," while Waters quoted himself, "Shine On". Or perhaps it was just that old Floyd perennial – English, middle class reserve. Gilmour never did make the trip to see his old pal before it was too late, and none of the band were invited to his funeral. Barrett continued to dominate the news in the months thereafter as his house was sold and his possessions auctioned off. They raised £120,000. He was said to have left £1.2 million in his will.

Despite the stated wishes of both Wright and Mason, it now looks unlikely in the aftermath of Live 8 and Barrett's death that Gilmour and Waters will reunite again; the former having returned to family life, saying he's in no rush to record another album; the latter now seemingly almost on his own never-ending tour, although he keeps promising another rock album, not to mention the Broadway production of *The Wall*. But one thing by now is clear is that the only thing that can be ruled out for sure in the continuing story of Pink Floyd is that the original lineup of will now never reform. But while Syd Barrett remains as mysterious in death as in life, even he now seems more corporeal than before, the ubiquity of his story personalizing him to a degree. Most people recognize him now. As they also recognize his former colleagues too. In the noughties, Pink Floyd feel very much *present*. On record, in the charts, on stage, on the television, in the press. Less there but not there, but *here, now*

Part 2:
The Music

The Albums

The Piper At The Gates Of Dawn

ASTRONOMY DOMINE/LUCIFER SAM/MATILDA MOTHER/
FLAMING/POW R TOC H/TAKE UP THY STETHOSCOPE AND
WALK/INTERSTELLAR OVERDRIVE/THE GNOME/CHAPTER
24/THE SCARECROW/BIKE
EMI; recorded March 15–June 27 1967; released August 4
1967; available on CD

The first voice on Pink Floyd's first album may be manager Peter Jenner's, the first notes may be Rick Wright's, but the album is absolutely dominated by Syd Barrett. Bar two group compositions and one by Roger Waters, the album is written by Barrett, sung by Barrett (assisted by Wright), and (in terms of featured solos) played by Barrett. More than anything, however, *Piper At The Gates Of Dawn* is *conceived* by Barrett: it is his vision, his mindset – from the title's allusion to *The Wind In The Willows* to the whimsy of much of the material and the lyrical and musical disorientation that is apparent from the off.

Though much has been made of the way *Piper* was a refinement – indeed containment – of the improvisational abandon of the Floyd's contemporaneous psychedelic live set, any album that starts with the spacey expansiveness of "Astronomy Domine", ends with the sound-effects meltdown of "Bike" and manages to find space for the nine-minute freakout "Interstellar Overdrive" in between, is still a pretty mind-bending affair (see p.179). And though the tunes are mostly pared down to a three-minute pop length, there is little that is conventional about either the playful, effects-driven instrumental "Pow R Toc H" or the shimmering, phantasmagoric "Flaming" (see p.180). Right down to the latter's lyrics, where lines like 'travelling by telephone' find Barrett's mind freed from linear logic, a poetic reordering of language that would, in time, connect with darker, more disturbing shifts in the singer's fracturing psyche.

Even "Lucifer Sam", perhaps the closest here to conventional beat-group pop (not least for being the only song to boast a proper chorus) takes its **James Bond** riff and **Duane Eddy** guitar somewhere slightly sinister. Waters' somewhat scrappy "Take Up Thy Stethoscope" is even darker: while it may be lopped down from its live incarnation, Barrett's guitar interjections are both extraordinary and disturbing, their closest cousin being Lou Reed's contemporaneous work with **The Velvet Underground.**

But if there is darkness here there is also light: this was *still* the Summer of Love, after all. Contemporary hippiedom finds its expression in the placid evocation of I-Ching mysticism in "Chapter 24", in the tilts at the cosmic of "Astronomy" and in the preoccupation with childhood throughout. "Matilda Mother" (its verses sung by Wright, sounding uncan-

Floyd in the recording studio, 1967: Waters, Wright, Barrett, Mason

nily like Barrett) evokes a child being told goodnight stories by his mother, a fairytale world entirely at one with the acid imagination, while "Flaming" makes more explicit links between childhood games and acid giddiness. "The Gnome", inspired by hippie bible *The Lord Of The Rings*, dives headlong into fairytale tweeness, however, as does the similar "The Scarecrow". More vaudeville than folk, both tracks are forerunners of the pastoral-

ism Floyd would do better after Barrett had departed. Indeed, these two numbers constitute the album's main flaw, making the second half (the original vinyl's side two) unbalanced, even schizoid – terms that would attach to the album's author almost immediately *Piper* was completed. "Bike", however, manages to combine the childlike and the twee with the spacey and sinister, and thus closes the album with a sense of cohesion. As such, "Bike" serves as a kind of summary of the album while reflecting the delicate but doomed psychic balancing act its creator was enacting throughout. Which makes *Piper* one of the most sparklingly imaginative but also slightly sad artefacts of the psychedelic era.

A Saucerful Of Secrets

LET THERE BE MORE LIGHT/REMEMBER A DAY/SET THE CONTROLS FOR THE HEART OF THE SUN/CORPORAL CLEGG/ A SAUCERFUL OF SECRETS/SEE SAW/JUGBAND BLUES
EMI; recorded 7–8 August, 8–24 October 1967 and January18–May 6 1968; released: 29 June 1968; available on CD

Even the most well-grounded of bands invariably experience difficult second album syndrome, and Pink Floyd had more stacked against them than most: namely the loss of their lead singer, songwriter and most charismatic member during its recording. Nevertheless, *Saucerful* makes a surprisingly successful fist of overcoming such a severe setback. Although it intermittently clings nervously to its Syd Barrett past, it also simultaneously manages to suggest a perfectly workable way forward.

As both singer and songwriter, Rick Wright stays closest to Barrett's legacy. Indeed his "Remember A Day" is the only song here, apart from "Jugband Blues", to definitely feature input from Barrett himself (on guitar). It's infused with the same Summer of Love spirit as "See Emily Play" – the same childlike wonder and the same space-pastoral mood, thanks to Barrett's spectacular slide guitar work – without ever quite achieving "Emily"'s transcendence. Attempting

to repeat the trick, Wright's "See Saw" manages only to be saccharine and somewhat forgettable, though its tempo shifts and **Mellotron**-orchestrations have their period charms, and its tape-log listing as "The Most Boring Song I've Ever Heard Bar Two" seems unnecessarily harsh.

It is Roger Waters who, while not immune to mimicry, manages to actually *build* upon Barrett's legacy, however. Both "Let There Be More Light" and "Set The Controls" pursue the space-rock of "Astronomy Domine", but while the former is distinctly Barrett-esque (and may even feature him on slide guitar), Waters' vocal on the latter (which even more probably features Barrett on guitar) is universes away from Barrett and pushes into mesmeric, mantric territory that moves firmly forward towards prog rock. On the other hand, while the anti-war "Corporal Clegg" may contain the foundations of *The Wall*, its kazoo-driven vaudeville, rumbling guitar and mannered vocals are so Barrett that many insist that it's the madcap laugher himself who sings the bridges. The chronology – and the wobbly pitching – suggest Waters, however.

In the midst of all this, new recruit David Gilmour had only a minor input. While he sings on "Light" and "Clegg" (adding some fine guitar to the latter) he is absent altogether from "Remember" and "Jugband", inaudible on "Set The Controls" and only a nominal presence on "See Saw". His sole compositional credit is on the album's group-composed title track, which, crucially, alongside "Controls", lays out the Floyd's immediate future. The last cut to be completed, "Saucerful" pools the talents of the reconfigured line-up to create a piece of *musique*

Suites You, Sir

The Man and *The Journey* were Pink Floyd's first attempts at creating lengthy suites of music, building out of "Saucerful Of Secrets" into something more varied and all-encompassing. Both are rooted in prog but, while The Journey is suitably portentous, pseudo-classical and fantastical, The Man concerns mundane everyday life in a way not dissimilar to *Dark Side Of The Moon*. These suites became the basis of their live set throughout 1969, but also laid the foundations for *Atom Heart Mother* (not least by The Journey's use of brass and choir at the Albert Hall), *Echoes*, and ultimately *Dark Side Of The Moon* itself.

The Man:

"Daybreak" (group version of *Ummagumma's* "Grantchester Meadows", with Gilmour singing harmonies and sometimes alternate leads)

"Work" (percussive instrumental with steam whistle etc

"Afternoon" ("Biding My Time", a Waters track recorded on July 9, 1969, remaining unissued until the 1971 *Relics* compilation)

"Doing It" (drum solo, also titled "Up The Khyber", as per the *More* track, in the Royal Festival Hall programme)

"Sleeping" (freeform keyboard instrumental,

referred to as "Quicksilver" in the RFH programme; inaccurately listed on some bootlegs as "The Narrow Way, Part 2". It would develop an identity of its own as time went on.)

"Nightmare" (an extended "Cymbaline" from *More* with taped effects of clocks ticking and a Scottish voice that shouted, "If you don't eat your meat, you can't have any pudding.")

"Daybreak" (reprise – little more than an alarm clock)

The Journey:

"The Beginning" ("Green Is The Colour" from *More*)

"Beset By The Creatures Of The Deep" ("Careful With That Axe, Eugéne")

"The Narrow Way" (a band version of Part 3 of Gilmour's track from *Ummagumma*)

"The Pink Jungle" ("Pow R Toc H")

"The Labyrinths Of Auximines" (the mid-section of "Interstellar Overdrive", but also used as the "Moonhead" improvisation for the Apollo Moon Landings programmes)

"Behold The Temple of Light" (instrumental)

"The End Of The Beginning" ("Celestial Voices" section of *Saucerful*)

---

concrète that's stricter of structure but looser of harmony than Barrett's improvisations and would be a cornerstone of the progressive Pink Floyd rock.

Finally, on "Jugband Blues", there is Barrett himself, arriving late and sounding like a ghost at the album's feast. For as good as the song is, it sounds like a coda, like nostalgia, like a throwback. For on *Saucerful*, Barrett's input and his vision are slowly but surely being sidelined. And the saddest thing is that, despite this song dating back to October 1967, Barrett sounds like he *knows* it too. Set the controls…

More (Original Soundtrack)

CIRRUS MINOR/THE NILE SONG/CRYING SONG/UP THE KHYBER/GREEN IS THE COLOUR/CYMBALINE/PARTY SEQUENCE MAIN THEME/IBIZA BAR/MORE BLUES/ QUICKSILVER/A SPANISH PIECE/DRAMATIC THEME
EMI; recorded March 1969; released: July 27 1969; available on CD

Back in the late 60s, folk was just as fashionable a way forward for psychedelia as progressive rock. With **Fairport Convention, Nick Drake, Incredible String Band** and even **Led Zeppelin** providing a British equivalent to the back-to-the-land approach of The Band in the States, it's little remarked that the years 1969– 72 were also as much Pink Floyd's pastoral as their prog period.

Although the pastoral had always been a part of Pink Floyd's music (as heard in "Emily", "Gnome", "Scarecrow", "Remember A Day", and "Julia Dream"), this soundtrack for **Barbet Schroeder**'s Ibizan hippie flick was folky in a simpler, sunnily lazy way – an approach the Floyd would revisit throughout the 1970s. Although mainly Waters' work (he writes all the actual *songs*), this laidback approach suited David Gilmour (who sings all of them) far better than psychedelia had, allowing him to find his own voice: slightly husky, soulful and yearning. Although opener "Cirrus Minor" manages to merge the pastoral and the spacey, "Crying Song" is almost country, Wright's vibraphone sounding anything but *avant* in this context. (Incidentally, the phrase "help me roll away the stone" is the first use of a Waters'

perennial symbol, "the stone" featuring on both *Animals'* "Dogs" and *The Wall*'s "Hey You".) "Green Is The Colour", meanwhile, is lent a slightly fey folkiness via the amateurish tin whistle of Nick Mason's wife Lindy. Finally, "Cymbaline" builds pop from pastoral via shimmering Farfisa organ and a buoyant chorus wistfully but assertively sung by Gilmour. It hints at the classic Floyd's magisterial, midpace approach, while also touching lyrically upon another future Floyd favourite: the music industry machine. This point is reiterated by the reference to a "butterfly with broken wings", a line which – while recalling **William Rees Mogg**'s famous *Times* editorial about the incarceration of **Mick Jagger** – may well refer to the author of "Flutter By Butterfly" and music-industry casualty Syd Barrett.

The space-rock legacy of "Saucerful" is still intact however, audible on the organ coda to "Cirrus Minor", on the rather pedestrian piano/drum/organ extemporisation "Up The Khyber", on *More*'s slightly ominous "Main Theme" and throughout "Quicksilver". A track that considerably develops the Floyd's electronic credentials, the glimmering organ, pulsing vibraphone and gong splashes of "Quicksilver" make it a key step between "Saucerful" and "Echoes", while hinting at "On The Run", while its seven-minute atmospheric sprawl was clearly carefully studied by incipient Krautrockers.

Amidst all this an entirely new direction is signposted by "The Nile Song" and "Ibiza Bar". Two variants on the same song, they're by far the heaviest things Pink Floyd had recorded thus far, revealing a rawer, rockier side to Gilmour's vocals and a Hendrix-esque aggression to his guitar playing. Waters' "Ibiza Bar" lyric, meanwhile, foreshadows neuroses to come ("I'm so afraid/of mistakes that I've made ... shaking every time that I awake"). These crunchy rockers, alongside a pivotal clutch of pastoral numbers, make *More* a somewhat anomalous release at the start of Pink Floyd's progressive rock period – but also a rather charming one.

Ummagumma

ASTRONOMY DOMINE/CAREFUL WITH THAT AXE, EUGENE/SET THE CONTROLS FOR THE HEART OF THE SUN/A SAUCERFUL OF SECRETS: A. SOMETHING ELSE/B. SYNCOPATED PANDEMONIUM/C. STORM SIGNAL/ D. CELESTIAL VOICES/SYSYPHUS PARTS I–IV/GRANTCHESTER MEADOWS/SEVERAL SPECIES OF SMALL FURRY ANIMALS GATHERED TOGETHER IN A CAVE AND GROOVING WITH A PICT/THE NARROW WAY PARTS 1-III/THE GRAND VIZIER'S GARDEN PARTY, PART ONE: ENTRANCE; PART TWO: ENTERTAINMENT; PART THREE: EXIT
Harvest; live album recorded April 27, Mother's Club, Birmingham, and May 2 1969, Manchester College of Commerce; studio album recorded January–June 1969, Abbey Road, London; released October 25 1969; available on CD.

It's almost impossible to imagine anyone making an album like *Ummagumma* in the 21st century. Releasing a live set a mere four albums into a career would be seen by modern record companies as indulgence enough: but to add a second album dedicated to solo experiments, half of the band *never* having written a tune before, and none of them being instrumen-

tal virtuosi? If ever there was a progressive rock folly, *Ummagumma* was it. Chucking out the rock'n'roll rule-book – and with it such fripperies as songs, melodies and often vocals – *Ummagumma* is a long, long way from "Louie Louie". Oh, and the rather challenging title (redolent of the **Grateful Dead**'s equally uninviting *Aoxomoxa*) is apparently a slang word for sex, courtesy of Cambridge scenester and Gilmour pal **Ian "Emo" Moore**, though it's hard to imagine a less sexy album than *Ummagumma*. Or a less amusing one, if humour was the intention.

That said, the live album isn't actually bad at all, recasting old favourites in mildly progressive mould. "Astronomy Domine" is successfully extended via some new keyboard passages, Gilmour doing a fine Barrett impression on guitar, Wright singing Barrett's lead vocal, Gilmour singing Wright's old harmony part. "Careful With That Axe" is longer and creepier than its studio sibling: Waters' screams are truly bloodcurdling, Mason's drumming particularly dramatic and Gilmour's guitar suitably stabbing, though it doesn't eclipse the studio version. While "Set The Controls" seems little different to its studio original, it does in fact contain a curiously forgettable white-noise middle section.

Surprisingly, given that it's on an album of such hubristic experimentation, instead of diving headlong into freeform noise "A Saucerful of Secrets" actually resembles a *song* rather more than its studio incarnation: it culminates in the emotive peak of Gilmour's superbly sung

"Celestial Voices" section, barer and more vulnerable than the choral album version. It's all far from being an essential addition to anyone's collection, but, as live progressive rock goes, is at least listenable and accessible.

That's something that cannot be said of the studio album, however. Rick Wright's instrumental suite, "Sysyphus", is both a descendant of the *avant* experimentalism of "Saucerful" and an attempt at fashionable classicism (one which would have beaten **King Crimson** to their "pioneer" status if the other Floyds had worked at Wright's rate). Shame Wright couldn't spell his classical reference. And that, by contrast to the live "Saucerful", "Sysyphus" manages to be both pompous *and* unlistenable.

Nick Mason's half-side, meanwhile, contents itself with being merely unlistenable. Restricted to percussion and sound effects, even his use of his wife **Lindy** on flute and – somewhat surprisingly – studio album producer Norman Smith on percussion can't save "The Grand Vizier's Garden Party" from experiment-for-experiment's-sake redundancy.

Conventional wisdom has Roger Waters as *Ummagumma*'s sole convincing contributor. But the fact is that the mouth-noise experiment "Several Species Of Small Furry Animals Gathered Together In A Cave And Grooving With A Pict" (which owes much to the work of Waters' golf partner Ron Geesin) is a one-listen joke – and not a particularly funny one. It's of interest primarily for its preview of Waters' deranged Scottish accent (to be recycled on *The*

Wall ten years later). "Grantchester Meadows" is Waters' second full lead vocal for the band, and was first performed as the "Daybreak" section of *The Man* in April 1969, making its folky evocation of the River Cam a spawn of "Cirrus Minor", with which it shares both a chromatic chordal structure and chirruping sound-effects-library birdsong. A relief on *Ummagumma* for its employment of conventional song-structure, "Grantchester" remains a fairly average *song*, however, brought to life largely by its sound effects (especially the stereo simulation of a bird splashing across the river).

Conventional wisdom also has it that David Gilmour's contribution to *Ummagumma* was a failure. But while "The Narrow Way" came to the guitarist with difficulty, and he dithered long enough to make it one of the last to be completed, the track is actually the strongest on the studio album. Indeed the vocal section, "Part 3", manages, bar some strained high notes, to perfectly define the classic Pink Floyd sound of the 1970s.

The truth is that conventional wisdom isn't much use when it comes to *Ummagumma*. From title to concept to execution, there's little that's conventional about it. That there is relatively little that is *appealing* about it either makes *Ummagumma* a product very much of its time and place, one in which it could be regarded as a creative peak by critics and even make the UK Top 10. A time and place in which, live album aside, few are likely to wish they were there.

Atom Heart Mother

ATOM HEART MOTHER (FATHER'S SHOUT; BREAST MILKY; MOTHER FORE; FUNKY DUNG; MIND YOUR THROATS PLEASE/REEMERGENCE)IF/SUMMER '68/FAT OLD SUN/ALAN'S PSYCHEDELIC BREAKFAST (RISE AND SHINE; SUNNY SIDE UP; MORNING GLORY)
Harvest; recorded February to August 1970; released October 10, 1970; available on CD.

Back in the early 1970s, symphonic sweep and classical aspiration were the vogue. Coming hard on the Achilles heels of a clutch of classicist opuses by **The Moody Blues** and **King Crimson**, not to mention **Deep Purple**'s *Concerto For Group And Orchestra*, *Atom Heart Mother*'s suite-length title track, full choir and orchestra cause it to be routinely dismissed as a typical prog folly of its pretentious era. Not even the Floyd themselves appear to like it much.

And yet *Atom Heart* is – alongside *Meddle* – the most creative product of Pink Floyd's progressive period. Despite its side-long duration, the album's title track is neither pompous, nor particularly esoteric, especially compared to the pretension and flashiness of Pink Floyd's prog peers. What's more, the title track tends to overshadow the album's second half, an unpretentious four-song pastoral sequence that beautifully balances the epic scale of the title track. Finally making good the misguided democracy of *Ummagumma*, this second half features proper songs from Waters, Wright and Gilmour apiece, plus a combined-force closing instrumental, "Alan's Psychedelic Breakfast", which effectively gives Nick Mason *his* own track via his creating and recording the effects

in his kitchen. Waters' "If" is another instalment in his folky oeuvre and another minor Floyd gem, prefiguring "Brain Damage" both musically (via its simple folk finger-picking style, Anglicised blues progression and Waters' deliberately understated vocal) and lyrically, with its fear of insanity and society's treatment of it. Barrett's blundering into the studio during the *Atom Heart Mother* sessions was by no means the only way he made his presence felt on the album: his spectre haunts this song, which not for the first or last time, engages the caustic Waters' empathy. "If" also has a line that would be echoed years later, voiced by Pink's wife in "The Trial" (from *The Wall*): "If I were a good man I'd talk to you more often than I do" (nice use of the subjunctive).

Wright, meanwhile, makes a welcome songwriting return with the ebullient pop-psyche of "Summer '68" (see p.193), while the swelteringly hot summer of 1970 continues to exert its influence via Gilmour's plangently folky "Fat Old Sun" (see p.193). "Alan's Psychedelic Breakfast" again has received brickbats from both band and critics. But while the music is slightly bland, with its vague acoustic picking and lilting piano doodles, it also possesses a period warmth entirely at one with the summery mood hitherto; a warmth enhanced by the voice of roadie – and Cambridge alumnus – Alan Styles making his breakfast in his trailer. The sound effects are fun, the idea of the dripping tap as a rhythm track is ingenious, while the song attains a brief magic at 1:08 as Rick Wright's Hammond evokes the gas igniting.

Ultimately, rather than being a prog-rock indulgence, *Atom Heart Mother* is, as the glum cow on the cover suggests, a rather humble, almost down-to-earth affair compared to the music of most of Pink Floyd's prog peers, an album that oozes a summery, pastoral, lazy, faintly melancholy joyfulness. And where is the folly in that?

Meddle

ONE OF THESE DAYS/A PILLOW OF WINDS/FEARLESS/SAN TROPEZ/SEAMUS/ECHOES
Harvest; recorded August 1971; released November 13, 1971; available on CD

On the gatefold of the original vinyl release of *Meddle*, the members of Pink Floyd stand shoulder to shoulder, gazing slightly challengingly at the camera. Bespeaking new confidence amongst its individuals, the picture also suggested a new group solidarity, albeit one nobody needed to know was tenuous at best.

For one thing, this was the first time since *Saucerful Of Secrets* that the band had worked on an album side by side in the studio, unassisted by outside musicians – or indeed producers, this being their first entirely self-produced effort. It was also a return to the horses-for-courses approach of *More*, with vocals provided by the best singer for the job, rather than the song's composer. Further evidence of a more developed band dynamic on *Meddle* lies in the reconvening of Gilmour and Waters' songwriting partnership for the first time since "Point Me At The Sky" over a year previously.

If collaboration and competition between these two would later become indistinguish-able, here the pairing is perfectly complementary. The haunting, acoustic, slide guitar-saturated music of "Pillow Of Winds" is signature Gilmour, but it's Waters' words that give the song its lilt. The stop-start motion and Kop crowd singing "You'll Never Walk Alone" on "Fearless" are pure Waters, but it's Gilmour's chorus that gives it depth. An increasingly confident Gilmour is in the compositional ascendant here and yet Waters plays guitar on both "Fearless" and "San Tropez" suggesting an underlying jockeying for position.

As the Waters and Gilmour pairing became the essence of Pink Floyd, the residual influence of Syd Barrett receded further. Although Barrett taught Waters the guitar-tuning and partly inspired the lyric of "Fearless" (in the shape of the idiot who fearlessly faces the crowd, smiling), his musical influence is now a distant memory: the jazzily amiable "San Tropez" is worlds away from psychedelia, and hears Waters' increasingly distinctive vocal style (complete with new American accent) at its best yet.

However, the album's most successful – and most popular – tracks are the two major group-written numbers. "One Of These Days" takes the band's patented space-rock and gives it both a 1970s rock muscularity and an electronic sheen that justifies Pink Floyd's proto-techno reputation (see p.194). "Echoes", meanwhile, takes the prog suite into simultaneously more *avant* and more accessible waters, the sound-effects are outré, the West Coast/home counties harmonies are humanly warm; Gilmour's liquid lead guitar and Wright's expressive piano intricate enough for musos but melodic enough for newcomers (see p.195).

The only real howler here (literally) is "Seamus", a lazy blues accompanied by the baying of Steve Marriott's hound. A doodle from David Gilmour, the fact that the group put their joint names to it suggests just how busy they were being a band at this time. And for the most part, whatever tensions may have simmered between those touching shoulders, *Meddle* was an indicator of just what coherence could be achieved when Pink Floyd's talents were properly pooled.

Obscured By Clouds

OBSCURED BY CLOUDS/WHEN YOU'RE IN/BURNING BRIDGES/THE GOLD IT'S IN THE.../WOT'S...UH THE DEAL/ MUDMEN/CHILDHOOD'S END/FREE FOUR/STAY/ABSOLUTELY CURTAINS
Harvest; recorded February 23–29, March 22–27; released June 3, 1972; available on CD

America has never really taken to art rock. In a country so colossal conservatism dominates, and music tends to succeed only when bets are hedged, knottiness is unravelled and sharp edges softened. Witness the early 1970s stateside failure of the British phenomenon of glam rock and the mid-1970s success of the recycled, ham-fisted "pantomime rock" of **Alice Cooper** and **Kiss**.

So it was far from coincidental that it was Pink Floyd's most conventional album that broke them in America. Like their other Barbet Schroeder soundtrack, *More* (with which it bookends Floyd's progressive period), *Obscured By Clouds* finds the band returning to shorter, simpler songs, and this time even largely avoiding their standard sonic experimentation for something considerably more immediate.

Indeed the Floyd had never previously essayed anything quite so conventionally, mainstream rock as "The Gold It's In The..." or the instrumental "When You're In". That these are both lumpen and unengaging says less about the Floyd's ability to rock (though it's curious Gilmour didn't use his grunting rock pig voice on "Gold") than their absorption of the American music of their era – an era in which the approach of country-folkies such as **The Eagles** and **Jackson Browne** to uptempo rock was both ungainly and unconvincing.

Constitutionally attuned to such laid-back West Coast acts, the compositional hand of Gilmour is heavy upon these tracks, as it is on the fine acoustic ballad "Wot's ... Uh The Deal", pushing Floyd's folksiness further West Coastwards. Indeed, were the influence of **Crosby, Stills & Nash** not already apparent, the vocal interplay of a double-tracked Gilmour on the 'mile after mile' section is a direct quotation from CSN&Y's 1970 song "Our House". Gilmour's "Childhood's End", meanwhile, also has a lethargic, sun-baked West Coast feel: he even sings the song in something resembling an American accent.

Wright, muted on **Meddle**, appears to have rather taken to this mainstream approach, turning in two hauntingly melodic ballads, "Burning Bridges" and "Stay" (both co-written by Waters) plus the moody instrumental "Mudmen" (essentially the middle section of "Burning Bridges"). Gilmour is all over these tracks, his harmonies adding richness to "Bridges", his echo-drenched guitar so dominating "Mudmen" he gained a co-writing credit, his wah-wah work saturating the FM-friendly "Stay" with the requisite Californian flavour.

Which leaves Roger Waters. While he busily contributes lyrics and arrangements throughout, he can't help but put a sardonic sting in the tail of all this relaxed, radio-friendliness. Musically "Free Four" is a throwaway, chorus-less three-chord country chugger; lyri-

cally it's Waters flailing at future favourite themes like his father's death, mortality and the music industry machine. "All aboard for the American tour", he sneers. Slathered with Gilmour's rock-out guitar, with a delicious irony it was this very song that American FM radio-programmers took to their hearts, playing the track consistently over the autumn, and opening the way for the Floyd with their next release. With Floyd seeming to have thrown everything at the mainstream, while keeping their fingers crossed behind their backs, this was mission accomplished. No one ever suggested it would make any of them happy, however.

Chris Parry on sax, and Roger Waters on bass

David Gilmour, Storm Thorgerson and Roger Waters enjoying a bottle or two in 1974

The Dark Side Of The Moon

SPEAK TO ME/BREATHE/ON THE RUN/TIME/BREATHE (REPRISE)/THE GREAT GIG IN THE SKY/MONEY/US AND THEM/ ANY COLOUR YOU LIKE/BRAIN DAMAGE/ECLIPSE
Harvest; recorded June 1–3, 6–10, 13–17, 20–24 1972; October 10–12, 17, 25–27 1972; January 13–14, 18–21, 24–27, 29–31, 1973; February 1, 1973; released March 10 (US), March 23, 1973 (UK); available on CD

Looking back at *The Dark Side Of The Moon*, it seems as if nothing was left to chance. From its taut visual package in, *Dark Side* drew a clean graphic line under the experimental approach of Pink Floyd's last four years and its embrace of happy – and not so happy – accident. Instead the album was planned meticulously, making its mainstream success seem rather less random than its authors suggest.

Dark Side was carefully worked out – from its central, cohering concept to the fact that actual songs were composed beforehand (rather than tracks being left to studio doodling) and the careful apportioning of responsibility in proportion to aptitude. Thus Waters took care of the lyrics (foregrounding a slightly sardonic simplicity) and Gilmour took the bulk of the lead vocals (providing warmth and prettiness) while, instrumentally, Wright and Gilmour were given free rein to create big splashes of harmonic and melodic colour throughout. This direct, accessible approach was underscored by the use of female soul singers, **Dick Parry**'s warm, breathy sax, the spoken passages to illustrate the concept, and the purchase of a crucial commercial sheen from outside mixer **Chris Thomas**.

As a consequence of all this care, even the hyper self-critical Floyd find it hard to fault the album, though Waters has called the lyrics "lower sixth", and Gilmour sometimes mumbles about the drum sound. In fact the only real dips in quality occur with "Money" (sound effects more interesting than song; instrumental section overlong) – and "Any Colour You Like" (filler), though even these sit happily amidst the linking dialogue and the album's signature musical segues. And if *Dark Side*'s lofty musings on life, death and madness also sometimes appear a little pompous – English grammar school boys potting philosophy for homely, happy Americans – then a cursory comparison to The Who's *Tommy*, Jethro Tull's *A Passion Play* or Genesis's *Lamb Lies Down On Broadway* soon puts such criticism into context. For unlike more abstract progressive conceits the album's concept was, as Waters stated, "the first one that had a heart". A heart that subtly affected the music of this previously

most head-orientated of bands way beyond the literalness of the opening and closing heartbeat, saturating their always imaginative music with some depth and emotion.

As such *Dark Side* has outlasted almost all vagaries of fashion. Punk pilloried it, but the CD age rescued it; the hardcore late 1980s spat upon it, but the chemical generation spaced out to it; Britpop made it obsolete, but **Radiohead** made it more relevant than ever. And not for one second did it ever stop selling. Indeed, after 2003's best ever (2.1) remastering, which alone shifted a million copies, *Dark Side Of The Moon* couldn't now be in a more unassailable position if Pink Floyd had planned it that way.

Wish You Were Here

SHINE ON YOU CRAZY DIAMOND PART 1/WELCOME TO THE MACHINE HAVE A CIGAR/WISH YOU WERE HERE/SHINE ON YOU CRAZY DIAMOND PART 2
Harvest (US: Columbia); recorded January 6–9, February 3–6, March 3, May 5–9, June 2–3, 5–6, July 7–11, 1975; released: September 15, 1975; available on CD

So confident and cohesive a work is *Wish You Were Here*, so much of itself both musically and conceptually, that it's positively claustrophobic. It's almost impossible to imagine the yawning acres of self-doubt and confusion that actually beset its creation. For rather than recharging Pink Floyd's creative batteries, *Dark Side*'s success seemed to sap them. Unbelievably, to follow up their multi-million-seller, the band messed about for months with the patently going-nowhere *Household Objects* project, then junked half an album's-worth of material,

The Music

only to then find themselves almost incapable of injecting life into the one song they did have, the Syd Barrett tribute "Shine On You Crazy Diamond".

Paradoxically energized by the enervation, inspired by the lack of inspiration, and revved-up by the mechanical nature of the sessions, Roger Waters came up with the concept for an album about absence, alienation and mechanisation, starting from the spectre of Barrett, then spiralling out into new songs about the music industry machine.

For while *Wish You Were Here* may be another favourite with stoners – with tempos even more hydroponically lethargic than *Dark Side* – its sleek, synthesized surface contains a cold steeliness sufficient to induce a creeping unease. An unease given alarm-bell anxiety by even the most cursory reference to the lyric sheet. Notwithstanding its soulful guitar solos, "Shine On You Crazy Diamond" is no reassuring Syd eulogy, becoming more clinical as it ticks over into its second half (or just runs out of ideas). Ostensibly an attack on money-grubbing music industry moguls, "Have A Cigar" is as much a "Money"-laundering joke at fans' expense, cynically recycling the Floyd's biggest hit's bluesy feel and fruity guitar solos (though it actually stalled as a single). Equally, the cold metallic finger of "Welcome To The Machine" is pointed as much at Floyd fans as the music industry itself, and however trippy the music's swooshing, stereo-straddling synths may be, it is claustrophobia rather than escape that's evoked. Even the title track is, beneath its pastoral prettiness, a song of desperate alienation,

albeit one that appears to be seeking another soul to share it. As on "Machine", the track's acoustic guitars – an element shunned on *Dark Side* – sound frail and lonely amidst the steely splendour of *Wish You Were Here*'s synthetics. Trapped between banks of synthesizers, acoustic guitars emerge out of tinny transistor radios, or are swamped in whooshing wind – a forlorn flag of human hope in the face of the crushing Machine.

Not itself quite the crushing commercial machine that *Dark Side* was, *Wish You Were Here*'s mere 18 million sales initially put it in its predecessor's shadow. But while it is decidedly the work of the same group, *Wish You Were Here* is a considerably chillier, more cynical, and even more impressive album than *Dark Side*. Certainly Wright and Gilmour think so, for both now rate it their favourite Floyd album, despite Gilmour's opposition to Waters' concept at the time. Which comes close to celebrating their own self-doubt and confusion. Or just adroitly turning weakness into strength.

Animals

PIGS ON THE WING/DOGS/PIGS (THREE DIFFERENT ONES)/ SHEEP/PIGS ON THE WING
Harvest (US: Columbia); recorded May–December 1976; released January 23, 1977

The late 1970s was a dark time for Britain, rife with unemployment, rising racism and industrial unrest. Despite emerging from disappointed 60s idealism rather than 70s defeatism, Pink Floyd's *Animals* was as much a distillation of this darkness as **The Sex Pistols'** *Never*

Mind The Bollocks – an equally angry, equally nihilistic reaction to a dystopian era.

While hardly Pink Floyd's punk album (punk albums do not contain four-minute synthesizer solos), *Animals* is initially an unprepossessing prospect for a Floyd fan. Bleak, misanthropic, musically monochrome, its bitter pill is unsugared by any of the Floyd's lusher trademarks. There are no harmonies – let alone female backing vocals – no saxophones, and even the sound effects are restricted to rather literal evocations of their titles. Amidst all this oinking, barking and bleating, *Animals'* music eschews the usual Floydean glide for something uncharacteristically uptempo and guitar-heavy. What's more, while the sweet-voiced Gilmour sings half of "Dogs", Waters sings everything else: by far his greatest vocal input thus far, this first usage of his sneering, slightly hysterical whine separating the sheep from the goats.

Conceptually Waters brusquely simplifies **George Orwell's** *Animal Farm*, to divide the human race into pigs, sheep and dogs – essentially the ruling classes, the masses and those who manage to work the system. With these characterised by greed, clueless conformity and murderous self-advancement respectively, Waters' scorched earth disgust is tempered only by the book-ending, almost-love song "Pigs On The Wing", though even here there is something in Waters' mordant tones – and the title's intimation of the expression "pigs might fly" – that doesn't sound entirely hopeful.

As such *Animals'* concept manages to be both crude and unclear – pigs being employed as symbols of both hope and oppression. And

that's not the full extent of *Animals'* flaws: "Pigs On The Wing" is a somewhat throwaway strumalong; the monotonous, one-chord chorus of "Pigs (Three Different Ones)" doesn't match its stinging verse, while the equally musically mono-dimensional "Sheep" is severely over-extended (see p.208). Even so, *Animals* has surprising staying power: there's a magnetism to its monochrome world, a compulsion to its grim, caustic humour, while there's also a subtler musicality discernible beneath its simplistic surface. Deprived of its traditional trademarks, the classic Floyd enigma takes time to emerge, but it's here: in the dreamy intricacy of the melody of "Dogs" and in its hallucinogenic, vocodered barking section; in the intro keyboard noodlings of "Sheep"; even in the churchy organ and oinking sections of "Pigs".

But herein lies not so much Animals' soft underbelly as its hidden claw: the whole album can be seen as a caustic upending of the cuddlier aspects of previous Pink Floyds. "Pigs" goes one further than the cynical recycling of "Money" on "Have A Cigar": by contemptuously recycling the latter's chord sequence verbatim, "Dogs" is a grotesque mutation of *Meddle*'s "Seamus" and "Sheep", a twisted take on Pink Floyd's patented pastoral, a wolf in sheep's clothing. This musical "fuck you" to a more innocent, more hopeful, post-60s past makes it a perfect match to the album's cynically sneering concept. But if this seemed dark, *Animals* proved only the first missive in a miserable trilogy: Pink Floyd were about to get a whole lot darker.

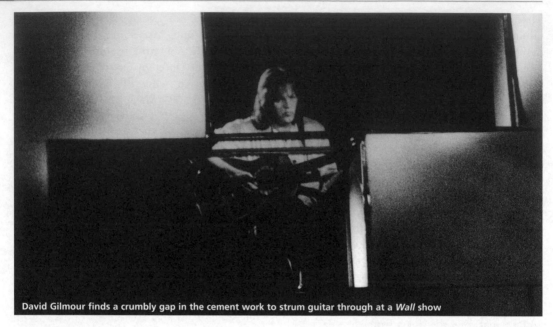

David Gilmour finds a crumbly gap in the cement work to strum guitar through at a *Wall* show

The Wall

IN THE FLESH?/THE THIN ICE/ANOTHER BRICK IN THE WALL PART 1/THE HAPPIEST DAYS OF OUR LIVES/ANOTHER BRICK IN THE WALL PART 2/MOTHER/GOODBYE BLUE SKY/EMPTY SPACES/YOUNG LUST/ONE OF MY TURNS/DON'T LEAVE ME NOW/ANOTHER BRICK IN THE WALL PART 3/GOODBYE CRUEL WORLD/HEY YOU/IS THERE ANYBODY OUT THERE?/ NOBODY HOME/VERA/BRING THE BOYS BACK HOME/ COMFORTABLY NUMB/THE SHOW MUST GO ON/IN THE FLESH/RUN LIKE HELL/WAITING FOR THE WORMS/STOP/THE TRIAL/OUTSIDE THE WALL

Harvest/EMI (US: Columbia) Recorded: April–November 1979; released November 30, 1979.

When Roger Waters spat in a fan's face in Montreal on Pink Floyd's 1977 stadium tour, he dramatically broke with the Floyd's established, coolly English – indeed, phlegmatic – detachment from messy emotional display. Waters had already begun this work with the generalized anger of *Animals*, but the spitting incident sparked the cathartic, primal scream of unleashed emotion that is *The Wall*: this time it was personal. Ostensibly the story of a rock star called "Pink Floyd" (oh, *come on!*) who builds a psychological wall between himself and the world, the album is more a platform for Roger Waters to spit figuratively upon everyone in his immediate line of fire – parents, teachers, wives, groupies, bandmates, himself and, yes, those pesky fans as well.

That such a concept was embraced so wholeheartedly by millions reveals less mass masochism than how carefully Waters tailored his disgust to appeal to the very masses he reviled. For compared to the relatively adult *Dark Side Of The Moon* or *Wish You Were Here,* there is something so fundamentally *teenage* about *The Wall* that it must have been intentional – Roger Waters was after all a 36-year-old man. The whingeing about teachers and parents, the "it wasn't me!" offloading of responsibility, the fearful distaste for female sexuality, and perhaps even protagonist Pink's flirtation with fascism – all are guaranteed to give any red-blooded teen a frisson. More specifically, *American* teens. Although the use of iconic US TV shows as sound effects throughout *The Wall* could be regarded as simply documenting the arena-rock hotel life Waters is satirising, the use of American vocabulary ("space cadet", "mama", "break my balls"), and stronger-than-ever US accents throughout (all soft Ts and dropped Gs) most definitely cannot. Furthermore, just to make sure Pink Floyd properly pushed American buttons after *Animals'* relative failure, the employment of stadium rock hit-maker Bob Ezrin as producer gave the album a stadium-filling sound that withstood comparison to previous Ezrin clients – and US heartland hits – Alice Cooper, Aerosmith and Kiss.

But as silly, self-indulgent and just plain unpleasant as it can be, *The Wall* works. For all that Rick Wright decried its monotony, *The Wall* is considerably more musically varied than, say, *Wish You Were Here*. Yes, it encompasses its fair share of bombastic stadium rock ("In the Flesh?" "Young Lust"), but also features disco ("Another Brick", "Run Like Hell"), delicate folk ("Goodbye Blue Sky"),

Beach Boys vocal harmonies ("The Show Must Go On", "In The Flesh"), and – sneaking arty touches in by the stage door – Tin Pan Alley tunesmithery ("Nobody Home"), 1940s pop ("Bring The Boys Back Home") and even Gilbert and Sullivan operetta ("The Trial").

What's more, *The Wall* is packed with even more aural treats than *Dark Side Of The Moon*: orgies of orchestration, bipping, parping, electronics, and whole layered, wedding cakes of backing vocals. And there's a stunning panoply of sound effects: helicopters, aeroplanes, Waters' deranged Scottish screaming, babies crying, groupies gushing, and that constantly squawking television set in Pink's hotel room as the singer sinks into navel-gazing catatonia. Then there are the guitar solos, David Gilmour suddenly sounding like something Pink Floyd had never had before: a virtuoso. If Gilmour's guitar work is a many-faceted delight throughout (his spiralling, echo-drenched playing on "Another Brick Part 1" alone is astonishing) on "Another Brick in the Wall Part 2" and "Comfortably Numb", it's as good as electric guitar gets.

Indeed, if *The Wall* is Waters' baby and Ezrin its midwife, then Gilmour can claim a vital nurturing role. His three compositional contributions include the album's highlight ("Comfortably Numb"), a crucial enlivening of a slightly flat second side ("Young Lust"), and the musical high-point of the grim final quarter ("Run Like Hell"). And while Waters takes the bulk of the lead vocals, Gilmour's singing sweetens the deal throughout: softening up "Mother", sexing up "Young Lust",

The Music

lifting up the floundering "Don't Leave Me Now", and suffusing "The Thin Ice", "Hey You" and "Comfortably Numb" with a soulfulness that subtly offsets Waters' cynicism and allows some humanity to enter all that endless, claustrophobic catharting.

In truth, the unrelenting cynicism and musical bleakness render *The Wall*'s last act a slog, but it's saved by a certain viewed-between-the-fingers fascination about quite how far Waters will go. For Waters makes a rather too convincing audience-goading Nazi on the reprise of "In The Flesh"; has rather too much fun rabble-rousing on the ungainly "Waiting For The Worms"; while absolutely *inhabiting* the parade of Freudian grotesque he portrays in the lurching mini-opera "The Trial". Waters' words may fit the music only by sheer bloody-mindedness, but "The Trial" compares to nothing much else in the entire history of rock, revealing the theatricality of Ezrin clients **Alice Cooper** and **Peter Gabriel** or even rock's pantomime dame, **David Bowie**, as that of mere understudies. When that's followed by the crashing collapse of the Wall itself, and then the fragile, hymn-like "Outside the Wall", the listener is left simultaneously exhausted and exhilarated, but – as a generation of grunge grumblers (Smashing Pumpkins, Nine Inch Nails) and its status as Pink Floyd's second biggest seller attest – somehow changed.

As an edifice *The Wall* is not pretty, but it *is* pretty compelling. Over-the-top, unpleasant, and anything but phlegmatic, *The Wall* is ultimately a rather monstrously impressive monument to the cathartic power of rock music.

The Final Cut

THE POST WAR DREAM/YOUR POSSIBLE PASTS/ONE OF THE FEW/WHEN THE TIGERS BROKE FREE (CD REISSUE ONLY)/THE HERO'S RETURN/THE GUNNERS DREAM/PARANOID EYES/ GET YOUR FILTHY HANDS OFF MY DESERT/THE FLETCHER MEMORIAL HOME/SOUTHAMPTON DOCK/THE FINAL CUT/ NOT NOW JOHN/TWO SUNS IN THE SUNSET
Harvest EMI (US: Columbia); recorded June–December, 1982; released March 21, 1983; available on CD

In cinema, the term "final cut" denotes control of the finished product. Fresh from his experience of losing control over just that with *The Wall* film, Roger Waters was determined to keep absolute control over Pink Floyd's next album. "I was on a roll, I was going to make *this* album," he later said. As such, *The Final Cut*'s subtitle *A Requiem for the Post War Dream by Roger Waters – performed by Pink Floyd*, speaks volumes. Of the *Animals/Wall/Cut* trilogy, this is the most Waters-dominated, with Gilmour and Mason reduced to just two of a team of clocking-on sidemen.

But rather than this being the flaw attested to by most critics (and David Gilmour) *The Final Cut*'s monomaniacal intensity is actually its major strength. Waters' fixity of vision gives this hugely underrated album a claustrophobic integrity, a character all of its own – a peculiarly English blend of bitterness, like stewed tea leaves. An Englishness that's enhanced throughout by **Michael Kamen**'s stately, brass-led orchestrations. Consequently, Waters' somewhat anomalous American accent and the album's state-of-the-art Holophonic sound effects are the only

Pink Floyd and the CD age

If anyone was going to embrace the CD, it was Pink Floyd. Their laborious, polished production was made for state-of-the-art equipment, and the crackle-free CD – first introduced in 1983 – suited them down to a T. Indeed, "Learning To Fly" was, in 1987, the first-ever CD-only single, while each subsequent CD reissue has hugely boosted their back catalogue sales. However, the Floyd went against the grain of the CD era by refusing to add extra tracks to their reissues, *The Final Cut* being the sole exception. Of their peers, only **The Beatles**, **Stones**, **Genesis** and **Led Zeppelin** have honoured their original albums' integrity in this way. While cynics might point out that Floyd often tended to have barely enough material for one album, let alone extra tracks, this isn't entirely true.

In a parallel universe of fantasy Floyd reissues, *Piper* would be augmented by "Arnold", "Emily" and their B-sides. Indeed, there's a plethora of unreleased Barrett-era material: "Scream Thy Last Scream", "Vegetable Man" and "John Latham" could have been added to *Saucerful*, alongside singles "It Would Be So Nice" and "Point Me At The Sky" – plus B-sides. Thereafter, "Seabirds" could be restored to the *More* soundtrack; "Embryo", "Moonhead" and "Biding My Time" added to *Ummagumma*; "Pigs On The Wing" Parts 1 and 2 to *Animals*; and "What Shall We Do Now", "Death Of Sisco" and the film soundtrack's re-recordings added to *The Wall*. Alternatively, why not round up the singles material onto a thorough, affordable compilation (cf. *Relics* and *Shine On*) and then release a chunky rarities album? Judging by the bootleg trade and the circulation of internet tracks of dubious veracity, there's certainly a market for it. Would that be too prosaically obvious a solution for the mysterious Pink Floyd?

hangover from *The Wall*: funereally-paced, Waters-voiced, melodically understated, there is no easy entry for the casual fan here. For if *The Wall* was grim, it was at least grimness filmed in gloriously lurid technicolor. *The Final Cut* by contrast is a cold, sepia-tinted morning after – perfectly evoking waking up from the communal consensus of the postwar dream into the atomized anomie of the Thatcherite 1980s.

But for those prepared to enter its chilly embrace, *The Final Cut*'s rewards are not inconsiderable. For a start, Waters is on top lyrical form throughout. "The fish-eyed lens of tear-stained eyes"; "the silver in her hair shines in the cold November air" – the lingering lines are endless. The sound effects meanwhile are stunning: the shout of "take care" on "Your Possible Pasts"; the explosions and terrorized intercom chatter on "The Gunners Dream"; and, most famously, the missile that flies across the room on "Get Your Filthy Hands Off My Desert", all making *The Final Cut* a truly cinematic experience.

What's more, Waters' always idiosyncratic singing is strangely compelling throughout:

the way his low, shruggingly resigned voice and his higher, emotionally deranged one combine on "The Hero's Return"; the way his restraint speaks volumes in "The Gunners Dream"; the way he screeches his harmony on "Southampton Dock"; and the absolute ball he has bellowing his head off at the end of "Not Now John".

The album is marred only by its closing track, "Two Suns In The Sunset", and not so much for ending the album on a downer (post-war dream – and world – dying forever in nuclear meltdown) as on a musical mis-fire. For once, Waters the composer really does let down Waters the conceptualist. But this time there would be no test-screenings to see how the ending played: Waters had absolute control of *The Final Cut*. And overall he does a pretty good job. Re-released in 2004 with the single "When The Tigers Broke Free" added to make it something resembling a director's cut, *The Final Cut* is, in the final analysis, a neglected masterwork.

A Momentary Lapse Of Reason

SIGNS OF LIFE/LEARNING TO FLY/THE DOGS OF WAR/ONE SLIP/ON THE TURNING AWAY/YET ANOTHER MOVIE/ROUND AND AROUND/A NEW MACHINE PART 1/TERMINAL FROST/ A NEW MACHINE PART 2/SORROW
Recorded April 1986–June 1987; released September 7, 1987; available on CD

At the time, Roger Waters compared the 1980s reformation of Pink Floyd to The Beatles reuniting without John Lennon. While Waters couldn't have known that in a mere eight years Lennon would be electronically exhumed for a "full" Fabs reunion, he should have known that by his demise Lennon was very far from the peak of his creative powers.

So that favourite Floyd fan parlour game, "What Would *A Momentary Lapse Of Reason* Have Sounded Like With Roger Waters?" (one played, according to producer Bob Ezrin, even by the re-formed Floyd themselves), is best quelled by a quick referral to Waters' concurrent album *Radio K.A.O.S.* Satisfying neither as contemporary 1980s releases nor as nostalgic Floyd artefacts, both albums are flabby with 80s production excess, lacking in songs of any substance whilst – in very different ways – utterly clueless in the concept department.

In fact *Momentary Lapse*'s not-so-secret intention was to return Pink Floyd to a time when Waters was *not* the band's sole creative force. If this goal aggrandizes Gilmour's own role, then the results do not. For with Gilmour as far from his creative peak as Waters, and Mason's and Wright's contributions nominal, *Momentary Lapse*'s attempts to revisit *Wish You Were Here* rarely get closer than mere wishing. Alternately twinkling and glowering in the woefully optimistic hope that it's being atmospheric, *Momentary Lapse* is certainly intangible and evanescent, but only in a bad way – being vague, insubstantial and bland. Just add 1980s production bombast for that nasty hole-in-the-middle effect. "On The Turning Away" is portentous supermarket-aisle folk. "Dogs of War" is a synthetic pub-rock plod, with Gilmour's throaty singing making him sound like someone bellowing about nothing. "One Slip" is U2-lite arena rock, courtesy of another 1980s casualty, Roxy Music's **Phil Manzanera**, further stymied by some vile slap-bass from Waters' sub **Guy Pratt**. You can practically hear the double thumbs-up from the control room. The glitz and glamour-obsessed 1980s seemed to prematurely age people: Gilmour sounds like a man hopelessly lost in the Linn drum department at Curry's.

Amidst all this, the quality of the lyrics really is neither here nor there. For the record, despite a host of hired hands, they're mired in Gilmour's favoured sonorous-sounding clichés ("the march of fate", "the wings of the night" and "the wind of change"), while it might have been nice if he'd spent some time trying to at least make them fit the music. It's only when Gilmour engages with the current situation that the lyrics, and (coincidentally?) the music step up to the mark. The engaging syncopated chug of "Learning To Fly" testifies to Gilmour's and Mason's shared love of flying (featuring sound effects from Mason's flying lessons) while also reflecting upon Gilmour's new piloting role in Pink Floyd. Equally "Sorrow" is an enjoyably moody return to "Comfortably Numb" terrain, complete with grungy guitar solo, that sounds like it reflects upon Waters' absence with more smugness than sorrow. On this evidence, however, Gilmour had little to be smug about. Very far from Fab.

Delicate Sound of Thunder (Live)

SHINE ON YOU CRAZY DIAMOND/LEARNING TO FLY/YET ANOTHER MOVIE/ROUND AND AROUND/SORROW/THE DOGS OF WAR/ON THE TURNING AWAY/ONE OF THESE DAYS/ TIME/ON THE RUN/THE GREAT GIG IN THE SKY/WISH YOU WERE HERE/US AND THEM/MONEY/ANOTHER BRICK IN THE WALL PART II/COMFORTABLY NUMB/RUN LIKE HELL
EMI; Recorded August 1988 at Nassau Coliseum; released November 22, 1988; available on CD, video and DVD

Although live performance is rock music's life-support system, it's curious how rarely the addition of an audience actually inspires musicians to surpass their studio performances. Consequently, unless composed of new material (**Jackson Browne**'s *Running On Empty*) or radically reinterpreting old material (**The Velvet Underground**'s *Live 1969*) live albums are largely a rather redundant affair. And there are few more redundant than *Delicate Sound Of Thunder*. A "document" of Pink Floyd's endless Momentary Lapse tour, it's the kind of release that rather justifies Roger Waters' view of the Floyd re-formation as being motivated by financial rather than artistic reasons.

As such, surely the pure appeal of the Pink Floyd brand to ageing 1980s audiences was the oldies? But, curiously, it's the new material – which dominates CD 1 – that works best, albeit recreating the album versions note-for-note, although "Sorrow" is effectively extended via additional female vocals.

The old material gets it wrong both ways, however. "Shine On You Crazy Diamond" sticks too tribute-act closely to the original

The Music

for its instrumental overture, before Gilmour's inappropriately throaty – yet strangely detached – vocal erases the original's emotional engagement. Worse, during the saxophone solo you can practically hear **Scott Page**'s mullet flapping, while Gilmour's whoops are about as un-Floyd as you can get. Equally, "Money" starts off like a frozen replica, before veering into a vile reggaefied jam, complete with bass solo from new boy Guy Pratt. Two oldies in and you're missing Waters' already: it's not inability that stopped Waters playing a bass solo. Similarly, Gilmour and Pratt's line-trading vocal performance on "Run Like Hell" substitutes the menace of the original for macho chest-beating. You even miss Waters on "Another Brick" – Gilmour on his own sounds like he simply doesn't understand the song, while a noodlesome ending just underlines the air of session muso anonymity. As for poor old Rick Wright, he manages to make his vocal on "Comfortably Numb" sound like a punishment for his failure to contribute to the studio original. The tortuously slow pace doesn't help.

An utterly pointless project then and a messy blot on the discography. Who would have guessed the Floyd would actually go on to eclipse this pointlessness in two releases' time? Put your hand down, Waters, we've seen you.

A through-the-porthole view of David Gilmour at work on *The Division Bell*

The Music

The Division Bell

CLUSTER ONE/WHAT DO YOU WANT FROM ME/POLES APART/ MAROONED/A GREAT DAY FOR FREEDOM/WEARING THE INSIDE OUT/TAKE IT BACK/COMING BACK TO LIFE/KEEP TALKING/LOST FOR WORDS/HIGH HOPES
EMI (US: Columbia); recorded January–May 1994; released March 30, 1994; available on CD

Like bingeing on chocolate or sleeping with a former partner, some albums are a slightly hollow pleasure. *The Division Bell* is one of those. A largely irrelevant release at the height of Britpop (a year prior to **Radiohead** and Smashing Pumpkins' reassertion of grandiosity), *The Division Bell* isn't even amongst the front rank of Floyd albums.

And yet *The Division Bell* successfully creates its own solipsistic little universe – that old Floyd franchise – which is strangely soothing in a manner *Momentary Lapse Of Reason* largely failed to achieve. This may have something to do with the greater percentage of Pinks involved, with Nick Mason actually playing this time and Rick Wright finally reinstated as a full member, co-writing a full five tracks. It may even have something to do with the presence of **Polly Samson**, Gilmour's partner, as lyrical foil: while unlikely to be inscribed on any bedroom walls, the lyrics here at least have consistency.

That they should be scoured for references to Gilmour's former writing partner was inevitable and – with the whole album's lyrics being concerned with communication – the couple duly oblige: "Lost For Words" referencing someone afflicted by "a fever of

spite"; "Poles Apart" talks of "[staring] out the steel" in its addressee's eyes. With its references to the Wall coming down, "A Great Day For Freedom" was also seen by many as a swipe at Waters: those aware of greater events than Floyd fallouts might imagine the lyric concerns the collapse of the Berlin wall, an event for which not even Roger Waters claims responsibility (he just made it look that way).

But an album can stand or fall only on its music. Although it largely avoids the taste transgressions of *Momentary Lapse*, and mutes the bombast, much of *The Division Bell* is still distinctly bland. "Lost For Words" appears to have been equally lost for music, rather reminiscent of **Jackson Browne**'s "Before The Deluge", while "Poles Apart" is a somewhat pedestrian recycling of "Goodbye Blue Sky" (also featuring a formulaic quotation from "Dogs"). But there are only two outright failures. "Take It Back" and "Keep Talking" are both attempts to update the Floyd formula via U2 circa 1986, the latter awkwardly embellished by Professor Stephen Hawking's synthesized voice.

On the plus side, "What Do You Want From Me" is potent and soulful stuff (despite its recycling of the riff from "Raise My Rent", from Gilmour's first solo album). The album's big ballad, "High Hopes" is magisterial and atmospheric (even if its words don't quite fit its music), while Wright's "Wearing The Inside Out" features a lovely vocal from its author (his first in 21 years) and a fine "Comfortably Numb"-style solo from Gilmour (see p.218). Indeed the sympathy between Wright and

Gilmour is the album's secret strength, the piano/guitar interplay on the opening instrumentals "Cluster One" and "Marooned" being particularly fetching. Like the album as a whole, these tracks are not especially ambitious (being essentially rewrites of "Shine On"), but the compound effect is curiously comforting. And thus it beats chocolate comedowns – or waking up with a former partner – hands down.

Pulse (Live)

SHINE ON YOU CRAZY DIAMOND/ASTRONOMY DOMINE/ WHAT DO YOU WANT FROM ME/LEARNING TO FLY/KEEP TALKING/HEY YOU/COMING BACK TO LIFE/A GREAT DAY FOR FREEDOM/SORROW/HIGH HOPES/ANOTHER BRICK IN THE WALL (PART TWO)/THE DARK SIDE OF THE MOON: SPEAK TO ME/BREATHE/ON THE RUN/TIME/GREAT GIG IN THE SKY/MONEY/US AND THEM/ANY COLOUR YOU LIKE/BRAIN DAMAGE/ECLIPSE/WISH YOU WERE HERE/COMFORTABLY NUMB/RUN LIKE HELL

EMI (US: Columbia); recorded Earl's Court Arena, October 20 1994; released May 30 1995; available on CD, VHS and DVD

To let loose one live album of the Gilmour Floyd is a misfortune; to let loose two looks like carelessness. For if *Delicate Sound Of Thunder* was a redundant addition to the Pink Floyd discography, then *Pulse* has all the artistic integrity of a tour T-shirt. *Pulse* is simply a restocking-up of Pink Floyd's coffers – albeit, as per the stringent corporate ethos of Pink Floyd™, an artfully executed, beautifully produced and immaculately packaged one. Repeating no fewer than ten *Thunder* tracks, *Pulse*'s unique selling points consist of five live versions of *Division Bell* tracks, a complete performance of *The Dark Side Of The Moon* and the novelty of a resuscitated "Astronomy Domine".

These are, respectively, distinguishable only via their dental records from the album versions, as bloodlessly proficient as a tribute band, and cosmically unspectacular. On *Pulse*'s scant plus side, Gilmour makes a much better job of the "Shine On" vocal this time, while Dick Parry's sax is a huge improvement on Scott Page's. But this is to ignore the elephant in the living room: on the considerably more substantial minus side, "Comfortably Numb" sounds even more "Recently Dead" than on *Thunder*, while the less said about Guy Pratt's attempt to duplicate Waters' more deranged vocals (on "Run Like Hell" and "Hey You") the better.

Consequently *Pulse*'s interest goes only cover-deep: the blinking red light embedded in the sleeve (an interest, let's face it, unlikely to stretch even to its limited battery life) and what's been done to the songwriting credits. For "Speak To Me" and "Great Gig In The Sky" gain a Waters co-credit, while Wright gets added to "On The Run". A mistake – or a rectifying of past misattributions? Gilmour blames **Storm Thorgerson**'s lousy proofreading. In any event, such quibbles really are as interesting as this album gets.

Ultimately little more than a retirement fund, on *Pulse* Pink Floyd sound like they're already metaphorically enjoying pipe and slippers. *Moribund* might have made a more accurate and appropriate title.

Floyd's Finest 50
The inside track

1. Arnold Layne

(Syd Barrett)

Recorded February 27, 1967; released as single March 11, 1967; available on *Relics, Masters Of Rock, Works, Echoes* and *Shine On*

When Roger Waters' mother noticed that underwear belonging to her female lodgers kept vanishing from her washing-line during the night, and he mentioned it to Barrett in London, the "Cambridge Knicker-Snatcher" became transmuted in Barrett's busy mind into cross-dresser "Arnold Layne".

Despite being banned by **Radio London** for being "smutty", there is in fact nothing sordid about this delightful little pop song: everything is entirely implicit in the fractured, impressionistic lyric, while Barrett's debauched child delivery – with its rolled Rs and overenunciated vowels – hovers impishly between innocence and smirking knowingness throughout, managing thus to appear both satirical of and sympathetic to Arnold's peccadilloes. That Barrett would later go through his own cross-dressing phase at one of his lowest ebbs is a rather pathetic instance of life imitating art.

There were some contemporary mutterings that "Arnold Layne" was not psychedelic enough; that it was too "pop". But at its best ("Strawberry Fields Forever"; the **Stones'** "Ruby Tuesday") British psychedelia was *always* consummately perfect pop: melodic, intricately-crafted music pushed and pulled to giddy imaginative heights. So while the sound of "Arnold" is rooted in a Duane Eddy-ish post-beat pop, **Joe Boyd**'s production, manages to make the band's performance sound feathery and evanescent, as if heard through water. Which makes it *indelibly* psychedelic. What's more, with its unconventional, mildly risqué subject matter, the song was entirely attuned to the permissive times. Not to mention giving glam a few pointers: **David Bowie** would later call his proto-Ziggy Stardust project Arnold Corns in Layne's honour, having been pop's very first cross-dresser.

2. Interstellar Overdrive

(Barrett, Waters, Wright, Mason)

Recorded, March 16, 1967; released on *The Piper At The Gates Of Dawn*; also available on *Relics*

While there had been precedents for the nine-minute sprawl of "Interstellar Overdrive" in **The Rolling Stones'** eleven-minute "Goin' Home", **The Butterfield Blues Band**'s thirteen-minute "East-West", **Love**'s side-long "Revelation", and **The Grateful Dead's** ten-minute "Viola Lee Blues", these were mostly just extended blues jams. With its freeform extemporisation and psychedelic spaceyness, the only true peers of "Interstellar Overdrive" are **The Mothers of Invention's** twelve-minute "Return Of The Son Of Monster Magnet" and **The Velvet Underground's** "European Son", putting the Floyd right at the vanguard of 1960s experimentalism.

Although Barrett is said to have derived the melody from Peter Jenner's out-of-tune rendition of **Love's** cover version of Burt Bacharach's "My Little Red Book", it's equally likely that Barrett heard the track first-hand on Love's debut album at Earlham Street – or even that he had **Ron Grainer's** *Steptoe And Son* sitcom theme in mind, as Waters has suggested. Either way, "Interstellar Overdrive" features one of the all-time great garage rock guitar riffs, before it leaves whatever original inspirations it might have had earthbound by shooting off into rock's outer space for its improvised middle section.

Rather than restraining the track, "conservative" producer Norman Smith deliberately courts chaos – drum skins buzzing from lack of separation between tracks, and a delay effect created by a second entire version of the track being superimposed on top of the first. While the mono version gains a further layer of organ and guitar, it loses the stereo version's spacey swirling from speaker to speaker, an effect which would soon become a key component of Pink Floyd's live sound (via their Azimuth Converter). As such, this is where Pink Floyd's progressive period started.

3. Flaming
(Syd Barrett)
Recorded, March 16, June 7, 27, 1967; released on *The Piper At The Gates Of Dawn*

What was it with the English and LSD? Where American acid culture was typically a rather adult affair of astral journeying and earnest jamming, its English counterpart dived straight down the rabbit hole back to childhood.

"Flaming" is one of the points on *Piper* – and in English psychedelic culture in general – where childlike whimsy chimes with acid weirdness in perfect synchronicity. Syd Barrett's lyric mixes the memory of drug-fuelled picnics on the banks of the Cam in autumn 1965 with childhood games of hide-and-seek with his sister Rosemary: childhood revisited – and revised – through the portal – or the veil – of acid. "Flaming" would have been an expression familiar to all 60s acid heads, denoting the common hallucinogenic vision of sparks that appeared to be detonated by fingers waggling.

Perfectly complementary, the track's music is an amalgam of the puerile and the sophisticated. The puerility lies in the singer being at his most Master Barrett-ish, by overenunciating madly, and singing slightly louder than absolutely necessary, while nagging away at a patented nursery-rhyme melody. The sophistication is to be found in the song's dazzling array of effects. There are bells, percussion, acres of echo, lovely Rick Wright harmonies, dabs of phasing and the Floyd's then ubiquitous sped-up piano, while the rumbling feedback introduction might possibly be a fleeting reference to *avant* ensemble **AMM**'s Jenner-produced "Later During A Flaming Riviera Sunset".

One of *Piper*'s oddest but most engaging tracks, "Flaming" was perceived as just too childish, English and eccentric for American audiences and thus was cut from the album's rather straight-laced American edition.

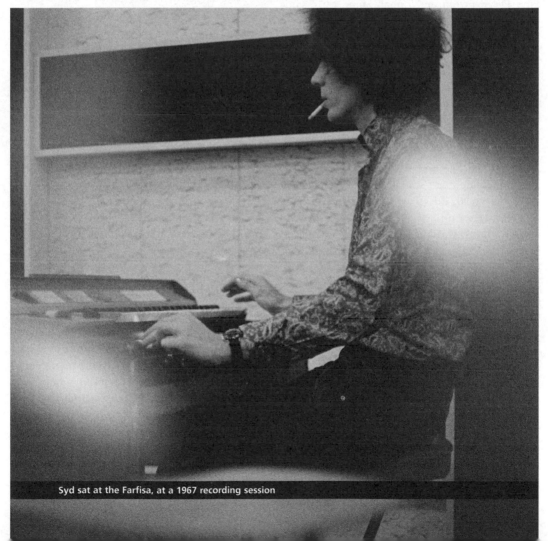

Syd sat at the Farfisa, at a 1967 recording session

4. Pow R Toc H
(Barrett, Waters, Wright, Mason)

Recorded, March 20–21, 1967; released on *The Piper At The Gates of Dawn*

Pink Floyd producer Norman Smith once said of Roger Waters that he was only "adequate" on his chosen instrument, but that "he made much more interesting noises with his mouth." Indeed, this facility not only gave Waters an area of "expertise" during the Barrett era but, in an odd way, pointed forward to his future leadership.

Primarily Waters' work, "Pow R Toc H" was inspired by an addled audience member grabbing the mic and making vocal noises at a regional gig that spring. Barrett sets up a rhythmic vocal, answered by Waters' 'quack', Barrett's cartoon sci-fi hoots and Waters' over-excited monkey impression. While Wright is given free rein in the contrastingly pastoral piano fills (prefiguring his work on *More*) and in the central section's more intense organ freak-out, the hand of Waters is heavy at the controls. His circular, descending bass-line commandingly brings the freak-out back to the melodic theme, with Wright's organ and Mason's plodding drum fills following meekly in what would become a patented Pink Floyd approach.

As regards the much-disputed title, it could just be dated stoner speak ("power tokage"), it could refer – given Waters' war obsession – to the Toc H organisation for soldiers (founded near Flanders in 1915) or it could just be a silly psychedelic spelling of "power torch". Though it's said Peter Jenner had a poor opinion of Waters, the tune was one of the co-manager's favourites, and he commended the band for its "avant-gardey-ness". Comic, melodic yet mildly disturbing, it's an object lesson in psychedelia's ability to merge the *avant-garde* with the pop.

5. Astronomy Domine
(Syd Barrett)

Recorded, April 11/12, 17, 1967; released on *Piper At The Gates Of Dawn*; also available on *Echoes*

Where there's LSD, the cosmic is sure to follow. During Syd Barrett's very first acid trip in a friend's Cambridge garden, he hoarded a plum and an orange, seeing them as planets in his own self-created universe. A universe he arguably never entirely left again – thus Storm Thorgerson's rather poignant visual joke in including both items on the cover of the 1970s reissue of Barrett's solo albums.

Although a direct connection to this experience can only be speculative, "Astronomy" simply couldn't have occurred without LSD. The lyric alone is so fractured as to be almost a reconception of language: a list of astral bodies from a Book of Planets; a touch of Dan Dare complemented by cartoon non-words ("Blam! Pow!"), allied to Barrett's own evocative, colourful, non-linear lyricism. The words **Peter Jenner** declaims through a megaphone at the start (and again at 2:38) are even more abstruse – a jumble of astrology, astronomy and random interjections worthy of **William Burroughs** ("All twelve houses ... low viscosity"). And is that the word "plum" Jenner is saying, nine seconds in?

The music is just as acid-infused. There's the fish-eyed warp of Jenner's splintered voice alongside the garbled morse code of Wright's Farfisa, the eerie keen of Barrett's and Wright's harmonies, the rumbling drama of Mason's drums, and the way Barrett's guitar shifts from cosmic **Duane Eddy** to unpredictable rhythm stabs – a wayward spaceship piloted by a mad professor. And then there's an audacious total stop at 1:34, followed by an extraordinary surge of echo, and a flailing freeform freak-out. Despite being brought gradually back to earth by the slowing, calming closure of the voices, this brief glimpse of Barrett's universe is beautiful, disorientating and slightly sinister. Perfect for a four-minute visit but not for prolonged habitation.

6. Bike

(Syd Barrett)

Recorded, May 21, 1967; released on *The Piper At The Gates Of Dawn*; also available on *Relics* and *Echoes*

If Barrett's childish whimsy does occasionally pall on *Piper*, it all comes right at the end in this psychedelic masterwork. Despite being inspired by girlfriend **Jenny Spires**' Raleigh bicycle and allied to a melody of nursery-rhyme simplicity, "Bike" is no exercise in mere tweeness, possessed of a wayward grace that has nothing to do with stability.

It's notable firstly for its quick-snapping internal rhymes. This was a favoured Barrett trick, probably derived from **Hillaire Belloc**, and later revisited regularly by Waters who admired "the way the lyric attaches to the meter in a very satisfying way". The lyric then regularly breaks out of rhythm and rhyme-scheme in wonderfully eccentric comic colloquialisms such as "I don't know why I call him Gerald" which finally drop any pretence at fitting the music.

The wittily chaotic wordplay is echoed by the chaotic double-tracking of the vocals, ricocheting from ear to ear before bundling into a free-for-all on the final verse.

But it's the sound-effects coda that cycles "Bike" off into another dimension: one that's equal parts comic (recalling The Beatles' contemporary Goons-derived sound effects in the same studio) and sinister. The cacophony of plucked piano strings, harmoniums, percussive plunks and the tape-delayed cry of a goose endlessly circling, manages to suggest not just chaos, but an undertow of fear and, ultimately, madness. So bewilderingly effective is "Bike" as an album closer that it was also chosen to close both the *Relics* and *Echoes* compilations.

7. See Emily Play

(Syd Barrett)

Recorded May 18–21, 1967; released as single June 16, 1967; available on US version of *The Piper At The Gates Of Dawn*, *Relics*, *Masters Of Rock*, *Works*, *Echoes* and *Shine On*.

Perhaps the single best example of English psychedelia, "See Emily Play" manages to encapsulate almost every aspect of the Summer of Love in just under three minutes: the sunny positivity, the childlike innocence, the veneration of fairy tales and paganism *and* the snooty attitude towards "day trippers". And that's only the lyrics.

The music manages to incorporate aspects of classic rock'n'roll (**Duane Eddy**-ish guitar; Waters' muscular, high-mixed Rickenbacker bass), folk and space-rock plus suggestions of classicism in Wright's extraordinary sped-up piano solo (a trick derived from **The Beatles**' Bach-like solo on "In My Life"), also engineered by **Norman Smith**, at the same studio. The whole sounds like several songs rolled into one slice of perfect summery pop.

Recorded just after the *Piper* sessions, but released before as a quick follow-up to "Arnold Layne", if it was a struggle for Smith to recapture the effect of **Joe Boyd**'s "Arnold" production (involving a shift from EMI to Sound Techniques studios), then the effortless-sounding end result was amply worth it.

Although Barrett claimed – tongue-in-elfin-cheek – that the song derived from a vision he had when he fell asleep in a wood, other sources suggest it concerned errant aristocratic teen **Emily Kennet**, best friend of **Anjelica Houston** (daughter of director John, later to become a Hollywood star), the two being notorious underground figures. While gently chiding ("Emily tries, but misunderstands") the song suggests less hipster condescension than sibling sympathy: naughty children, who know slightly more than they should, colluding on an exciting, slightly scary adventure into a version of adulthood their parents could never understand.

Recorded and released at the giddy pinnacle of the Summer of Love's sunny optimism, "Emily" was also the pinnacle of Syd Barrett's creativity: for both it would be a steady decline into darkness hereafter.

8. Scream Thy Last Scream
(Syd Barrett)

Recorded August 7–8, 1967; unreleased; available on *Total Eclipse* bootleg

"Scream Thy Last Scream" is conventionally seen as representing the breakdown of Syd Barrett. Yet former Floyd manager **Andrew King** believes that it represents the start of what should have been Pink Floyd Phase II. The sad fact is that this supremely strange song may actually be both: to create this tune's psychedelic scariness Barrett needed to have travelled so far out that there was no way back.

Amongst the song's oddities is the fact it's sung, uniquely, by Nick Mason (Barrett adding the last line of each verse). In fact Mason doesn't sound all that different to Barrett at his most theatrically camp – madly overenunciating the deliberately cod-Shakespearean lyric. (Was the entire group separated at vocal birth?) The Varispeed vocals that sometimes echo, sometimes duet with Mason are the song's signature, however, and still sound extraordinary nearly forty years on.

The song's tempo shifts are also unique. Initially stealing a Beatles trick of time-shifts from waltz-time to 4/4 (as in "We Can Work It Out"), the music gradually speeds up throughout the instrumental. A trick that prefigures

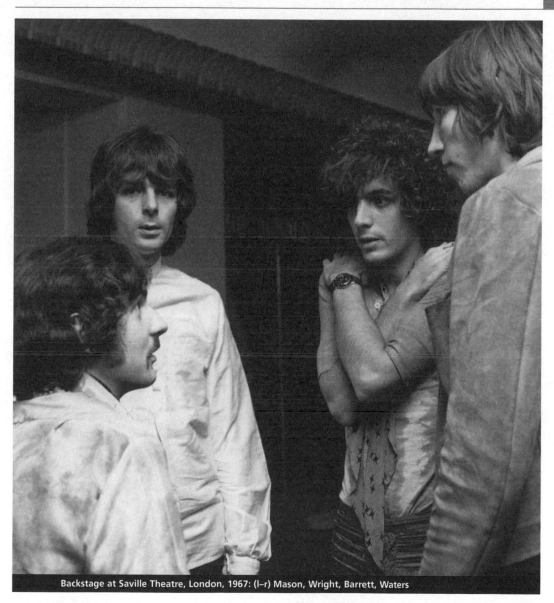

Backstage at Saville Theatre, London, 1967: (l–r) Mason, Wright, Barrett, Waters

The Music

Barrett's later wayward timing, here used to deliberately disorientating effect. The song's other signature is Wright's spectral organ, lavishly splashed with wah-wah, making this the Floyd's most Soft Machine-esque track.

Unreleased at the time and blocked by the band from both *Saucerful* and *Opel*, it would be left to **David Bowie** to pursue the song's psychedelic insanity, specifically his use of Varispeed on "All The Madmen" and "After All" on his 1970 album *The Man Who Sold The World* and again on his extraordinary "The Bewlay Brothers" on 1971's *Hunky Dory*. Bowie deployed the technique once more, bringing the debt back home on his 1973 cover of "See Emily Play".

9. Set The Controls For The Heart Of The Sun

(Roger Waters)

Recorded, August 7–8, 1967, Jan 11, 1968; released on *A Saucerful of Secrets*; also available on *Works*; *Echoes*

Although it did so quietly, almost unobtrusively, "Set The Controls" heralded a new voice within Pink Floyd – that of Roger Waters. That it did so on the very same day Syd Barrett was forecasting another potential Floydian future with "Scream Thy Last Scream" is all the more fascinating.

This new voice was, for a start, exactly that – "Controls" being Waters' first full lead vocal for the band. Low in the mix though it may be, merging melodically with his bassline, Waters' low-registered, almost conversational style is nevertheless already utterly distinctive.

But "Controls" also ushered in a new song-writing voice. Waters' second full composition for the band finds him considerably less in Barrett's psychedelic shadow than his first ("Take Up Thy Stethoscope"). Although still anchored in "Astronomy" spaceyness, it sets out Waters' stylistic musical stall via the entire melody being defined by a remedially simple four-note bass riff, whilst sacrificing nothing in mystery – indeed, it suggests entire universes of strangeness. The seagull sound effects are clearly a Waters touch too. Only the gnomic, haiku-like lyric – derived from an unspecified ancient Chinese poem – is untypical of his later caustic style. The title is usually attributed to **William Burroughs** but is actually taken from the novel *Fireclown*, by underground sci-fi novelist **Michael Moorcock**.

Although the guitar is sidelined (to the extent that no one can actually tell whether Barrett or Gilmour plays on the track), Wright and Mason both efficiently fall in behind Waters. Wright makes full use of the song's chordal openness to fly off into the blue yonder, with several layers of wah-wahed organ supplemented by vibraphone (a jazz instrument milked here for its shimmering, spacey, near-distorted tremelo), while Mason adds atmospheric, expressive drumming that was inspired by "Blue Sands" by jazz legend **Chico Hamilton** (from *Jazz On A Summer's Day*). A perfect piece of space-rock, "Controls" would steer the Floyd through all the set-lists of their progressive rock period.

10. Jugband Blues
(Syd Barrett)

Recorded, October 19–21, 1967; released on *A Saucerful Of Secrets*; also available on *Echoes*

"It's awfully considerate of you to think of me here," Barrett sings on his final Pink Floyd song, with almost unbearable poignancy, "and I'm most obliged to you for making it clear that I'm not here."

Not released until long after Barrett had left the band, these lines are often read as reproaches to Barrett's bandmates, particularly when allied to, "and I'm wondering who could be writing this song". But as, at the time of its recording, Barrett, however barmy, was still unchallenged band-leader, **Andrew King** says, "It's not directed to the band, it's addressed to the whole world. He was completely cut off." As such, the song gains even greater poignancy.

A compromise between Barrett's desire for a "freeform Salvation Army freak-out" (King's words) and producer **Norman Smith**'s insistence on something more scripted (aided by Mason on kazoo and Wright on tin whistle), the result manages to be both comical and touching.

But then there's the coda: Barrett alone with an acoustic guitar, his echoey, wispy voice almost ectoplasmic. "What exactly is a dream, and what exactly is a joke?" he muses. It might just be whimsical nonsense, but it could also be a cry for help. "Jugband Blues" was used by the Central Office of Information for a pro- motional film about Britain distributed in the US and Canada. While instructive of nothing about Britain, it is highly instructive about the state of Syd Barrett's psyche at the time. Co-manager with King, **Peter Jenner** called it, "a portrait of a nervous breakdown".

11. Let There Be More Light
(Roger Waters)

Recorded January 17–18, 1968; released on *A Saucerful Of Secrets*

Most listeners could be forgiven for failing to notice David Gilmour's arrival in Pink Floyd on this opening cut of their first post-Barrett album. For "Light" is a pretty seamless continuation of *Piper*'s spacier moments. The opening bass riff echoes motifs from the central section of "Interstellar Overdrive", Wright and Gilmour essay a Barrett tag-team vocal impression on verse and chorus respectively while Gilmour's almost comically overenunciated RS are closer to parody than tribute. Gilmour's one truly arresting moment on the track – the culminating dramatic slide guitar solo – may possibly be the work of Barrett himself.

Such an undramatic entry into the fold is a typical bit of Floydian elusiveness, fudging the issue of personality in order to put music first. On these terms, "Light" is a spectacular success. Waters' popping, pumping bass intro is exciting, the verse is haunting in the patented Floyd Eastern manner, while the chorus, despite lacking a simple hook to make it single material, lifts off like a spaceship.

As such, the music does a better job of illustrating the theme of alien visitations than the lyrics. Despite some nice Barrett-esque touches (the absurdist and evocative "glowing slightly from his toes"), they stall on a gauche reference to The Beatles' "Lucy In The Sky With Diamonds", while the less said about the use of the word "'twas", the better. Not so much alien visitation as friendly familiarity, "Let There Be More Light" quietly, seamlessly assimilates Gilmour into the Pink Floyd line-up.

12. A Saucerful Of Secrets
(Waters, Wright, Mason, Gilmour)
Recorded May 1968; released on *A Saucerful Of Secrets*; live version available on *Ummagumma*

During the sessions for their second album's last-completed track, Roger Waters and Nick Mason rolled a piece of paper onto the studio floor and drew the piece's structure out as an architectural diagram. Using a series of already existing brief extemporisations as a basis, they added elements then spliced each one together to fill the album's last 12 minutes. This music-as-building-blocks approach so alienated **Norman Smith** that he effectively left the band to produce themselves – a key precedent.

Both Gilmour and Wright threw themselves into the project: Gilmour holding the cymbal Waters bashed to create the overtones on the opening segment (which EMI probably logged as "Richard's Rave Up", and which was titled

"Something Else" on *Ummagumma*); Wright adding spectral horror movie organ. Gilmour added the ricocheting feedback to the drum loop Mason had recorded as "Nick's Boogie" (called "Syncopated Pandemonium" on Ummagumma) while Wright got to let loose on some *avant* jazz piano. Once again, the pair absolutely *make* the final section (called "Celestial Voices" on *Ummagumma*), in which an oceanic Wright organ sequence is overlaid with a heavenly host of David Gilmours harmonising with the mellotron's voice effect.

If the last section of "Saucerful" uncannily anticipates **The Moody Blues**, the piece as a whole anticipates **The Beatles**' tape collage "Revolution No. 9", whilst Krautrockers **Tangerine Dream** and **Klaus Schulze** arguably built entire careers upon it. Harmonically freer but structurally more rigid than the Barrett-era improvisations, "Saucerful" became a live staple until Autumn 1972. But while its structural approach led to "Echoes" and ultimately Dark Side, it's equally arguable that its musical approach led only to the blinder *avant* alleys of Floyd's prog years.

13. Point Me At The Sky
(Waters, Gilmour)
Recorded November 4, 1968; released as single December 17, 1968; available on *Shine On*

Stanley Kubrick's 1968 film *2001 – A Space Odyssey* had a profound effect on the 60s generation. The film's dazzling depiction of outer space, its suspicion of technology and the military-industrial complex and its climactic suggestion of escape into the void made it for many – as the adverts declared – "the ultimate trip".

Although Waters was far too grounded for acid, the film nevertheless chimed with both his socialism and his sci-fi fixation to inspire this song about a man who decides to desert the rat-race and head off into space. With this grabby concept, its wit and its perfect internal rhymes, this song boasts Waters' first truly great lyric.

The first compositional collaboration between Waters and Gilmour makes something poppier of the "Let There Be More Light" approach. Verse melody fits lyric perfectly and finds a keen, yearning quality in Gilmour's expressive vocals. A bridge sung by Waters ups the dramatic ante, before the song resolves into a rare proper chorus – a shouted Beatles-y business that marks a rare instance of communal bonhomie for this band.

Intriguingly, **David Bowie** would score a substantial British hit the next year with the similarly-themed "Space Oddity", using a vocal style similar to Gilmour's here, and sharing the arrangement's musical evocation of a rocket taking off. Perhaps it's similarly coincidental that the Floyd's final salvo at the singles market before taking off for progressive space should conclude: "all we've got to say to you is goodbye." But in doing so, the band also turned their back on this song which, despite being the worst-served of all their early cuts (available almost nowhere), is actually amongst their best.

14. Careful With That Axe, Eugene
(Waters, Wright, Gilmour, Mason)

Recorded November 4, 1968; released December 17, 1968, B-side to "Point Me At The Sky"; available on *Relics & Shine On*; live version on *Ummagumma*; remake on *Zabriskie Point*

Roger Waters' lyrical preoccupations with madness and pathological behaviour long predated *Dark Side* and *The Wall*, and even predated his experiences with Syd Barrett. Syd was in perfectly good shape when "Take Up Thy Stethoscope" was created, while the paranoid hints on "Julia Dream" sound distinctly personal.

"Eugene" dated back to the tail-end of the Saucerful sessions. The piece evolved from a group-jammed two-minute, one-chord instrumental called "Murderistic Woman" (the song's theme in place from the off, then), recorded for a June 1968 BBC session. Essaying a sinister insouciance with a creepy jazziness that anticipates David Lynch's *Twin Peaks*, the piece is anchored on Waters' one-chord octave bass notes, and is overlaid with Gilmour's floating jazzy chords, Wright's lounge organ and that almost cheesey jazz staple the vibraphone. The laidback-ness is undercut by a suggestion of menace in the drums, and by Waters' creepy whispering of the title line. After nearly two minutes of simmering tension, the track boils over abruptly when Waters emits an absolutely bloodcurdling stream and Gilmour's guitar suddenly turns nasty, blundering about the mix with bloody intent.

For a mere B-side, "Eugene" proved to have considerable legs (especially compared

The Music

to its ill-fated flip). Apart from reappearing on *Relics*, and on *Ummagumma*, it formed the "Beset By The Creatures of the Deep" section of *The Journey* suite, and was played at almost every show from 1968–73. It proved equally popular with filmmakers, and was featured in Peter Sykes' 1968 movie *The Committee*, **Michelangelo Antonioni**'s 1970 *Zabriskie Point* (re-recorded and renamed "Come In Number 51, Your Time Is Up") whilst also featuring prominently in *Pompeii*. Intriguingly, "Eugene" was revived for the 1977 In the Flesh tour, and, according to Mason, it was calls for the tune on that same tour that, in an uncanny echo of the tune's sentiments, caused Waters to snap, spitting in a fan's face. As such, the titular axe of "Eugene" can be seen as the same as Pink's "favourite axe" in *The Wall*'s "One of My Turns".

15. Cirrus Minor
(Roger Waters)
Recorded March 1969; released on *More*; also available on *Relics*

Proof positive of his wife's view that he was "good at everything", when Pink Floyd's resident "straight" Roger Waters set his mind to writing songs of druggy reverie, he came up trumps with this quiet classic. Perfectly suggesting a transcendence simultaneously easeful and deathly – rendered explicit by it's use in the heroin scenes in *More* – the sliver of a lyric starts with a lazy summer day lolling in a churchyard by a river (the Cam?), before drifting out into the universe at large.

This transcendent theme is beautifully mirrored by the song's performance. With the recording of *More* being a hurried affair, the music is a simple cyclical construction of descending chromatic chords, and features only half the group (Wright and Gilmour, plus some sound library birdsong). But the performance utterly transcends these humble origins to create a yearning epic. Over his lovely plucked acoustic, Gilmour sings an awed-sounding imitation of Waters. At the hunched low-end of his range, and deferential to each syllable of the lyric, reverence evokes reverie – especially when bathed in echo at the end. Transcending his lack of interest in the *More* project, Wright's stunning coda of sustained, oceanic Hammond organ chords builds on the end of "Saucerful", while the twittering, spacey vibrations of his Farfisa build on those in "Julia Dream", merging with the birdsong to create a phantasmagoric piece of cosmic pastoral.

As such, in both form and content the song also entirely transcends the rather earthbound account of the hippie narcotic counterculture it was created for.

16. The Nile Song
(Roger Waters)
Recorded March 1969; released on *More*; also available on *Relics*

The lyrical conventions of the late 1960s represent women as curiously uncorporeal. From **Crosby, Stills & Nash** to **Leonard Cohen**, women tend to be vague, semi-mythological muse-figures – either soft and delicate or siren-like and dangerous. Derived in part from the character of the heroin-addicted Estelle from the movie *More*, the female subject of Roger Waters' "Nile Song" belongs to the latter category. Featuring nowhere in the film, the Nile is simply a suitably mythic-sounding location.

If the lyric doesn't transcend its era, the music does – "The Nile Song" prefigures the 1970s by being the Floyd's first out-and-out rocker, and couldn't have taken them further from Syd Barrett's musical legacy. Utilized to soundtrack a hippie party in *More*, where the movie's central couple first meet, the song finds Gilmour letting rip with a hoarsely full-throated vocal, a raunchy rock touch engagingly at odds with his RP diction. He also attacks his axe in a hunkily Hendrix-esque manner. Waters later claimed to have deliberately echoed this song on *The Wall*'s "Young Lust".

Oddly, a slightly gentler reprise of *Nile Song* – "Ibiza Bar" on the *More* album – is credited to all four Floyds but, with its identical tune and riff and its paranoid lyrics, is plainly Waters' work. Possibly due to the rushed, piecemeal nature of *More's* recording, Wright is absent from "The Nile Song" altogether, though this probably also reflects his distaste for a song that isn't so much unprogressive as actively atavistic. Punchy, crunchy and visceral, "The Nile Song" is Wright's loss.

17. The Narrow Way Parts 1–3
(David Gilmour)
Recorded April–June 1969; released on *Ummagumma*

Pushed into having to create a quarter of an album's solo material, neophyte songwriter Gilmour quickly discovered himself in difficulty. He begged Waters for help, but the bassist refused, insisting Gilmour stick to the concept, defining their future Floyd roles – Waters the conceptualist, Gilmour the muso. As such it's strange that the song is so overlooked (not least by Gilmour himself), as it also defines Pink Floyd's classic sound of the 1970s.

The instrumental "Part 1" was ready by a December 1968 BBC session as "Baby Blue Shuffle in D Major". Quickening the tempo, Gilmour added backwards guitar surges and some wonderfully outré slide guitar. "Part 2" is anchored by an ugly unison electric guitar riff, echo-laden drums pattering behind like following footsteps, strangely suggestive of contemporaries Black Sabbath's gothic heavy rock.

But it's "Part 3" (completed by April 69 for *The Journey*) that's the highlight. The lyrics won't win any Novello awards (indeed they're the only words left off the 1994 *Ummagumma* CD repackage), but they're nonetheless a perfectly effective texture in a beautifully atmospheric piece. Boasting a haunting, ethereal melody, it features a lovely breathy vocal from Gilmour, albeit pitched so high he often struggled to reach the notes live. If Gilmour was unusual in attempting a song on *Ummagumma*, he was unique in evoking a band playing it, adding not just his signature spacey slide, but

The Music

piano, Mellotron, bass and drums, engagingly echoing Mason's spaciously plodding style. Consequently it sounds very like Pink Floyd – albeit a Pink Floyd that didn't quite exist yet. How on earth did Gilmour miss this one when later claiming he was the heart and soul of Pink Floyd?

18. Atom Heart Mother
(Mason, Gilmour, Waters, Wright & Geesin)

Recorded June 10, 16, 19, 20, 21, 1970; released on *Atom Heart Mother*

Poor old "Atom Heart Mother". Nobody seems to like it much. Not critics, who dismiss it as a failed piece of prog pomposity; not orchestrator and co-writer **Ron Geesin**, who thinks his score was performed poorly by second-rate Abbey Road clock-watchers; and not Pink Floyd themselves. "God it's shit, possibly our lowest point artistically," is a typical Gilmour utterance on the topic.

While the Floyd and Geesin both have the excuse of being self-critical perfectionists, music critics are simply guilty of accepted received wisdom as fact – thus "Atom Heart Mother" remains forever a prog rock folly. Some things are undeniable, of course. Yes, "Atom Heart Mother" is that ultimate prog indulgence, a side-long suite. Yes, it does feature an orchestra and a choir, and yes, the middle funky section does get a bit dull. But, in reverse order: said funky section only accounts for a mere three minutes out of 25; the piece's symphonic aspects add power rather than pomposity (no

one calls **Ennio Morricone**'s music, which it recalls, pretentious); and finally, in the realm of music at least, it's not how long it is that matters, but what you do with it.

Despite being rushed, despite the jobsworth brass players who rebelled at the upstart Geesin's baton, despite Geesin's complaint that the beat was misplaced, "Atom Heart Mother" achieves all kinds of wonderful – and many weird – things. "Father's Shout" boasts a joyful brass fanfare in which Geesin builds brilliantly on Gilmour's Morricone-like melody; "Breast Milky" (from 2:59) is a compelling cross-hatch of wheeling cello and Wright's organ curlicues, with Gilmour's slide solo here being his best guitar work to date. Then "Mother Fore" (from 5:19) peaks in an eerily lovely melody for two sopranos.

OK, so "Funky Dung" (from 10:16) errs towards the latter part of its title, with Waters and Mason creating a plodding white funk groove and Gilmour waffling on guitar, but it's rescued at 13:22 by Geesin's inspired choir-chanted gobbledegook and the return of the brass theme. The electronic "Mind Your Throats Please" (from 15:30), is an atmospheric work reminiscent of "Quicksilver", while "Remergence" (from 17:45) is a clever assembly of all the previous elements. Then Mason's mangled voice, at 19:10, announces "silence in the studio", heralding the triumphant return of the brass, more lovely Gilmour slide-guitar, and brass and choir bringing matters to a magnificent close on a climactic shift from E minor to E major à la **The Beatles**' "A Day In The Life".

It may not be on quite the same plane as The Beatles' classic, but "Atom Heart Mother" deserves to be rehabilitated from the ravages of an intense – and inaccurate – whispering campaign. No wonder the cow on the cover looks glum.

19. Summer '68
(Rick Wright)
Recorded July 1970, released on *Atom Heart Mother*

Rick Wright was the main source of disgruntlement with Pink Floyd's attempts to address the singles market post-Barrett. He was also one of that market's main sources of material. So it's intriguing that, having got the classical pretensions of *Ummagumma*'s "Sysyphus" and "Atom Heart Mother" itself out of his system, Wright returned to the very pop songwriting he apparently despised – the pop-psyche of the 1967/68 singles tracks "Paintbox" and "It Would Be So Nice". The title actually refers to the time when the Gilmour Floyd made their first proper Stateside foray.

Late 1960s America, and specifically LA's Sunset Strip, was a Shangri-La for what Robert Plant (in **Led Zeppelin**'s "Going to California") and Bernie Taupin (**Elton John**'s "Tiny Dancer") depicted as a relatively innocent era of sexual freedom. The hypersensitive (and married) Wright appears to have found the experience rather more debilitating, judging by the world-weariness that weighs down both lyrics and plaintive vocal in the piano-based verse here. But as the contrastingly jaunty chorus adds a swath of burbling Beach Boys harmonies

from multiple Wrights and Gilmours, then soars even higher with ebullient Mellotron and (real?) brass, the mood is ultimately one of joyful melancholy, of bittersweet nostalgia – not for the girl in the song in particular (or even free love in general) but perhaps for the flawed innocence of the 60s itself.

Incidentally, Gilmour's acoustic guitar link to the slow bridge is particularly deft. His constantly-shifting tempo recalls Barrett's solo work, except Gilmour sounds like he knows exactly where he's going. Followed by a quite stunning sequence of harmonies and a final blast of brass, the only question mark next to "Summer '68" is why Wright couldn't produce more of this kind of thing?

20. Fat Old Sun
(David Gilmour)
Recorded August 1970, released on *Atom Heart Mother*

Grantchester Meadows is the rural, riverside area outside Cambridge in which Gilmour grew up, and a place central to pastoral Floydian iconography. A conscious sequel to Waters' "Grantchester Meadows", it's as if Gilmour, bored of being the new boy, is, in this first struggle-free solo composition, both reasserting his songwriterly stake in his childhood haunts *and* in his band.

Gilmour strums a countryish acoustic pattern not dissimilar to the Western theme of "Atom Heart", showing what would prove to be a consistently American influence on the guitarist of this most English of bands. That said, the song is still very English, with its dusk chorus

The Music

of church bells, its poetically bucolic lyric and Gilmour's Home Counties voice pitched high like someone sleepily humming to himself. Too much has been made of the song's supposed similarities to one by an even more English of bands – "Lazy Old Sun" by The Kinks (from their 1967 album *Something Else By…*). The songs share little but similar titles.

As organ then Beatlesy drums enter, the song builds up to a brilliantly incongruous climactic guitar solo, hinting at Hendrix (whose Isle of Wight set Gilmour had recently mixed) and recalling *Zabriskie Point*'s unreleased "Country Song". The solo is backed by ever more woozy slide-guitar and falsetto backing vocals, before the church bells ring in the end. Not sufficiently transcendent to make complete classic status, "Fat Old Sun" is a quiet joy nonetheless.

21. One Of These Days
(Mason, Gilmour, Waters, Wright)

Recorded January–August 1971; released on *Meddle*; also available on *A Collection Of Great Dance Songs*, *Works* and *Echoes*

Pop quiz: what links TV theme-writer **Ron Grainer** with Pink Floyd? One point only for his *Steptoe And Son* theme's influence on "Interstellar Overdrive", three for adding the *Dr Who* theme's key role within "One Of These Days".

Cutting through the indolence of the *Meddle* sessions, "One of These Days" is the audible product of a rare studio excitement. When Roger Waters played a muscular one-note bass-

riff through the band's trademark **Binson echo unit**, Gilmour was inspired to grab a second bass, the others quickly embellishing the tune. So quickly, in fact, that a roadie dispatched to buy new strings for Waters' bass returned to find recording complete. Consequently, the dull-toned, plodding bass of Waters (in the left channel), and the bright-toned sprightly bass of Gilmour (on the right) combined to create their first out-and-out rocker since "The Nile Song". Topped with Wright's exhilarating backward-surging organ chords, and Gilmour's evil-sounding lap-steel, the track was – in a first, post-prog sign of cutting to the chase – edited down at Morgan studios. It was also now given its knowing nod to Grainer's *Dr Who* theme-tune in a barer, electronic middle section (actually created by guitar and tape delay) that points forward to "On the Run".

Likely it was this *Dr Who* reference that prompted the band to put the Dalek effect on Nick Mason's rare vocal turn. Sometimes known by its full lyric – "one of these days I'm going to cut you into little pieces" – "Days" continues the theme of madness and violence that runs through "Eugene" and into the heart of Waters' darkness on *Animals* and *The Wall*. It quickly became a live favourite.

22. Echoes
(Mason, Gilmour, Waters, Wright)

Recorded January to August 1971; released on *Meddle*; also available on *Echoes*

Though not all bands can spend their studio time hoovering up drugs or being pleasured by obliging groupies, Pink Floyd must be unique in spending it reading the newspaper. "Pink Floyd sessions had a reputation for being boring," attests *Meddle* engineer John Leckie. The hedonistic Faces the Floyd were not.

If *Meddle* ultimately revealed a new sense of purpose within Pink Floyd, it wasn't always apparent during its recording. Many months were spent simply waiting around for ideas, while the working title they gave the snippets they *did* record – "Nothing Parts 1-36" – hardly indicated huge inspiration. "Because of our previous experience of things being developed in the studio, we thought that that was the Way Forward," says Nick Mason somewhat apologetically.

And in a strange way it was. From the small acorn of a Rick Wright *ping*-ing piano B-note put through a Binson echo unit, the mighty "Echoes" grew – the key link between the progressive and the populist Pink Floyd. That "ping" is certainly a nice noise, as crystalline as icy water droplets on rock, but unlike the dripping tap on "Alan's Psychedelic Breakfast", it's a noise that, crucially, prompted Pink Floyd to create some purposeful-sounding music. Despite utilizing the suite structure of "Atom Heart Mother", "Echoes" does so with a melodic directness that perfectly prefigures *Dark Side Of The Moon*.

For a start, the Gilmour guitar solo that bubbles over Wright's lovely minor chords is the first airing of the liquid, light-fingered but icily-precise style that would become his signature, whilst also adhering to a song-like melodic arc in immediate contrast to more diffuse previous

solos. Then suddenly, just before the three-minute mark, there really *is* a song. What's more, it has vocals from Gilmour and Wright in warmly precise harmony, and even has a chorus, summoning a Sunday morning sleepiness that rises to radiance via a climactic chromatic sequence (sounding like Waters' work).

While to many listeners, Waters' words here sound like plangent post-psychedelic whimsy – warm, vaguely peace'n'love poeticism to complement the gentle, atmospheric music – to their author, they evidence the emergence of his humanist theme. The line "Strangers passing on the street, by chance two separate glances meet/And I am you and what I see is me" suggests the connections that exist between the remotest of people. This was a theme that would receive fuller expression on *Dark Side*'s "Us And Them" and "Brain Damage" and on Waters' solo "Every Stranger's Eyes" – sentiments their own author once deprecated as "airy fairy mystical bollocks from the 60s".

If, in truth, the funky section that follows (7:00–11:24) is little more successful than that of "Atom Heart Mother", you need to be more than a merely curious Floyd fan to warm to the central section (11:25-14:36), with its synthesizer whale-cries, cawing birds and Gilmour's backwards wah-wah guitar evoking that Floyd favourite, screeching seagulls (see "Controls" or "Embryo"). Even to devotees it can seem more impressive than entirely listenable, functioning largely to make what follows the more rewarding: a classic sequence of sustained Rick Wright organ chords, building to a wheeling, ever-intensify-

The Music

ing bass pattern before surging breathlessly back into the reprised vocal section. With the voices flanged for further wateriness, the piece then eddies gently away on further lovely Gilmour lead-guitar lines, echoing Wright's rippling piano.

A cornerstone of their live set for five years, "Echoes" was one of only two tracks from Pink Floyd's progressive era that the rigorously revisionist Gilmour allowed into the band's 80s and 90s canon, even giving its name to the band's most comprehensive career compilation. Well worth waiting for, "Echoes" is both prog Pink Floyd's peak *and* its last post. For while there would be further epics, experiments and studio longueurs in the future, never would Pink Floyd again sound like a band operating outside the musical mainstream.

23. Burning Bridges

(Wright, Waters)

Recorded February–March 1972; released on *Obscured By Clouds*

Given that enigma is, by definition, "that which is not easily understood", pinpointing it – let alone summoning it up to order – can be a slippery business. And although enigma is the essence of Pink Floyd, as "Echoes" revealed, the band themselves had little more clue how they managed to create it than the rest of us, largely trusting to space and time magically to induce it.

Paradoxically then, the object lesson in the elliptical and evanescent that is "Burning Bridges" was created in a rather prosaic rush,

for the soundtrack of **Barbet Schroeder**'s film *La Vallée*, in a mere two weeks in a castle-cum-studio in France. Indeed it's arguable that "Burning Bridges" is less elliptical than simply unfinished. Featuring a bare-bones organ, bass, guitar and four-square drums arrangement, it lacks the usual Floydian filigree of layers, and there is no chorus. The lyrics, by Waters, hint promisingly at connections between personal choice and military strategy ("ancient bonds are breaking", for example – and of course the song's title) without ever quite properly pursuing them.

As it is, the song simply makes the most of Wright's haunting melody, with its subtle, cyclical key-changes, the lyrical rather than the literal quality of Waters' words, and the heavenly, baton-passing harmonic interplay between Dave Gilmour's and Rick Wright's voices. "...His voice in harmony with mine works very well," Gilmour has commented. The rest is left to the listener. For as their former collaborator **Ron Geesin** once said, "what Floyd's music does is it allows you space to think within it." There but not there. "Burning Bridges" is a minor yet enchanting example of how they did just that.

24. Childhood's End

(David Gilmour)

Recorded February–March 1972; released on *Obscured By Clouds*

"Roger said, 'Well haven't you got anything?'," Gilmour once said, in explaining how he came up with "Childhood's End". "I said, 'Well, it's only half done.' He said 'Get it out!" In fact, the song sounds rather in hock to its galvanizer, Roger Waters, from the start. If its music makes its contemporaneity with the *Dark Side Of The Moon* sessions blatantly clear (sharing a similar, faded-in VCS3 drone and tempo to "Time"), its lyrical theme of ageing and mortality makes it virtually a *Dark Side* track *manqué*, right down to two particularly Waters-esque touches: the quick-firing rhymes in the second verse, and the self-referentiality of "so the song will end" in the third, is cousin to "the song is over" in "Time". What's more, "Childhood's End" is named after a 1953 novel by Waters' favourite **Arthur C. Clarke**, about humans giving way to more highly evolved beings – a relative of his *2001*, which had already inspired Waters' "Embryo" and "Point Me At The Sky". While Gilmour does a commendable job of taking Waters on on his own territory, neither lyric nor music (a livelier version of the "Atom Heart"/"Echoes" funk) achieve quite the same transcendence as "Time" – perhaps inevitable given the song's brusque creation. Like the childhood it hymns, "Childhood's End" is, in Gilmour's phrase, "only half-formed" – but charmingly so.

25. Stay

(Wright, Waters)

Recorded March 1971; released on *Obscured By Clouds*

Although it's hard to imagine a more constitutionally contrasting pair, Rick Wright and Roger Waters' creative partnership was on an absolute roll in 1972 – "Burning Bridges"

was behind them and *Dark Side*'s "Us And Them" and "Breathe" were already written. "Stay" was written quickly for the album *Obscured By Clouds* and, if not the best, is certainly the most completely collaborative of this quartet.

Although Waters had taken the lyrical helm for *Dark Side*, the verse of "Stay" sounds way too close to "Summer '68" to be anything but Wright's work, with its tenderly world-weary treatment of an on-the-road liaison. Not that groupies were a subject Waters was ignorant of (despite the Floyd's gentlemanly reputation) – it's more that the chorus's more poetic flights ("midnight blue/burning gold" et al.) sound more like Wright turns of phrase. Stranger still, the music sounds like a collaboration too: for if the chorus's key-shift and soulful melancholy suggest the delicate, musically-trained Wright, the simplistic, three-chord verse fingers the straight-up, no-messing Waters.

But Gilmour was, by *Obscured*, not to be left out either, making his vocal presence felt on the chorus via a soothing harmony, whilst absolutely saturating the song with plangent wah-wah lap steel, faintly reminiscent of **Jerry Garcia**'s steel-work on CSN&Y's "Teach Your Children". It's less country than pure California. Indeed, with Wright essaying his first American accent, Pink Floyd had rarely sounded less English than they did on this almost custom-made AOR ballad, and they were rewarded with considerable radio play. Despite this success, Waters and Wright would never again work so closely together as they did on "Stay". Indeed, in a few years' time Waters would be making quite the reverse recommendation to his collaborator.

26. Breathe (In The Air)
(Waters, Gilmour, Wright)
Recorded June 1972–Jan 1973; released on *Dark Side Of The Moon*

For all of Waters' preliminary talk of "coming back down to earth" for *Dark Side Of The Moon*, "Breathe" is amongst the most ethereal, celestial and least grounded pieces in the entire Pink Floyd canon. And it's all the better for it.

Musically, this ethereality is achieved by Gilmour's wafting, surging pedal steel, which manages to combine both the pastoral and the space rock approaches of the previous four years, and by the filigreeing of layers (Gilmour's three vocal and three guitar tracks, Wright's three keyboard tracks), building a magic castle out of humble two-chord rock. The Wright-penned chorus opens out to six harmonically expansive chords (partly inspired by **Miles Davis**' jazz classic *Kind Of Blue*): Earth viewed from air, free from gravity's pull.

Waters' symbiotically complementary lyrics may have gravity, but they are very far from being down-to-earth. Although closely related to his songs for the film *The Body* and their connections between man's corporeality and his environment, the lyric of "Breathe" encompasses the pastoral ("run rabbit run"), whilst also being spacey and elusive. Living long and flying high suggests spiritual ease, but it's conditional ("only if you ride the tide") suggesting a simultaneous material stress. The lyrics are perhaps best not analysed too closely: it's evocative and enigmatic in the patented Pink Floyd style, with sufficient hints of Waters' humanism ("don't be afraid to care") not to feel abstract.

Waters could huff and puff all he liked about Pink Floyd being perceived as a space rock act (indeed the online music encyclopedia *All Music still* calls them "the premier space rock band"), but when music is so far off into the ether as "Breathe", classifications become as intangible as the song itself.

27. On The Run
(Gilmour, Waters)
Recorded January 1973; released on *Dark Side Of The Moon*

"On The Run" is a key departure from Pink Floyd's signature laid-back style, a precursor of the more edgy and tense elements that would intrude during Waters' later takeover of the band.

The hints of paranoia in "Julia Dream", "Eugene" and "One Of These Days" are here given full musical rein; the tune's clipped electronic minimalism all the more startling coming after the leisurely Floydian lushness of the preceding *DSOTM* track "Breathe".

Replacing the jammed "Travel" of early live versions, "On The Run" kept the concept (one close to any touring band's mind, if not heart) but broadened it to its attendant stress and ultimately madness.

The music similarly expanded on what began as a rudimentary synthesizer doodle. Fiddling with the new VCS3 Synthi-A briefcase, Gilmour came up with a sequence of notes he then sped up to a blur; the ever-competitive Waters, listening, proceeded to play a different sequence. "I hate to say, it was marginally better," Gilmour conceded. Despite its apparent minimalism, "On The Run" is actually a complex mesh of seventeen instrumental tracks, from a conventional set-up of electric guitar, bass, drums and piano amalgamated with electronics to suggest the frenzied motion of travel. But it's the sound effects that give the tune its depth, a cinematic montage of hurrying footsteps, heavy breathing, mumbling roadies and Waters' deranged cackling.

The use of the VCS3 synthesizer (see p.83) would have been innovative enough in itself, but it was truly pioneering in such a brutally minimalist form, prefiguring techno pretty accurately. Waters was later dismissive of this genre, suggesting its creators did little more than plug the machines in. Given that this was an accusation levelled at the Floyd themselves, this sounds a little like defensiveness. But whether music be electronic or organic, technical accomplishment is less important than what is chosen and how it is presented, as this tune conclusively proves. It was perhaps Gilmour's insufficient recognition of this fact in the 1980s and 1990s, however, that engaged Waters defensiveness, or, one might even say, his paranoia.

28. Time
(Mason, Waters, Wright, Gilmour)
Recorded June 8, 1972; released on *Dark Side Of The Moon*; also available on *Echoes*

One of the curious effects of *Dark Side Of The Moon*'s ubiquity is that such everyday sounds as a heartbeat or a ticking clock can now summon up Pink Floyd. While they couldn't, of course, copyright these sounds (not least because it was engineer **Alan Parsons** who recorded the clocks), "Time" is still trademark Floyd – simultaneously cool yet emotional, confident but questioning. The song's introduction alone is testament to this, its VCS3 drone, drum-machine like clicks from Waters' Fender Precision bass and Mason's ringing, tuned roto-toms being intensely dramatic, its clock-chime electric piano and sheer length being almost lackadaisically leisurely. Waters later said that "there was a serious lack of panic about losing the listener's attention here". Two minutes and twelve seconds' lack, to be precise.

The song's lyrics derived from Waters' realisation, aged 29, that "there isn't suddenly a line when the training stops and life starts." As such, Gilmour's assertive bark adds a chiding urgency to the verse ("fritter", "waste", run", "death"), while Wright's softer, more self-effacing tones utterly inhabit the introspection of the chorus, the filtered, disembodied backing vocals sounding simultaneously soulfully alive and creepily spectral.

Credited to the group, the demo aired on the *Making Of Dark Side Of The Moon* DVD sug-

The Music

gests Waters wrote the basic song of "Time", which the others finessed into something more epic. These inputs include Wright's opening chord decorations (he was probably also responsible for tweaking the chorus chords from major to minor), Gilmour's economical but effective guitar work and Mason's dramatic roto-tom intro. Splicing said intro to the song's end on the US B-side to "Us And Them" might have made "Time" more immediate for radio programmers, but it ruined the brilliantly bathetic climax: "thought I'd something more to say…" To make subverting pomposity itself sound pompous – now that was something the Floyd really *could* have copyrighted.

29. The Great Gig In The Sky
(Rick Wright)

Recorded June 25, 1972, October 1972 & January 21, 1973; released on *Dark Side Of The Moon*; also available on *Echoes*

After a series of rushed records, Pink Floyd had, since *Meddle*, acquired a reputation for taking an age to finish anything. A Freudian would equate this Floydian completion anxiety with fears about mortality, a subject foremost in the Floyd's minds via a shared fear of flying, and heightened as both Wright and Waters now approached 30. That death should be the subject of *Dark Side*'s longest gestating tune is thus entirely appropriate.

It didn't start that way, however. Indeed Wright has attested that, had death been in his mind, he wouldn't have created such a beatifically beautiful chord sequence. The tune's churchy sonority slotted perfectly into the incipient *Dark Side*, however, following the religious references of "Breathe Reprise". Known as "Religion" in early 1972 live performances, it featured only organ, taped religious readings and the voice of British conservative religious broadcaster **Malcolm Muggeridge** (a sure Waters touch). By the Floyd's autumn American tour, the voices had been ditched, the sequence shifted to piano, the segue from "Breathe Reprise" rendered more seamless by redeploying its chords (transposed) in the introduction, and the tune had finally gained its theme, as "The Mortality Sequence".

But still the existential tinkering continued – the tune gaining Gilmour's deliberate echo of his "Breathe" pedal steel part that October. Still discontent, they set to it again at the mixing stage. If Jerry Driscoll's and Pete Watts' spoken comments about death were key elements to what Waters now dubbed "The Great Gig In The Sky", the vocals of session singer **Clare Torry** were conclusive. Torry's jaw-dropping, almost orgasmic wails levitated "Gig" from atmospheric dirge to ecstatic eulogy, not so much quelling fear of death as making it actively appealing. In fact, so lambently soothing is the track that a re-recorded version was used to advertise Nurofen painkillers in the 1990s. The most seductive song about death until **Radiohead**'s (distinctly Floydian) "Pyramid Song" twenty years later, as PR for the Grim Reaper, "Great Gig" takes some beating.

30. Money
(Roger Waters)

Recorded June 7/October 1972; released on *Dark Side Of The Moon* and US single; also available on *A Collection Of Great Dance Songs* (re-recorded) and *Echoes*

Although there'd been hints as far back as "Corporal Clegg", and more recently in "Free Four", "Money" represented the first full public flowering of George Roger Waters' soon-to-be-characteristic cynicism. As such, it must have given its author some satisfaction that "Money" followed in the sardonic footsteps of "Free Four" in opening up America for the Floyd. Given heavy rotation on FM radio, this song about wealth and greed was the key to *Dark Side Of The Moon*'s American success, climbing to #13, and helping make the Floyd richer than even Waters' sarcastically loaded lyric could hypothesize.

So far, so ironic. Or was it? It's hard not to suspect that "Money" was a move as cynical as its sentiments. OK, it employs a slightly outré 7/8 tempo, but it remains in essence the kind of mid-70s blues-rock beloved of heartland American stoners, especially when it digs into a double-time boogie for the guitar solo (an idea of Gilmour's suggestive of a space-rock **Allman Brothers**). And any fool knew that sax meant hits in the 1970s. What's more, Gilmour's box-fresh American accent smacks of trying too hard, though he's only acting up to Waters' US-steeped lyrics ("a gas", "bullshit" et al.). Indeed, "Money" could pass for the work of an American group were it not for Gilmour's significant stumble on the word "class". You can

take the boy out of the Home Counties…

As for that lyric – is it *really* so sarcastic? Waters says the band had "a shared goal, which was to become rich and famous", often citing their "avarice" in continuing after *Dark Side* made riches and fame a reality. So perhaps those annoying audience members who took the lyric literally, as he and Gilmour complained, were just poetic justice for such a sustained – and dodgy – double-bluff. "It was the track that made us guilty of what it propounds," Gilmour later said.

All of which would make this melodically monotonous song more interesting conceptually than musically, were it not for the combined efforts of another bravura production job, the song's sound effects (so adroitly executed that they become the song's hook) and the "violence" monologues, which distract from the song's more self-indulgent instrumental noodling. On this track at least, Gilmour's earnest muso-ness is rather less appealing than Waters' cynicism.

31. Us And Them
(Waters, Wright)

Recorded June 1, October 1972; released on *Dark Side Of The Moon*; also on *Echoes*

Rarely has such harsh subject matter been presented in so mellow a manner as on "Us And Them". This disparity derives from Rick Wright's delicate piano chord sequence's origin as the cleverly contrasting soundtrack to the police-student violence in *Zabriskie Point*. Though unused in the film, Pink Floyd played the piece live intermittently through the early 70s as "The Violent Sequence".

Zabriskie's loss was very much *Dark Side*'s gain: exhumed at Broadhurst Gardens in late 1971, the sequence – swapped to organ – inspired a similarly contrasting Roger Waters' lyric. This concerned not just violence but the perceived differences – or contrasts – that cause it: between ordinary men on opposing sides in war (the most direct expression yet of Waters' anger about his father's death); between races (racist violence was on the increase in the early 1970s with the rise of the National Front); and between society's haves and have-nots (a more complex, implicit violence in allowing the old man to die "for want of the price of tea and a slice"). A fiercely humanist lyric then, but one delivered with contrasting dispassion by Gilmour's vocal.

Although Waters had sung lead on 1972 live versions' verses, back in the studio the verses were given to Gilmour, his smoother, more clinical delivery more sharply contrasting with the lyric than the more subjective Waters, a detachment enhanced by the distancing delay effect ("Us, us, us..."). Tackling the chorus more sweetly than disharmonious live versions, Wright and Gilmour's clipped Home Counties harmonies cool both the lyric's anger and the levitational lift of the black backing singers.

The other musical additions stick to this script. Although the saxophone is usually a warm touch, Dick Parry's gorgeous playing derives its inspiration from "cool jazz" legend **Gerry Mulligan**. Wright's own piano solo is cut from similar hotel lobby cloth, pulling against roadie **Roger the Hat**'s amiably shock-ing "short sharp shock" violence monologue. In all then, "Us And Them" is a quite brilliantly rendered study in contrasts – Pink Floyd at their creative peak.

32. Brain Damage

(Roger Waters)

Recorded June 1972–January 1973; released on *Dark Side Of The Moon*; also on *Works*

During the making of *Dark Side Of The Moon*, Rick Wright found himself unable to relate to the lyrics of "Brain Damage", and considered the track to be the album's "weakest link". In fact this empathetic invocation of Syd Barrett's condition is *Dark Side*'s emotional core and Waters could not but take Wright's disinterest personally, particularly when Wright began broadcasting his overall lack of interest in lyrics in interviews. As such, the creation of this song can be seen to contain the seeds of the pair's future falingl-out.

Doubtless the fact that "Brain Damage" is simplistic by muso, would-be-jazzer Wright's standards, was crucial in its failure to engage his sympathy. The four-chord verse is rooted in Waters' vein of folky fingerpickers, like "Grantchester Meadows" and "If" – notwithstanding the fact that, like "Breathe", its pastoralism is refracted by the pattern being played on an electric by Gilmour. But the song's music combines particularly potently with its lyrics, whose "lunatic on the grass" again refracts the riverside innocence of "Grantchester" through the fear of madness of "If". Waters had said both that the grass is a specific patch

The Music

by the Cam he was told to keep off as a child, and that the lunatic is Barrett, whose "crazed insights" Waters more than equals here in the surreal imagery of newspapers holding their faces to the floor. Equally, by extension, the lunatic is all of us.

If, despite his own mental fragility, Wright felt himself exempted from this, he didn't bunk off from the band's all-hands approach to the four-chord chorus, adding his Mini Moog and shimmering Hammond to the pile of drums,

guitar arpeggios, vocal harmonies and female backing singers. It was as if the band was grabbing the listener by the lapels to ensure an emotional response. But, *pace* Wright, it's the way the music combines with Waters' final spelling-it-out statement of empathy – "I'll see you on the dark side of the moon" – that's the key to *Dark Side Of The Moon's* success, and consequently the difference between cult attraction and commercial breakthrough.

Rick Wright at his keyboards, 1973

The Music

33. Eclipse
(Roger Waters)

Recorded June 1972–January 1973; released on *Dark Side Of The Moon*; also available on *Works*

It's hard to imagine *Dark Side Of The Moon* could ever have existed without "Eclipse", so perfect an ending is it. But "Eclipse" wasn't added until *Dark Side's* ninth performance, when Waters allegedly said to the others "here

David Gilmour kills some time with a spot of backgammon, 1973

it is, boys, I've written the ending." Bumptious as Waters was now becoming, he was so obviously correct that no one argued.

Waters has described "Eclipse" as a "*recitative* of the ideas that preceded it". While one can argue with his terminology (he means a lyrical recapitulation), one can't argue with the track's effectiveness. This lyrical summation of "Breathe", "Time", "Money", and "Us And Them" forms a mantric cycle broken only by the closing couplet in which life's positive aspects (symbolized by the sun) are eclipsed by the negative (the moon). This "depressing ending" (as Waters described it) doesn't stop the song feeling euphoric however.

Across a purposeful chorus-less, four-chord pattern, the vocal and lyric have a sheer incantatory momentum, and the Floyd pull out all the musical stops. Literally so, in the case of Wright's Hammond – it absolutely surges out of "Brain Damage". Gilmour's stately guitar arpeggios echo *Abbey Road's* "Long Medley" and a further push is added every four lines: first the backing vocalists' "oohs"; then Doris Troy letting rip; then Gilmour's harmony; finally everyone joining forces at the journey's end. "I'm only going to charge you £100 for my thing at the end," Troy quipped to an apparently frosty Floyd upon her departure. In fact they were very happy with the result. In what would prove to be a temporary mood of communal accord, "Eclipse" stands as godless gospel, a downbeat anthem, and a negative celebration – Pink Floyd in excelsis.

34. Shine On You Crazy Diamond Parts 1–5

(Gilmour, Waters, Wright)

Recorded June/July 1975; released on *Wish You Were Here*; also available on *Works* (edited version of both parts) and *Echoes*

Somewhere deep inside "Shine On You Crazy Diamond", the ghost of Pink Floyd's preposterously misconceived *Household Objects* project lurks. At 2:05 and 4:18 to be precise – where the whistling tone of multiple wine glass rims can clearly be heard amidst Wright's stately synthesized string and trumpet overture.

But it's another ghost that haunts this song more overtly. The spirit of Roger Keith Barrett had wreathed itself around *The Dark Side Of The Moon*, but it took up residence in *Wish You Were Here*. If the whole album can be seen as addressing Barrett's fate in some form or other, "Shine On" is the song that does so most directly.

Waters' lyric was written in an emotional response to Gilmour's chanced-upon, mournful four-note guitar motif that, in early versions, opened the song. It now opens "Part 2" at 3:54 (confusingly listed as "Part 3" on vinyl versions). Indeed, the topic seemed to inspire Gilmour to the best guitar of his career. After Part One's extraordinary, liquid-toned solo, the more conventional blues solo over Part Two's four-note motif adds grit; while the coolly volatile solo on Part 3 (which starts at 6:27), with its deliberately half-hit notes, carefully manipulated string-catches (a recurring open G from 8:16) and oozing feedback, bring the instru-

mental section to a spectacular climax. While Gilmour's work here is rooted in blues, its tone shimmers with a kind of elegant passion that is very "white". The over-amped nuances of his playing – every strike of his plectrum seemingly audible – essays a kind of chamber earthiness: blues without mess, emotion without tears. A very Floydian series of conundra.

Equally, the ensuing vocal section (Part Four, from 8:52) manages to be simultaneously passionate and poetically detached. Both eulogy and elegy, Waters' lyric undoubtedly proffers sympathy, reaching its apogee in the lines from the vocal reprise – its "pile on many more layers and I'll be joining you there" being this album's "I'll see you on the dark side", its empathetic emotional peak. And, as on "Brain Damage", the closer Waters gets to Barrett in terms of subject matter, the closer he gets to him artistically – the lyrics of "Shine On" being an absolute triumph. Unsurprisingly, given both Waters' personality and his personal history with Barrett, there's also an underlying flintiness to the words, however. "Random precision" is an oxymoron that suggests the method in Barrett's madness, while the rest of the line makes it clear that the invocation of the chorus is certainly not an invitation to rejoin the band. Indeed, from the Floyd's reaction when Barrett really *did* return to Abbey Road – during the recording of this very track – they didn't wish the real Barrett was there at all. Which, if you think about it, is quite unimaginably sad.

Taking a rare lead vocal turn, Waters' vulnerable yet faintly sardonic singing does his lyric proud (however many hours of studio time it may have taken to achieve). In the post-Waters Floyd, Gilmour would struggle to convey the song's passionate detachment without sounding either sentimental or clinical. The baritone sax solo is a neat concluding touch, its intricate dazzle of notes managing simultaneously to suggest shining and fading away.

The Floyd made a sensible decision in splitting this track in two: "Parts 1–5" ("Part 1" on recent CDs) is by far the stronger, almost every note rivetingly relevant, before less focused jamming takes over on "Parts 6–9". If the only flaw in "Part 1" therefore is the dated sound of some of Wright's keyboard parts (particularly the fruity **Moog French horn** on "Part 3"), then it's a small quibble, and still a quite unimaginable improvement on the sound of twanging, plunking *Household Objects*.

35. Welcome To The Machine
(Roger Waters)

Recorded July 1975; released on *Wish You Were Here*

It's conventionally held that when musicians start writing about the music industry, they've lost the plot. If so, plot loss has never sounded so pleasing as with late-period Pink Floyd, two out of four songs on *Wish You Were Here* addressing the music industry (three if you count "Shine On"), with "Welcome To The Machine" being one of the album's highlights.

If quite how the idea of musicians and fans being cogs in the music industry machine fits into Waters' stated theme of "absence" is somewhat fuzzy ("there but not there"?), the song itself is anything but. Gilmour's echoing VCS3 throb renders the machine concept musical (and provides the song rhythmic backbone) while sounding for all the world like a giant fan oven, complete with buzzing timer. Flitting across the stereo spectrum between Wright's steely electronic sound-washes, Gilmour's acoustic guitar acts as vulnerable, human, contrast (**ABBA** would soon use the same sonic cold/hot trick on 1977's "Knowing Me, Knowing You").

Amidst all this, it takes time to realize it's not Waters singing but Gilmour: two vocal lines, an octave apart, the higher being at the ragged edge of Gilmour's range so that – with a delicious irony – he was forced to seek mechanical help to hit the notes. As for the lyrics, they're Waters' second full-on cynical assault. Taking the voice of the omniscient "Machine" the lyrics steelily and sardonically describe/create the life/fantasy of the rock star/Pink Floyd fan.

Quite unlike anything they'd done before, "Machine" is an intimation of Waters' work to come: a bitter lyric and deranged vocal married to a crushingly simple two-chord line. You can almost hear Wright's muso sniff. Nevertheless, the keyboardist's work here is crucial, leaving prog behind for something approaching krautrock's **VCS3** experiments and 90s listening techno: coldly angry, spaciously claustrophobic and balefully beautiful.

The Music

36. Wish You Were Here

(Waters, Gilmour)

Recorded July 1975; released on *Wish You Were Here*; also available on *A Collection of Great Dance Songs*; *Echoes*

The only Pink Floyd song to become a buskers' favourite, such is the country-tinged immediacy of "Wish You Were Here" that it also influenced the very West Coast wellspring it drew from (The Eagles' "Hotel California") whilst even eliciting a cover from hip-hop eclectic Wyclef Jean, positioning the band squarely in the musical mainstream.

And yet the song is also archetypal Pink Floyd: that instantly memorable acoustic riff being heard first through a tinny transistor radio, distorted and mechanized; then the rare acoustic solo that suddenly emerges being typically Gilmour in spaciousness and nuance, plectrum audibly knocking wood.

Abetted by acoustic piano and acoustic slide, "Wish" is also the pinnacle of Pink Floyd's longstanding pastoral style, nostalgia absolutely infusing Gilmour's husky, warmly wistful singing. If this unalloyed warmth again is rare, so is the passionate, irony-free lyric. And yet it's still suffused with Floydian enigma and familiar obsessions. At **Live 8**, Waters dedicated the song to "everyone who's not here, but particularly for Syd" and while its lines about "a lead role in a cage" suggest the isolated singer, its ambiguous questions about authenticity and fakery more could be seen as being addressed to Waters' wool-gathering colleagues. Or, as Waters suggests, it could be an internal dialogue, the misanthrope calling for the humanist, "to search within [himself] for the empathetic part, to fight the desire to drive other people off the road".

Ultimately what emerges from the song's absolute symbiosis of lyric, music and performance is a plea for comradeship, for connection, which – in the world beyond its ironically, increasingly estranged co-authors – unironically and unambiguously achieved its aim.

37. Dogs

(Gilmour, Waters)

Recorded April–December 1976, released on *Animals*

Back in the mid-60s, lodging in manager Andrew King's house, Roger Waters used to terrorize King's cats with what he called "big bird practice" – essentially, leaping on them when they least expected it. "He said it would toughen them up," says King. "Roger always believed everyone needed toughening up."

As such, though apparently a condemnation of ruthless corporate-climbers – what would soon be termed "yuppies" – "Dogs" is actually a considerably more complex beast. The competitive, hard-carapaced Waters probably wasn't being entirely sarcastic in the song's opening verses' predatory, dog-eat-dog survival manual. That Gilmour, despite being increasingly annoyed by this very pushiness of Waters, sings these lyrics with such soul is key to the song's appeal. For Waters' lyric doesn't just relish the nastiness, it also expresses sympathy for its protagonist's ultimate fate: the sad, cancer-ridden old man who is "dragged

The Music

down by the stone" – that personal Waters' perennial. That Waters later calls himself a "dog" in "Pigs On The Wing (Part 2)" makes the situation plain: "Dogs", with its otherwise incoherent shifts from first to second person, is essentially Waters' internal dialogue, another push and pull between the humanist and the misanthrope, and thus a direct sequel to "Wish You Were Here".

This heavy weight is carried with surprising lightness by the music. Gilmour's breezily intricate chord sequence – simultaneously jazzy and folky – is one of the most fluid and engaging in the Floyd discography, while also possessed of a haunting depth. Gilmour also contributes some of his best lead guitar work: a melodic solo at 2:00 and a beautifully expressive melody on the slower section from 3:42 suggestive of **Fleetwood Mac**'s "Albatross". For his pains, the synthesized barking and whining that begins at 4:54 sounds like a dig at Gilmour's "Seamus", though the guitarist's insouciant evocation of a dog's whine (at 6:19) suggests he's tough enough to take it. There's more synthetic barking on the mesmeric middle section (from 7:59), a series of keening synth-lines being the one moment the very far from tough **Rick Wright** is allowed to shine on the album. The ensuing lines' assertions concerning people's expendability, and the illusory nature of friendship, must have struck him sharply in retrospect.

As the song returns to Gilmour's jazzy sequence, Waters takes over the vocals, premiering his future style, which abandons his lower register to make an inverted virtue of an inability to hit the high notes, sounding slightly deranged. With the lyrics also more self-doubting and vulnerable now, there's no sacrifice of soulfulness, particularly when the song returns to the lush, layered "Albatross" section, Waters now singing an almost liturgical lyric, a repeated "who was…" formulation which echoes **Allen Ginsberg**'s poem *Howl*. It's a brilliant ending, climaxing in an entirely appropriate howl of feedback from Gilmour.

No member (or variant of) Pink Floyd would ever attempt anything on the scale of "Dogs" again. Only Waters would even *play* it again, and even then not until 2000. Gilmour declared it not one of his real favourites, while compilations neglect it altogether. It's a shame, for the complex and majestic "Dogs" is very far from being a dog.

38. Sheep
(Roger Waters)
Recorded April, May and July 1976; released on *Animals*

Animals can sometimes seem like an extended joke at Pink Floyd fans' expense. Caricaturing "Seamus" on "Dogs", while cynically recycling "Cigar" on "Pigs", and "One Of These Days" on "Sheep", in its 1974 Tour incarnation as "Raving and Drooling", "Sheep" had seemed a direct attack on the stoner fans picked up post-*Dark Side*.

Dusting the track down to fit the new *Animals* concept two years later, Waters widened his crosshairs to target the masses as a whole. Evincing no sympathy for them as they willingly file off to the slaughter, it even implies

David Gilmour, *Animals* tour, 1977

that their ultimate uprising in the song's final verse is merely the conformist's cud-chewing fantasy. As such "Sheep" perfectly demonstrates Waters' ongoing philosophical dilemma: a human-scorning humanist, a socially-isolated socialist, "connecting" with an audience with whom he felt no connection.

Indicative of this scorn, "Sheep" is one of Waters' most poorly-crafted songs, not only lazily re-using "One Of These Days" bass-line and chord sequence but herding new words so randomly into the tune's new, one-chord "chorus" that it's only Waters' bloody-minded vocal bravura that makes this torrent of inconsistent-length lines and random rhyme-schemes work. And if, instead of the *Dr Who* re-run of "Raving", "Sheep" has the clever idea of caricaturing Pink Floyd's pastoral moments (a *pastorale* being, classically, a poem supposedly recited by a shepherd), it is executed a trifle tokenistically: a dab of Wright's "Western Theme" electric piano alongside bleating sheep at the start; some of the Floyd's favourite sound library birdsong at the end; while inbetween, the 23rd Psalm pastiche ("the Lord is my shepherd") is – somewhat pointlessly – largely inaudible.

Despite all this, "Sheep" remains compelling: Gilmour's pounding bass riff, Waters' savage vocal and Gilmour's slashing guitar work, which climaxes in an absolute riot of ringing chords. Like the masses it describes, "Sheep" may not be pretty or clever, but it's a powerful force to be reckoned with.

39. In the Flesh?

(Roger Waters)

Recorded April–November 1979; available on *The Wall*

"Alienation Effect' was 1920s playwright **Bertolt Brecht**'s technique of highlighting the artificiality of performance – using masks, songs and direct audience addresses – in order to alert minds to the realities of power, and to focus them on his anti-fascist political message.

Redeployed in rock, such a technique is often undermined by the sheer brain-bypassing power of music. Does anyone truly trouble themselves with the distancing quotation marks on **David Bowie**'s "Heroes" or the intended mocking obviousness of **Nirvana**'s "Smells Like Teen Spirit" riff? With fans already missing the irony in Pink Floyd calling their disengaged 1977 stadium tour In The Flesh, Waters' alienated addition of a question mark to this audience-addressing song doesn't exactly help him to make his point, and the "ironic" deployment of an uncharactersistic heavy rock demotic probably even hinders him.

For there's a pure, visceral thrill to Gilmour's primal guitar riff, to the dual attack of the doubled-drum kit, to the simmering tension in the slower vocal sections, and to Waters' hysterical climactic shouts ("roll the sound-effects!"); while there's no irony in Bob Ezrin's production, an American density of sound that pummels the note-for-note Britannia Row demo to a Limey pulp. Even when Waters sarcastically plays up the inherent "fascism" of the rock spectacle in the song's reprise, many still, apparently failed to realise he wasn't being serious.

So, just to hammer the point home, at the ensuing *Wall* shows Waters had the song performed by session musicians in Brecht-ian Floyd facemasks, the "real" Floyd appearing behind them at its conclusion. The "point", presumably, is that his audience are unable to tell the real deal from the money-motivated motions. Small wonder most "failed" to fully understand it.

40. The Thin Ice
(Roger Waters)
Recorded April–November 1979; available on *The Wall*

Songs about the writer's children are usually mawkishly sentimental affairs, flooring even once tough guys like **John Lennon** ("Beautiful Boy"), Paul Weller ("Moon On Your Pyjamas"), Liam Gallagher ("Little James") and Eminem ("Hailie's Song").

But not Roger Waters, whose first song since becoming a father was anything but mawkish, bordering, in fact, almost on mordant glee. From "Embryo", through the cycle of life songs on *The Body* to "Breathe", children in Pink Floyd are presented as blank slates upon which the world will scrawl obscenities given half the chance. "The Thin Ice" is in fact, lyrically, almost a rehash of "Breathe". The first verse – sung by Gilmour from the off, presumably because Waters couldn't convey its tenderness – invokes parents' love for their newborn child, but the cautionary note of "Breathe" is here even stronger. By Waters' delivery of the second verse, it is less cautionary than sardoni-

cally pessimistic, implying that slipping out of one's depth – and one's mind – is inevitable.

Musically much simpler than "Breathe", "The Thin Ice" is nevertheless highly effective: from its lullaby first verse, through its snappier second verse, propelled by choppy piano chords (**Bob Ezrin** depping for the absent Wright), to the marvellous melodramatic entry of Gilmour's mammoth guitar riff, relentless and grinding as the Grim Reaper. Going from birth to death in a mere two-and-a-half minutes "The Thin Ice" doesn't offer young Pink much of an innings. Looks like fatherhood hadn't mellowed Roger Waters much then.

41. Another Brick in the Wall Part 2
(Roger Waters)
Recorded April–November 1979; released as single on WHEN and on *The Wall, A Collection Of Great Dance Songs* and *Echoes*

As befits a song about education, "Another Brick in the Wall Part 2" is simultaneously gifted and remedial. Top of the class is Bob Ezrin. It was the producer who underlined Waters' lunkhead melody with a guitar-line whose almost comic insistence evokes the bouncing ball on singalong TV shows. It was Ezrin who blended the voices of Waters and Gilmour into an *über* Floyd voice, an indivisible unity between a warring pair possible only on a recording. It was Ezrin who added the disco beat, created a second verse by looping the first in the Floyd's absence, and hit upon the idea of children singing – a classic pop touch in

The Music

the school of **Alice Cooper**'s similarly-themed "School's Out" (another Ezrin production), **Keith West**'s "Excerpt From A Teenage Opera" and **Clive Dunn**'s lamentable "Grandad".

The remedial elements are mostly Waters' work. If the double-negatives are deliberate, teacher-baiting bad grammar, the rhyme of

A Gerald Scarfe puppet from the 1980 *Wall* tour

"control" with "alone" brings to mind the line in "School's Out" boasting of not being able to think up a word that rhymes" – only without bothering with the wit. The mis-stressing of 'sar-*cas*-um' meanwhile is just simple bad craftsmanship. As his derided teachers doubtless would have said: "could do better". While remedial lyrics are themselves a classic pop touch ("A Wop Bop A Loo Bop" etc), at six lines, "Another Brick" must have the least lyrics of any #1 in pop history outside instrumentals, which makes it, of course, instantly memorable.

A further piece of giftedness is left to the last minute however: Gilmour's guitar solo. A cleverly out-of-context return to the liquid style of "Echoes" and "Shine On", played on his 1959 Gibson Goldtop, its dexterity, melodicism and limpid, latex-esque note-stretches (perfect for **Gerald Scarfe**'s video's cartoon footage) absolutely lifts the song, and almost alone takes it from being a Floyd staple to a Floyd classic.

42. Hey You!

(Roger Waters)

Recorded April–November 1979; available on *The Wall* and *Echoes*

The consummate "good cop/bad cop" routine, David Gilmour's and Roger Waters' contrasting styles became, on *The Wall*, the band's essence. If the light and dark, soothing and alarming, sane and deranged contrasts of their vocal styles appear to prefer Gilmour, then everyone knows that, in rock'n'roll, of all media, the dark is just as important as the light.

For "Hey You', like "Wish You Were Here" and "Dogs", directly addresses that battle between the light and darkness within Waters' own personality: the humanist, still hopeful of human contact, and the isolated, despairing cynic. As such, Gilmour's vocal adds a genuine wistfulness to the opening verses. He's backed by his own delicate acoustic guitar (given real sparkle by Ezrin's pristine production) and his curiously yearning fretless bass. "Bad cop" Waters then returns, in the middle eight, to dismiss such pleas as "fantasy" (bizarrely mangling the word's pronunciation in the process), before his last verse re-voices the opening verses' humanism ("together we stand, divided we fall") in tones so hysterical as to dispel any hope.

"Hey You" is marred only by a slightly routine Gilmour guitar solo over an ominous rendering of the "Another Brick" riff. Though written by Waters, the song is another testament to his and Gilmour's collaborative strength, one reflected in its regular resurrection in the set-lists of the Gilmour Floyd.

43. Nobody Home
(Roger Waters)
Recorded April–November 1979; available on *The Wall*

Deriving from the colloquial name for the late 19th century professional songwriting district of West 28th Street, New York, the term "Tin Pan Alley" has subsequently been applied to any professionally-crafted, pre-rock'n'roll music. Roger Waters has long possessed a rare-in-rock ability to work to order. "Nobody Home", created to meet David Gilmour's demand for more substance in *The Wall*'s third quarter, is a brilliant example. And one which, aptly enough, has more than a suggestion of the Tin Pan Alley about it – a piano-based torch song that shares with **Randy Newman**'s work an air of acerbic show-tune. To this is matched one of Waters' career-best lyrics. Ostensibly referring to narrator Pink's attempts to contact his estranged wife, the phrase "Nobody Home" also refers to Pink's own catatonic condition, and, more resonantly still, recalls **Joe Boyd**'s description of Syd Barrett back in 1967 – "It was like somebody had pulled the blinds – you know, nobody home." Indeed, the song's personality profile is pure Barrett: the elastic bands keeping his shoes on, the 60s hipster Gohills boots, "the obligatory Hendrix perm", and, most of all, those "wild staring eyes".

The subject of Syd Barrett always re-connects Waters to his humanity, and "Nobody Home" produces one of the bassist's best vocals. The verse sticks to his lower, Dylanesque register, sounding simultaneously sad and sardonic, rising to hysterical upper pitch for the chorus, before lapsing back to a shrugging baritone for the title line. A brilliant performance is perfected by the album's best sound-effects, evoking the "13 channels of shit on the TV" in Pink's hotel room. Indeed, the climactic deployment of **Jim Nabors**' 60s *Gomer Pyle Show* catchphrase "surprise, surprise, surprise" at 3:00 is amongst the best use of sound-effects in rock. An argument for perspiration over inspiration if ever there was one.

The Music

44. Comfortably Numb

(Waters, Gilmour)

Recorded April–November 1979; released on *The Wall*;
also available on *Echoes*

Although Pink Floyd can often appear curmudgeonly, it's worth noting that, unlike **Led Zeppelin**, they have never rejected or refused to play their signature song. And if ever there were a signature Pink Floyd song, it is "Comfortably Numb". Remaining rightly proud of it, all permutations of Pink Floyd, and both of its authors, have included it in every set-list since its creation, right up to choosing it to climax their Live 8 reunion.

Musically, "Comfortably Numb" is signature Pink Floyd for its rich harmonies, its gliding 4/4 pace and its two astonishing Gilmour guitar solos. It is also signature at this stage of the Floyd's career for the complementary contrast of its co-writers' voices. Gilmour plays the catatonic Pink, unable to perform, yearning for the simplicities of childhood; Waters, playing the dodgy doctor, is sardonic and a little threatening, cynically pumping his million-dollar patient with drugs to get him through the show.

While the lyric is suffused with Waters' own experience (a close encounter with a Doctor Feelgood in Philadelphia) it also, in equally signature Floydian manner, touches strongly on the spectre of Roger K. Barrett. Specifically the latter's withdrawal prior to July 1967's International Love-In at Alexandra Palace – right down to the voice calling "time to go" at the knocking door. But the sense of enigma,

of the mysterious, of the not-quite-grasped is pure *post*-Barrett Floyd. Intangible and slipping from view, but – like that "distant ship smoke" – all the more haunting for it, it is quite rightly described by Bob Ezrin as "one of the greatest lyrics ever written to a song".

Sadly, "Comfortably Numb" is also signature Floyd in that its authorship is hotly contested. Waters excommunicated a friend who attributed the entire song to Gilmour in print, while Gilmour flatly contradicts Waters' claims to have co-authored the music. For what it's worth, Gilmour's demo suggests he provided the melody for the chorus and the chords for the verse, while Waters wrote the lyric and the verse's vocal melody. As Mason says, "there's never enough credit to go round", and the *point* is the level of investment both parties have in the song.

For similar reasons, the pair bickered about the arrangement from the beginning. Predictably Waters preferred a looser take, Gilmour a tighter – Ezrin finally simply spliced the two together. To make an educated guess, the loose version lasts to the end of the first guitar solo (2:45). It's used in full in the film's soundtrack, wherein Mason's dragging beat and Waters' two bass fumbles immediately before the climactic solo lessen the dramatic impact.

But if Gilmour was right on this point, he was wrong in his desire for a bare-bones backing and a grungier guitar sound. For the orchestration is just perfect – dreamy and nostalgic – and if Gilmour's first solo is glorious, his second is guitar nirvana, with just the right degree

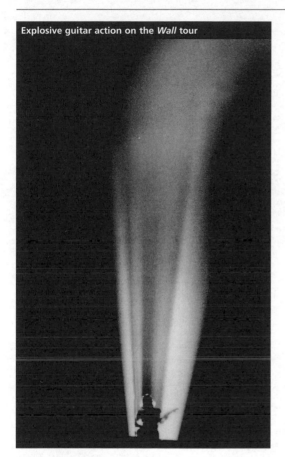

Explosive guitar action on the *Wall* tour

The Music

45. Run Like Hell
(Waters, Gilmour)

Recorded April–November 1979; released on *The Wall*;
also available on *Echoes*

When **John Lydon** paraded around in a "I Hate Pink Floyd" T-shirt in 1976, it would have been impossible to imagine that a mere three years later, these two opposing poles should find themselves on a similar musical alignment. **Public Image Ltd**'s July 1979 UK hit, "Death Disco" was the most commercially successful of a number of new wave disco subversions from bands such as **Gang of Four** and **Throbbing Gristle**, the song later giving its name to an entire 21st-century subgenre. Strangely, in the same year, Pink Floyd produced "Run Like Hell", a similar subversion of that most feelgood of all genres.

It was actually Bob Ezrin's idea to add the disco beat, despite Gilmour's distaste for the genre ("gawd awful") to a track originating, like "Comfortably Numb", from Gilmour's demos for his previous year's solo album. Reflecting this positioning, it's a clear development of Gilmour's crashing chordal work at the climax of "Sheep", and of the solo album's "Short and Sweet" (both tunes have the guitar's bottom E-string tuned down to a D).

But though the instrumental Britannia Row version was already slightly creepy, the lyrics Waters added in France were positively crazed. Making it the manifesto of the drug-addled, fascistic Pink as he and his heavies go on the rampage, Waters topped this with his most hysterically outré vocal, Gilmour's breathless

of grit against sheer swooning sweetness, a solo as memorably melodic as a vocal chorus.

Exuding menace and yearning in equal measures, "Comfortably Numb" is subtly, serenely colossal, Pink Floyd's very own "Stairway to Heaven" – but one that, for all their snootiness, for all their distance, Pink Floyd are never going to deny their audience.

"run run run"s adding additional urgency (unusual in a Pink Floyd song), both made the more dramatic by being drenched in dizzyingly cyclical reverb.

As such "Run Like Hell" provided a crucial enlivening of *The Wall's* somewhat leaden last quarter, and would be a regular in post-Waters set-lists. It also inspired Ezrin to redeploy the disco trick on "Another Brick In The Wall Part 2" to still mildly subversive, but considerably more commercial ends.

46. The Post-War Dream
(Roger Waters)

Recorded June–December 1982; released on *The Final Cut*

Look up "the post-war dream" on Google, and all you get is Pink Floyd links. Though this says a lot about the cultural impact of Pink Floyd, it's also rather sad that Roger Waters' song has so eclipsed its subject matter. For servicemen like Waters' father, who began as a conscientious objector but then volunteered, World War II was fought for a better world, a notion which developed such strength for a battered nation that, at the war's end, the Conservative Prime Minister **Winston Churchill** was swept from office in a landslide victory for a Labour government dedicated to a vast programme of social reform.

In this overture to the album, a newsreader reports that the contract to replace *Atlantic Conveyor*, sunk during the Falklands conflict, has gone to Japan rather than to the Clyde's struggling shipbuilding industry. Against

Michael Kamen's very British-sounding brass, redolent both of coal pits and the Proms, Waters ponders these events and demands of British Prime Minister **Margaret Thatcher** "what happened to the post-war dream?"

Even thirty years on, such bald political statements are startling in a Pink Floyd record. Where's the enigma? But that's the thing: even here Waters manages to summon up mysterious, irrational feelings in the listener, particularly through the climactic, questioning plea, which remains spine-tingling stuff long after its specific political issues became irrelevant. The only complaint really is why, on such an English album, Waters felt compelled to retain his American accent ("Eng-luhnd") making his questions sound curiously anomalous.

47. Your Possible Pasts
(Roger Waters)

Recorded June–December 1982; released on *The Final Cut*

The past and the present constantly act upon each other, modifying our perception of both. In 1999, **Marianne Faithfull** released a song called "Incarceration Of A Flower Child". Credited to Roger Waters, it boasted a chorus curiously similar to 1982's "Your Possible Pasts", but Faithfull claimed that it harked back even further into Waters' past, written back in 1968 about Syd Barrett.

If this is not a case of Waters modifying *his* possible pasts, it certainly sheds some light on "Your Possible Pasts". At the time of its release, the song appeared to be tracing the *Final Cut's* teacher/hero's survival of his (possible) past as war casualty only to find himself alienated and unloved in the 1980s, albeit in so elliptical a fashion as to be almost impenetrable. Listened to now, the song appears to be articulating Waters' "there-but-for-fortune-go-I" empathy for Barrett's condition: the possible pasts that are "wild eyed and crazy … frightened and lost" suddenly leaping to life like recovered memories. The lines about sexual guilt could thus apply as equally to Waters' and Barrett's austere 1940s upbringing as the song's hero's, while the questions of the chorus – nostalgic, and tinged with regret and a tiny hint of the accusatory – could refer equally to the hero's or Waters' estranged wife, to Waters' then estranged band-mates, or indeed to Syd Barrett.

This multi-layered suggestiveness helps make "Pasts" the most classically Floydian cut on *The Final Cut*, aided by Mason's plodding drum fills, a all-stops-out chorus, **Andy Bown**'s spooky Rick Wright impression on Hammond and a consummate soaring Dave Gilmour guitar solo. As such, surely Gilmour's unaccountably poor opinion of "Your Possible Pasts" is itself due for some modification?

48. The Gunners Dream
(Roger Waters)

Recorded June–December 1982; released on *The Final Cut*

He might be no one's idea of a technically-accomplished singer, but one thing is undeniable: no one screams quite like Roger Waters, from "Pow R" to "Eugene", from "Another Brick" to "Comfortably Numb". But perhaps his best is the scream that occurs near the end of "The Gunners Dream", on the almost sociopathically elongated word "insane".

For the rest of the song, Waters' vocal is surprisingly restrained, considering the closeness to home of the lyric. For the Gunner is surely Waters' father, his dream the post-war dream. The "corner of some foreign field" that he inhabits echoes the words of Cambridge war poet **Rupert Brookes** ("there is a corner of some foreign field that is forever England"). And as the Gunner watches his family at a Remembrance Day service, Waters produces some of the most vivid and moving words of his career, fashioning a wintry poetry out of a slow walk to the car, using tiny details such as the catching of the light on silver hair, and the feel of the silk in a smart suit.

As the Gunner now invokes the dream for which he died, it's increasingly undercut not just by Waters' magnificently moronic background shouting but the brutal reality of the bandsmen being blown up is a reference to the IRA's Hyde Park bombing of 1981. Then, after a sax solo by **Rafael "Baker Street" Ravenscroft**, the song's protagonist suddenly switches to Waters himself, his voice becoming increasingly hysterical until he hits that final screamed "insane". The word carries on through the calmer, more hopeful lyrics of the conclusion, seemingly mocking their naïve impossibility.

The Music

49. Not Now John
(Roger Waters)
Recorded June–December 1982; released on *The Final Cut* and as a single

The reputation of Pink Floyd as a band not renowned for their sense of humour nowadays pains Pink Floyd's former conceptualist. "I may have been pissed off", Waters says, "but I was always deeply involved in the humour of all the situations."

"Not Now John" is a perfect example. There shouldn't be many laughs in a song about the decline of British industrial power, but if getting a phalanx of female soul singers to chorus "fuck all that" wasn't funny enough, Waters' chant of "clickety click, hold on, oh no, bingo!" has an acidly acerbic effervescence, while his climactic send-up of xenophobic Brits is as funny for its seething class snobbery as its actual accuracy.

But perhaps the funniest aspect of "Not Now John" is the way Waters hands over the vocal of *The Final Cut*'s self-critique to its most vocal critic. For, in his sole vocal on the album, David Gilmour gets to say "fuck all that" to the whingeing about the state of the world, and urge getting on with the job. Although barely speaking, Gilmour and Waters make a quite brilliant comic double act, Waters' own vocal regularly popping back up, like some insistent coat-grabbing irritant from Floyd favourites **Monty Python**, before Gilmour punches back in with another bilious, expletive-venting verse.

Gilmour, sadly, appears not to have got it –

or perhaps got it only too well – having no love for the song. Sadly, the public felt the same, with a censored version ("*stuff* all that") struggling to #30 in the UK charts. Nevertheless, "Not Now John" serves as a very funny farewell to the Waters era.

50. Wearing The Inside Out
(Wright, Moore)
Recorded January 1993–July 1994; released on *The Division Bell*

Whatever happened to Rick Wright? Once pegged as the band's likely leader after Syd Barrett's departure, then a vocal and compositional level-pegger with Roger Waters, by 1975 Wright was mute, by 1977 compositionally dry, and by 1979 so disengaged he was pushed out of the band he co-founded.

This song, Wright's first Floyd vocal for 21 years, and the utterly unexpected highlight of 1994's *The Division Bell*, provides some of the answers. Elliptically so, of course (it being the Floyd), and by using outside help (it being the *1990s* Floyd), but old Blackhill cohort **Anthony Moore** does a marvellously empathetic job of articulating Wright's experience. Which appears to amount to a morbid withdrawal, and an inability to function socially, let alone assert himself against bullish bass-players. Indeed the line "this bleeding heart's not beating much" sounds like a tender upending of a favourite, visceral phrase of Waters. Indeed, without interference from Gilmour, the lyric manages to be delicate without dulling any sharp edges.

The song's music repeats this delicate/edgy trick, enhanced by some brilliantly breathy sax from old pal Dick Parry, plus two splendidly abrasive Gilmour guitar solos. And it's a delight to hear Wright sing again, wistful and gentle as ever – age giving his voice the conversational quality of another old friend of theirs, **Robert Wyatt**. Brilliantly intertwining with the female backing vocals (courtesy of **Sam Brown, Durga McBroom, Carol Kenyon, Jackie Sheridan** and **Rebecca Leigh White**) and with a verse sung by Gilmour, the effect is gently warm, effacingly empathetic, and subtly communal. If Waters didn't feel left out, he should have.

The spectacle that was Pink Floyd live, in Chantilly Park, 1994

Soundtracks, compilations & bootlegs

Note: both *More* and *The Wall* are reviewed in the Albums section proper.

Soundtracks

Tonite Let's All Make Love In London (OST)

INTERSTELLAR OVERDRIVE [FULL LENGTH VERSION]/ MICHAEL CAINE/CHANGING OF THE GUARD/MARQUESS OF KENSINGTON (INTERVIEW)/NIGHT TIME GIRL (TWICE AS MUCH)/"DOLLY BIRD" INTERVIEW/ OUT OF TIME (CHRIS FARLOWE)/EDNA O'BRIEN INTERVIEW/INTERSTELLAR OVERDRIVE (REPRISE)/ANDREW LOOG OLDHAM INTERVIEW/ WINTER IS BLUE (VASHTI)/ANDREW LOOG OLDHAM INTERVIEW/WINTER IS BLUE (REPRISE) (VASHTI)/MICK JAGGER INTERVIEW/JULIE CHRISTIE INTERVIEW/MICHAEL CAINE INTERVIEW/PAINT IT BLACK (CHRIS FARLOWE/ALAN ALDRIDGE INTERVIEW/PAINT IT BLACK [INSTRUMENTAL REPRISE] (CHRIS FARLOWE)/DAVID HOCKNEY/HERE COMES THE NICE (SMALL FACES)/LEE MARVIN (INTERVIEW)/ INTERSTELLAR OVERDRIVE (REPRISE)/TONITE LET'S ALL MAKE LOVE IN LONDON (ALLEN GINSBERG)/NICK'S BOOGIE
Recorded January 1967; released July 19 1968; reissued on See For Miles CD 1990

Two Pink Floyd tracks were included in **Peter Whitehead**'s 1967 attempt to capture the Swinging London scene on film. The documentary's original vinyl soundtrack album featured acts from **Rolling Stones** manager **Andrew Loog Oldham**'s Immediate label (all readily available elsewhere, bar Vashti – aka

Vashti Bunyan, over whom a small cult would form in the 2000s), alongside interviews with celebrity scenesters like **Julie Christie, Michael Caine** and **Mick Jagger,** plus snippets from two specially recorded Pink Floyd songs. The 1990 CD reissue added the full-length versions of both tunes but remains a thoroughly unsatisfying listen – the tracks best purchased on the *In London* CD/DVD.

In London 1966–1967

INTERSTELLAR OVERDRIVE/NICK'S BOOGIE
See For Miles; Recorded January 1967; released 1999

The best way of obtaining Pink Floyd's studio performances for *Tonite Let's All Make Love,* sans extraneous baggage, and with the benefit of DVD footage of the band recording the tracks at **Sound Techniques,** intercut with (unheard) performances at **UFO** and the **14 Hour Technicolor Dream.** "Interstellar Overdrive" is a sprawling 16-minute version which lacks the power of Barrett's guitar riff in the *Piper* cut, while Rick Wright's organ still possesses a rinky dink, fairground feel which falls short of psychedelia. "Nick's Boogie" is more of the same, but slightly less focused. The visuals reflect a similarly half-formed psychedelic act: Barrett every inch the psychedelic princeling, Mason looking like he should be scrumping apples while playing truant from some expensive prep school, while Waters, in blue shades and stripey trousers. looks like he's just bought a tourist's psychedelic kit in Carnaby Street.

Zabriskie Point (OST)

HEART BEAT, PIG MEAT (THE PINK FLOYD)/BROTHER MARY (THE KALEIDOSCOPE)/DARK STAR (EXCERPT) (THE GRATEFUL DEAD)/CRUMBLING LAND (THE PINK FLOYD)/TENNESSEE WALTZ (PATTI PAGE)/SUGAR BABE (THE YOUNGBLOODS)/ LOVE SCENE (JERRY GARCIA)/I WISH I WAS A SINGLE GIRL AGAIN (ROSCOE HOLCOMB)/MICKEY'S TUNE (THE KALEIDOSCOPE)/DANCE OF DEATH (JOHN FAHEY)/COME IN NUMBER 51, YOUR TIME IS UP (THE PINK FLOYD) LOVE SCENE IMPROVISATION VERSION 1/2/3/4 (JERRY GARCIA)/COUNTRY SONG (THE PINK FLOYD)/UNKNOWN SONG (THE PINK FLOYD)/LOVE SCENE – VERSION 6 (THE PINK FLOYD)/LOVE SCENE – VERSION 4 (THE PINK FLOYD)
Rhino Records; Recorded November/December 1969; released: May 30, 1970; Re-released on CD with additional tracks1997; available on CD

Michelangelo Antonioni's attempt to capture the Californian counterculture at its fist-clenching, free-loving apotheosis, gave Pink Floyd a crucial opportunity to address a hitherto-elusive American audience.

This explains, for a start, the Floyd going country-rock on "Crumbling Land": it's an attempt to speak both the film's language and – crucially – America's language. Although "Crumbling Land", complete with street noise

recorded by Mason in Rome, was used in the film, the self-explanatory "Country Song" (aka "Red Queen Theme" on bootlegs) was rejected in favour of tracks by Californian acts with greater country credentials. You can see Antonioni's point. But hearing "Country Song" on the 1997 reissue, the track's folk-to-guitar-freakout trajectory is revealed as another important step for the Floyd, prefiguring both "Biding My Time" and "Fat Old Sun", whilst also marking Gilmour's first Floyd use of country staple the pedal-steel guitar, which would play a key part in future work (from "One of These Days" and "Breathe" to the second half of "Shine On") and a rare outing for his throaty vocal style on the chorus. What's more, Gilmour and Wright's harmonies on "Crumbling Land" reveal a West Coast influence (reminiscent of **Crosby Stills & Nash**, whose debut was released that May) that would become a crucial component in the records that ultimately broke them Stateside. Something else that'd come in useful later was the tape collage instrumental "Heart Beat Pig Meat", the "heartbeat" created by Mason with a padded beater recurring on *Dark Side*.

Conversely, two other cuts find the Floyd reusing earlier material: "Come In Number 51 Your Time Is Up" is a rather fine remake of "Careful With That Axe Eugene" (up a tone; less falsetto; more screams); "Unknown Song", (aka "Rain in the Country" on bootlegs), is a remake of Gilmour's finger-picked acoustic instrumental "The Narrow Way Part 1" (with just a hint of the funk of "Atom Heart Mother" section "Funky Dung").

Of the other unreleased material, "Love Scene Version 6" is a fairly uninspiring slow blues jam – anything but erotic, but "Love Scene Version 4" is a lovely solo Wright piano piece with a sort of classical jazz feel. There was another Wright piano piece recorded for this soundtrack but never used, the fabled "The Violent Sequence" (which would have sound-tracked the movie's riots on the UCLA campus) later morphing into "Us and Them". The Floyd's continued refusal to release this track even on this reissue seems curmudgeonly in the extreme, as does the absence of other bootleg staples such as "Fingal's Cave" and "Oneone". Still, this album is near essential for Floyd fans as an intriguing clue to future paths, particularly those that led to America.

Is There Anybody Out There? – The Wall Live

MC: ATMOS/IN THE FLESH?/THE THIN ICE/ANOTHER BRICK IN THE WALL – PART 1/ THE HAPPIEST DAYS OF OUR LIVES/ ANOTHER BRICK IN THE WALL – PART 2/MOTHER/GOODBYE BLUE SKY/EMPTY SPACES/WHAT SHALL WE DO NOW?/YOUNG LUST/ONE OF MY TURNS/DON'T LEAVE ME NOW/ANOTHER BRICK IN THE3 WALL, PART 3/THE LAST FEW BRICKS/ GOODBYE CRUEL WORLD/HEY YOU/IS THERE ANYBODY OUT THERE?/NOBODY HOME/VERA/BRING THE BOYS BACK HOME/COMFORTABLY NUMB/THE SHOW MUST GO ON/IN THE FLESH/RUN LIKE HELL/WAITING FOR THE WORMS/STOP/ THE TRIAL/OUTSIDE THE WALL

EMI; recorded 1980–1981; released April 18, 2000; available on CD

"Are there any paranoids in the audience?" demands Roger Waters just before "Run Like Hell" on this live document of the 1980–81 *The Wall* tour. "This is for all the weak people in the audience," he spits, before, screaming dementedly, "Enjoy yourselves!" This diatribe alone is almost worth the exorbitant price of this largely redundant recording.

A lavish box and book package, encasing equally lovingly-executed music, *Is There Anybody...* is hard not to enjoy, but, being a note-for-note re-creation, it's also hard to see how it's any more enjoyable than the original. OK, so there's the restoration of various last-minute cuts from the original: "What Shall We Do Now" (good, but the movie soundtrack version is better); and an extra verse on "The Show Must Go On". There's also a new instrumental "Last Few Bricks" the time-filling function of which is clearly audible.

Otherwise "Run Like Hell", performed as a vicious, nose-to-nose duet by Gilmour and Waters is the only track close to bettering the album version. But on the other hand, the guitar solo on "Another Brick" is unthrillingly-extended. Waters sounds perfunctory on "One Of My Turns", "Hey You!" is taken too fast for its dignity, while "Outside the Wall" is made into a harmony-laced, hand-holding finale (it worked better downbeat and depressing).

Very much the product of the post-Waters Heritage Floyd, prizing quantity of product over coherence of catalogue, *Is There Anybody Out There?* is enough to make any Pink Floyd fan paranoid.

Compilation Albums

Masters Of Rock

*CHAPTER 24/MATILDA MOTHER/ARNOLD LAYNE/CANDY
AND A CURRANT BUN/THE SCARECROW/APPLES AND
ORANGES/IT WOULD BE SO NICE/PAINTBOX/JULIA DREAM/
SEE EMILY PLAY*
Harvest; released 1970; currently unavailable

Masters is an early odds'n'sods compilation, released only in Europe in a vile gold sleeve and reissued in 1974 using the *Meddle* group portrait. It was, until *Relics*, the only album to include "Arnold", "Emily", "Paintbox" and "Julia Dream" (the latter track and "Embryo" being the only innocent sounding songs Waters ever wrote), while it remained the only source for "Apples", "Candy" and "It Would Be So Nice" until *Shine On*. Although handy for this reason, it is too scrappily packaged and programmed to be deemed essential, particularly as it was quickly outclassed by *Relics*.

Why the prejudice against "Point Me At The Sky", though, a precedent maintained by all future compilations?

Relics

*ARNOLD LAYNE/INTERSTELLAR OVERDRIVE/SEE EMILY
PLAY/REMEMBER A DAY/PAINTBOX/JULIA DREAM/CAREFUL
WITH THAT AXE, EUGENE/CIRRUS MINOR/THE NILE SONG/
BIDING MY TIME/BIKE*
Starline, then Music For Pleasure; released May 14, 1971;
available on CD

This "Collection of Bizarre Antiques and Curios" overlaps extensively with *Masters Of Rock,* and is an even less complete compendium of the early singles. But, being better programmed and packaged, and the sole residence of post-*Ummagumma* out-take "Biding My Time", it is an essential purchase for even mildly curious Floyd fans. Content perfectly matches title and cover (a Nick Mason ink drawing of an antiquated invention): pop psychedelia like "Arnold" and "Emily" nuzzling up against rockier numbers like *More*'s "Nile Song" and the aforementioned "Biding", which shifts from jazzy song to blistering Gilmour guitar solo (backed by a rare Wright trombone performance). The only complaint is how much more of a must-have this would have been had it included "Point Me At The Sky", "Nice" and "Apples And Oranges".

A Nice Pair

*PIPER AT THE GATES OF DAWN
A SAUCERFUL OF SECRETS*
Harvest (US: Capitol); released December 1973, available
on vinyl only

Straightforward twofer repackage of the first two Floyd albums, created to capitalize on the interest in the band post *Dark Side*. The title was Waters' idea, and Hipgnosis' sleeve concept ran with it, beginning with an image of breasts and then a whole series of other visual jokes, double entendres and deliberate mistakes. The band had wanted to use a photograph of boxer Floyd Patterson but he wanted $5000 for the usage. The original US vinyl version managed to substitute the live, *Ummagumma*, version of "Astronomy Domine", sans Barrett, for the original. American shops also banned the cover.

A Collection Of Great Dance Songs

ONE OF THESE DAYS/MONEY/SHEEP/SHINE ON YOU CRAZY DIAMOND/WISH YOU WERE HERE/ANOTHER BRICK IN THE WALL PART 2
Harvest/EMI; released November 23, 1981; available on CD

A post *Wall* compilation demanded by the record company, in which Waters took no interest. Beware: "Wish You Were Here" is slightly trimmed and "Shine On" is an edited composite of parts 1–3, 5 and 7. "Another Brick" is a splice of the single version's drum intro and the album version's sound effects outro. And, for contractual reasons, "Money" is a re-recorded version by Gilmour alone alongside original saxophonist Dick Parry – as it includes the original sound effects, it is almost indistinguishable from the original. The set is a rather sorry affair, right down to its gauche title and cover, which Gilmour later admitted was "awful".

Works

ONE OF THESE DAYS/ARNOLD LAYNE/FEARLESS/BRAIN DAMAGE/ECLIPSE/SET THE CONTROLS FOR THE HEART OF THE SUN/SEE EMILY PLAY/SEVERAL SPECIES OF SMALL FURRY ANIMALS GATHERED TOGETHER IN A CAVE AND GROOVING WITH A PICT/FREE FOUR/EMBRYO
Capitol; released 1983; available on CD

This is an oddity released only in the US by Capitol, as an attempt to capitalize on *Dark Side* after losing the Floyd to Columbia. Long the easiest way to obtain out-take "Embryo", otherwise only available on the hard-to-find 1970 *Picnic* Harvest sampler, it is now readily available via the Internet. A demo for *Ummagumma*, whose release was unsanctioned by the band, probably due to Gilmour's slightly hesitant vocal, "Embryo" has an appealing innocence that works well with the live-from-the-womb subject matter. The only other purchase-incentive is quadraphonic mixes of the *Dark Side* cuts. And what on earth were they thinking including "Several Species..."?

Shine On (box set)

A SAUCERFUL OF SECRETS/MEDDLE/DARK SIDE OF THE MOON/WISH YOU WERE HERE/ANIMALS/THE WALL/A MOMENTARY LAPSE OF REASON
EMI; released November 17, 1992; available on CD box set

A box set that manages two insults to Floyd fans. It short-changes them because it lacks rarities and it rewrites history for political and commercial ends. Is *Momentary Lapse* really more essential than *Piper*? In truth, it's inferior even to *Ummagumma*, but not to have included it would have been tantamount to admitting this and considered bad marketing. The only rarities here are on the *Early Singles* disc, which should by rights have been made available separately.

Echoes – The Best Of Pink Floyd

ASTRONOMY DOMINE/SEE EMILY PLAY/THE HAPPIEST DAYS OF OUR LIVES/ANOTHER BRICK IN THE WALL PART 2/ECHOES/HEY YOU/MAROONED/THE GREAT GIG IN THE SKY/SET THE CONTROLS FOR THE HEART OF THE SUN/ MONEY/KEEP TALKING/SHEEP/SORROW/SHINE ON YOU CRAZY DIAMOND PARTS 1–5/TIME/THE FLETCHER MEMORIAL HOME/COMFORTABLY NUMB/WHEN THE TIGERS BROKE FREE/ONE OF THESE DAYS/US AND THEM/LEARNING TO FLY/ARNOLD LAYNE/WISH YOU WERE HERE/JUGBAND BLUES/ HIGH HOPES/BIKE
EMI; released November 6, 2001

It's a testament to the generosity of the Gilmour-led Floyd that they included no less than five songs by Syd Barrett in this 2001 cross-career retrospective – indeed, opening and closing with the same tracks that opened and closed *Piper*. Less to their credit is the self-justifying excess of post-Waters content (a further five, alongside Barrett's cuts, as if to make a custodial point), the dismissal of *The Final Cut* (only one track) and the cull of the progressive period (two tracks, with *More*, *Ummagumma*, *Atom Heart Mother* and *Obscured By Clouds* all excised from history). As a result, the sense of being pushed around outweighs any pleasure in the music.

Bootlegs & ROIOs

So cabbalistic are bootleg-buyers that not only do they never use the B-word these days – it's strictly ROIO ("recordings of illegitimate origin") – they even have their own audio criteria (so average sound quality is "sup" and poor quality "VG") in the quest for rarity.

Although, as befits their status, Pink Floyd are one of the most heavily bootlegged bands in history, their bootleg output falls far short of the sonic and performance standards of their official output. Live shows tend to be dogged either by poor sound (the Barrett era and intermittently through the 70s) or poor performance (the mid 70s). Oddly, the early 1970s seem to represent the best of Floyd's live work: hence that period's dominance in this list.

Unfortunately, by the time studio-level standards had been attained in live sound and performance for the Gilmour-led spectaculars of the 80s and 90s, the soul of the band had been pretty much lost. And, apart from anything else, their live act was well documented by two live albums and two live DVDs. Hence the absence of Gilmour-era bootlegs here.

Inevitably, studio out-takes tend to be better quality all round, but they can't match the presentation level of the Floyd's *official* output and in any case are dispersed inconveniently across various mixed-bag collections. But because many of these do contain essential tracks for the committed Floyd fan, the best of them are listed here.

10 Best unreleased rarities

1 **"Scream Thy Last Scream"** One thing Gilmour and Waters can agree on: this missing link in the Floyd story should never receive a release. Peter Jenner feels otherwise. (From *Total Eclipse*.)

2 **"Vegetable Man"** Often said to be "the intended B-side of "Scream", "Vegetable" actually emanates from some months later and, while still of psychological interest, is of less musical merit. (From *Total Eclipse*.)

3 **"One In A Million"** A missing sonic link between "Scream" and "Cirrus Minor", this 1967 live cut is simultaneously dreamy and aggressive, with shimmering organ, stabbing guitar work and what sounds like Waters on vocals. (From *Rare Tracks and Live*.)

4 **"Moonhead"** Mesmeric six-minute bass-led improvisation that some see as a forerunner of "Money", from the July 1968 *Omnibus* moon landing documentary. (From *On The Air*.)

5 **"Seabirds"** From the *More* film, this Beatlesy, uptempo, stop-start Waters' composition featuring wah-wah organ, a big guitar solo and a Gilmour vocal. It can be heard in the background of the Paris party scene, but never made it onto the film's soundtrack release.

The Complete Top Gear Sessions 1967–69/Pink Floyd Archives 1967–1969

This is the largest collection of studio material on bootleg – all from 1960s and 1970s BBC Sessions – but the performances and sound quality of the Barrett-era recordings are poor. The Gilmour May 1968 recordings are much better, especially "Murderistic Women" (another "Eugene"), and "Julia Dream", plus a sufficiently different "Let There Be More Light" to suggest the studio original may have featured Barrett. The December '68 session isn't so good: the sound is somewhat submariney on "Baby Blue Shuffle In D Major" though an organ-suffused "Embryo" outshines the released *Picnic* version. A rather fine May 1969 *The Man* session is disappointingly murky and the similar *Archives* omits "Apples And Oranges" but boasts somewhat better sound quality throughout.

The Complete Paradiso Tapes

Caught in interesting transition between Barrett and Gilmour on May 23, 1968 in Amsterdam, this OK-quality live bootleg features some great playing on the proto-

6 **"The Violence Sequence"** This live version from Paris is the prototype for "Us And Them" featuring some lovely Waters bass work. Somewhere or other the Zabriskie Point version languishes in an archive. (From *On The Air.*)

7 **"Oneone/Fingal's Cave"** A *Zabriskie Point* out-take medley: "Oneone" is like a more melodic "Quicksilver", while "Fingal's Cave" is a more uptempo, gnarlier, bluesy number. (From *Total Eclipse.*)

8 **"Embryo"** The December 1968 studio version remained unfinished but the song gained a new life live from 1969 to 1971.Though the harmonies are uncertain on this 1970 version, the keyboard and guitar work are excellent, especially Gilmour's seagull effects. (From *Interstellar Encore.*)

9 **"Cymbaline"** Utterly transformed in live performance, this *More* ditty became an eerie epic. This 1970 version finds Gilmour in soulfully dramatic voice and Wright in ethereal mode, while the footsteps section is commendably creepy. (From *Interstellar Encore.*)

10 **"What Shall We Do Now?"** This song, with lyrics listing urgent tasks to perform, was dropped from *The Wall* album too late to lose its lyrics: the version remixed for *The Wall* soundtrack betters the live versions. (From *Total Eclipse.*)

"Eugene", "Keep Smiling People" and what sounds like "Saucerful", with Gilmour's guitar work shining, despite his reputedly tentative role in proceedings at this stage. The disc is marred by vocals being horribly murky throughout, however.

The Man And The Journey

Sadly, the most commonly available bootleg of these suites – that of September 17, 1969 at Concertgebouw, Amsterdam – is often incomplete. It leaves out "The Labyrinths Of Auximenes", "Behold The Temple Of Light" and "The End Of The Beginning", somewhat dulling the impact of the overall concept. The sound quality is good, however, even if Rick Wright's trombone on "Biding My Time" does sound like a kazoo. Wright more than makes up for this with a superb "Sleep", while Gilmour is in particularly fine voice throughout, giving "Cymbaline" and "Green" real soul, and lifting "Grantchester Meadows" with his harmony.

Interstellar Encore

This soundboard recording from just before *Atom Heart Mother* was recorded at Fillmore West, San Francisco, on April 29, 1970. It's notable for Waters and Gilmour's traded vocals on "Grantchester Meadows", an early – rather flat – version of "Atom Heart Mother", a superb "Cymbaline" and the hilariously mincing poshness of Roger Waters' stage pronouncements.

Smoking Blues

Much revered amongst bootleggers, this Montreux Casino show on November 21 1970, is only just about acceptable quality (despite being a rare soundboard recording) but contains several key cuts. First is a fine extended "Cymbaline" – complete with echoing footsteps section (as well as a horrific aural glitch) and a jazzy "The Embryo" (sic), which is revealed to be a prototype "Echoes", complete with funky section and screeching seagull wah-wah effects. Collectors drool over the first version of "Just Another 12 Bar" (a derivative of "Biding My Time"); others might feel its title says it all.

Live In London 1971

In actual fact this recording was made live in London, July 16, 1970. This regularly rebroadcast BBC recording from the Paris Theatre features an early, rather fine, performance of "Atom Heart Mother" with brass. *The Pink Floyd BBC Archives 1970–1971* comprises both this and a September 30 show from the previous year, which contains the first ever performance of "One Of These Days" and has high-quality sound.

Best Of Tour 1972

Confusingly titled, this is actually the Rainbow performance of *DSOTM* (not its premiere, as often claimed). At this early stage, "On The Run" is still a guitar-organ jam, "Any Colour" is still "Scat" (with Gilmour humming to his axe). "Money" has its tape effects already in place and sounds grungier than the finished version; it also features an organ solo that would be dropped on the studio cut. Sadly "Time", "Us And Them" and "Eclipse" are all abruptly curtailed. Sound quality is pretty good.

Scratch The Silence

A high-quality *DSOTM* bootleg which gives a fascinating insight into the piece's development. From September 22, 1972 at the Hollywood Bowl, Los Angeles, "Breathe" has briefly gained a guitar solo in the introduction; "Time" is faster for the first time (though still contains the lyric "lying supine in the sunshine"); "Great Gig" is now on piano, but goes into a horrible organ solo backed by even uglier bass; the chorus of "Us And Them" is a chaotic three-part harmony, with Gilmour bellowing above it all.

Cold Front

A high-quality audience recording of the still gestating *Dark Side Of The Moon* on March 13, 1972 from Nagazhima Sports Center, Sapporo, Japan. *Home Again* from the same tour has a smoother performance but a more cavernous sound.

Brain Damage

Often mislabelled as being from 1972, this recording is actually from the British Winter Tour, recorded on November 16, 1974 and is a BBC broadcast of the entirety of *Dark Side Of The Moon*. Sound quality, playing and singing are all excellent, with Waters' bass on "Us And Them" reminiscent of **The Beatles'** "Sun King", belying his poor reputation on the instrument. The Work label version of this show includes "Shine On", though none of the others do. Loved by fanatical fans, this post-*DSOTM* bootleg, with few discernible differences from the studio version, may be mystifying to others.

British Winter Tour '74

The story that many bought this bootleg, of November 19, 1974, Trentham Gardens, Stoke, in the belief that it was the Floyd's next official release is rather hard to believe. Would the Floyd's attention to detail have failed them so completely that they released something of, not just poor sonic quality, but second-rate performance quality too? "Gotta Be Crazy" in particular is a cacophonous mess. Yet it's this and "Raving And Drooling" which are the purchase incentives here, the latter being primarily instrumental at this stage, very close to "One Of These Days" with lots of spacey slide and some siren-like synth from Wright.

Echoes In The Gardens

Audience tape of decent quality from Boston, June 18, 1975. This sees further development of "Raving And Drooling" and "Gotta Be Crazy" from the previous year's versions. "Raving" sounds more like a song now but lacks a singer, with Waters' repeated shrieking of the same nine lines wearing thin. "Crazy" is also inestimably better – recognisably "Dogs" now, though Gilmour's vocals are done few favours by, in this case, an excess of Waters' words. Rated highly by many fans for the extended version of "Any Colour You Like", with the backing singers letting rip, though others may find this somewhat indulgent.

Under Construction

The 1978 Britannia Row *Wall* demos. "Goodbye Cruel World", "Don't Leave Me Now", "Waiting For The Worms", "Mother", "Stop!" and "The Trial" are largely complete. "The Thin Ice" features an additional simultaneous second verse, "Hey You" is sung by Waters, and "The Show Must Go On" has different lyrics (some of which were reused in the live shows). "Comfortably Numb" is here in very embryonic form (as "The Doctor") and there are also three songs – "What Shall We Do Now", "Sitting By The Telephone" and "Anyone Out There" – which would be cut from the ultimate piece. A fascinating document rather than something you're likely to listen to regularly.

The hirsute Floyd, 1973

Total Eclipse

Although it's something of a holy grail among Floyd collectors, shouldn't a four-disc ROIO contain more *unavailable* material? All the early singles are available officially, as is "Nick's Boogie", while the *Top Gear* and live *Dark Side* cuts are available on other common ROIOs. Nevertheless, this is a useful bootleg-of-bootlegs compilation. It contains the essential studio versions of "Scream Thy Last Scream" and "Vegetable Man", various *Zabriskie Point* out-takes, "Oneone" (a "Quicksilver" relative) and the churning "Fingal's Cave", though the recording of "Violence Sequence" from Paris is inferior to that from *On The Air*. The quadraphonic mix of "Brain Damage" features the lead guitar lines heard on the *Pompeii* film, and "Raving And Drooling" and "You Gotta Be Crazy" from Nassau Coliseum, June 1975, make for interesting – but not especially pretty – listening. *The Wall* soundtrack cuts are also fairly essential.

On The Air

Somewhat thrown together and of ridiculously varied sound quality, *OTA* is mainly of value for the January 23, 1970 Paris recording, including a stunning "The Violence Sequence", alongside an "Amazing Pudding", the highlight being Wright and Gilmour harmonizing in falsetto countermelodies. There's also the essential "Moonhead" moon landing improv.

Solo Projects

Syd Barrett

The Madcap Laughs

TERRAPIN/NO GOOD TRYING/LOVE YOU/NO MAN'S LAND/ DARK GLOBE/HERE I GO/OCTOPUS/GOLDEN HAIR/LONG GONE/SHE TOOK A LONG COLD LOOK/FEEL/IF IT'S IN YOU/ LATE NIGHT
Harvest; recorded April and July 1969; released January 3, 1970; available on CD

For those familiar with *Piper At The Gates Of Dawn* and the idea of Syd Barrett the psyche-delic maverick, *The Madcap Laughs* can come as a surprise. Not for its eccentricity but for its conventionality. For Syd Barrett's first solo album is rooted in fairly standard – if rickety – 1970s folk-rock, with little of the texturing or spaciness of psychedelia. Furthermore, when the weirdness does commence, a full two-thirds of the way through *Madcap*, it's less psyche-delic than simply sad.

Opener "Terrapin" sets the tone: a simple, strummed acoustic twelve-bar blues, possessed of a very English summer day laziness, only slightly undermined by its time elisions and surreally lovely lyrics ("fangs all 'round the clown is dark below the boulders hiding all"). "Here I Go", written in minutes at the same first sessions with producer **Malcolm Jones**, is fun but fairly standard pop-vaudeville, as is the flighty, frivolous "Love You". For the album's first half, only "No Good Trying" sounds

psychedelic (thanks largely to **Soft Machine**'s backing), and only "No Man's Land" sug-gests any darkness, with its spiky, distorted guitar, muffled spoken passage and fractured language ("under all we awful, awful crawl"). Of the barer tracks produced by Dave Gilmour and Roger Waters, "Feel" and "Dark Globe" are folky makeweights, fairly conventional for all the latter's stumbling tempos and rather desperate sounding singing.

But then things start to get odder. "Octopus" begins as a rollicking, almost poppy number, before tripping over itself into one of Barrett's best, most evocative lyrics – ("Isn't it good to be lost in the wood, isn't it good so quiet there?") – pantheistic, nostalgic and plain disturbing. The brilliant "Long Gone" is stranger still, start-ing off scraping the bottom of Barrett's range, then hitting a chorus in which a high-pitched, slightly deranged Barrett duets with himself (a trick Waters would utilize to fine effect in due course), the song's drama underpinned by Rick Wright's shimmering organ. If this is outré, then rarely has anything so on-the-edge been record-ed as "If It's In You". Its infamous false start is as excruciatingly compelling as anything the post-Alan Partridge vogue for cringe-inducing comedy has created. Surely Gilmour and Waters should have spared Barrett's blushes as he veers

Syd Barrett, live at the Olympia in 1967

from dying mid-note to lunging wildly at the tune? Then, in the middle of a song whose use of language is already lateral, Barrett suddenly departs from human speech altogether, "yummie, yam, yum yum, youm, yom" he yowls, somewhere between insanity and genius.

After this harrowing experience, everything is tucked up neatly with "Late Night", another Jones-produced track. Barrett's singing is low and sweet, his slide guitar sighing sleepily in the background, and for three gorgeous minutes you can almost convince yourself this is a rather quaint singer-songwriter album of the early 1970s. If you can ignore the lines, "inside me I feel alone and unreal", that is.

Barrett

BABY LEMONADE/LOVE SONG/DOMINOES/IT IS OBVIOUS/
RATS/MAISIE/GIGOLO AUNT/WAVING MY ARMS IN THE
AIR/I NEVER LIED TO YOU/WINED AND DINED/WOLFPACK/
EFFERVESCING ELEPHANT
Harvest, recorded February–July 1970; released November
14, 1970; available on CD

As a result of the subjective, slightly creepy cult that has spun itself around Syd Barrett, it is never noted quite how *little* top-flight material this troubled songwriter actually turned out. A couple of sparkling 1960s singles, a few first Floyd album gems and a clutch of rough solo album diamonds... And then there is *Barrett* – an album that, were it by, say, Pete Brown's Battered Ornaments, would be forgotten alongside a host of other Harvest indulgences of the era.

Barrett is virtually manic depression inscribed in wax: dispiritingly flat on the one hand,

disturbingly frantic on the other. The numbers that fit between inevitably constitute the album's highlights: the scrappily poppy "Baby Lemonade", the jaunty "Gigolo Aunt" (with its brilliantly abrasive, off-blues guitar work,) and the lovely, lilting "Dominoes" (again featuring some intermittently great Barrett guitar). But despite having a more consistent production team in a returning **David Gilmour**, with **Rick Wright** replacing an exasperated Roger Waters, not one of these quite matches *The Madcap Laughs'* highlights, however.

Far too much of the album finds Barrett sounding almost catatonically subdued. "Waving My Arms In The Air" wants to be jaunty but can't quite manage it, before slumping into the dead-on-its-feet "I Never Lied To You". Were "It Is Obvious" a "Have You Got It Yet"-style joke about its melody being the same four notes endlessly repeated, it might be funny; as it is, it sounds painfully unaware of its own limitations. Meanwhile, the ballad "Wined And Dined" (inspired by girlfriend, **Gala Pinion**) aims for sweetness, but founders on the flat inexpression of Barrett's vocals. All these tracks feature Barrett playing and singing to rather pedestrian prerecorded backing tracks, which might lead one to expect that the numbers where the musicians attempt to overdub onto of Barrett's tracks might be better.

Not a bit of it. The Barrett-led tracks simply swing to the opposite end of the manic depressive scale. On "Rats", both Barrett's guitar rhythm *and* his mind seem to stumble incoherently around the song, backing musicians – and probably most listeners – floundering as they attempt to follow the pied piper. The baritone drone of "Maisie" meanwhile manages the feat of being both disturbing and dull, and "Wolfpack" quickly becomes cacophonous after a promising opening. Even more than *Madcap*'s "If It's In You" for furthering the Barrett freak-show factor, these tracks should probably never have been released – Barrett wearing his sanity on his sleeve for cultists to peck at.

But just as *Madcap* managed to end on a high, so does *Barrett*. Syd's solo career ends where it started, with one of the first songs he wrote, "Effervescing Elephant". A lovely children's song, displaying the influence of Edward Lear in its witty word games, Barrett's vocal is as knowing and playful as Vic Saywell's frolicsome tuba. Engaging as this is, however, "Elephant" doesn't manage to give the album a pleasant aftertaste, instead offering a sad reminder of what is now, in Barrett's own words, long, long gone.

The Radio One Sessions

TERRAPIN/GIGOLO AUNT/ BABY LEMONADE/EFFERVESCING ELEPHANT/TWO OF A KIND/BABY LEMONADE/DOMINOES/ LOVE SONG
Strange Fruit; recorded February 24, 1970 and February 16, 1971; released 1987 on vinyl, then with extra tracks May 11, 2004; available on CD.

The main purchase-incentive for these *Top Gear* and *Sounds Of The Seventies* sessions from 1970 and 1971 is the otherwise unavailable "Two Of A Kind", a fascinatingly archetypal Floyd mystery. Rick Wright reportedly wrote the song, but Barrett became convinced *he'd* written it, and

Wright himself professed characteristic confusion when asked about the subject in 1996.

Lyrically at least, "Two Of A Kind" sounds like Wright's work, however, possessing none of Barrett's signature wordplay. It also fades away mid-way through, as if Barrett had forgotten it. Otherwise though, apart from wavering mic technique on "Effervescing Elephant", Barrett is in reasonably together form on the 1970 sessions. Backed by David Gilmour and **Jerry Shirley** (and some reports say Floyd roadie **Alan Styles** on guitar), and featuring overdubbed mouth noises from Barrett, the stripped-down "Terrapin" heard here is actually more precisely played than the original. Of the previously unreleased *Sounds Of The Seventies* session (featuring just Barrett and Gilmour), the sound is poor due to being recorded from the broadcast not the masters, but the performances themselves also sound rather flat. Unofficial release number one, and barrel is already being scraped.

Opel

OPEL/CLOWNS AND JUGGLERS/RATS/GOLDEN HAIR/ DOLLY ROCKER/WORD SONG/WINED AND DINED/SWAN LEE (SILAS LANG)/BIRDIE HOP/LET'S SPLIT/LANKY (PART ONE)/WOULDN'T YOU MISS ME (DARK GLOBE)/MILKY WAY/ GOLDEN HAIR
Released April 1989; CD version with extra tracks 1994; available on CD

If even his *official* releases often exceed the boundaries of seemly interest in Syd Barrett, the raiding of the vaults occupies an even more questionable area. This collection jus-

The Music

tifies its existence by the inclusion of eight previously unreleased songs, though plans to include "Vegetable Man' and "Scream Thy Last Scream" – the two most essential Barrett rarities – were apparently scuppered by spoilsports the Floyd.

Malcolm Jones recorded "Opel" for *The Madcap Laughs*. Forced to leave the project, he was surprised when Gilmour and Waters excised it in favour of *Madcap*'s more harrowing moments. It's a sweet song, revealing Barrett at his most poetic, backed only by his mildly wayward acoustic guitar playing. "Lanky" and "Swan Lee" derive from the original post-Floyd Peter Jenner sessions of 1968. Despite Jenner's assessment, "Swan Lee" is actually rather fine, a surreal *Children's Hiawatha* complete with twanging Western guitar. "Lanky" is a quite enjoyable jam, featuring twinkling xylophone and grittily effective guitar from Barrett, though at 5:30 it outstays its welcome.

Of less merit are the other previously unreleased tracks: "Birdie Hop" starts off cute but its one-chord melody soon becomes tedious; the litany of unrelated words in "Word Song" sounds more like a psychiatry session than a song; while "Let's Split" is further freak-show fare, barely making it to mid-point before Barrett stops altogether, sighs and then begins whistling. Deep breath: "Milky Way" is poppily vaudevillian and mildly engaging, while "Dolly Rocker" is notable mainly for the line "she's as cute as a squirrel's nut".

The alternate takes are even more redundant: "Dark Globe" is sung at a lower register with none of the magic of the *Madcap* version; an attempt at "Octopus" ("Clowns And Jugglers") is erratic and tuneless; the band-free "Rats" isn't much of an improvement on the released version; while there's a fairly similar "Golden Hair". The other alternate takes added for the 1994 reissue are even more depressing: while a first take of "Octopus" without musicians is interesting, after a horribly lifeless "It Is Obvious" sung at the bottom of his range, Barrett begins a new version in a lovely return to his higher range but then seems to run out of steam. Sadly that is more than could be said for the Barrett compilation demand and supply. Ultimately this collection feels like the musical equivalent of doorstepping this determined recluse. As David Gilmour says, "Why can't they just leave him alone?"

Wouldn't You Miss Me: The Best Of Syd Barrett

OCTOPUS/LATE NIGHT/TERRAPIN/SWAN LEE/WOLFPACK/ GOLDEN HAIR/HERE I GO/LONG GONE/NO GOOD TRYING/ OPEL/BABY LEMONADE/GIGOLO AUNT/DOMINOES/ WOULDN'T YOU MISS ME/WINED AND DINED/EFFERVESCING ELEPHANT/WAVING MY ARMS IN THE AIR/I NEVER LIED TO YOU/LOVE SONG/TWO OF A KIND/BOB DYLAN BLUES/ GOLDEN HAIR (INSTRUMENTAL)
Harvest/EMI; released March 27, 2001; available on CD

Superseding the earlier, less thorough *Octopus* compilation, this collection is taken from Barrett's solo albums, the BBC Sessions and *Opel* and thus doesn't make a bad one-stop shop for Barrett's work. It's also notable for the inclusion of a long-lost rarity, "Bob Dylan Blues", donated from David Gilmour's vaults. But as neither "Dylan" nor BBC track "Two Of A Kind" are remotely essential, and the *Opel* tracks only very vaguely so, isn't it almost as simple just to buy Barrett's scant two solo albums?

Crazy Diamond – The Complete Syd Barrett

TERRAPIN/NO GOOD TRYING/LOVE YOU/NO MAN'S LAND/ DARK GLOBE/HERE I GO/OCTOPUS/GOLDEN HAIR/LONG GONE/SHE TOOK A LONG COLD LOOK/FEEL/IF IT'S IN YOU/LATE NIGHT/OCTOPUS/NO GOOD TRYING/LOVE YOU/ LOVE YOU/SHE TOOK A LONG A COLD LOOK/GOLDEN HAIR/BABY LEMONADE/LOVE SONG/DOMINOES/IT IS OBVIOUS/RATS/MAISIE/GIGOLO AUNT/WAVING MY ARMS IN THE AIR/I NEVER LIED TO YOU//WINED AND DINED/

WOLFPACK/EFFERVESCING ELEPHANT/BABY LEMONADE/ WAVING MY ARMS IN THE AIR/I NEVER LIED TO YOU/LOVE SONG/DOMINOES/DOMINOES/IT IS OBVIOUS/OPEL/CLOWNS AND JUGGLERS/RATS/GOLDEN HAIR/DOLLY ROCKER/WORD SONG/WINED AND DINED/SWAN LEE (SILAS LANG)/BIRDIE HOP/LET'S SPLIT/LANKY PT 1/WOULDN'T YOU MISS ME (DARK GLOBE)/MILKY WAY/GOLDEN HAIR/GIGOLO AUNT/IT IS OBVIOUS/IT IS OBVIOUS/CLOWNS AND JUGGLERS/LATE NIGHT/EFFERVESCING ELEPHANT
Released April 26, 1993 on Harvest; available on 3-CD box set

This 3-CD box set comprises Barrett's two solo albums, *Opel,* and 19 previously unreleased alternate takes. Although the unreleased material is entirely dispensable, this format does, bizarrely, actually represent the most economical way of obtaining all three Barrett albums.

Rick Wright

Wet Dream

MEDITERRANEAN C/AGAINST THE ODDS/CAT CRUISE/ SUMMER ELEGY/WAVES/ HOLIDAY/MAD YANNIS DANCE/DROP IN FROM THE TOP/PINK'S SONG/FUNKY DEUX
Recorded January 10–February 14 1978; released May 1978; unavailable

There's not much sex in the world of Pink Floyd. But if the title of Rick Wright's first solo album implies that Pink Floyd fans' fantasies will be fulfilled, then it equally suggests private guilty pleasure – a suggestion the album's content, sadly, confirms. A release supposedly born of repression – Wright bemoaning Waters blocking his contributions to the immediately

preceding *Animals* – *Wet Dream* is hardly evidence of overflowing wells of creativity.

Aiming for the classic 1970s Pink Floyd sound, Wright essays not one but *two* retreads of the Floyd's patented white funk plod. But without the nuances of Gilmour's guitar or Mason's amiable percussive clump, "Drop In From The Top" and "Funky Deux" are strictly self-indulgences rather than public-pleasers. On these tracks and throughout *Wet Dream*, Wright makes way too much use of sessioneers, taste lapses that rather justify Waters' subsequent challenge to Wright's producer's credentials during *The Wall*. Overfeatured Floyd sec-

Zee

Identity

CONFUSION/VOICES/PRIVATE PERSON/STRANGE RHYTHM/CUTS LIKE
A DIAMOND/BY TOUCHING/HOW DO YOU DO IT/SEEMS WE WERE
DREAMING/EYES OF A GIPSY (CASSETTE VERSION ONLY)
Recorded 1983–84; released April 9, 1984 on Harvest;
unavailable

There are few instruments more 1980s than the
Fairlight Synthesizer. The first digital sampling synthe-
sizer, the CMI Fairlight's use in pop was pioneered by
Peter Gabriel and **Duran Duran** in the early eighties,
becoming as standard a production device as the Linn
Drum Synthesizer as the decade progressed.

An album born of a shared interest in the Fairlight
was only ever going to be a casualty of its era.
An unlikely collaboration between **Fashion** casualty **Dave Harris** (New Romantics who'd had some
minor funk-pop hits) and an 80s casualty of a rather
different kind, Rick Wright, this album is, conse-

quently, as dated as deely boppers. The sole product
of Wright's post-Pink Floyd wilderness years, Identity
perhaps inevitably defers to Wright's collaborator
throughout. Harris co-wrote all the music, sang all
the songs and wrote all the lyrics – despite some
tantalizingly Wright-esque titles like "Confusion"
and "Private Person". Wright's low profile on his
own album can only be seen as an indicator of quite
how shot away his personality was by the success of
Dark Side Of The Moon and its troubled aftermath.
As such any assertiveness detectable in the album's
title, Identity, can only be regarded retrospectively
as ironic.

Not even a sympathy vote for Wright can make
this album worth excavating from its 1980s landfill.
True to its times, it manages to be both tinny and
bombastic, beyond the reach of even the most
determined 80s revival.

ond unit guitarist **Snowy White** lacks Gilmour's
soulfulness, simply sounding like he's filling
gaps for pay rather than pursuing any kind of
inspiration. Sax player **Mel Collins** is of similar
ilk: sessioneer for everyone from **King Crimson**
to **Dire Straits**, he may be technically Dick
Parry's superior, but he's emotionally his inferior. There is nothing of the depth of "Us And
Them", let alone "Great Gig" here.

What's more, amongst the album's scant
four actual *songs*, the tantalizingly titled
"Pink's Song" transpires not to be about
Wright's alma mater, but about the Wright
children's tutor, while the focus of "Against
The Odds" and "Summer Elegy" is equally

inward, addressing Wright's crumbling marriage to Juliette (who pens the lyrics to "Pink's
Song"). While these songs are slightly better
than the instrumentals, they're still flimsy
affairs, less a Floyd fan's wet dream than simply wet, lacking a single memorable melody.
It's a problem compounded by Wright's voice
seemingly having lost some of its character
– the very richness of its reedy vulnerability,
the tenderness that made even songs about
groupies sound strangely soulful is missing.
His singing here is curiously charmless, as is
the playing, and consequently, it's no surprise
that *Wet Dream* had all the public impact of
a private nocturnal emission.

The Music

The Music

Broken China

BREAKING WATERS/NIGHT OF A THOUSAND FURRY TOYS/
HIDDEN FEAR/RUNAWAY/UNFAIR GROUND/SATELLITE/
WOMAN OF CUSTOM/INTERLUDE/BLACK CLOUD/FAR FROM
THE HARBOUR WALL/DROWNING/REACHING FOR THE
RAIL/BLUE ROOM IN VENICE/SWEET JULY/ALONG THE
SHORELINE/BREAKTHROUGH
EMI; recorded March 1995-April 1996; released November
26, 1996; available on CD

For someone who has experienced such intense withdrawal, Rick Wright has latterly excelled at finding simpatico collaborators. Having forged a partnership with **Anthony Moore** on his vocal reawakening, "Wearing The Inside Out" on *The Division Bell*, Wright took its style and content as a starting point for this entire album – his first solo album in eighteen years.

This time Moore is co-opted not just as co-writer, but as co-producer *and* co-keyboard player (having previously played that role in **Slapp Happy**). The lyrics continue the exploration of mental frailty of "Inside Out", although *Broken China* purports to explore Wright's *wife*'s experience of clinical depression.

Pink Floyd hangs heavy over the entire enterprise, naturally. As with *Wet Dream*, Wright employs the Floyd's current Gilmour guitar foil, this time **Tim Renwick**, on guitar, as well as Floyd regular **James Guthrie** on mixing duties, with album design covered by **Storm**

Thorgerson. There's also something Floydian about the concept and the dense layers of sound effects. That said, *Broken China* is a far more electronic, ambient, even new age affair than anything the other Floyds have essayed. As with much else in the genre, the overall impact is somewhat wispy – a wash of vague keyboards, effects and fragile vocals that often fails properly to connect, with almost nothing as immediate or memorable as "Wearing The Inside Out". The only time the music ever attempts anything edgier, on "Along The Shoreline", Wright's vocals almost give out under the strain.

But it's Wright's discovery of another empathetic collaborator that saves the album. **Sinead O'Connor** had proved decidedly *un*simpatico with Roger Waters at the Berlin *Wall,* but here she proves a superbly sensitive interpreter of both "Reaching For The Rail" and "Breakthrough" (O'Connor had her own dark times during the 1990s). "Breakthrough" is by some distance the best track here, and was later performed very effectively by Wright with Gilmour on his *In Concert* DVD. A yearningly melodic ballad, it says more in 4 minutes 19 seconds than the rest of *Broken China* manages in an hour. For all its New-Ageiness, Broken China is a long way from being a complete Rick Wright rebirth.

Nick Mason

Fictitious Sports

CAN'T GET MY MOTOR TO START/I WAS WRONG/SIAM/HOT RIVER/BOO TO YOU TOO/DO YA?/WERVIN'/I'M A MINERALIST
Harvest (US: Columbia). Recorded October 1979; released 1981; limited availability

It's perhaps no surprise that Nick Mason's sole solo album should contain not a single Nick Mason composition. Mason was never really a composer within the Floyd – apart from his drumming duties, he often acted as a kind of second-unit producer to Waters and Gilmour, often overseeing sound effects. Consequently, more than any other Floyd member, Mason developed an extensive extra-curricular career as a producer rather than a solo artist, making the Canterbury *avant* jazz scene centred on **Robert Wyatt** his particular production metier. And this album is, essentially, a Nick Mason production rather than a Nick Mason creation.

Through Wyatt, Mason had already worked with jazz composer/trumpeter **Michael Mantler** and his wife, composer/keyboardist **Carla Bley**. Lending his name to what was essentially a Carla Bley album that Mason produced and drummed on was a generous gesture intended to assist sales. Wyatt was again on hand to sing these rather silly songs. But while Bley's self-consciously wacky work is an often uninviting prospect, there is one major exception: Bley's returning of Mason's favour via the Pink Floyd pastiche "Hot River". "It has all my favourite clichés of the last fourteen years", said Mason, "a vocal track lifted straight off the *Dark Side Of The Moon*." Possessed of a scorching melody, it has fine vocal interplay between Wyatt and Karen Kraft, and **Chris Spedding** again proves himself a fine Gilmour sub (he'd played the same role on **Roy Harper**'s 1975 "The Game").

This is barely enough to satisfy the few Floyd fans who did buy the record on the basis of Mason's name, however, while Bley's jazz fans were largely unimpressed by her attempts at impure pop.

Profiles

MALTA/LIE FOR A LIE/RHODA/PROFILES PARTS 1 & 2/ISRAEL/ AND THE ADDRESS/MUMBO JUMBO/ZIP CODE/BLACK ICE/AT THE END OF THE DAY/PROFILES PART 3
Recorded 1984; released August 19, 1985 on Harvest (UK) and Sony (US); currently unavailable

Nick Mason's extra-curricular activities often appear to be less an attempt to make money than simply to spend it. Alongside his car collection, his motor racing, his investment in racing teams and his aeroplanes, Mason's two meagre-selling but expensively produced "solo" albums must surely have cost more than they made.

Still, it was game of Mason not to want to be left out of the Floyd's 1984–85 solo album splurge. *Profiles* was another collaborative effort, this time with Rick Fenn – guitarist for **Mike Oldfield** and **10CC** and, equally importantly, Mason's film soundtrack business partner. Even so, *Profiles* has more right to be called a Nick Mason album than did *Fictitious Sports*, Mason lending his name to all but one composition ("Israel"). In fact, this effort is actually somewhat better than Wright's Zee project, composed mostly of slight doodles created for film soundtracks and adverts (not least the *Life Could Be A Dream* documentary on Mason himself), and featuring contributions from Floyd acolyte **Mel Collins** on saxophone and one **Danny Peyronel** on vocals on "Israel". Peyronel also wrote the lyrics for the other vocal track, "Lie For A Lie", upon which David Gilmour sings – the first recorded collaboration between Floyd members since *The Final Cut*. Pleasant but hardly essential, the song is at least of historical interest in defining what no one could have known at the time would be the future power basis of the next formation of the Floyd. A formation which, while providing somewhere for Mason to sink his money, would also inconveniently make him a whole heap more of the stuff.

Production and session work

The Floyd's most outgoing member, Mason was the first to work properly outside the band, carving out a fairly impressive production career for himself in the 1970s.

Principal Edwards Magic Theatre

Mason's first production forays were 1971's *Asmoto Running Band* (Dandelion) and 1974's *Round One* (Harvest) by this **John Peel**-endorsed fifteen-strong ensemble of Exeter university students, mixing theatre, music and general hippie wackiness.

Robert Wyatt

Former drummer with Floyd chums **Soft Machine**, Wyatt had a fall from a block of flats in 1973 that disabled him for life. The only Floyd collaboration likely to appear in any Best Albums Of All Time lists, 1974's stunning *Rock Bottom* (Virgin) was Wyatt's recuperation record, finding him at a compositional high, aided by the employment of such Canterbury-scene talent as **Mike Oldfield**. Mason captured all this immaculately. He also produced a Wyatt cover of the Monkees' "I'm A Believer", which became an unlikely UK hit.

Gary Windo

More Canterbury-scene jazz fare. Saxophonist Windo, Wyatt and **Carla Bley** were the first to use the Floyd's Britannia Row, in 1975, although the tracks they recorded weren't released until 1996 on *His Master's Bones*. Not recommended.

Michael Mantler

Mason engineered and mixed a collection of Edmund Gorey poems set to music by New York trumpeter **Mantler**, called *The Hapless*

Child (Watt, 1976) at Britannia Row. Mantler's wife Carla Bley plays keyboards; Wyatt sings. "The Doubtful Guest" is recommended (and features Mason speaking). Mason would also drum on Mantler's *Something There* (1982) and *Live* the next year, which also featured Mason's friend **Rick Fenn**.

Gong

Another Canterbury act, founded and led by old Floyd cohort **Daevid Allen**. After his departure, Gong became a vehicle for the band's jazzier, proggier instrumentalists. Mason produced 1976's *Shamal* (Virgin) brightly and cleanly, catching the band at a mid point between hippie twaddle and cold muso jazz-funk.

Steve Hillage

Mason continued to be the Canterbury scene's producer *du jour*, co-producing former Gong guitarist Hillage's somewhat Floydian *Green* (Virgin, 1978) and drumming on "Leylines To Glassdom" (recommended). Mason also produced a version of **The Beatles'** "Getting Better" on Hillage's *Open* (Virgin, 1979; not recommended).

The Damned

In total contrast to his proggy Canterbury scene work, Mason produced The Damned's 1977 second album, *Music For Pleasure*, at Britannia Row – one of their entourage scoring the walls in an anti-prog-dinosaur protest. Slackly produced, poor material, it's not of great interest to either punk or Pink fans.

David Gilmour

Jokers Wild

WHY DO FOOLS FALL IN LOVE/WALK LIKE A MAN/DON'T ASK ME (WHAT I SAY)/BIG GIRLS DON'T CRY/BEAUTIFUL DELILAH Private pressing; recorded and released 1965; unavailable (though some tracks are on bootlegs)

Blindfolded and forced to guess who was responsible for these tracks in classic 1960s pop paper style, few people would pick a future member of Pink Floyd. For David Gilmour's first recordings comprise a clutch of covers concentrating on the light end of sixties R&B: the bouncy, throwaway "Don't Ask Me" by **Manfred Mann**, "Beautiful Delilah" by **Chuck Berry**, and "Big Girls Don't Cry" and "Walk Like A Man" by MOR soulsters **The Four Seasons**, plus Frankie Lymon and the Teenagers' international doo-wop hit, "Why Do Fools Fall in Love". Even so, this music is too earthy, and let's face it, too black for any member of the whiter-than-white Pink Floyd past or future to carry off convincingly. A mil-

The Music

lion miles away from psychedelia then, let alone space rock, Gilmour would never again sound as camp and affected as he does on "Why Do Fools Fall". Which is, if only for humorous rather than musical reasons, a shame.

David Gilmour

MIHALIS/THERE'S NO WAY OUT OF HERE/CRY FROM THE STREET/SO FAR AWAY/SHORT AND SWEET/RAISE MY RENT/NO WAY/DEAFINITELY/I CAN'T BREATHE ANYMORE
Harvest; recorded 1977–78; released May 25, 1978; available on CD

Long blocked compositionally by his older bandmates, Beatles junior **George Harrison** responded by making his first solo album proper a triple, *All Things Must Pass*. That Floyd's "new boy" David Gilmour splurged his first solo opus between the Waters-dominated Floyd albums *Animals* and *The Wall* might suggest a similar compositional overflow. But the fact is there are only three self-composed songs here – the rest of the album comprising three instrumentals, two co-writes and a cover; the latter, "There's No Way Out Of Here", also being by some distance the album's best track.

Despite being born of "a crazy desire to express [himself]", Gilmour was clearly stuck to do so, firstly asking **Ken Baker**, of his protégés **Unicorn**, to contribute lyrics. When Baker declined, Gilmour contented himself with co-opting Baker's "No Way Out of Here", making it sound like a Floyd original, and summoning his old Jokers Wild muckers to their French stomping ground to do so. Still stuck, Gilmour asked **Roy Harper** to co-write the album's sec-

ond-best track, "Short And Sweet", a majestic mid-pacer in patented Pink Floyd style. To be fair, the lovely – and entirely self-composed – ballad "So Far Away" runs both songs close, another Floydian cut complete with soulful female backing vocals (**Vanetta Carlton** being a Floyd regular), while aspects of the melody would be recalled on Gilmour's "Comfortably Numb" solo, a basic version of that song being demoed late in this album's sessions.

Other Floydian echoes are Gilmour's organ work on "No Way", the lyrics of which ("it's my show" etc) could be taken to refer to the increasingly fraught Gilmour/Waters relationship, as could the evocation of one of the Floyd's most famous compositions in "I Can't Breathe Anymore". But for all this, *David Gilmour* is largely Floyd-lite. The most conventional, least arty-sounding album in the entire Floyd 1970s discography bar *Wet Dream*, it mostly sticks to a straight bass/guitar/drums format, lacking any of the band's signature sound effects or atmospherics (only "Deafinitely" even employs synthesizers) and consequently largely lacking any interest.

Unlike George Harrison's opus, *David Gilmour* is a long way from being the creative high point of the guitarist's career. But for those three aforementioned tracks alone, plucking familiar Floydian enigma from austere ingredients, it is, curiously, as fundamental to the Floyd canon as *All Things Must Pass* to the Beatles'.

About Face

*UNTIL WE SLEEP/MURDER/LOVE ON THE AIR/BLUE LIGHT/
OUT OF THE BLUE/ALL LOVERS ARE DERANGED/YOU KNOW
I'M RIGHT/CRUISE/LET'S GET METAPHYSICAL/NEAR THE END*
Harvest (US: Columbia); recorded 1983–4; released March
5, 1984; available on CD

Assertiveness training makes a crucial distinction between being assertive and simply being aggressive. But if David Gilmour's debut album found the laid-back, long-term "new boy" asserting himself, then his second effort finds him blundering headlong into aggression. With its big 1980s FM rock sound, its militaristic title, its high ratio of rockers and its extensive use of Gilmour's blustering bark, *About Face* is one of the ballsiest efforts in the Floyd canon. But it's by no means the best.

Coming hard on the final humiliation of Gilmour's sidelining during *The Final Cut*, *About Face*'s aggression sounds as if it was directed squarely at **Roger Waters**. As such, *About Face*'s sound could be seen as an attempt to refute Waters' accusations of blandness – while Gilmour's creation of ten pieces in a year faces down Waters' assertion he'd not written anything for five years (Gilmour's two major *Wall* contributions dated back to 1977). What's more, in writing more lyrics for this album than in his entire career hitherto (albeit with help from **Pete Townshend** on two numbers), Gilmour is also directly challenging Waters' power base, while in "Cruise", he even attempts to take on Waters' accusations of being apolitical, creating an – ahem – love song to Britain's stock of American nuclear missiles.

The problem is that no amount of high protein production (take a very brief bow, **Bob Ezrin**) can bulk up lightweight material, the feeble white skank of "Cruise" being the worst offender, while bellowing doesn't make "All Lovers Are Deranged" any more convincing a proposition. The 80s touches don't help either, especially the risibly funky "Blue Light" with its blasting 80s brass and booming Linn drums. What's more, Gilmour often comes closer to imitating Waters than emulating him: notably the blistering ballad "Murder" echoing "Your Possible Pasts" in both melody and lyrical cadence.

As for the lyrics, Gilmour doesn't just tread on Waters' turf here, he takes him on directly: if

David Gilmour and Polly Samson

"Near The End" probably applies to the pair's relationship, even Gilmour admits "You Know I'm Right" addresses Waters. Petulant rather than piercing, neither is likely to cause Waters sleepless nights, while on a purely artistic level the string of clichés in "Out Of The Blue" is more likely to send him to sleep.

The sound of someone banging the table to be heard, it's little surprise no one much listened to *About Face* (selling a mere half million copies), a musical case study in how utterly unassertive aggression can be.

On An Island

CASTELLORIZON/ON AN ISLAND/THE BLUE/TAKE A BREATH/
RED SKY AT NIGHT/THIS HEAVEN/THEN I CLOSE MY EYES/
SMILE/POCKETFUL OF STONE/WHERE WE START
EMI; recorded 2002–2005; released March 6, 2006; available on CD

David Gilmour's fear that Pink Floyd's Live 8 performance would overshadow his projected solo album seems curious in retrospect. For Live 8's *actual* effect was to *boost* Gilmour's personal profile to such an all-time career high that his album couldn't but benefit. With pleasing Pink Floyd paradox, this occurred largely as a result of the very squabbles Gilmour and Waters put aside in order to perform, providing the coolly remote Pink Floyd, for the first time in their history, with a human, directly emotional dimension.

So it's an unexpected pleasure that Gilmour should rise to the occasion with an album, following on from his subtler, more introspective 2002 South Bank shows, that is itself suf-

fused with emotion. Specifically nostalgia and yearning. Released on his 60th birthday, and gilded with guests from throughout Gilmour's life, if *On An Island* is not quite the career peak he claims, it's far better than anyone had a right to expect from him – or any musician – at the dawn of his seventh decade.

The Floydian title track surges and sweeps with Rick Wright's oceanic organ, while the harmonies of **David Crosby** and **Graham Nash** are the summit of Gilmour's lifelong West Coast fixation; Wright adds fragile harmonies to the liquidly lovely "The Blue", which recalls enduring Gilmour favourite – **Fleetwood Mac**'s "Albatross" (and thus "Dogs"); old Cambridge connection **Bob Klose** guests on guitar on both tracks. Another Cambridge alumnus, Jokers Wild's **Willie Wilson** drums on the lilting, irresistible "Smile" – as premiered at Robert Wyatt's Meltdown. Wyatt himself plays cornet on "Then I Close My Eyes" alongside Gilmour's own autumnal sax on "Red Sky At Night", both tracks boasting an artiness that harks back to Pink Floyd's rarely revisited prog period. Finally, Roxy Music's **Phil Manzanera** plays intermittently throughout and co-produces.

Manzanera last guested on *Momentary Lapse Of Reason,* and it's only on the revisits to that era that *On An Island* really falters: "This Heaven" is the "Dogs Of War" retread no one was longing for, while "Take A Breath" is a token attempt at another "Sorrow", complete with late Floyd regular **Guy Pratt** on bass.

Gilmour doesn't *need* to reassert his rock

credentials, however – the arty, atmospheric instrumentals and the ballads in particular are quietly, sufficiently, assertive. Beautifully, soulfully sung, with better lyrics than any other Gilmour-helmed album, and naturally boasting quietly dramatic guitar work, "The Blue", "Smile", "A Pocketful Of Stones", "Where We Start" and the title track are the best pieces Gilmour has written since *The Wall*. If this seems a momentous claim, it should be noted they have only *About Face* and two fairly undistinguished Floyd albums to compete with. But, crucially, Gilmour sounds for the first time like he genuinely doesn't need Roger Waters any more. And that's the last legacy of **Live 8** anyone might have expected.

Production and session work

While Gilmour has occasionally produced, his main non-Floyd work has been as a guest guitarist, in which capacity his credits are voluminous, especially during his convivial 1980s.

Unicorn

Gilmour's first production foray was these country-rockers' *Blue Pine Trees* (Charisma, 1974), also playing pedal steel. He also produced 1975's *Too Many Crooks* (Harvest) and 1978's *One More Tomorrow* (Harvest), at BritRow. Not recommended.

Sutherland Brothers and Quiver

Featuring Cambridge cohort and future Floyd second guitarist, **Tim Renwick**, Gilmour produced and played guitar on 1975's *Reach For The Sky* (CBS). Rather soggy AOR folk rock, this is not recommended to Floyd fans.

Roy Harper

An absolutely key Floyd collaborator: Floyd fans should own Harper's classic *HQ* (Harvest, 1975) if only for Gilmour's playing on "The Game" and, even more crucially, *The Unknown Soldier* (Harvest 1980) upon which, apart from playing guitar throughout, Gilmour also co-wrote "Playing Games", "True Story" and the stunning "You" (featuring **Kate Bush**). Gilmour also played on "Once", "Once In The Middle Of Nowhere" and "Berliners" on *Once* (1990).

Kate Bush

An equally important Floyd collaborator, Gilmour officially "discovered" Kate Bush. In fact, **Ricky Hopper** recommended the 13-year-old singer-songwriter, while Gilmour recorded some of her songs, including "**Man With The Child In His Eyes**". Gilmour brought her to his Essex home studio in August 1973, where they recorded "Passing Through Air", with Unicorn and Gilmour on guitar (available as B-side to "Army Dreamers" and on *This Woman's Work* box set). Gilmour booked AIR studios in June 1975, bringing in arranger Andrew Powell, then presenting the tapes to his label, EMI. "Man With The Child" ended up on *The Kick Inside* (EMI, 1977), on which Gilmour is listed as executive producer.

Gilmour also added backing vocals to *The Dreaming*'s "Pull Out The Pin" and played lead guitar on *The Sensual World*'s "Rocket Tail" and "Love And Anger" (all recommended). He also appeared with Bush at the Secret Policeman's Third Ball, playing "Running Up That Hill".

Paul McCartney

For all the talk of Lennon and Barrett's links, it is Gilmour who has the only longstanding relationship with any Beatle, playing on **Wings**' "Rockestra Theme" and "So Glad To See You Here" on *Back To The Egg* (EMI, 1979). He played soaring lead on McCartney's 1984 hit "**No More Lonely Nights** (Ballad Version)" – recommended – (*Give My Regards To Broad Street*, EMI, 1984), played on "We Got Married" on *Flowers In The Dirt* (EMI, 1979) and contributed lead guitar throughout McCartney's *Run Devil Run* set of rock'n'roll covers (EMI, 1999).

Pete Townshend

Another heavyweight connection. After recording at Townshend's Eel Pie studio during *Final Cut*, the two became friends. Gilmour

played on "**Give Blood**" on Townshend's 1985's *White City* (ATCO) and co-wrote the title track with him, an out-take from Gilmour's solo album *About Face*. *White City*'s music also appears on Roy Harper's 1984 *Jugula* as "Hope". Gilmour also played lead guitar for a series of London concerts in Townshend's band, available on the *Deep End Live* video.

The Dream Academy

Via his brother Peter, Gilmour produced **Nick Laird-Clowes**' 1985 album *The Dream Academy* (Blanco y Negro), featuring the big hit "**Life In A Northern Town**" and 1990's *A Different Kind Of Weather* (Blanco y Negro). Laird-Clowes would later work on *The Division Bell*, while Academy bassist **Guy Pratt** joined Pink Floyd.

Bryan Ferry

Gilmour played guitar on Bryan Ferry's album *Boys And Girls*, was the sole Floyd to appear at **Live Aid** – in Ferry's band – and also contributed to Ferry's 1987 *Bête Noire*, produced by Pat Leonard (who'd work on both *Momentary Lapse* and Waters' *Amused To Death*). Gilmour later took Ferry's keyboard player **Jon Carin** off to the Floyd. Ferry and Gilmour also collaborated on "Is Your Love Strong Enough" for Ridley Scott's 1985 film, *Legend* (recommended).

The 1980s and 1990s

As guest musician, Gilmour played on the title track of Supertramp's *Brother Where You Bound* (A&M, 1985); the title track on Grace Jones' *Slave To The Rhythm* (Island, 1985); on "The Promise" with Sting; on Duran Duran side-project Arcadia's *So Red The Rose* (Capitol, 1985); the Bob Ezrin-produced Berlin's "Pink and Velvet" from *Count Three And Pray* (Mercury, 1996); Warren Zevon's "Run Straight Down" on *Transverse City* (1989, Virgin); Propaganda's

"Only One Word" (Virgin, 1990); Elton John's "Understanding Woman" on *The One* (Rocket, 1990); Paul Young's *Other Voices* (CBS, 1990); Floyd backing singers Blue Pearl's *Naked* (Big Life, 1990); All About Eve's *Touched by Jesus* (Vertigo, 1991); Jimmy Nail's *Growing Up In Public* (Eastwest, 1992); while also guesting on John Martyn's unpopular remakes of his 1970s classics on *No Little Boy* (Permanent, 1993). Apart from the Grace Jones and Zevon tracks (the latter very Floydesque), none of these is recommended to Floyd fans.

Roger Waters

Music From The Body

OUR SONG/SEA SHELL AND STONE/RED STUFF WRITHE/ A GENTLE BREEZE BLEW THROUGH LIFE/LICK YOUR PARTNERS/BRIDGE PASSAGE FOR THREE PLASTIC TEETH/ CHAIN OF LIFE/THE WOMB BIT/EMBRYO THOUGHT/MARCH PAST OF THE EMBRYOS/MORE THAN SEVEN DWARFS IN PENIS-LAND/DANCE OF THE RED CORPUSCLES/BODY TRANSPORT/ HAND DANCE – FULL EVENING DRESS/BREATHE/OLD FOLKS ASCENSION/BEDTIME-DREAM-CLIME/PIDDLE IN PERSPEX/ EMBRYONIC WOMB-WALK/MRS THROAT GOES WALKING/SEA SHELL AND SOFT STONE/GIVE BIRTH TO A SMILE
Harvest; recorded January–March, August–September 1970; released November 18, 1970; available on CD

This first full outside venture by any Floyd bar Barrett was, in retrospect, highly significant, providing Roger Waters with some useful compositional lessons, providing key conceptual ideas, while also giving him a freedom and degree of control that impacted fundamentally on his future Floyd work.

With Ron Geesin having influenced Waters' experimental "Several Species", on *Ummagumma*, Geesin in turn called in a little conventional songcraft from Waters for this soundtrack commission. Consequently the collaboration is nicely balanced between quirky doodles from Geesin and "Grantchester Meadows"-style folky numbers from Waters. The pair also try out a couple of aural japes, "Our Song" and "Body Transport", making good use of Waters' facility for mouth noises, while also co-composing two instrumentals – the lovely cello and acoustic guitar piece "Sea Shell And Soft Stone" and the experimental "Womb Bit".

Geesin's compositions, for piano, cello, sound effects and guitar, are object lessons in combining experimentalism and listenability – lessons Waters remembered on *Atom Heart Mother* (at least insofar as enlisting Geesin's assistance). The songs Waters sings here gave the bass player an opportunity to flex his vocal muscles (singing an unprecedented four lead vocals on an album) and to play guitar (something he'd now do on almost every Floyd release). The broad themes of birth and life built upon his recent "Embryo" track and would play a key part in *Dark Side*'s genesis – not just the obvious "Breathe" but the invocation of ageing and of human interconnection in "Chain Of Life". The link is plainest on "Give Birth To A Smile", however, for this anthemically life-affirming ballad not only features an uncredited Pink Floyd, but a troupe of female backing singers, and sounds like a dress rehearsal for "Eclipse". This Waters sounds like one to watch.

The Pros And Cons Of Hitchhiking

4.30AM (APPARENTLY THEY WERE TRAVELLING ABROAD)/ 4.33AM (RUNNING SHOES)/4.37AM (ARABS WITH KNIVES AND WET GERMAN SKIES)/4.39AM (FOR THE FIRST TIME TODAY – PART 2)/4.41AM (SEXUAL REVOLUTION)/4.47AM (THE REMAINS OF OUR LOVE)/ 4:50AM (GO FISHING)/4:56 (FOR THE FIRST TIME TODAY – PART 1)/ 4:58AM (DUNROAMIN, DUNCARIN, DUNLIVIN)/ 5:01AM (THE PROS AND CONS OF HITCHHIKING PART 10) / 5:06AM (EVERY STRANGERS EYES) / 5:11AM (THE MOMENT OF CLARITY)
Harvest; recorded February–December 1983; released May 8, 1984; available on CD

If *The Final Cut* is a Roger Waters solo album in all but name, then, equally, then *Pros And Cons* is a Pink Floyd album in all but personnel. Waters wrote and demoed the song-cycle at the same time as *The Wall*, with which *Pros* shares lyrical and musical themes (the opening riffs of both are identical). Gilmour says he worked on the songs, and *Pros* boasts the same sonic setup as *Final Cut* (heavy of sound effect; sluggish of tempo), as well as much the same additional players (**Raphael Ravenscroft, Andy Bown** and **Michael Kamen**). What's more, with Gilmour's guitar interludes replaced by **Eric Clapton**'s, what, for Pink Floyd fans, is there *not* to like?

Apparently a great deal, given *Pros'* unloved status. Gilmour called it "too much the same"; critics complained of a lack of tunes; fans remain largely silent on the subject. But while *Pros* has a unity of mood (the same melody recurring on five different tracks), this casts an aptly somnambulant spell, seamlessly linked by sound effects, and, when it does become monochrome it is largely lifted by Clapton's excellent playing (especially on "For The First Time Today", "Sexual Revolution" and the title track).

It's also the case that Waters' vocals are even more tortuous than hitherto, barking, shrieking and wailing throughout. But Waters has always barked, shrieked and wailed with some aplomb, his voice operating more as dramatic texture than for dulcet tonality. His background shriek of "leave us alone, leave us alone" on "Arabs With Knives" is

Raymond Briggs' *When The Wind Blows OST*

THE RUSSIAN MISSILE/TOWERS OF FAITH/HILDA'S DREAM/THE AMERICAN BOMBER/THE ANDERSON SHELTER/THE BRITISH SUBMARINE/THE ATTACK/THE FALLOUT/HILDA'S HAIR/FOLDED FLAGS
Virgin; released October 10, 1986; available on CD

It's perhaps appropriate that Waters' first official post-Pink Floyd product should have addressed the Cold War full on, and be suffused with (political) paranoia. For, while sharing the billing with **David Bowie**, **Hugh Cornwell**, **Genesis**, **Squeeze** and **Paul Hardcastle**, Waters provided the bulk of the music for this soundtrack to Raymond Briggs' gloomy animated nuclear war film. Beating Gilmour only in a numbers rather than creativity game, it's by no means essential, most of the tunes being fairly forgettable instrumentals overlaid with film dialogue. The acoustic guitar piece, "Hilda's Dream" has a somnambulant prettiness that recalls "Brain Damage", however, and "Hilda's Hair" sounds like a more caustic version of Part 1 of "Shine On", featuring some fine electric guitar from **Jay Stapley**, whilst actor **John Mills** recites The Lord's Prayer.

As for the *songs*... while on "Towers Of Faith" Waters apparently points to competing claims over Israel as the potential catalyst of nuclear conflict (crude but not absurd), the way he follows a quotation from **Woody Guthrie**'s "This Land Is Your Land" with "this band is my band", makes the parallels between world and Pink Floyd politics plain. A plainness enhanced by the vocal presence of "Great Gig In The Sky" singer **Clare Torry** and a cheekily Gilmour-esque guitar solo by Stapley. Shame the track isn't so hot. Being a vocal version of the same "Brain Damage"-esque acoustic piece as "Hilda's Dream", "Folded Flags" is another Floydian slip. Just as its fingerpicking harks back to Pink Floyd's long submerged pastoralism, so does it invoke another folk standard, "Hey Joe", to produce the rather forced line "Hey Joe where you going with that dogma in your hand?" Very far from being one of Waters' best lyrics, "Flags" is actually one of Waters' better solo songs, guest vocalist **Paul Carrack** giving the penultimate verse a suitably climactic urgency, and it deserves a wider audience than this album gave it. But if change was around the corner for the real world's Cold War, it was about to get a whole lot colder in the Floyd's.

particularly effective, his deranged panting on "Sexual Revolution" creepily hilarious, while there's something heart-rending about his wail of "stay with me" on "First Time Today Part 2". What's more his vocals on highlights "Pros And Cons" itself and "Every Strangers Eyes" are both more conventionally melodious affairs. Waters also has the sense to sweeten the deal throughout with the mellifluous voices of **Madeleine Bell, Katie Kissoon** and **Doreen Chanter**.

Furthermore, the concept is Waters' most convoluted yet, offering no entry for the merely curious. But once you realize the whole thing is a dream, and that the narrative follows dream logic – characters randomly appearing, disappearing and merging, locations shifting abruptly – *Pros* becomes easier both to understand *and* to love. A concept album about sex, the subconscious and indeed love, Waters is on top lyrical form throughout: alternately witty, lascivious (a new dimension to his writing) and scabrous. Indeed, "Every Strangers Eyes" is one of his best lyrics, a typically Watersian cascade of images linked as tautly by their characteristic internal rhymes as their associative sense. Again that problem with the apostrophe (in the title), but again that assertion of humanism, however scuffed and scarred: it's not so much that Waters sees the best in people, but that he sees the worst of them in *himself*.

If "Dunroamin" is a repeated melodic motif too far, perhaps the *most* offputting aspect of *Pros* is the cover: a tacky attempt at soft-porn populism, that may instead have helped the public agree with Gilmour's assessment. It might have at least given Waters some satisfaction that said public didn't take Gilmour's contemporary fan-friendly opus to their hearts any more than this more challenging – but infinitely superior – album.

Radio K.A.O.S.

RADIO WAVES/WHO NEEDS INFORMATION/ME OR HIM/THE POWERS THAT BE/SUNSET STRIP/HOME/FOUR MINUTES/THE TIDE IS TURNING (AFTER LIVE AID)
Harvest (US: Columbia); released June 5, 1987; available on CD

If *Radio K.A.O.S.* can be said to prove anything in the competitive aftermath of the Floyd's reformation, it's that Roger Waters knows how to end an album. If he hadn't already proved this with "Brain Damage"/"Eclipse", "Outside the Wall" and "Every Strangers Eyes"/"The Moment of Clarity", then he proves it conclusively here, with "The Tide Is Turning". For "Tide" is one of Waters' most stirring, most anthemic, most singable songs, and quite why it wasn't a hit is beyond imagining. Which isn't – crucially – to say that the song is one of his best. It's sentimental, breast-beatingly "big" and distinctly saccharine – in short it' archetypically 80s. That's simply the best you can say about this deeply flawed album.

If *Pros And Cons'* concept was convoluted, it at least had the excuse of dream logic: *Radio K.A.O.S.*'s story supposedly takes place in the real world. A real world of simple-minded boys (our Welsh hero, Billy) with telepathic gifts; a real world where a simulated nuclear war teaches everyone it's not what they want after all, thanks. Quite what Waters is trying to say here is frustratingly foggy (nuclear war is bad?), a fogginess not helped by Billy's synthesized voice being utterly incomprehensible (indeed Waters' usually impeccable use of sound effects is disappointing throughout).

The music is equally hard on the ear, possessed of few tunes, while being even more in hock to 1980s production values than Pink Floyd's contemporaneous *A Momentary Lapse Of Reason* – all Fairlight synthesizers, booming Linn drums and portentous tinniness.

Waters' voice, meanwhile, is at its worst. Many attributed its new gruffness to age – if so, he must have discovered the elixir of youth before he undertook the Berlin *Wall* performances three years later. Waters' use of session singer **Paul Carrack** on "The Powers That Be" doesn't really help: Carrack's voice sounds like someone's flipped the automaton's switch to "Angry", making what should be a hard-hitting song strangely bland. It is interesting to note, though, how much faster most of this material is than Floyd's familiarly glacial pace – even if "Radio Waves" simply sounds like a testosterone-deprived **ZZ Top** and "Sunset Strip" summons the tight-white-T-shirted spectre of **Bryan Adams**. (Perhaps Waters thought so too: Adams would later appear at the Berlin *Wall*.) Another uptempo, electro-fuelled tune, "Home", at least has something resembling a tune, lifted by the presence of *Dark Side*'s **Clare Torry**, but it rambles so much that its impact is muddied.

"Me Or Him" initially suggests an acoustic respite from the technology, but the *shakuhachi* – a Japanese bamboo flute, played by Waters – also sounds very much of its world music-lite time. "Who Needs Information" at least has a decent female-sung chorus, with horns and male voice choir adding interest. Which brings us back to where we started, and "The Tide Is Turning", for which "the album's standout track" really isn't much of a compliment. By some distance, Roger Waters' worst solo album.

The Wall Live In Berlin

IN THE FLESH?/THE THIN ICE/ ANOTHER BRICK IN THE WALL PT 1 / THE HAPPIEST DAYS OF OUR LIVES / ANOTHER BRICK IN THE WALL PT 2 / MOTHER / GOODBYE BLUE SKY/ WHAT SHALL WE DO/YOUNG LUST/ ONE OF MY TURNS/ DON'T LEAVE ME NOW/ ANOTHER BRICK IN THE WALL PT 3/ GOODBYE CRUEL WORLD / HEY YOU/ IS THERE ANYBODY OUT THERE?/NOBODY HOME/VERA/BRING THE BOYS BACK HOME/ COMFORTABLY NUMB/ IN THE FLESH/ RUN LIKE HELL/WAITING FOR THE WORMS/ STOP!/THE TRIAL/ THE TIDE IS TURNING
Universal; recorded July 21, 1990; released September 17, 1990; available on CD/DVD

A spectacle intended to celebrate a new era (the collapse of Communism and the Berlin Wall) which ends up unwittingly hymning the *previous* era: the 1980s. From the mullets that adorn the musicians' heads, to Waters' power-dressed designer suit/shades/trainers combo, to the air of jet-set indulgence that overhangs proceedings, this event screams "80s" from build to collapse.

As such, perhaps paradoxically, the Berlin *Wall* views seem better now than they did then. In 1990, with a dressed-down, back-to-basics apoliticism dominating youth culture via hardcore and acid house, *The Wall* just looked like a bunch of middle-aged men in yesterday's OTT fashions, re-enacting the day-before-yesterday's OTT concept album in quest of Political Significance. But the 1990s themselves are now dated, while our abhorrence of the 80s has softened the further they've receded.

Available as a combined DVD and CD, *The Wall Live In Berlin* is best enjoyed visually. The inflatables look incredible; the bricks are bigger

The Music

and better than the original staging; and the collapse at the end is truly stunning. And the guest stars are fun to watch: **The Scorpions** being just the kind of comedy metal band "In The Flesh" was satirizing, **Bryan Adams'** performing "Young Lust" sans irony, and luvvies **Ute Lemper** and **Marianne Faithfull** camping up the album's cabaret elements. And if **Cyndi Lauper's** delivery of "Another Brick" is disappointing, it's fun watching the hyperactive singer annoying **Rick Di Fonzo** as he does a note-perfect imitation of Gilmour's guitar solo. Otherwise it's a mixed bag: **Sinead O'Connor** (with **The Band**) makes good work of "Mother" (due to technical hitches, her performance is from the dress rehearsal); **Joni Mitchell** never quite gels with "Goodbye Blue Sky"; **Jerry Hall** makes a hash of the groupie monologue from "One Of My Turns", while **Van Morrison** and The Band do a surprisingly soulful job of "Comfortably Numb". The arrival of the East Berlin Radio Choir and Soviet Orchestra (in full uniform) for "Bring The Boys Back Home" manages to float somewhere at a precise mid-point between insult and inspiration. As does Waters' performance at the rally scene: he's just that bit too comfortable in Nazi regalia, and the "joke" is a bit too queasy as he spouts sarcastic fascist rhetoric on the very spot where Hitler died.

And, of course, there's something embarrassingly eighties about the climactic communal sing-song of "The Tide Is Turning", though it's actually performed far more professionally than Live Aid's finale, with Lauper and Mitchell now acquitting themselves well. As with the finale, so with the whole thing however, The

Wall making for uncomfortable but compelling viewing – and thus functioning as a fond footnote to an odd era.

Amused To Death

THE BALLAD OF BILL HUBBARD/WHAT GOD WANTS, PART 1/
PERFECT SENSE, PART 1/PERFECT SENSE PART II/THE BRAVERY
OF BEING OUT OF RANGE/LATE HOME TONIGHT, PART 1/
LATE HOME TONIGHT PART II/TOO MUCH ROPE/WHAT GOD
WANTS, PART II/WHAT GOD WANTS, PART III/WATCHING TV/
THREE WISHES/IT'S A MIRACLE/AMUSED TO DEATH
Columbia; recorded 1987–1992; released September 7,
(11, US) 1992; available on CD

Roger Waters regards *Amused To Death* as his third claim upon posterity, alongside *Dark Side* and *The Wall*. And in sheer size, scope and impact, *Amused To Death* is certainly a major work, even if at times it feels this is accomplished simply through sheer bludgeoning force of will.

For if *Amused To Death*'s concept is less chaotic than *Radio K.A.O.S.*, it's still as heavy-handed as its title suggests: war, religion and government repression via the filter of mass media. Oh, and then, viewed through the eyes of a monkey. Waters may be a more political animal than his 1960s self, but he's clearly still a *2001* devotee.

The music is equally big and bombastic – courtesy of slick Madonna producer **Patrick Leonard** and two Floyd cohorts – **Nick Griffiths** and **James Guthrie** – co-producing and mixing respectively. "What God Wants" Parts I and II both sound as if they were recorded in a stadium, with the crowd chanting the chorus (actually another of Waters'

Welsh male voice choirs). A hectoringly preachy diatribe against right wing religious evangelists ("what God wants, God gets"), with Waters' voice at its most unappealingly gruff, it is however still hard to resist. What Rog wants, Rog gets. "Perfect Sense", meanwhile, already taken to soaring heights by **P.P. Arnold**'s superb second vocal, adds in "Part II" another sports crowd singing along, and even deploys an overexcited sports commentator. By the time this trick is repeated a *fourth* time on the superb, **Michael Kamen**-orchestrated ballad "Late Home Tonight" you begin to feel Waters is not simply hitting home his theme of world-events as mass spectator sport but asserting that his own music should be fulfilling a similar function. That for all his disavowals, *he*, like Pink Floyd, should be filling sports stadiums, thus getting his message heard by the masses once again.

All this heavy-handedness does occasionally pall. "The Bravery Of Being Out Of Range" is a lumbering heavy rock recycling of "What God Wants" spliced to a cruder take on the firt verse of "Us And Them", while "Watching TV" is a gauche treatment of the Tiananmen Square massacre – rather too lascivious about the girl killed on live TV for taste. It's a nice tune, however, its return to country featuring harmonies from Eagle **Don Henley**, belatedly repaying the debt owed "Wish You Were Here' by "Hotel California".

Waters saves a knockout triptych for the end, however: bravely piling three ballads

Roger Waters and daughter, 1995

atop one another. They're all sprawling affairs, lyrics popping out all over the place, "It's A Miracle" swerving tangentially to a random attack on **Sir Andrew Lloyd Webber**, but these tunes are as powerful as they are polemical. "Three Wishes" rises to a fantastic, female-sung hook line, while "Amused To Death" features a lovely **Rita Coolidge** vocal, a lyrical dig at the Floyd fiasco and shows Waters still knows how to close an album in anthemic style.

The public wouldn't agree with Waters' estimation of this album and, apparently peeved by *ATD*'s poor commercial performance (albeit his best so far), Waters refused

The Music

to tour for seven years. Fourteen years later, he still hasn't released a follow-up to this rather splendid album.

In the Flesh – Live

IN THE FLESH/THE HAPPIEST DAYS OF OUR LIVES/ANOTHER BRICK IN THE WALL PART 2/MOTHER/GET YOUR FILTHY HANDS OFF MY DESERT/SOUTHAMPTON DOCK/PIGS ON THE WING, PART 1/DOGS/WELCOME TO THE MACHINE/WISH YOU WERE HERE/SHINE ON YOU CRAZY DIAMOND (PARTS 1-8)/SET THE CONTROLS FOR THE HEART OF THE SUN/BREATHE (IN THE AIR)/TIME/MONEY/THE PROS AND CONS OF HITCHHIKING – PART 11 (AKA 5:06 AM – EVERY$ STRANGERS EYES)/PERFECT SENSE (PARTS 1 AND II) / THE BRAVERY OF BEING OUT OF RANGE/IT'S A MIRACLE/AMUSED TO DEATH/BRAIN DAMAGE/ECLIPSE/COMFORTABLY NUMB/EACH SMALL CANDLE
Recorded, summer 1999, summer 2000; released December 5, 2000; available on CD, SACD and DVD

If Waters had finally reached, as he says in the sleeve notes here, an accommodation with his audience, finally consenting to play live after a petulant seven-year absence, he was far from reaching an accommodation with Pink Floyd – either its members or its legacy.

For, with the record-shop shelves already stuffed with needless live albums of Pink Floyd catalogue retreads, *In The Flesh* often feels like its only *real* reason for existing is as a "touché" to Pink Floyd's *Pulse*. Waters is apparently not done proving which one's Pink: provocatively, he re-uses a Floyd tour title; crosses over on a whopping *nine* out of 24 tracks; and utilizes Gilmour's own stunt double **Snowy White**, Rick Wright stand-in **Jon Carin** *and* the same producer as *Pulse* (**James Guthrie**, strangely unassisted for once by Waters).

And where Gilmour employed **Guy Pratt** and Carin to sing and play Waters' parts, here Waters enlists Carin and **Doyle Bramhall** to sing Gilmour's. But, as with Gilmour's roll-call of diluted Waters, Gilmour cannot himself be replaced so easily. Despite approaching the problem mob-handedly, the "three-man Gilmour" demonstrates that Gil-more is ultimately Gil-less, making *In The Flesh* sound even more like a Pink Floyd tribute band than the Gilmour Floyd. While Waters does trot out some tracks the modern Floyd won't touch, all succeed or fail in a precise ratio to Gilmour's involvement in the original. Thus *Final Cut* fare is fine, "Dogs" is a dog, and "Mother" floats in the middle – the song being sufficiently refreshing to hear live that Gilmour's replacement by **P.P. Arnold**, **Katie Kissoon** and **Susannah Melvoin** offfering a fair compensation for the lack of Gilmour. The one exception to this rule, Waters' surprisingly decent solo fist of "Wish You Were Here", is still unlikely to cause Gilmour sleepless nights.

All this Pyrrhic point-proving wastes not just time but space, leaving Waters room for only six tracks from his solo albums, blowing the chance to redress *Radio K.A.O.S*'s techno overkill with new arrangements by ignoring it altogether, including instead a fairly forgettable unreleased track, "Each Small Candle". With the solo tracks being by far the best here, and "Perfect Sense" and "It's A Miracle" sounding particularly spectacular, Waters could have concentrated on solo material and made a much better album. But Pink

Floyd is obviously a spectre not too easily put to rest. Not that the Floyd content helped sales much.

Flickering Flame: The Solo Years Volume 1

KNOCKIN' ON HEAVEN'S DOOR/TOO MUCH ROPE/THE TIDE IS TURNING/PERFECT SENSE PTS 1 AND 2/THREE WISHES/5.06 AM (EVERY STRANGERS EYES)/WHO NEEDS INFORMATION/ EACH SMALL CANDLE/FLICKERING FLAME/TOWERS OF FAITH/RADIO WAVES/LOST BOYS CALLING (DEMO)
Released April 2002; currently not available in any format

Seemingly buying time as the gap since *Amused To Death* grew and grew, Waters released this Australian/Japanese compilation of his solo work. The choices are questionable however: three from *K.A.O.S.* is two too many (and wouldn't this have been a great time to remix or re-record them?); one from *Pros And Cons* is rather cowardly; while "Towers Of Faith" is simply the wrong song from *When The Wind Blows*. The version of **Bob Dylan**'s "Knockin' On Heaven's Door" is interesting, with its characteristic use of sound effects, but sadly Waters' original demo of "Lost Boys Calling" is included rather than the far superior **Morricone** and **Eddie Van Halen** version from *The Legend Of 1900*; while "Each Small Candle" is the same track that appeared on *In The Flesh*. The title track is, however, rather more inviting – despite being only a demo. Another Dylan-inspired track, it's essentially a state-of-Waters address for 2002, encompassing the death of his friend Philippe Constantin

in 1996, his divorce, his love of sport and his ambivalent feelings about returning to the rock fray. It's one of his best lyrics, full of characteristic quick-snapping rhymes, but it's also very moving. However, as of 2006, there's still no indication of it being given a proper recording: the flame less flickering than close to sputtering out altogether.

Internet-only tracks

TO KILL A CHILD/LEAVING BEIRUT
Recorded 2004; released 2004; available online only

Released in response to the Gulf War, these are the only new products from Roger Waters, bar "Each Small Candle" and "Flickering Flame", since *Amused To Death* in 1992. Though not as heavy ("Beirut" is, again, only a demo), they are very much in the *Amused* vein, with their political themes and heavy use of backing vocals and synthesizers. And yet the twelve-minute "Beirut" in particular shows both a more personal approach to politics and a more literary approach to music. For "Beirut" approaches the war via a long spoken passage about the young Waters' encounter with a Lebanese family in 1961. If it is, ultimately, overlong, the story is well told and moving, while the sung sections pack a fine melodic punch, even if they are occasionally lyrically crude ("not in my name Tony/you great war leader, you"). Although "To Kill A Child" is a finished song, it still lacks the clout of *Amused*, while finding Waters sounding curiously like the

The Music

late **Warren Zevon**. Again it relies heavily on black backing singers but its sentiments are too crude, while any witticism in Waters' wordplay is rather undermined by his increasingly irritating US accent.

Ça Ira : "There Is Hope" (An Opera In Three Acts)

Released on Sony Classical/Columbia on September 2005; available on CD and SACD

While ostensibly tangential to his work in Pink Floyd and solo, Roger Waters' opera (brewing, significantly, since as long ago as 1989) could be seen as his ultimate touché to David Gilmour. For a start, Waters has achieved the ultimate coup in the high cultural approbation this most middle class of bands has always craved: an opera. Featuring **Bryn Terfel** in the lead role, and is about no less a subject than the French Revolution. Waters doesn't need to so much as *hint* that his former bandmate couldn't even consider such a concept. The closest Gilmour has got is a short but sweet stab at a single Bizet aria. But even more importantly, in composing the music to *someone else's* concept and lyrics (those of French librettist **Etienne Roda-Gil**) for the first time in his career, Waters is mounting the "Waters-the-conceptualist, Gilmour-the-composer" idea.

That much rides on this project is apparent in Waters' rather defensive promotion of the album. "Of course the knives will come out," he predicted. "People defend their own little islands of culture with great panache." In fact *Ça Ira* was largely positively reviewed by the classical press, going to #1 in the classical chart, even if it elicited bafflement from the rock establishment. For, even allowing for an unfamiliarity with opera, the music here doesn't initially appear overburdened with memorable tunes, and when it does – on "The Letter" – the melody is borrowed from *Pros And Cons'* "Every Strangers Eyes".

But things get better on the second disc, which is suddenly packed with fine tunes, with something familiarly Floydian about the rollicking "The Fugitive King" in particular and the anthemic "Vive Le Commune De Paris", with its positive assertions of the power to change things of every individual under the sun. Inevitably, in translating Roda-Gil's libretto, Waters has added his own personality to lyrics as well as music. In particular, Waters' sees his lines in "France In Disarray" to be the ultimate expression of his philosophical humanism, addressing the conflict between brute instincts and human choice.

Of course, this could be seen as *just* as important a gauntlet to Gilmour as the music: the assertion that Waters is a humanist not a misanthropist, a champion of the light, not the darkness – the good guy, not the grumpy one. And back and forth it goes on, with Gilmour's solo album and hopefully, maybe one day another Roger Waters rock album. Which, given the increasingly remote likelihood of a Floyd reunion album, is probably about the best we can hope for. Just a thought.

Part 3:
Floydology

Floyd on film

True to snooty form, Pink Floyd have never been over generous in parcelling their songs out to film soundtracks, but this most visually-orientated and atmospheric of bands have enjoyed a rich relationship with the screen, from film through TV soundtracks to concert films.

Apart from the movies and documentaries listed here, there are of course also the promos that were shot for "Arnold Layne", "See Emily Play", "Apples And Oranges" and "Point Me At The Sky", which, alongside the moon landing soundtrack "Moonhead" and an abundance of late 1960s/early 1970s European TV footage would make a fine DVD collection (the "Another Brick" video is available on *The Wall* DVD), while there's a less rewarding DVD to be made of **Storm Thorgerson**'s Gilmour-era promos for singles.

   Indeed, mirroring their career, Pink Floyd-related films tend in the early years to be interesting but flawed, tepidly experimental in the middle period, heavy-handed in the Waters era and artily bland during the Gilmour years, while a series of (admittedly unauthorized) rehashes of their history put as nasty a blot on their filmography as the 1990s live albums do on their discography.

Syd's First Trip

(Nigel Lesmoir-Gordon, 1966; Music Video Dist. DVD)

Why let accuracy get in the way of a tantalizing title? While by no means a record of Syd Barrett's first trip, this is still a fascinating document for any Barrett aficionado. Shot in summer 1966, it features a young, short-haired, immaculately dressed Barrett tripping in a copper mine in the Gog Magog Hills near Cambridge. Beautifully captured by his filmmaker friend and acid proselytizer **Nigel Lesmoir-Gordon**, Barrett is simultaneously dandyishly dapper and boyishly vulnerable. There's a charming but slightly sinister innocence in his placing mushrooms over his eyes and staring at his own hands in endless fascination. There's no dialogue, though the 1980s video gives the footage an effective ambient soundtrack by electronic act **Dilate**. Midway through, the action suddenly shifts to London, with shots of Barrett outside EMI. Although this section is less essential, there's an eerie purity to the mine footage: a moment of youthful optimism and excitement captured forever.

Tonite Let's All Make Love In London

(Peter Whitehead, 1967)

Pink Floyd provided the incidental music and some live footage for Whitehead's Swinging London documentary. The original, rather uneven, film is currently unavailable on DVD, but the Floyd's contributions are available as a CD/DVD release, *In London 1966–1967* (See For Miles, 1999).

This comprises January 1967 **Sound Techniques** session footage in addition to shots from UFO and of the crowd at Alexandra Palace's **24-hour Technicolor Dream** (Whitehead failed to capture the Floyd). It makes for fascinating viewing.

Barrett looks tremendous in stripy red T-shirt, striped trousers and pencil moustache. Although he's absorbed in his music, he also looks entirely, refreshingly together – signalling to the others when to stop at the end of "Interstellar Overdrive", and mouthing out instructions during "Nick's Boogie".

Waters is cool and detached in blue shades, black high-collared shirt and stripy trousers; Wright appears a little self-conscious; and Mason, especially in the studio footage, looks downright incongruous – like a prep-school boy, his puce roll-neck pullover making him look like he's bought his Swinging London look at M&S.

The Committee

(Peter Sykes, 1968; Basho DVD)

A curious 1960s period piece, *The Committee* is of interest to Floyd fans for capturing some of the first fruits of the post-Barrett line-up. **Manfred Mann**'s **Paul Jones** (who'd starred in the previous year's *Privilege*) is an alienated 60s youth whose casual murder of an older, more conventional man prompts the formation of the slightly sinister Kafka-esque committee, which convenes at a country house.

Shot in black and white, and featuring long sections of dialogue concerning the individual's relationship with society, the film is heavily stylized, a blend of the *nouvelle vague* directorial style of Alan Resnais and the surreal dialogue of playwright Harold Pinter. Within this rather pretentious setting, the Floyd's music – electronic bleeps, cyclical organ riffs and staccato guitar – is highly effective and, bar a prototype "Eugene", all unavailable elsewhere. The otherwise interminable interviews on the DVD extras reveal, amusingly, that for this low-budget film the Floyd "demanded the most expensive soundtrack studio in London".

More

(Barbet Schroeder, 1969; BFI DVD)

The use of Pink Floyd's music is the only clever thing about this rather dim-witted film. Concerning a naive hippie called Stefan (**Klaus Grunberg**), drawn into the fatal embrace of heroin/heroine Estelle (**Mimsy Farmer**) in an Ibizan hippie enclave, whatever its intentions, it manages to suggest a distinctly conservative, rather sexist, take on the hippie counterculture.

For the film's first half, Pink Floyd's music is used diegetically, incorporated as part of the film: "Nile Song" emanates from a party cassette player, "Ibiza Bar" from a Paris bar radio, "Party Sequence" is an Ibizan bongo jam, and "Cymbaline" a record played on Estelle's stereo. All are earlier versions than the ones featured on the *More* album, with the singing more uncertain. This is especially apparent on "Cymbaline" which, usually reported as being Waters' vocal, is actually Gilmour having a reedy day. As the action drifts into the unreal, interior world of heroin addiction, however, so the music emerges from the ether, specifically the trippy "Quicksilver" and the transcendent "Cirrus Minor".

If only the acting were so sharp. As Stefan, Grunberg shifts from blankness to bellowing with much resting on his hangdog handsomeness and hip haircut, while Farmer struggles to bring an Estelle to life whose only characteristic is siren-esque nihilism.

The English-as-second-language dialogue doesn't help either. *More* does intermittently look good: the couple's villa hideaway, a scene where the couple cavort on a windmill's wheel and Ibiza's alluringly dangerous shoreline (plot parallel alert). Somewhat surprisingly, the film got positive US reviews, with *The New York Times* calling it, "a very beautiful, very romantic movie", though its X rating affected its box office performance. Although

it became a minor hit in Europe, *More* has long been eclipsed by its soundtrack.

Zabriskie Point

(Michelangelo Antonioni, 1970; MGM VHS)

This is Italian New Wave director Antonioni's attempt to do for the Californian counterculture what his *Blow Up* had done for Swinging London: reconfigure it as art. With a post-*Easy Rider* Hollywood briefly but busily throwing money at the underground, the lavish, MGM-financed *Zabriskie Point* is an oddity rather more appealing than its reputation – or commercial fortunes – suggest.

The film follows one UCLA riot participant (the blankly handsome **Mark Frechette**) after he kills a cop, steals a helicopter and escapes to Death Valley, where he encounters a lissom young hippie girl (**Daria Halprin**). They roll personably around in the sand for an incredibly long time (no surprise to find out they were an item off-screen too). After Frechette's death at the hands of the LAPD, Halprin envisages revenge upon the bourgeois "straight" world with the explosion of an opulent desert mansion.

The latter scene is one of the occasions when Pink Floyd's music ("Come In Number 51", a remade "Eugene") is used – highly effectively. Others include the opening title sequence at a political meeting (set to "Heart Beat Pig Meat") and a sequence in which "Crumbling Land" briefly emerges from a radio. It's just a shame Antonioni didn't use the now notorious "Violent Sequence" (better known today as "Us And Them"). A series of compelling set-pieces rather than a coherent narrative, the film is perfect for the DVD age. Or rather, it would be were the thing available on DVD, which, considering it's one of the more interesting artefacts of a fascinating era and one of the best film projects Pink Floyd were involved in, is a lamentable state of affairs.

Stamping Ground (aka Rock Fieber)

(Jason Pohland 1970; UFA DVD)

A fairly straight documentary record of the 1970 Holland Pop Festival, featuring **Santana**, **T-Rex** and **The Byrds**, as well as the Floyd, this is included as one of the few legitimately available performances from the Eurocentric phase of the Floyd's career. It's Waters and Mason who are the stars of the Floyd's performance here. Waters plays muscular bass on both "Eugene" and "Saucerful" while Mason flails dramatically at his kit on the latter, the song only spoiled by Gilmour's thin, slightly off-key singing. This footage makes regular appearances in all unauthorised Floyd documentaries (see below).

Pink Floyd Live At Pompeii

(Adrian Maben, 1972; Universal DVD [Director's Cut])

What began as a simple – if epic – concept (Pink Floyd play in the ruins of Pompeii) has become a rather complex item in the Floyd canon, and one disowned altogether by David Gilmour. The Floyd's original October 1971 Pompeii footage was supplemented with sequences shot on an empty sound stage in Paris in early 1972. Then, when delays dated the film, this was spliced with interviews from *Dark Side Of The Moon* interviews. Various video versions further confused matters by often excluding the Abbey Road footage, and substituting different pieces of music in the intro. Then for the DVD director's cut (approved only by Waters), director Maben reassembled the footage yet again, partly because some of the original rushes had been destroyed. So what is gained in – somewhat spurious – new material (Hubble telescope shots; shots of the Underground; black-and-white interviews during the Paris sessions) is lost in original footage, thus explaining the somewhat homoerotic intensity of focus on a half-dressed David Gilmour: the shots of the other members were lost.

But it's still an eminently watchable film. The wreaths of mist from the bubbling mud provide a perfect backdrop for a superb "Echoes", while the gorgeous morning light during "Saucerful" adds a haunting quality, making even **Roger Waters**' gong-bashing a nostalgia-tinted snapshot of the 1970s. The interviews conducted during the *Dark Side* sessions, meanwhile, are entirely fascinating, revealing the band in snooty, insular, slightly smug and frosty form. Seen today, they appear curiously like **Radiohead**, who must have studied this film before making their *Meeting People Is Easy* documentary.

La Vallée/The Valley (Obscured By Clouds)

(Barbet Schroeder, 1972; HVE DVD)

"Paradise is a place with many exits but no entrances…" says hippie Olivier (**Michael Gothard**) to bored, bourgeois Viviane (**Bulle Ogier**) as they go in search of a paradisiacal valley. Simultaneously of its time and entirely up to date, *La Vallée* is inestimably better than *More*, Schroeder's previous Floyd-related film. While its questing, free-lovin' European hippie subjects place it firmly in the post-sixties spiritual vacuum, its exploration of whether man has a place in the Garden of Eden was replicated by 2000 blockbuster *The Beach*, while its entranced but critical ethnocentricity lends it a subtlety and complexity most hippie period pieces lack.

The Papua New Guinea locations are beautifully and dramatically shot by **Nestor Almendros**, its portrayal of the hippies naturalistic and convincing. Viviane's transformation from bread-head hobbyist to free spirit is well portrayed, especially against the other more cardboard females. The Floyd's music is utilized superbly throughout. "Obscured By Clouds" itself makes a suitably ominous, sulphurous opening and closing; the lyrics of "Burning Bridges" comment directly upon the action, so the lyric "she breaks the golden band" marks Viviane's decision not to return to her husband but to stay with Olivier. Similarly "The Gold It's In The…" soundtracks the moment when Viviane decides to accompany the hippies for the promise of bird feathers. "Wot's… Uh The Deal" meanwhile soundtracks the first sex scene, and the final reel is accompanied by one of Wright's trademark oceanic organ chord sequences – an extended version of "Absolutely Curtains". This film is as unfairly underrated as its soundtrack.

The Wall

(Alan Parker, 1982; Sony DVD)

The Wall is a curious beast: a drama with almost no dialogue, a rock opera with no libretto, a live action film that keeps switching to animation. Its only obvious precursor, **Ken Russell**'s *Tommy*, at least featured musical dialogue. But *The Wall* album is a series of interior monologues, right down to the voices of Pink's mother (in "Mother") and the Judge (in "The Trial"). Only the doctor (in "Comfortably Numb") is given his own musical voice. In the film, this serves to highlight the album's self-indulgent subjectivity, its inability to escape the scrambled, ugly mind of Pink.

The film also inadvertently highlights how the album's few spoken word sections jar with this internal monologue approach: in the film, the groupie on "One Of My Turns" sounds mechanical, and the film's donation of an additional spoken passage to the teacher (Alex McAvoy) – the ridiculing of young Pink's poems – is just plain embarrassing. The "poem" is the second verse of "Money", which, read aloud, rather proves his point. The film's other key break into dialogue is

Floydology

equally awkward, as Pink, in prison, mumbles a medley of Waters' lyrics (*Pros And Cons'* "The Moment Of Clarity", *The Final Cut's* "Your Possible Pasts" and "Stop!"). Couldn't we have had a break from Waters' words?

Even the more moving scenes can't transcend this mismatch between visuals and music: the song "When The Tigers Broke Free" simply tells what the film's opening sequence shows. And as for the most praised aspect of the film – Scarfe's animated sequences – they never quite gel with the live action, which essentially involves Geldof stumbling from music video to music video with lots of shots of blood and mud between. Rather than criticizing Geldof's performance or Parker's direction, it's questionable whether *The Wall* should ever have been filmed at all.

The Final Cut

(Willie Christie, 1983)

Distressed by what Alan Parker had done to *The Wall*, Waters exercised more control over the film of the album's follow-up: it was directed by his brother-in-law. But with *The Final Cut* material even less cinematic, with an ill-defined "story", and even fewer dramatic voices, *The Final Cut* film is just as unsatisfying a hybrid as *The Wall* – with poorer production values. *The Final Cut* album's plot focuses on *The Wall's* teacher (again played here by **Alex McAvoy**), who, it transpires, is one of "the few", the flyers in the Battle of Britain, whose brutalization of his pupils is born of his disenchantment that the post-war dream had not been realized. Beyond "One Of The Few", "The Hero's Return" and "Paranoid Eyes", however, everything else only relates politically, rather than making sense in narrative terms.

Nevertheless Waters attempts to lend a running narrative to the film, via the teacher, who, it's revealed in the opening "Gunners Dream", has lost his son in the Falklands War. A tangential jibe at *The Wall* film confuses the issue, however. Waters himself is seen talking to a psychiatrist named "A. Parker-Marshall" – a reference to **Alan Parker** that is presumably related to Waters feelings of the betrayal of his personal vision by commercially minded opportunists._"The Final Cut", while ostensibly a documentary on women through the ages viewed by the insomniac teacher, seems equally tangential. The trite images of lazy British workmen in "Not Now John" does at least loosely fit the post-war dream theme, the teacher making a token cameo. But if "The Fletcher Memorial Home" was already a heavy-handed satire on record, it fares even worse here: as the world's massed "dictators" parade in schoolboy-crude grotesques, the teacher fantasizes assassinating them. Unavailable on DVD, but viewable on Pink Floyd's website, there's the ghost of something interesting here, though it'd require a seance to discover it.

Floydology

David Gilmour Live

(Michael Hurll/Norman Stone, 1984)

By far the most interesting aspect of this document of Gilmour's first – and until 2006 only – non-Floyd tour is the title of the accompanying home movie.

With the packaging also making reference to Gilmour's "new solo career", the overall implication is that Gilmour was not altogether sure the Floyd would continue post *Final Cut*. Currently unavailable on DVD, included in the VHS package are promos for "Blue Light" and "All Lovers Are Deranged" by **Storm Thorgerson**.

But the main feature is a cheap and cheerful film of Gilmour and band in concert at the Hammersmith Odeon, London, on April 30, 1984, running efficiently through his *About Face* set, plus "Run Like Hell" and "Comfortably Numb" (with Nick Mason on drums) in stark, stripped-back visual settings far removed from Floyd live spectaculars before and since.

It's as if Gilmour were experimenting to see how far he could redress things in a musical rather than conceptual direction, staging personality against spectacle. Album and ticket sales presumably gave him a fairly definite answer. A year later, the Floyd were active once again.

Delicate Sound Of Thunder

(Wayne Isham, 1989; EMI VHS)

A visual companion-piece to the album of the same name, this is the re-formed Floyd's performance from Nassau Coliseum in the summer of 1988. It differs from the album in several respects. Only "Part 1" of "Shine On" is shown. "Signs Of Life", "On The Run" and "Great Gig" – with three vocalists attempting a Torry and added fireworks from the Versailles gig – are on the video but not the album. "Yet Another Movie", "Round And Around", "Money", "Another Brick" are on the album but not the video.

If there's no great musical incentive to buy the video then neither is there much visual incentive. Viewers get only to glimpse Storm Thorgerson's filmed back projections, see a blur of the inflatable pig (which despite added bollocks, has to attest "original pig concept by R. Waters") and can only vaguely make out the enormous mirror ball that rises during Gilmour's "Comfortably Numb" solo and opens like a flower.

Otherwise what you see is a bunch of rather ungainly, occasionally bemused middle-aged men, flanked by a gang of tasteless younger sessioneers. Attention-seeking percussionist **Gary Wallis** and foully be-mulleted saxophonist **Scott Page** are the worst offenders. As its current unavailability on DVD suggests (those versions on eBay are fakes), this is deemed very far from essential even by the Floyd themselves.

Floydology

Pink Floyd In Venice

(Wayne Isham/Egbert Von Rees, 1989)

The climax of the Floyd's endless *Delicate Sound Of Thunder* tour took place in the suitably dramatic environs of St Mark's Square, Venice. The subsequent European TV special, despite the addition of an orchestra, doesn't, in truth, add much to the already dispensable *Delicate Sound* video.

Live At Knebworth

(Chuck LaBella [Producer]; Eagle Rock DVD)

The Floyd headlined the biggest concert spectacular since Live Aid on June 30, 1990, in aid of Nordoff-Robbins Music Therapy.

Playing higher up the bill than **Paul McCartney, Phil Collins, Genesis, Dire Straits, Eric Clapton,** and **Robert Plant** and **Jimmy Page,** the Floyd appear in the third volume of the video and financed the £60,000 firework display from their own pockets.

Unfortunately, the performance itself was a distinct damp squib, thanks to a relentless rainstorm, affecting both picture and sound quality. What's more, the sight of a portly, besuited Gilmour with extremely bad hair, "rocking out" to "Run Like Hell" is, in all, rather an unpleasant one.

La Carrera Panamericana

(Ian McArthur, 1992; VHS)

The closest Nick Mason ever came to a takeover of Pink Floyd, this entire project was a reflection of his – and manager **Steve O'Rourke**'s – tastes. And for the first time in nearly 20 years, Mason even got his name back on the songwriting credits.

Mason and O'Rourke's 1991 entry in the 3000km motor race from near the border of Guatemala to the US border found Gilmour (literally) along for the ride, alongside a film crew. There was some high drama – Gilmour crashed his and O'Rourke's car – but it all happened off-camera. Consequently, the main appeal lies in the otherwise unavailable Floyd music, albeit often obscured by dialogue.

Alongside various *Momentary Lapse Of Reason* tracks, there are a series of instrumentals – all credited to Gilmour/Wright/Mason for the first (and only) time since "Any Colour You Like". Of these, "Country Theme" reasserts Gilmour's Eagles-eyed ability to knock out West Coast-sounding material; "Small Theme" is rather too laden with 80s keyboards for appeal; the guitar-heavy "Big Theme" recalls some of *Momentary Lapse*'s more grandiose moments; "Slow Blues" is just that; while "Pan Am Shuffle" burbles along amiably enough on guitar and Hammond solos without ever being remotely memorable. None of this stuff is essential, but in combination with the film it is at least mildly diverting.

Pink Floyd – The Story

(Jacques Peretti, 1994; VHS)

This 40-minute BBC *Omnibus* special was the first of a whole spate of turn-of-the-century Floyd documentaries, and thus established the template – and the stock of clips – to which future efforts would largely stick.

Narrated by **Richard E. Grant**, the programme is not available on DVD. But it is worth tracking down for its first section alone, featuring an unusual interview with **Rick Wright,** footage from the obscure "Scarecrow" promotional film, and interviews with the rarely interviewed **Andrew King** and **Joe Boyd**. The film's major flaw is that Waters does not contribute, thus making it, as part of *The Division Bell* promotional round, distinctly Gilmour-biased.

But while Gilmour takes the opportunity for various pot-shots at Waters without the latter having a chance to retaliate (specifically regarding *The Wall*), Mason at least speaks fondly of his and Waters' former friendship. This would, of course, stand him in good stead, and, arguably, ultimately pave the way for the **Live 8** re-formation.

The Gilmour bias is further echoed in the narrative's fast-forward from *Piper* to *Dark Side,* reflecting Gilmour's continuing purging of Pink Floyd's progressive years, and the – albeit brief – trumpeting of their current formation. A useful template, it would be improved upon by later BBC programmes.

The Colours Of Infinity

(Nigel Lesmoir-Gordon, 1995; VHS)

This eye-crossingly abstruse television documentary about the Mandelbrot set features music by David Gilmour. Directed by long-standing Cambridge alumnus Lesmoir-Gordon and presented by Waters favourite **Arthur C. Clarke,** *Colours* explores the key discovery by mathematician Mandelbrot which launched fractal geometry.

Foundering on the fact that the subject is never actually precisely defined – where is it? what is it? – the music will still be of interest to Floydophiles, being essentially a pastiche of the "Crazy Diamond" keyboard overture, along with fruity French horn, Moog doodlings and lots of spacey guitar.

The overall effect of all these pastel graphics and wafty music is all rather New Age, however, and the film can't be seriously recommended to any but 1990s Floyd fanatics.

In The Flesh – Roger Waters In Concert

(Ernie Fritz, 2002; Sony DVD)

Having failed to win the argument that he "is" Pink, Roger Waters has, in the 21st century, appeared to shift the ground – painting himself as amiable and Gilmour as "the grumpy one". Underlining this point, this film of the Portland, Oregon, show of his 2000 tour kicks off with Waters in the dress-

Floydology

ing room, looking relaxed, and singing a jazzy, "San Tropez"-ish number.

Indeed, the DVD is considerably more enjoyable than the audio version. For although the retreads of Floyd numbers remain primarily pointless, it's great to see Waters playing bass again – and if anyone were in doubt, his playing on both "Another Brick" and "Breathe" proves him a quite brilliant exponent of his instrument.

What's more, while "Dogs" remains redundant, it's at least leavened by Waters and his bandmates sitting down in the middle to play a hand of cards, leaving **Jon Carin** to shoulder both Wright's and Gilmour's parts, saying, one can only assume, "Which one's Pink? Who cares?" But, in truth, Waters looks like he's trying a bit too hard to look relaxed: watching him here, it's hard not to conjecture he's spent his time away practising benevolent facial gestures in the mirror.

What's more, during the largely more successful solo segment, there's a moment of rather awkward pathos when the "crowd" starts singing along to "Perfect Sense". For it isn't the Portland crowd that's singing along, it's a taped crowd, the sound of Roger Waters' fantasies faked into life. Still, those benevolent facial expressions would soon come in handy at Live 8.

David Gilmour In Concert

(David Mallet, 2002; EMI DVD)

Few would expect anything very much from a David Gilmour solo show, and yet this appearance at Robert Wyatt's Meltdown festival found Gilmour at his best in years. Small scale, compared to recent Floyd spectaculars, the set begins with Gilmour performing a surprisingly effective "Shine On" on his own, his vocal more expressive and emotive than he'd ever previously managed, and joined at the end by **Dick Parry**.

Then, after a touching solo rendition of Barrett's "Terrapin", he's joined by a band of double-bassist Chucho Merchan, drummer Nic France, and keyboard player Michael Kamen, plus Kirsty McColl's brother Neil on guitar and backing vocals.

The only concession to Floydian scope is a huge troupe of female backing vocalists who particularly benefit "Coming Back To Life" and "High Hopes". More surprising is a rather stunning rendition – in French – of an aria from **Georges Bizet**'s opera *The Pearl Fishers*.

The only real misfires are a dull workout of the second section of "Shine On" and two underrehearsed attempts at "Comfortably Numb", one with Wyatt and another with **Bob Geldof**. Yes, Bob Geldof. Gilmour has never found an adequate replacement for Waters on this song.

If the Geldof appearance weren't sufficient, the auguries of Floyd's re-formation are everywhere. Wright comes on to sing "Breakthrough" from *Broken China*, and Gilmour's harmony and solo reveal quite how much magic is left in the old formula. In retrospect, this DVD was a real "watch this space" moment.

Pink Floyd: The Making of Dark Side Of The Moon

(Matthew Longfellow [Classic Albums], 2003; Eagle Rock DVD)

An object lesson in documentary filmmaking, this single-album study is helped inestimably by the input of all four Floyds. They, alongside key personnel **Chris Thomas** and **Alan Parsons**, plus a couple of journalists for broader context, talk the viewer through the album, track by track, accompanied by the visuals the Floyd themselves projected during performances of the piece, plus some modern-day re-creations by the individual Floyds.

Among the documentary's highlights are Parsons separating the vocal tracks of "Breathe". Ever wondered why Gilmour sang the harmony with himself rather than Wright? Separated into a cappella parts like this, there's a soulful perfection about Gilmour's layering that's so gorgeous you can see exactly why Wright deferred. There's also a lovely moment when contemporary footage of Wright playing "Great Gig" is joined in split-screen by Gilmour playing the pedal steel part. Waters' performance of "Brain Damage" is also rather touching (though why he insists he can't sing the higher chorus is a bit mystifying). Meanwhile, tucked among the extras is something of a bombshell: what is apparently Waters' original demo of "Time", which bar the odd minor/major substitution, is revealed as largely identical to the (group-credited) finished version. Fascinating filmmaking.

The Pink Floyd And Syd Barrett Story

(John Edginton, 2003; Direct Video DVD)

Finally, the Pink Floyd story as it, largely, should be told. Narrated by **Kirsty Wark**, this follows the format of the *Omnibus* documentary but betters it via input from all four Floyds, as well as from **Bob Klose** and Barrett's early girlfriend, **Libby Gausden**. Focusing so closely on Barrett, the documentary brings out the best in its contributors, Gilmour waxing so lyrical about his old friend he feels compelled to say that, "it's not meant to sound like a love song", while Wright makes the most articulate speech of his life when recounting Barrett's visit to the *Wish You Were Here* sessions. If Mason seems a little too considered and smug, then Waters, while engaging, rather glosses the level of his Cambridge friendship with Barrett. It also contains some rather bizarre extras – not least of which is Gilmour bumbling interminably around his guitar room searching for the right guitar with which to perform "Wish You Were Here". Overall, however, this is a moving and thoughtful documentary, as well as providing a useful entry point for new fans.

Inside Pink Floyd: A Critical Review 1967–1996

(Bob Carruthers, 2004; Ragnarock DVD)

"This project requires total independent editorial control" boasts the blurb on the back of this 2-CD set of quite astonishing amateurishness. In other words, this first of several cheapo documentaries from the *Classic Rock* stable didn't get the rights to any official Pink Floyd audio or visual material.

Thus the Floyd themselves appear only on footage from other documentaries, reproduced so badly you can only surmise they were filmed off the television screen. The only other talking heads come from obscure critics and musicians, particularly – count 'em! – three members of a Floyd tribute act called **Mostly Autumn** whose "analyses" of their music are bland beyond belief. There's a quite interminable section where the keyboard player recites the entire chord sequence of "Great Gig". Thanks for that.

Not that the other contributions fare much better, offering such judgements as: "Gilmour is the real genius in Pink Floyd"; *Piper* "is not really essential"; and *Momentary Lapse* and *Delicate Sound Of Thunder* are as good as *Dark Side Of The Moon*. As for the music, well, because Carruthers was unable to gain the rights to the studio versions, all of it emanates from film of the Floyd performing live or cover versions. Worse, having patently failed to get the rights to show the *Dark Side* artwork, the film repeatedly shows a piss-poor primary-school mock-up of it. Oddly, the accompanying booklet is much better – rather nicely packaged with entertaining commentaries on all the albums and songs – if still sometimes inaccurate. But Carruthers and crew were far from finished yet.

The World's Greatest Albums: Atom Heart Mother

(Bob Carruthers, 2005; Art House Classics DVD)

Refining the formula, this DVD from the *Inside Pink Floyd* team is a slight improvement. While the scudding cloud graphics are merely tacky, the comic cow images are downright insulting.

Once again, they couldn't get the rights to play the album versions, all the audio coming either from murky film footage of *AHM*'s premiere at the Bath Festival or from tribute act performances. *Classic Rock* scribe "Krusher" is a not entirely convincing presenter but the musicological analyses are, this time, intermittently interesting. Adding to the general confusion about how "Atom Heart Mother" itself divides up, however, the film features **Ron Geesin** outlining it in one way, while the subtitles contradict him entirely.

Pink Floyd In Their Own Words/Reflections On The Wall (aka Pink Floyd's The Wall – The Ultimate Critical Review)

(James Fowler, 2005; Art House Classics DVD)

Yet another Bob Carruthers-conceived Floyd film, this again makes great use of the cheapest, nastiest graphics available, the favoured swirling clouds and, in a stunning innovation, shifting bricks. Despite these disadvantages, *The Wall* is built on firmer foundations than its companions, presenter **Graham McTavish** lending a degree of authority, more established journalists such as **Chris Welch** and (Carruthers' boss) **Geoff Barton** giving additional weight.

Reflections On The Wall is hampered again by the problem of lack of access to the original songs, meaning lots of footage of the Gilmour Floyd and performances by tribute acts. The musicological analysis is again rather better here then on *Inside Pink Floyd*, **Mostly Autumn** thankfully relegated simply to musical "interpretations" of Pink Floyd on the extras. There are still inaccuracies, however – **Bob Ezrin** was *not* present at the Montreal spitting incident, for instance. A second disc meanwhile is a remarkably cut-price experience – the voices of the Floyd matched to visuals of revolving tape spools. As with *Inside Pink Floyd*, this double disc set is lavishly packaged in a book which contains reams of additional – if not always accurate – information.

Pink Floyd Rock Review

(Samuel M Donald, 2005; Angry Penguin)

Again from the Carruthers/*Classic Rock* stable, this retelling of the oft-told Floyd tale is lent a degree of gravitas by the late **Tommy Vance** as presenter, though the combination of Carruthers' script and Vance's melodramatic style make for a number of Chris Morris-esque moments ("taking L – S – D – and *anything* else he could get his hands on").

With additional contributions from the same team as the *Atom Heart Mother* documentary – **Krusher** and music producer **Nick Tauber** – there's little that's revelatory here, and, as usual, no access to the songs' original studio versions, which leads to a number of mismatches between audio and visuals, the worst of which is when *The Wall* stage show is discussed alongside footage from Roger Waters' Berlin *Wall* show. Carruthers also takes the opportunity to recycle some of his favourite mistakes (that **Norman Smith** was merely executive producer on *Saucerful*, for instance) and repeat some of his favourite dubious assertions – that there was "no sad decline into mediocrity" for the Floyd, and that *Momentary Lapse* and the late live albums are as good as *Dark Side*. Furthering the general aura of opportunism, the film comes right up to date via footage of **Live 8**.

Books & websites

Books

Pink Floyd take a dim view of books about themselves. Where they will, on occasion, contribute to television programmes (of sufficiently high cultural standing), they almost never collaborate with authors on books, with the exception of Nick Mason.

Mason was so off-message in this regard he even decided to publish his own book, which eventually came out in 2004 – a decision that may have driven a wedge between him and David Gilmour. What's the source of the band's opposition to these books? Most likely, it's to do with preserving privacy, and more importantly still, maintaining the Pink Floyd brand's most essential – and most fragile – component: enigma.

Barry Miles: Pink Floyd – A Visual Documentary
Omnibus Press

For years this was the standard book on the Floyd, published in 1980 by veteran psychedelic kingpin **Barry Miles** and since updated by *Amazing Pudding* co-editor **Andy Mabbett**. Going through their career almost day by day, it's packed with detailed quotes from the band and fabulous photos, but inevitably it's more detailed on the 60s, and is full of dates of dubious veracity. Also, no revisions have corrected the misattribution of a quote about electronically manipulating the vocal on "Welcome To The Machine" to Roger Waters, oft repeated elsewhere (it's Gilmour both speaking and singing). Such quibbles aside, even if you're not reading the Pink Floyd bibliography chronologically, this is still the perfect place to start.

Malcolm Jones: Syd Barrett – The Making Of The Madcap Laughs
Private printing; reprinted by Orange Sunshine Pill Press

In a rare instance of music literature impacting upon music production, this 1982 private pressing by the late former Harvest boss/producer directly resulted in the release of *Opel*. Not only does it reveal exactly what resided in the Barrett solo archive, it shows all the Barrett Floyd recordings logged at Abbey Road (the rarities here, alas, have not been released; indeed the Floyd have not allowed anyone in their archive since) but also provides a fascinating eyewitness account of Barrett post-Floyd – essentially depicting him as much saner than any other account. It's not immune to mistakes but, for fanatics, the detail will compensate. Now available as a download via www.brain-damage.co.uk.

Vernon Fitch: Pink Floyd – The Press Reports 1966–1983

Collectors Guide Publishing Inc

Producing this scholarly 1983 tome stood Vernon Fitch in good stead to create the Pink Floyd Archive (see p.280). Containing almost every interview or even bare-bones news pieces about the Floyd (up to *The Final Cut*), its only flaw is an inconsistency regarding quotes: sometimes they're unnecessarily full, sometimes frustratingly paraphrased. Essential for biographers, but of dubious usefulness to anybody else.

Karl Dallas: Bricks In The Wall

Shapolsky

Veteran music journalist Dallas essentially burned his bridges with Roger Waters via this 1987 book. The book has a rather slapdash attitude to accuracy (eg Robert Wyatt's song "Shipbuilder"; the painter *Charles* Munch) and Dallas attributes the lyrics of "Comfortably Numb" to Gilmour. Uh-oh! That aside, the book is attractively – if idiosyncratically – arranged, devoting interesting chapters to the Floyd's singles, and including several interviews with both Waters and Gilmour, alongside a sympathetic understanding of Waters' attitude to the post-war dream.

Nicholas Schaffner: Saucerful Of Secrets – The Pink Floyd Odyssey

Helter Skelter

First published in 1991, Schaffner's book is thoughtful, interesting and more accurate than many, if marred by both factual slips and a tendency to quote minor figures at inordinate length. Roger Waters was extremely irked by the book – the fact that Schaffner describes *Pros And Cons* as "an avalanche of verbiage" and that the book culminates in some rather crowing comments by Gilmour during the 1988 tour might not be unconnected. It was reissued in 2005 with an updated afterword by music journalist Michael Heatley.

Mike Watkinson & Pete Anderson: Crazy Diamond – Syd Barrett And The Dawn Of Pink Floyd

Omnibus Press

This first Barrett biography makes for interesting reading but is still rather disappointing. Published in 1991, it boasts a **Julian Cope** preface, and key contributions from close associates, but is often factually inaccurate (hopelessly confused about the goings-on at **Mike Leonard**'s Highgate house; making no attempt to qualify **Norman Smith**'s dismissal of Barrett during the *Piper* sessions), often poorly written and full of elementary errors (an inability to spell Storm Thorgerson). But perhaps the central problem – that Barrett never really comes alive – is not the fault of his first biographers: it's an inevitable problem for any Barrett scribe.

Chris Welch: Learning To Fly

Castle

Veteran prog journalist Welch's book, published in 1994, is indicative of the rather soft-edged journalism of his era, strong on long quotation (especially from **Ron Geesin**), soft on hard questions. Among Welch's mistakes are to place the *Dark Side* premiere in London and to assign the vocal on "Shine On You Crazy Diamond" to **Roy Harper**. Welch also has an ongoing problem with names (Michael Champing instead of Kamen; Magpie Thatcher; Eric Fleecier Waters, and thus the "Fleecier Memorial Home"). In all, combined with the A4 children's book format, a rather crude, rushed affair.

Andy Mabbett: The Complete Guide To The Music Of Pink Floyd

Omnibus Press

Handy guide to – almost – every song in the Floyd catalogue, this book is small enough to fit in your pocket but, inevitably, equally short on substance. It is mostly accurate in its wealth of factual detail, but it tends towards speculation about songs rather than proper analysis. You can also have fun spotting which songs it doesn't include. Its 1995 publication date means it doesn't run to *Pulse*.

Cliff Jones: Echoes – The Stories Behind Every Pink Floyd Song (aka Another Brick In The Wall)

Omnibus Press; Carlton

A book to inspire fear into all would-be Floyd biographers, this 1996 book had to be withdrawn and revised after incurring the legal wrath of David Gilmour, who cited both "inaccuracies" and "libels". True, the book had inaccuracies ("Eugene" is supposedly included on *Saucerful*; "Sheep" is credited to Gilmour/Waters; Waters is credited as Gilmour

in a photo caption). But the truth is that at this time Gilmour was in record-straightening mode, and Ron Geesin claims one of the key issues was a pictorial comparison between Geesin's and Gilmour's melodies for "Atom Heart Mother". This issue remains as opaque as much of the book itself.

Bruno MacDonald (ed): Pink Floyd – Through The Eyes Of ... The Band, Its Fans, Friends And Foes

Da Capo Press

First published in 1996 and compiled by the co-editor of *The Amazing Pudding* fanzine, this is a compilation of enjoyable – and often unfamiliar – articles which trace the Floyd's history. Particularly riveting is a 1992 Roger Waters interview by John Aizlewood for *Q*, which has enormous fun at the expense of the conceptualist at his most glum. More vital still is a track-by-track guide to each Pink Floyd song, in which the relaxed, scrapbooky, non-definitive style, although leaving many questions unanswered, is ultimately far more satisfying than Cliff Jones's approach.

Glenn Povey & Ian Russell: Pink Floyd: In The Flesh – The Complete Performance History

St Martin's Griffin

The very thing that might have made this 1997 book dull – a full listing of every Floyd gig, plus set-lists – is actually its forte. For, to achieve this, former Brain Damage fanzine founder Povey and contributor Russell have researched their facts more diligently than most

Floyd biographers. Going beyond the call, they also preface each period with a fine essay, using quotes and new interviews, yet are also not afraid to theorize – plausibly arguing that Barrett played up his madness for manipulative ends. Well laid-out and illustrated, the early years are covered more authoritatively and illuminatingly than the later ones, but the book remains one of the best available on the band.

Julian Palacios: Lost In The Woods – Syd Barrett And The Pink Floyd
Helter Skelter

This book is that most unlikely of all things – an account of a recluse that manages to be relatively unintrusive. Not that this 1998 Barrett biography shies away from the dark or the difficult: it simply balances its fact-digging diligence with sympathy for its subject. Elliptically, occasionally jerkily, written, it often gives way to passages of arresting beauty (musing on the fate of a flower child at the Technicolor Dream) and insight (Palacios's definition of English psychedelia; his analysis of individual songs, especially "Bike"). But at other times it simply leaves events and facts fuzzy. And Barrett himself, perhaps inevitably, remains fuzziest of all.

Phil Rose: Which One's Pink? An Analysis Of The Concept Albums Of Roger Waters And Pink Floyd
Collector's Guide Publishing

Wild interpretation is a temptation for any biographer – and, hell, Phil Rose isn't even thrown off the scent when he loses his subject,

Waters, in an interview. Rose throws everything at this 1998 volume – musicology, philosophy, sociology, psychology – but ultimately, despite some passing insights, it's a weight Waters' concept albums can't bear. Sometimes the analysis is bafflingly intellectual (*The Wall*). Sometimes it's just plan daft: *Animals* is, apparently, the story of a young "dog" who yearns to become a member of the ruling class of "pigs" who – and this is the best bit – regularly fly by on reconnaissance missions. And, no, he's not joking.

Nick Hodges & Ian Priston: Embryo – A Pink Floyd Chronology 1966–1971
Cherry Red Books

Did we really need a *third* Floyd chronology? The most interesting aspect of this book is the authors' assertion, in their introductory essay, that "to understand the early Floyd is to understand *The Man* and *The Journey*". While this, the collated quotes and such titbits as the differences between the album and movie versions of *More* are mildly diverting for devotees, even the keenest may be less interested in verbatim reproductions of stage announcements (right down to ums and ahs) from unnamed bootlegs. Simultaneously informative and curiously obfuscatory.

David Parker: Random Precision – Recording The Music Of Syd Barrett 1965–1974
Cherry Red Books

Cherry Red clearly has chronologies on the brain. This 2001 book crosses over with *Embryo* on a

Floydology

good fifty percent of its content. Where this book betters *Embryo* is in a large number of new quotes from secondary participants such as managers and engineers (**Jenner**, **King** and **John Leckie**, in particular, are always great value). Where it doesn't better *Embryo* is in an even drabber design, pages and pages of flat print unleavened by even the few pictures *Embryo* boasts. As such, this book is a distinctly daunting proposition to all but the more fanatical – and ideally, salaried – fact-checker.

Tim Willis: Madcap – The Half-Life Of Syd Barrett, Pink Floyd's Lost Genius
Short Books

Willis doesn't get any closer physically to Barrett than previous authors: this book closes with Barrett slamming his door in his face. But, through access to Barrett's letters to **Libby Gausden**, a healthy cynicism about accepted facts and by literary references (such as Kenneth Grahame and Henry Thoreau), Willis's slim 2002 book gets metaphysically closer to Barrett than many larger tomes do. Willis's facts aren't always accurate (he's confused about early recording dates), and he fails to pursue the rumour that Barrett's father suffered from mental problems too. In the end, though, this is a well written and rather moving book.

John Cavanagh: Piper At The Gates Of Dawn
Continuum

This study of the band's first album is not the best written book you'll read on the Floyd,

falling too often into first-person subjectivity, and it regurgitates some common fallacies. But in all it's an enjoyable read and contains some interesting insights and observations from Mason, Jenner and King, not least on the disastrous (and relatively rarely documented) **Hendrix** tour of November 1967.

Nick Mason: Inside Out – A Personal History Of Pink Floyd
Weidenfeld & Nicolson

Mason describes himself as "occupying the no-man's-land between diplomacy and duplicity", and this very English characteristic has marked his tenure in the band and his writing alike. So it's perhaps inevitable that the nearest thing we've had to an "official" Floyd history (first published in 2003) should be so unrevealing – not helped by Gilmour's initial opposition to the project. Barrett inhabits the text like a ghost, while Wright comes little more to life. Only Waters' consuming fire and Gilmour's ice really come across, with Mason – Spinal Tap never far from his mind – the lukewarm water in-between. Best Waters' story? Taking manager O'Rourke's declaration he was in such a good mood nothing could upset him as a challenge (seven minutes later O'Rourke had stormed out in a fury). But if the text is, as Waters has attested, bland, the pictures are beautiful – the scores of unseen shots from Mason's personal archive celebrating the little-noted fact that the sixties and seventies Floyd were a fabulously photogenic group.

DSOTM-era Roger Waters and David Gilmour backstage with Hipgnosis man Aubrey "Po" Powell

Jeff Bench & Daniel O'Brien: The Wall, In The Studio, On Stage And On Screen

(Reynolds and Hearn)

The Wall is the best documented album of the Floyd's career. Perhaps the reasons are the willingness of **Bob Ezrin** during the 1990s to offer a candid and informed overview – resulting in a spate of articles – and the fact that the album has been at the centre of the public slanging match between Waters and Gilmour since the late 1980s. Consequently, because it is derived from ample secondary sources, the wealth of detail in this 2004 volume is largely accurate. The authors add a worthy chapter on the development of the concept album, but like the analysis of *The Wall* itself, it seems plodding and pernickety rather than compelling and insightful.

Floydology

Vernon Fitch: The Pink Floyd Encyclopedia

Collector's Guide Publishing

An absolute Aladdin's Cave of Floyd ephemera and vital statistics, from the curator of the Pink Floyd Archives. A random rummage reveals, for instance, that Yes's **Steve Howe** almost stood in for Syd Barrett at a **UFO** gig back in '67; another unearths a synopsis of Storm Thorgerson's *Division Bell* tour film to accompany "Shine On"; another the overdub history of "Silas Lang". Now in its third edition, there are mistakes here and there, but they'll probably be corrected by the time you get round to spotting them. All this *and* a Hawkwind tribute to Pink Floyd CD. Like most free gifts, however, this last is dispensable.

John Harris: The Dark Side Of The Moon – The Making Of The Pink Floyd Masterpiece

HarperCollins

Published in 2005, and one of the best, this compact but compelling volume has an air of official endorsement: a **Storm Thorgerson** cover, access to Nick Mason's photographic archive and interviews with Waters, Gilmour and Mason. The interviews were all actually given for other projects, but Harris consolidates these advantages with thorough research, useful analyses of contemporary social/political events and a bracingly opinionated tone that's unafraid to confront the inconsistencies within *Dark Side's* concept. The book's only real flaw is that after a lengthy build-up the book ends rather abruptly.

The best Pink Floyd websites

Official Website
www.pinkfloyd.co.uk

It took the Floyd's official site six months to take down the Live 8 news announcement. It also rather gives the impression that their only albums are *The Final Cut* and *Dark Side Of The Moon*. It does contain some interesting stuff on both, however, especially *The Final Cut* short film. Won't let you back out once you're in, by the way. Beautifully designed, though.

Brain Damage
www.brain-damage.co.uk

By far the best fan site. It won't win any design awards, and isn't always easy to navigate, but the content is exemplary: a definitive news section; a jumbled but fascinating interviews and articles section (including the full transcription of Waters' essential 1979 Radio 1 *Wall* talk-through with **Tommy Vance**); lots of investigation and opinion; plus a free download of **Malcolm Jones'** book – all this and the *Echoes* FAQ too.

All Pink Floyd Fan Network
www.pinkfloydfan.net
It's poorly organized and designed, with too many intrusive ads, but it has much useful info – lots of articles (albeit chaotically presented), decent info on the albums (if not always entirely accurate), some nice little interview pieces (with roadie **Phil Taylor**, for instance), guitar chords and even bass tabs along with the absolutely essential *Amazing Pudding* song list (see also **Bruno MacDonald**'s book p.274).

Pink Floyd & Co
www.pinkfloyd-co.com
Despite nuggets of interest (interviews, and tabs and chords for all songs), this poorly designed site remains curiously unsatisfying (a bare-bones discography) and unengaging. Claims to be the largest Floyd site in the world.

The Pink Floyd Fandom
www.pinkfloyd.net
Austere fan site, with exceptionally little content – only pictures and purchasing links for the videos and just poorly written, uninformative reviews of the albums (example: "hey, who can't admit that *DSOTM* Rules?").

Pink Floyd Online
www.pinkfloydonline.com
Haphazardly updated, badly designed fan site with too many intrusive ads. On the plus side, the content includes informative album reviews plus quotes.

The Pink Floyd Archive
ourworld.compuserve.com/homepages/ PFArchives/
Curated by **Vernon Fitch** of *The Pink Floyd Encyclopedia*, this is splendid, thorough stuff: very much a research archive however – to any but fact-checkers it could feel like reading train timetables. Not brilliantly designed, it's also somewhat hard to navigate.

Pink Floyd ROIO Database
www.pf-roio.de
An excellent, informative database of Floyd bootlegs, it is thorough if not quite exhaustive (it's not actively maintained). The reviews are submitted by fans and, while sometimes invaluable, are presented chaotically – and could use some editing (especially the posts that promise to provide an opinion at a later date).

Neptune Pink Floyd
www.neptunepinkfloyd.co.uk
Claims to be the world's largest Pink Floyd community. Well maintained, though the features are disappointing, and you have to subscribe to view the interesting video content. Some good audio, however, including throwaway rarity "**Merry Christmas Song**". Contains a few interesting articles and has a link to Wikipedia's excellent Floyd entry (en. wikipedia.org/wiki/Pink_Floyd).

The Most Complete Pink Floyd Page
utopia.knoware.nl/users/ptr/pfloyd/ start.html
Very far from accurately titled, this is fandom gone awry. Although there's the odd interview of interest (that Tommy Vance/Waters *Wall* one again), this site is eccentrically designed and boasts an entirely empty Movies section.

Its centrepiece is a series of Midi files seemingly featuring webmaster Peter Houweling bashing through the songs on various keyboards.

Pink Floyd and the Publius Enigma
folk.uio.no/ericsp/floyd.html

Ostensibly dedicated to the Publius enigma, the enigmatic postings of "Publius" on alt. music.pink-floyd are supposedly clues to the enigma within *Division Bell*. Many millions of conspiracy posts later Nick Mason revealed that it was actually a record company publicity stunt. If the Publius enigma was ultimately a Publius banality, the website dedicated to it is surprisingly essential, mainly for including the *Echoes* FAQ, the most useful source of factual information outside the *Archive*, with the benefit of being more opinionated.

The Pink Floyd Fan Club
www.pink-floyd.org

An amateurish affair: poorly updated (latest news is still **Live 8**) with some horrible Casio keyboard intro music. It has a good number of interviews and articles, however, along with the essential *Echoes* FAQ. But will anyone ever compile a complete set of published press album reviews?

A Fleeting Glimpse
www.pinkfloydz.com

A long-established Australian site enthusiastically but chaotically presented, it's both difficult to load and daunting to navigate. Very strong on news (even if its presentation is jumbled and uninviting, it's refreshingly less reverential than most) with some interesting personal reminiscences of the 1960s by the site owner, and some info about such rarely covered topics as Roger Waters' daughter, **India**, who's a model. But there are no reviews of the DVDs and nothing on the albums.

Floydian Slip
www.floydianslip.com

Superbly-titled site connected to **Craig Bailey**'s Burlington, Vermont radio show. Ten years old, it's neatly designed and very simple to navigate, with an excellent news section and its centrepiece is a series of reviews. Refreshingly for the web, they're stronger on information than opinion, though the information is rarely revelatory.

Spare Bricks: The Pink Floyd Webzine
sparebricks.fika.org

One for the slightly highbrow Floyd fan, snootily avoiding the obvious to focus at length on ephemera: ***When The Wind Blows***, Gilmour's gear, an interview with archivist **Vernon Fitch** and a piece on the film ***The Committee***. This considered approach would work even better were it applied to a wider compass of material.

Floydology

Pink Floyd tributes

Tribute bands

This most anonymous-looking of bands was always going to be one of the ripest for tribute-dom. Hell, Pink Floyd even created their *own* tribute act! No, not the Gilmour Floyd, but the Surrogate Band, who opened the *Wall* shows in 1980–81.

But, in all seriousness, with both Gilmour and Waters casting around for replacements for each other for the last twenty years, punters have been paying top dollar to watch something not far from tribute Floyds since 1985. What's more, since 1995, with no version of the Floyd touring and only a scant few Waters shows, tribute bands have filled a Floydian void. Here's a select few of the hundreds riding the gravy train.

The Australian Pink Floyd
This act actually played at David Gilmour's fiftieth birthday party, being joined onstage by **Rick Wright** and **Guy Pratt** for "Comfortably Numb". Formed in 1988, they're the only world-touring Pink Floyd act. Their website features some amusing Aussie Floyd graphics.

The Surrogate Band
Michigan-based band cleverly taking their name from a lyric in "In The Flesh" and the name given to the fake Floyd who opened the *Wall* shows. Active since 2003.

Just Floyd
Formerly the more amusing **Pink Side Of The Moon**, this British Floyd aren't look-alikes, they just try and recreate the *nineties* Floyd sound. Yes. Really.

Wish You Were Here
Covering the whole era from Barrett to Gilmour, complete with female backing vocalists and ambitious light show, this Cleveland, Ohio, Floyd headlined Clear Channel's 2002 FakeFest tour. Get points for performing the whole of the usually ignored *Animals*.

Which One's Pink?
LA based; active since 1998; status indicated by **Alan Parsons** doing the live mix for their *Dark Side Of The Moon* performance in 2005; have since performed the whole of *The Wall*.

Think Floyd
British cover band which, er, covers all eras of the Floyd. Have done complete performances of *Wish You Were Here*. Confusingly, there's also a US tribute band with exactly the same

name (covering material only from *Meddle* on). Which one's Pink? Indeed.

Mostly Autumn

They don't regard themselves as a PF tribute act, but given that this British group seem to spend almost as much time playing Pink Floyd songs and talking about them on documenta-ries as they do playing their own material (of which they have recorded several albums), they are listed here accordingly.

Beyond The Darkside

Another Australian tribute band, active since 1995, and replicating the Gilmour-era tours and repertoire. Big of light show and of mullet.

Tribute albums

There are as many Pink Floyd tribute albums as there are Pink Floyd albums proper – even accounting for reissues with a sneaky name-change. But if the quantity is impressive, the quality is not. In chronological order:

Discoballs:
A Tribute To Pink Floyd

Rosebud (Atlantic Records, 1977)

Among the things *les françaises adore* are *le disco* and *le Pink Floyd*. So what wheeze would be more delightful than to combine the two? In fact, although intermittently amusing, the novelty soon wears thin. The Scissor Sisters this is not.

Beyond The Wildwood –
A Tribute To Syd Barrett

Various Artists (Imaginary, 1987)

As indie finally acknowledged the past in the mid-eighties, it did so with a preciousness that seemed to celebrate obscurity. Even the best-known acts here, **The Shamen, The Soup Dragons** and **The Mock Turtles,** would only gain success in the nineties by complete com-mercial overhaul. Thus the exploration of Barrett's more arcane work ("Two Of A Kind"; "Apples And Oranges") is annoying rather than a sign of authenticity – and the tinny, tre-bly, fey, inept performances are a tribute only to the grimness of this era of British indie music.

Objects Of Fantasy
(aka Orchestral Maneuvers)

David Palmer (RCA, 1989)

Orchestral versions of Pink Floyd songs arranged by **Jethro Tull's** Palmer, and also featuring for-mer Genesis guitarist **Steve Howe**, plus **Clare Torry** recreating her "Great Gig" vocal.

Us And Them:
Symphonic Pink Floyd

London Philharmonic Orchestra (Philips, 1995)

How punks learned to stop worrying and love the Floyd. Arranger **Jaz Coleman** was once a firebrand of **Killing Joke**, as was producer **Youth**. Ten years on, they're arranging the most obvious selection of Pink Floyd tracks for classical orchestra. With slightly more bite than others of its ilk, it still manages to combine blandness and pomposity. Just quite how much all this is like punk never happened, is illustrated – literally – by a **Roger Dean** cover.

A Saucerful Of Pink
(aka Other Side Of Pink)

Various Artists (Cherry Red, 1995)

Techno/industrial covers of the likes of "Set The Controls For The Heart Of The Sun" (**Psychic TV** – rather fine), "Echoes" (**Alien Sex Fiend** – not bad) and "Eugene" by Hawkwind flautist **Nick Turner**. A saucer's depth of interest.

Welcome To The Machine
The Electronic Tribute To Pink Floyd

Various Artists (Vitamin, 2000)

Given Pink Floyd's influence on electronic music, this could have been interesting. Given the usual array of nobodies, it isn't. And there's a *Volume 2* as well.

Pickin' On Pink Floyd

Various Artists (CMH, 2001)

Gaining points for tapping into Pink Floyd's paranoia theme, this bluegrass tribute, as usual, lacks big names. And while "Run Like Hell" is surprisingly effective in this form, it's really only of novelty value.

Pigs And Pyramids –
An Allstar Lineup Performing The Songs Of Pink Floyd

Various Artists (Musea, 2002)

Fabulously inaccurate title: not only are the artists here very far from "stars", the "songs of Pink Floyd" don't extend further than their three best-selling albums. Tribute packhorse and **Yes** member **Billy Sherwood**'s cast are only stars to other session musicians (various Toto and Peter Gabriel backroom boys). Sessioneer-slick, but sessioneer-vapid, this album simply sounds like non-copyright supermarket music.

Echoes Of Pink

Various Artists (Lakeshore, 2002)

Twelve utterly obscure female singer-songwriters do folky takes on the Floyd canon. At least making some interesting choices ("Cymbaline", "Stay"), it otherwise emphasizes the blander elements of the Floyd's music.

Floydology

Re-Build The Wall

Luther Wright and the Wrongs (Back Porch, 2002)

A country/bluegrass version of *The Wall* organized by Canadian novelty practitioner **Luther Wright**. Initially amusing, if only for the snook it cocks at Waters' pomposity, it ultimately feels like listening to **Rednex**'s "Cotton-Eyed Joe" 26 times in succession.

A Reggae Tribute To Pink Floyd

Various Artists (Snake Machine, 2002)

It's exactly what it says on the tin. What it doesn't say is how totally obscure all the artists are. Avoid.

The String Quartet Tribute To Pink Floyd

Various Artists (Vitamin, 2002)

Is it pedantic to point out that string quartets should not include guitars and that "tributes" should not make you start to wonder whether you actually dislike the originals after all? Oh well, at least they'd listened to something apart from *The Wall*: not many tribute albums dredge up "Take Up Thy Stethoscope".

A Chillout Tribute To Pink Floyd

Various Artists (Big Eye, 2002)

If the title alone suggests being trapped for eternity in Café Del Mar, the music, alas, isn't even *that* interesting – just a bunch of utterly obscure musicians rendering an utterly obvious selection of Floyd tracks into elevator music. Next.

A Fair Forgery Of Pink Floyd

Various Artists (Stanley, 2003)

The Waters-referencing title is by far the best thing about this Obscure Artists cover album. Only veteran British rocker **Graham Parker** has any pedigree, and his acoustic version of "Comfortably Numb" is a disappointment. Who on earth writes the rave reviews of these things on the Internet?

Dub Side Of The Moon

Easy Star All Stars (Easy Star, 2003)

At last some inspiration in a Floyd tribute – a rather loving, unironic rendering of *Dark Side Of The Moon* by this New York reggae label's house band, done with fantastic attention to detail (the spoken parts redone in patois, the loop on "Money" becoming bong hits and coughing). While everything works surprising well, "Great Gig" is probably the nearest the album gets to essential, with the tension, oddly, slackening the closer it gets to the climax. A surprising success, the album spent over a year on *Billboard's* reggae chart and became a regular between sets on Radiohead's tours.

Back Against The Wall

Various Artists (Cleopatra, 2005)

Again organized by **Billy Sherwood**, this rebuilding of *The Wall* features a more impressive array of talent than usual, at least for prog fans with long memories. It even tries a little in-joke by getting Jethro Tull's **Ian Anderson** to sing "The Thin Ice" – a song often compared to his own "Skating Away On The Thin Ice Of A New Day". Yes's **Chris Squire** does a decent job of "Comfortably Numb", **Rick Wakeman** pops up to add some pianistic icing to "Nobody Home" and Sherwood's own Waters' impression is so creepily close that Waters ought to slap a restraining order on the man. Impressive at first, *Back Against The Wall* soon becomes about as interesting as repointing.

The Influence

Pink Floyd's influence has been as inescapable as their music ever since they arrived on the music scene – and it's noticeable in genres as diverse as prog, punk, Krautrock, nu metal and dance. Here's a thorough, if necessarily subjective, roundup:

The Rolling Stones
Recorded for The Stones' sole psychedelic opus, 1967's *Their Satanic Majesties* (1967), "In Another Land" is a rare Bill Wyman composition. Even feyer than Jagger, **Wyman**'s vocal and lyrics are a dead ringer for Barrett.

Jeff Lynne
Future ELO mastermind **Jeff Lynne**'s psychedelic poppers Idle Race reveal a strong Barrett/Floyd influence on "Skeleton And The Roundabout" (*The Birthday Party*, 1968). And Wright's "Paintbox" shows its influence on "What?" (*Looking On*, 1971) by Lynne's next band, The Move.

Kevin Ayers
Ex-**Soft Machine** bassist Ayers' pastoral, whimsical vision owes much to his friend Barrett, a debt acknowledged in "O Wot A Dream" from 1974's *Banamour*.

Gong
Ayers' Soft Machine bandmate **Daevid Allen**'s spacey slide, "glissando" guitar style was, by his own admission, derived from watching Syd Barrett at **UFO**.

Tangerine Dream
1971's "Ultima Thule" was a rare, Barrettesque, single from the Krautrock experimen-

talists, while their early 1970s "cosmische" tracks owed much to the Floyd's "Saucerful Of Secrets".

Klaus Schultze

Former **Tangerine Dream** member Schultze's *Irrhlicht* (1972) and *Cyborg* (1973) are both highly recommended to fans of the Floyd's spacier, more improvisational side.

Marc Bolan

"One of the few people I'd actually call a genius," said Bolan of Barrett, the elfin one seeking out Blackhill management purely for the Barrett association: "...he inspired me beyond belief."

David Bowie

Bolan's pal Bowie was present at many early Floyd shows, probably got the idea for varispeeding voices from "**Scream Thy Last Scream**", and paid tribute on 1973's *Pin Ups* by covering "**See Emily Play**". Bowie's choice of Mick Rock as court photographer was almost certainly down to the Barrett connection too.

Can

Although these Krautrock kingpins were closely contemporaneous, "Mother Sky" (from 1970's *Soundtracks*) replicates Waters' simple but effective octave bass line from "**Eugene**", and a Floyd influence is apparent throughout their work.

George Harrison

A nice example of mutual influence: Harrison's "So Sad" (*Dark Horse*, 1974) nodded at "**Us And Them**", itself influenced by Harrison's own arpeggio-heavy guitar style.

ABBA

The all-conquering Swedish Euro-poppers' 1977 international #1, "Knowing Me Knowing You" borrowed its acoustic guitar/synth, sonic hot/cold trick from the Floyd's "Welcome To The Machine."

The Eagles

Although Gilmour had been getting Eagles-esque for some time, 1976's "**Hotel California**" reverses the influence, owing a clear debt to the riff from "**Wish You Were Here**". It was Waters that **Don Henley** would later become matey with, however, duetting on "Watching TV" in 1992.

Hawkwind

These freaks never came overground. Gilmour mixed their 1976 single, "Kerb Crawler", and the band's fondness for morse-code keyboards (on 1977's "Spirit Of The Age", and 1978's "Psy Power") was Floyd-derived. They also recorded a version of "**Interstellar Overdrive**" for the *Pink Floyd Encyclopedia*.

Alan Parsons Project

APP's bland AOR distillation of *Dark Side* was successful in the mid- to late 1970s, employing such Floydian motifs as sci-fi, pyramids *and* time. They even used *Dark Side*'s vocalists on 1979's *Eve* and David Gilmour himself on 2004's *A Valid Path* – a union of Floyd "forgers" that must have given Waters grim satisfaction.

Boomtown Rats

Despite **Bob Geldof**'s avowals that, as a punk he "never cared for Pink Floyd's music", his old band covered "**Arnold Layne**" on a 1977 TV performance, and the track was added to the CD reissue of *Mondo Bongo*.

Siouxsie and the Banshees

Even as punk morphed into new wave, it was still a shock to hear punk queenpin Siouxsie saying 1980's *Kaleidoscope* was influenced by early Pink Floyd.

Marc Almond

When Almond abandoned synthpop for a solo album (*Marc And The Mambas*, 1982), among the covers he chose was Syd Barrett's "**Terrapin**".

The Jesus and Mary Chain

Before anyone had quite spotted the pop classicists beneath the feedback, only Floyd obsessives could have been familiar with "**Vegetable Man**", B-side of the Mary Chain's very first, 1984 single, "Upside Down" (to this day only available on the flip of the single's limited 7" pressing).

Prefab Sprout

Unlikely as it seems, the acoustic guitar line on "Don't Sing", the 1984 single of this archetypal eighties act, is remarkably similar to that of "**Dogs**".

Julian Cope

When the former **Teardrop Explodes** heartthrob decamped to reclusion near his childhood home in Tamworth, with his Tonka toys and truckfuls of acid, the parallels with his idol Syd Barrett were disturbingly obvious. But the resultant 1984 albums *World Shut Your Mouth* and *Fried* were among Cope's best, sharing Barrett's skewed Englishness and psychedelic pastoralism, as well as a bubbling undercurrent of insanity.

Flaming Lips

The band deliberately challenged their punk following by playing the supposed antithesis, a cover of "Wish You Were Here", in 1985. "We never cared about what was cool," said **Wayne Coyne**, introducing *Q*'s 2004 Floyd Special, *We Loved Pink Floyd*.

XTC

When new wavers XTC decided to make a psychedelic album – 1986's *Skylarking* – **Andy Partridge** lent bandmate **Colin Moulding** some Barrett records. The result was "Grass", the perfect alliance of Swindon whimsy with Barrett's childlikeness.

U2

"OK, Edge, play the blues." In fact, The Edge's spacey slide guitar work on "Bullet The Blue Sky" (*Joshua Tree*, 1987) and "Silver And Gold" (*Rattle And Hum*, 1988) owes little to the blues and much more to one David Gilmour, making the Floyd's 1990s' aping of U2 on "Take It Back" pretty much a draw.

Robyn Hitchcock

Robyn Hitchcock has devoted a career to being Barrett-esque: his punk-era band **Soft Boys** being among the first to mine the 1960s, and recording "Vegetable Man". Culty but influential (not least on his friends REM), Hitchcock performed Barrett's "**Dominoes**" on the BBC's *Pink Floyd And Syd Barrett Story*.

REM

Michael Stipe sometimes sang Barrett's "Dark Globe" a cappella at 80s shows. There are also versions on B-sides ("Orange Crush" and "Everybody Hurts"), and flexidiscs of him performing the song with REM bassist **Mike Mills** on piano.

Megadeth

Pretty much anyone growing up in the US during the 1970s is Floyd-damaged: the archetypal thrash metallers' **Dave Mustaine** cites *Wish You Were Here* as one of his favourite albums.

Queensryche

The pop metallers' 1990 US top-five hit "Silent Lucidity" strongly echoed **"Comfortably Numb"**, while their *Empire* album frequently recalled *The Wall*. Some critics mark the Floyd becoming "cool" from this point.

This Mortal Coil

The goth supergroup played a large role in opening up indie ears to a broader musical canon during the 1980s, covering Barrett's **"Late Night"** on their final album, *Blood*, in 1991.

The Orb

The original ambient house act's 1991 debut, *The Orb's Adventures Beyond The Ultraworld*, showed a deep debt to the Floyd in its rich synthetic textures, a debt acknowledged in "Back Side Of The Moon".

Warp Records

Many on Sheffield label Warp's roster of electronic acts are Floyd-indebted. Indeed, the cover of their 1992 label collection, *Artificial Intelligence*, featured a copy of *Dark Side Of The Moon*. Aphex Twin's *Selected Ambient Works II* shows a particular debt to the Floyd's **"Quicksilver"**/**"Echoes"** approach.

Blur

It was a surprise in 1991 to hear the ubiquitous baggy beat allied to distinctly Barrett-like vocals on Blur's breakthrough single "There's No Other Way". The band subsequently allied themselves to Barrett's very English songwriting lineage, their career peak *Parklife* (1994) containing a space nursery rhyme "Far Out", which strongly evoked **"Astronomy Domine"**.

Oasis

The laddy Oasis seem a long way from the effete Floyd, but not only are Oasis Floyd fans, but, more bizarrely, their 1994 debut *Definitely Maybe*'s brutal "Columbia" suggests the influence of the rather delicate **"Sorrow"**.

Gorky's Zygotic Mynci

Early Floyd and Soft Machine are all over these mid-1990s Welsh psychedelicists, who, for a while, brought up the Welsh wing of Britpop.

Super Furry Animals

Similarly psychedelic-inspired as their countrymen, Gorky's: both the band's fried wordplay and the more proggy elements owe a debt to different eras of Pink Floyd.

Orbital

The brothers Hartnoll's conceptual arena dance was clearly influenced by Pink Floyd, never more apparently than on their 1996 album *In Sides*.

Smashing Pumpkins

Billy Corgan inducted Pink Floyd into the **Rock'n'Roll Hall of Fame** in 1996. "Pink Floyd is the band that I reach for when I've completely lost hope in music." His 1995 *Mellon Collie And The Infinite Sadness* was intended to be a 1990s *The Wall*. It wasn't.

Radiohead

If ever there were a 1990s Pink Floyd, it's Radiohead: classically middle-class (Oxford to the Floyd's Cambridge), achieving a surprise worldwide hit with a doomy state-of-the-world opus (1997's *OK Computer*). Radiohead even had their version of the spitting incident with 1999 fan-baiting *Meeting People Is Easy* documentary.

Nine Inch Nails

Revolver magazine arranged a meeting between glum industrial princeling **Trent Reznor** and his glummer hero Roger Waters in 2000, after Reznor had brought in Bob Ezrin to help on his ambitious 1999 double-CD *The Fragile*.

Marilyn Manson

The goth-glam superstar and Reznor protégé is a *Wall* fanatic and employs "**Another Brick In The Wall**" as his concert intro tape. "They're one of the bands I listen to the most," he says.

Monster Magnet

This archetypal stoner rock band covered "**There's No Way Out Of Here**" from *David Gilmour*, on 2004's *Monolithic Baby*, and in the sleeve notes called Gilmour's album "the last classic Pink Floyd album".

The Coral

The most successful outgrowth of Liverpool's 1990s "cosmic scallies" movement, whereby council estate kids discovered marijuana and *Dark Side Of The Moon*. The antic psychedelic spirit of Barrett runs throughout their work.

The Mars Volta

These contemporary Californian proggers show the strong influence of "Echoes" on the sonic blips and burbs of "Cygnus Vismund Cygnus" from 2005's *Frances The Mute*.

LCD Soundsystem

The one vogue electronic act in the noughties' dance doldrums featured a distinctly Floydian, or more specifically Gilmour-esque, track on their 2005 debut, "Never So Tired As When I'm Waking Up", right down to its harmonized lead guitar lines.

The Mystery Jets

These oddballs from Eel Pie Island's first performances included a cover of "Comfortably Numb". Their soundscapes owe much to Pink Floyd's prog years, and they perform beneath a picture of Syd Barrett.

10 Floyd covers

Given the following, it's a sobering thought that many Live 8 viewers would have been more familiar with Velvet Revolver's, the Scissor Sisters' and Wyclef Jean's versions of their set-list than the Pink Floyd originals.

Dan Reed Network: Money

Available on *The Heat*, 1991

Pacific Northwest funk-rock stalwarts do a workhorse version of Pink Floyd's most famous track. By removing the 7/8 time signature, they simply reveal the song's rather bland blues-rock heart.

Phish: Dark Side Of The Moon

Available on bootleg only

The grunge-era Grateful Dead, from Vermont, covered the entire *Dark Side Of The Moon* album in Utah in November 1998: they would do the same with Velvet Underground's *Loaded* the following night.

Class of 99: Another Brick In The Wall Part 2

Available on *The Faculty* OST, 1999

Nu metal supergroup that featured Alice in Chains' **Layne Staley** and Rage Against the Machine's **Tom Morello,** managing to sound almost catatonic, flattening the song's melody.

Foo Fighters featuring Brian May: Have A Cigar

Available on *Mission Impossible II* OST, 2000

Sludgy metal version sung by Foos drummer **Taylor Hawkins.** "The most punk rock thing Pink Floyd ever did," said **Dave Grohl,** inaccurately. The far-from-punk Queen guitarist Brian May guests on typically OTT lead guitar.

Wyclef Jean: Wish You Were Here

Available on *The Ecleftic: 2 Sides II A Book*, 2000

Having made a career of too-close-to-call covers, the hip-hop magpie insists that "this is no ordinary cover tune" with a quite risible rap about "Pink Floyd – a band from the British blocks".

Limp Bizkit: Wish You Were Here

Available on *America: A Tribute to Heroes*, 2001

Soulless nu metallers Limp Bizkit's contribution to a 9/11 tribute had to borrow their sensitivity from this tune: **Fred Durst** adds two ham-fisted extra verses ("we don't need any more pain/we just need to remain on the very same page"), but the end result is no kind of tribute to anyone.

Pearl Jam: Interstellar Overdrive

Available on *Live: 8-18-00*, 2001

Long a live favourite with the grunge lynchpins, this tune got even greater exposure when Pearl Jam beat the bootleggers by releasing each of their 2000 shows on CD.

Velvet Revolver: Money

Available on *The Italian Job* OST, 2003

The not quite reunited Guns'n'Roses super-group with Stone Temple Pilot's **Scott Weiland** on vocals offer a very reverent re-creation, with even the guitar solos largely note for note.

Scissor Sisters: Comfortably Numb

Available on *The Scissor Sisters*, 2004

Risking blasphemy for Floyd fans, this camp cover crossed the song with the disco rhythm of "Run Like Hell", while also referencing Frankie's "Relax" and the Bee Gees. A huge UK hit, it provided the Sisters' commercial breakthrough. The Floyd resisted the temptation to perform it in Sisters' style at Live 8.

Korn: Another Brick In The Wall Parts 1–3

Available on *Greatest Hits Vol 1*, 2005

This "new" track on Korn's *Greatest* is a surprisingly reverent take on *Part 1*, a more metallic *Part 2* (with note-for-note rendition of the guitar solo), and a more resigned *Part 3*, even ending with "Goodbye Cruel World".

Floydology

Index

Listen Up!

"You may be used to the Rough Guide series being comprehensive, but nothing will prepare you for the exhaustive Rough Guide to World Music . . . one of our books of the year."
Sunday Times, London

The filth • the fury • the fashion

THE ROUGH GUIDE to

Punk

Al Spicer

The songs • the singers • the stories • the soul

THE ROUGH GUIDE to

Soul and R&B

Peter Shapiro

ROUGH GUIDE MUSIC TITLES

Bob Dylan • The Beatles • Classical Music • Elvis • Frank Sinatra • Heavy Metal • Hip-Hop
iPods, iTunes & music online • Jazz • Book of Playlists • Opera • Pink Floyd • Punk • Reggae
Rock • The Rolling Stones • Soul and R&B • World Music

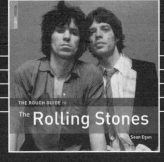

THE ROUGH GUIDE to

The **Rolling Stones**

Sean Egan

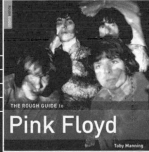

THE ROUGH GUIDE to

Pink Floyd

Toby Manning

The story • The songs • The solo years

THE ROUGH GUIDE TO

The **Beatles**

Chris Ingham

BROADEN YOUR HORIZONS

ROUGH GUIDES

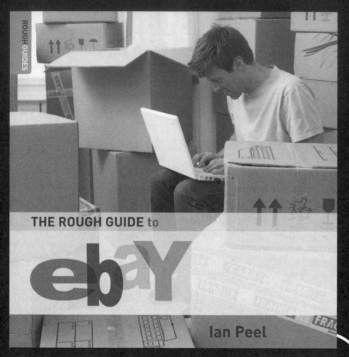

Rough Guides presents...